DR. A. S. BOSWORTH

A History of Randolph County West Virginia

From its Earliest Exploration and Settlement
to the Present Time

ILLUSTRATED

BY

DR. A. S. BOSWORTH

Southern Historical Press, Inc.
Greenville, South Carolina

Please direct all correspondence and orders to:

www.southernhistoricalpress.com
or
SOUTHERN HISTORICAL PRESS, Inc.
PO BOX 1267
375 West Broad Street
Greenville, SC   29601
southernhistoricalpress@gmail.com

Originally published: West Virginia 1916
ISBN #0-89308-902-8
All rights Reserved.
Printed in the United States of America

PREFACE

No literary merit is claimed in the presentation of this book. The purpose of the writer was to present facts and if any event of historical value will be saved to future generations, the author will feel compensated for his labors. An undertaking embodied within this volume involves labor and research little understood by the average individual. Encouragement and assistance have been received from many sources not practicable to enumerate, but none the less cherished and appreciated.

I acknowledge with gratitude assistance from the following individuals in procuring subscriptions: Jesse W. Bird, B. Y. White, G. W. White, Felix R. Tuning, Rev. Robert Greynolds, Wm. H. Conrad and Samuel H. Godwin.

Valuable assistance which the writer acknowledges with pleasure was given by Hon. T. J. Arnold, Capt. W. H. Cobb, Col. S. N. Bosworth, Jesse W. Robinson and Geo. W. Crawford.

In the preparation of this volume valuable information was obtained from Maxwell's History of Randolph, Haymond's History of Harrison, Price's History of Pocahontas, Morton's History of Pendleton and from Harper's Magazine.

A. S. BOSWORTH.

Elkins, W. Va., 1916.

TABLE OF CONTENTS

LIST OF ILLUSTRATIONS

CHAPTER I.

PHYSICAL FEATURES.

"This our life exempt from public haunts finds tongues in trees, books in running brooks, sermons in stones and good in everything."

THE pioneers of Randolph partook of their rugged environment in their mental, moral and physical characteristics That period produced a superior class of men because the struggle for existence was ameliorated by easy access to the soil, giving opportunity for culture and the social amenities and fostering a generous and hospitable spirit. The extent and direction in which man is compelled to expend his energy in obtaining food, shelter and raiment materially influence his life and belief. In the field of biology it is a well known law that every leaf, limb or branch is developed because of the necessity of the organism to obtain support from its environment. The organism is strong or feeble, depending upon the munificence with which the surroundings bestow their gifts.

The proverbial utterance that "mountaineers are always freemen" is largely true for the reason that a people living in the seclusion of valleys, surrounded by high mountains are enabled by Nature's fortresses to impel invading foes. Moreover, the birds in the illimitable air and the animals that roam at will in the wilds of the woods suggest to man the inherent right to freedom and independence.

Randolph is the largest county in the State with an area of 1,080 square miles. The contour of the county exhibits a series of mountain ranges with parallel valleys. The valleys are drained by the several forks of the Cheat, the Valley River, Middle Fork, Buckhannon, Elk and Gauley Rivers. Tygarts Valley is about 40 miles long and averages one mile in width. The head of the valley is known as Mingo Flats. The highest point in the county is Snyder's Knob in Mingo district on the Pocahontas line. Its altitude is 4,730 feet, being only 130 feet below Spruce Knob, in Pendleton County, the highest point in the State. The lowest point in the county is at the

Randolph-Tucker line, on Cheat River with an elevation of 1,765 feet. At the Southern extremity where the Elk River enters Randolph, the altitude is 2,390 feet and at the Randolph-Webster line it is 2,000 feet. The Valley River has a fall in Randolph of 1,325 feet. Cheat River has a fall in Randolph of 1,930 feet, more than it has in its subsequent course of 3,000 miles to the Gulf.

The following table will show the elevation of some of the places in Randolph:

Middle Fork Bridge	1,900
Elkins	1,950
Kerens	2,000
Beverly	2,000
Lick	2,000
Orlena	2,000
Montrose	2,050
Valley Bend	2,050
Huttonsville	2,080
Lee Bell	2,100
Cassity	2,100
Long	2,100
Crickard	2,100
Roaring Creek	2,100
Elkwater	2,200
West Huttonsville	2,300
Helvetia	2,400
Alpina	2,400
Harman	2,400
Day's Mills	2,450
Mouth Fishing Hawk	2,480
Valley Head	2,500
Kingsville	2,500
Job	2,600
Laurel Hill B. and B. Pike	2,600
Mingo Flats	2,700
Pickens	2,700
Blue Springs	2,900
Florence	2,900
Glady	2,900
Monterville	3,000
Rich Mountain Battle Field	3,000
Osceola	3,400
The Sinks	3,400
Rich Mountain	3,400
Nettly Mountain	3,400
Currence Knob	3,500
Lone Tree	3,570
Cheat Bridge	3,600
Bickle Knob	4,020
Bayard Knob	4,150
Yokum Knob	4,330
Ward Knob	4,400
Crouch Knob	4,600

The rocks of Randolph, with few exceptions, are limestone, sandstone and shale. Nearly all of these rocks are of sedimentary origin. Limestone was formed of the remains of the shells or skeletons of sea animals, more or less broken to fragments or even ground to powder in the waves of shallow waters. It is much more soluble in water than other rocks. Sandstone was formed from waste of such rocks as granite. The sand was washed into the sea or other body of

Big Falls of Cheat.

water and was there spread out into layers which in the course of ages accumulated in great thickness. Infiltering waters, carrying some mineral substance in solution was deposited between the grains and bound them more or less perfectly together. The finer waste of granite rocks formed shale and slate. Millions of years ago the only dry land in North America was a mountain ridge lying east of the Alleghenies. This primitive mountain by an internal force was forced up out of the bed of the ocean. The rocks forming this mountain were not sedimentary in origin. The action of air, wind and water in the course of a long period wore down this mountain to a base level and deposited its silt and sediment layer upon layer in the bottom of the ocean. The land formation crept steadily westward. There were alternate intervals of upheavals and subsidences. The coal beds of

Randolph formed by compressed vegetation, mark successive terrestial surfaces. At the time of the formation of the Appalachian plateau, there were no deep valleys or high mountains. The dry land was plastic and formative. There were anticlinals and synclinals that in the course of long periods of time by the action of floods, frosts and other agencies sculped out deep valleys and formed high mountains.

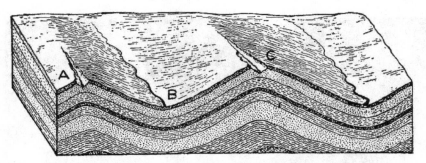

The Mountains and Valleys of Randolph as They Probably Appeared in an Early Geological Period.

No lake, probably, ever existed in the present formation of Tygarts Valley. The outlet of the Valley, with the exception of temporary land slides, perhaps, has ever been on a lower plane than its floor. However, that the flood plane of the valley has been gradually degrading or eroding, is evidenced by river terraces in different parts of the valley, covered by sandstones worn smooth by agitation in a stream with a rapid current. These terraces are particularly prominent on the M. J. Coberly farm two miles above Beverly and on the opposite side of the river on the farm of D. R. Baker. Cheat River as it passes through Randolph County is being eroded or degraded at the rate of two inches per annum.

The Sinks.

Perhaps the greatest natural curiosity in Randolph County is the sinks, where Gandy Creek makes a remarkable subterranean passage beneath a spur of the Allegheny mountains. The stream issues from its lethean channel in three arched passages side by side on the face of a perpendicular cliff, which abridges the glen by an arched opening fifty feet wide by twenty feet high. Into this orifice Gandy's waters incessantly glide. At a low stage of the water a few persons have succeeded in making their way from entrance to exit.

Entrance to the Tunnel of Gandy.

CHAPTER II.

PRE-HISTORIC RANDOLPH.

RANDOLPH COUNTY was never the settled abode of the Red Man. To him it was only a large game reservation, into which he made periodic incursions for the hunt and the chase. When the first white men visited the county there

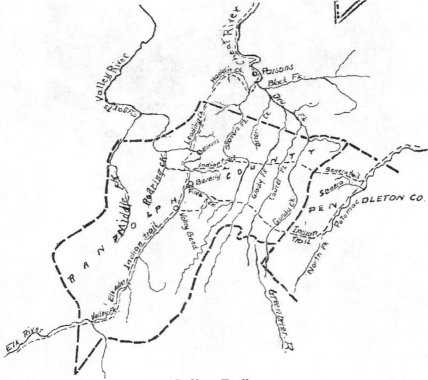

Indian Trails.

was little evidence of any except temporary occupation by the savages. Squaw patches, or small clearings were found in some localities; however they were of such a character as to indicate only transitory habitation. Indian mounds are

still to be seen in some localities, but as a rule are found on
or near old trails. A mound of considerable size is still visible
on the farm of Archibald Lytle, near where the old fort stood,
about three miles south of Elkins. This mound is on an
Indian trail which passed up Westfall Run to the West side
of Rich Mountain, through the Caplinger settlement on the
East side of the mountain, thence up Chenoweth's Creek.
Excavations in this mound have revealed fragments of human
skulls and stone implements. An Indian burial ground existed
also in Valley Bend district on the Currence farm, once owned
by Henry Clay Dean.

The Indian population in what are now the two Virginias
was never very dense. It is conjectured that at the time of
the discovery of America, the territory embraced in these two
states contained a population of about 8,000 savages. The
Shawnees were the white man's greatest foes during the first
half century of his occupancy of the New World. They were
a branch of the Algonquin family. The remnants of this
family live in the Indian Territory, in a condition of semi-
civilization. They are a superior race mentally and physically. Tecumseh, a member of this tribe, was a man skilled in
the arts of warfare and of dauntless courage. He was a
Brigadier General in the British army in the war of 1812,
and was killed in the battle of the Thames.

The ethnic stages as adopted by most archaeologists are
savagery, barbarism and civilization and in each of the two
lower stages there are three subordinate periods. The distinction between savagery and barbarism is marked by the
point where the manufacture of pottery is begun. In the
lower status of savagery men lived in their original restricted
habitat and subsisted on fruits and nuts. Articulate speech
may be supposed to have begun in this status. All existing
races of men had passed beyond it at an unknown antiquity.
In the middle status of savagery men had learned how to
catch fish and to use fire. The invention of the bow and
arrow marks its close. The upper status of savagery, in
which some of the lowest American tribes still continue, such
as the Athamaskans of Hudson Bay, ends, as above stated,
with the invention of pottery. They know nothing of horti-

culture, make no pottery and depend for subsistence entirely
on roots, fish and game. They have little or no village life.
The lower status of barbarism exhibits the domestication of
animals other than the dog. In 1492, at the time of the discovery of America, the dog was the only animal domesticated
by the North American Indians. This was true of all the
American aborigines, except the Peruvians. The absence of
domesticable animals is no doubt important among the causes
that retarded the development of the American Indians. The
horse, which is shown by fossil remains to have existed in
six or seven species, had become extinct, and was reintro-
duced by the invaders. The regular employment of tillage
with irrigation, and the use of adobe brick and stone in archi-
tecture, marked the end of the lower status of barbarism in
America. The middle status of barbarism was marked in
the Eastern Hemisphere by the domestication of other animals than the dog, and there as well as in the Western Hemisphere, by the development of irrigation in cultivation, and
the use of brick and stone in building, by great improvement
in the manufacture of stone implements, and ultimately the
introduction of implements of copper and bronze. The middle
status may be regarded as ending with the discovery of the
process of smelting iron ore; and this process becomes more
and more important through the upper status of barbarism
and is finally associated with the production of written records
by means of a phonetic alphabet or of advanced hieroglyphics.
Among the influences which have affected the more or less
rapid development of races the following suggest themselves:
The condition of soil and climate as favoring or impeding
the aquisition of ample and varied means of sustenance, the
existence or absence of the various animals suited for domestication, notably, sheep and cattle; the opportunities for con-
tact, by migration, commerce or war, with races occupying a
higher ethnic scale; inherent ethnological defects or advantages in special races.

The Indian that made incursions into this section, belonged to the lower status of barbarism. He practiced a
limited agriculture. However, he domesticated no animal
except the dog. He discovered the tobacco plant, smoked

but never chewed. Smoking was a civil and religious rite and was indulged as a means of communicating with the Great Spirit as well as emphasizing the sancity of treaties between tribes. Thus originated the phrase "smoking the pipe of peace." The Indian raised corn and had many ways of preparing it for food. "Green corn" was an important food with the Indians. Many tribes celebrated its season with festivals and religious ceremonies. The Indian cleared land by deadening the trees with the stone tomahawk. However, his main subsistence was upon game and fish. His hut was made of long poles bent together and fastened at the top, and covered with bark. There were two openings, a place to go in and out and a place for the smoke to escape. Clothing was made from the tanned skins of animals. His weapons were bone and stone instruments and the bow and arrow. He was unacquainted with firearms until the white man came. The tradition that the Indian visited lead and other mines has no foundation in fact. Implements used in the hunt and the chase were burried with the Indian because he believed that the soul took its flight to the happy hunting ground. The coward and the deformed were denied admittance to the Indian's paradise. In scalping and mutilating an enemy, he prevented his foe from entering this abode of bliss.

The Indian had great skill in finding his way through the forest. The moss and bark on the trees revealed to him the prevailing direction of the wind and the rays of the sun. In this way he was enabled to distinguish the points of the compass. Foot-paths were as a rule established along water courses, but in crossing from stream to stream dividing ridges were followed. Although not provincial, each tribe claimed a definite territory, and any infraction thereof was a cause of war with neighboring tribes. Individual ownership of land never prevailed and all claims thereto were of a tribal nature. However, individual rights to cultivated patches were respected, but his use of the land gave him no permanent title. Tribes consisted of groups, each living in a separate village. Their laws were founded upon custom. Matters of tribal interest were settled in council.

The Indian was sometimes a cannibal, but not often, and

was closely associated with economic necessity. The custom was practiced only under circumstances of the direst extremity. The custom of leaving old men in the woods to die, is bad enough but not as bad as supposed. They carried the old man with them until he himself grew tired of being a burden and begged to be killed. When this point was reached he was given more than his share of food and left in the woods to die. He believed in revenge, but it was to be measured by the offense. His revenge was only directed against his enemies and he at all times defended the members of his own tribe. Within the tribe everything was shared in common. However scant the food, it was shared by those present.

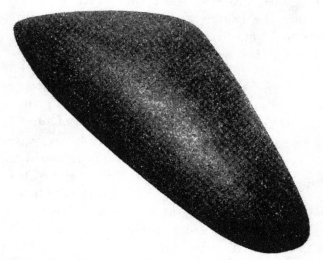

Stone Hatchet Taken from Indian Grave on Isner
Farm, Lower Cheat.

CHAPTER III.

PIONEER PERIOD.

ORANGE County, Virginia, was formed from Spottsylvania county in 1704 and was made to include all the territory West of the mountains. In 1744 that vast region was divided into the districts of Augusta and Frederick and was to be organized into counties as soon as they attained

A Pioneer Cabin.

sufficient population. Monongalia was formed from part of Augusta in 1776; Harrison was formed from part of Monongalia in 1784 and Randolph from part of Harrison in 1787.

In 1856 Randolph gave part of its territory to the formation
of Tucker county. Randolph also contributed part of its
territory along with other counties in the formation of Nicholas, Pocahontas, Upshur and Webster.

Although settlement was made in the adjoining county of
Pendleton in 1747, the first white men to visit the valley were
Files or Foyle and Tygart or Taggart, in 1753. Foyle located
his cabin in the present site of Beverly, a little north of the
Baker Mill, near the mouth of the creek that bears his name.
Tygart selected a location farther up the river, on the west
side, now the John D. Weese Brick House Place three miles

The Historic Site of Tygart Cabin, Weese Farm,
Valley Bend District.

from Beverly. Nothing is known of Tygart or Files that
would throw light on their antecedents; however, the tide
of emigration must necessarily have been from the east.
The Tygart family and young Files departed from the county
into Pendleton. These circumstances coupled with the fact
that the name was probably Taggart rather than Tygart
and the Taggarts were among the first settlers of Pendleton
and other eastern counties, the presumption is very strong in
favor of the hypothesis that these families came into the
valley from the settlements west of the Alleghenies.

Perhaps, Files and Tygart were induced to push into
the wilderness in pursuit of game. The fertile lands of the
valley, also no doubt, were an inducement.

The difficulties in the way of procuring breadstuffs for

their families, coupled with the perception of the dangers from Indians on a remote and unprotected border induced Files and Tygart to a determination to abandon the valley. Before they carried their plans into execution Robert Files, wife and five children, the youngest of which was ten years old, were murdered by the Indians, who were returning from the South Branch to the country west of the Ohio. An elder son not being at home escaped, but being nearby heard the disturbance and approaching the house learned of the horrible fate of his relatives, and realizing the utter impossibility of giving any assistance, resolved to give warning to the family of David Tygart, a few miles up the river. Young Files and the Tygart family immediately abandoned the country. Withers says that Files and Tygart had discovered that their location was near an Indian trail and an Indian village. No Indian village existed in dangerous proximity. Mingo on Mingo Run, 32 miles above, had been many years before the site of an Indian village. However, it had been abandoned by the Mingoes many years previous to 1753. Their cabins were near the trail that entered the valley at Elkwater and Huttonsville and passed down the river on the east side, and thence up Leading Creek and over the mountain to Cheat river.

Tygarts Valley did not attract emigrants for a period of eighteen years after the disaster attending the efforts of Files and Tygart. In the meantime hunters from Greenbrier visited the valley and on their return gave a glowing description of the region to the settlements. These reports induced many settlers to seek homes west of the mountains and most of the level land in the valley was occupied by permanent possessors during the year 1772. Withers mentions among those who were first to occupy the valley the names of Hadden, Conley, Whiteman, Warwick, Nelson, Westfall, Riffle, and Stalnaker. Westfall found and buried the remains of the Files family. Settlements were made in what is now Lewis, Taylor and Harrison counties in the same year. The region that now comprises Upshur County had been the abode of John and Samuel Pringle since 1764 and by several other families since 1769. John and Samuel Pringle were deserters from the army at Fort Pitt and sought safety in the seclusion of the wilderness by ascending the Monongahela and making their abode in the trunk of a sycamore tree on the west fork of the Buckhannon, near the mouth of Turkey Run. They made visits to the South Branch for amunition and their reports caused others to seek that section for settlement.

Indian hostilities, which had been in abeyance since 1765, were renewed in 1774. There is a diversion of opinion as to the cause. Some think that the unprovoked murder of several Indians caused them to seek revenge, while others are inclined to the opinion that they were instigated to outrages upon the whites by British emmisaries and that the savages who committed the deeds were ignorant of the outrages committed upon the members of their own race. Three Shawnees, friendly to the whites, were killed near Wheeling by the settlers. Three Indians were killed on the South Branch while on a friendly visit to that country. Among the number killed were Captain Peter and Bald Eagle, two Indians of prominence in their tribes. About the same time a few white men exterminated Chief Bull and five families of Indians on the Little Kanawha, in cold blood, in what is now Braxton county. Bull and his little band were on terms of intimate friendship with the settlers, visiting and hunting with them. The people expected renewed hostilities on the part of the Indians and in 1774 two forts were built in Randolph. The Westfall fort, evidences of which still remain on the farm of Daniel Baker, near the mouth of Files Creek and the Currence fort which was built near the present town of Mill Creek. These forts were constructed of logs, with chimneys on the inside to keep the Indians from reaching the roof. Holes were left between the logs to shoot through. There was no visitation this year from the Indians. However, the settlers kept scouts in the mountains, watching the trails leading into the valley. On the first indication of danger, the settlers took refuge in the forts. The Revolutionary war brought Indian troubles in 1777. On the frontier this year was known as the bloody year of the three sevens. The British were instrumental in causing the Indians to make an effort to exterminate or drive back the western settlers. The whites were apprehensive and vigilant. Leonard Pedro and William White were sent out as scouts to watch Indian trails leading into Randolph. They were watching the path that ascended the Little Kanawha, in Braxton County, when being pressed by the necessity for food, shot an elk. A number of Indians being in the neighborhood, heard the report of their gun and stealthily followed them to their camp, and were in the act of making an attack when they were discovered by White. A savage sprang upon them and White made a futile strike at the Indian with a tomahawk. Realizing that resistance was useless, White pretended that he had attempted to do the Indian harm only when half awake, and assumed an air of friendliness. He told the Indians that Pedro and himself were on their way to join the Indians. Perhaps his ruse would have been successful if Pedro's dejected countenance had not contradicted his pretentions. They were tied for the rest of the night. In the morning Pedro was marked for the tomahawk and scalping knife by being painted black. However, the Indian abandoned their purpose of killing Pedro and returned to Ohio, taking their two captives with them. White stole a gun, killed an Indian, appropriated the horse of his fallen foe and returned to Randolph in 1777. Pedro was never heard of afterward.

As a rule the settlements were free from Indian molestation during the months of winter, for the reason that they could be followed by their tracks, as well as from the fact that their scant clothing was not sufficient for the rigors of such a trip through the mountains. However, whether they followed White or came on an independent mission of massacre and plunder, a party of about twenty Indians approached to within about twenty miles of the settlements in November. A snow had fallen and they waited until December 15th. When it disappeared on that date, they attacked Darby Connoly's house in the upper valley, and having killed him, his wife and several of his children, they took the others prisoners. The graves of the Connoly family are still to be seen on the farm once owned by Harmon Conrad, on which there was a salt well drilled at one time. They next visited the house of John Stewart, and killed him, his wife and his child, carrying away his sister-in-law, Miss Hamilton, as a prisoner. John Hadden discovered the murder of the Stewart family and reported the fact to Colonel Benjamin Wilson at Wilson's Fort. Wilson's Fort was situated about thirty miles down the river. Colonel Wilson was an officer in the Revolutionary army. With thirty men Colonel Wilson followed the men five days through the rain and snow, often wading ice cold streams waist deep, but the Indians could not be overtaken. The settlers were not molested in 1778. But the next year the Indians shot and killed Lieutenant John White from the roadside. Colonel Benjamin Wilson with a party of men tried to intercept the Indians on their Westward return at the mouth of Sand Fork on the Little Kanawha, but the Indians returned by a different route.

Early in March, 1780, Jacob Warwick and others from Greenbrier county visited Randolph as Government surveyors. Kilbuck was scouting the mountains at the time with bands of Mingoes and Shawnees. Mr. Warwick and his company felt themselves in comparative safety on account of the snow, which would betray the Indians' tracks to the settlers. While the Greenbrier party was at Haddan's Fort, Thomas Lackey reported that he had seen moccasin tracks in the snow a few miles above the fort, and heard a voice say in an undertone, "Let him alone; he will go and bring more." An escort of men went with the Greenbrier party to the place where Lackey saw the Indian signs. When near the place Andrew Sitlington's horse showed signs of fright. Mr. Sitlington then saw the Indians, but for the moment could not speak from fright. Warrick's attention was attracted and he cried out, "Indians! INDIANS!!" Thereupon the Indians fired, wounding one member of the party and Mr. Warwick's horse. The horse sank to the ground and the rider was in the act of throwing off his cloak to facilitate his escape when the horse arose and started off at a rapid speed and away from their assailants. Jacob Warwick, James McLean, Thomas Cartwill and Andrew Sitlington comprised the party on horse back, all of whom escaped. John McLean, James Ralston and John Nelson were killed. This occurred on Windy Run. John McLean was killed about thirty yards from the brow of the hill. James Ralston was killed while ascending the hill. James Crouch was wounded near the summit of the hill, but escaped and recovered. John Nelson attempted to escape down the river, but was met by a stout warrior and after a severe struggle was killed. But the shattered gun stock, the uptorn earth and Indian hair still in his clinched fist gave evidence that he had fought bravely. Mr. Warwick's horse received only a slight wound in the thigh and carried him to his home in Greenbrier County the same day. The Indians occupied the road above and below where they were attacked, those on horseback were enabled to out-distance the Indians, but the foot men were compelled to cross the river and ascend a steep bluff on its opposite side. In attempting this several lost their lives.

Soon after this a family by the name of Gibson was attacked at their sugar camp, on a branch of the Valley River. They were made prisoners and the return trip to the country west of the Ohio with their captives was undertaken. Mrs. Gibson, being incapable of undergoing the fatigue of the trip, was tomahawked and scalped in the presence of her children. The other members of the family were carried into captivity and were never heard of afterward.

In April 1781, Indians attacked a party of five men who were returning to the present county of Tucker, from Clarksburg, where they had been to obtain deeds for their lands. John Minear, David Cameron, and a Mr. Cooper were killed. Messrs. Miller and Goff escaped, one returning to Clarksburg, the other to St. George. The Indians continued their course toward Cheat, but meeting Stephen Radcliff and James Brown, whom they could neither kill nor capture, and no longer believing that they could surprise the Cheat River settlements, changed their course and passed over to Leading Creek, and nearly destroyed the entire settlement. They killed Alexander Rooney, Mrs. Dougherty, Mrs. Hornbeck and her children as well as many others and made prisoners of Mrs. Alexander Rooney and her son, and Daniel Dougherty. Johnathan Buffington and Benjamin Hornbeck succeeded in escaping. Mr. Hornbeck lived about a quarter of a mile east of where White Station now stands, on the north bank

of Stalnaker Run. The remains of the chimney of Hornbeck's cabin is still visible on the farm of Obadiah Taylor.
It seems that the Hornbeck family had some intimation of the
presence of the Indians in the community and had left the
house and were in the woods on the hill nearby. The Indians
visited and plundered the house and were in the act of leaving,
when the whereabouts of the family was betrayed by the
barking of a dog that was with them. Mr. Hornbeck, fearing
to approach his house, mounted a horse in the field without
saddle or bridle and rode hurriedly to Wilson's Fort, six
miles up the valley. Colonel Wilson raised a company and
pursued the Indians, but the men becoming alarmed lest their
families be murdered in their absence, returned without overtaking the savages. In the meantime word had reached
Clarksburg of the murder of land claimants on their return
home and a number of scouts were sent out to intercept the
Indians on their return to the Ohio. Their trail was discovered on the West Fork River, near Isaac Creek, in the present
county of Harrison. Colonel William Lowther of Hacker's
Creek, raised a company to pursue them. They were overtaken on a branch of Hughes River, in Ritchie County in the
evening. They waited until the Indians were asleep and then
opened fire. Five were killed, the others escaped, leaving
everything in camp, except one gun. One white man, a
prisoner, was killed. He was the son of Alexander Rooney
and his sad fate was much regretted by the whites, who had
been very cautious in trying to prevent such an accident.
Withers relates the following amusing incident in connection
with the affair: "Daniel Daugherty, an Irishman, came near
being killed by the whites. The Indians had him tied down
and he was so cold he could scarcely speak. Colonel Lowther's party rushed forward after the first fire, and mistaking
Daugherty for a wounded Indian, they were about to dispatch him with a tomahawk, when fear loosened his tongue
and he exclaimed, 'Lord Jasus! and am Oi to be killed by
white people at last!' His life was saved. Mrs. Rooney was
overcome with the prospect of deliverance. She ran toward
the men saying. 'I'm Ellick Rooney's wife of the Valley! and
a pretty little woman too, if well dressed!'" She was not
aware that her son had been killed.

On this raid the Indians killed James Wilmoth. The Wilmoth's were at Wilson's Fort, either in anticipation of an Indian raid or as a result of the recent one on Leading Creek. James Wilmoth, leaving the other members of the family at the fort returned to his home on Cheat to attend to some skins he had in process of tanning. The barking of a dog which was with him betrayed him to the Indians and he was shot and killed, near where the Stone House now stands. Some of the Indians were afflicted with small pox and jumped into the ice cold water of Wilmoth's Millrace for relief. They died from the exposure.

A band of from twenty to thirty Indians visited the valley in the summer of 1782. They were led by a renegade white man by the name of Timothy Dorman. John Bush and his wife, Jacob Stalnaker and his son, Adam, were ambushed on the old road, as they were crossing a drain, on the old Hoy McLean place, about a mile south of Arnold station. Young Stalnaker was shot from his horse and killed, but his father, and Bush and his wife escaped. The fleeing party had a close race with the Indians to the river, being so near some times as to try and reach the bridle reins. The whites plunged into the river and the Indians abandoned pursuit. The Indians were followed by the aroused settlers. When near the crest of Rich Mountain, at a point which afterward became the scene of the Rich Mountain battle, the Indians were overtaken. When just east of the top of the mountain as an Indian stooped to drink from a spring, he was shot and killed by a man by the name of Morgan. The other savages escaped and were pursued no farther.

The Indians made their last hostile raid into the valley on May 11, 1781. Two or three families, as a measure of protection, lived with Joseph Kinnan, whose cabin was one mile above the mouth of Elkwater on the west side of the river on the land that afterward became the Adam See farm. Haddan's Fort was less than a mile down the river. The Indians approached the house a little after dark and finding the door open, walked in. Mr. Kinnan was sitting on the bed and the Indian extended his hand in a friendly manner saying, "How-

d-do, how-d-do?" Mr. Kinnan was in the act of extending
his hand when an Indian in the yard shot him dead. A young
man by the name of Ralston, who had been working in the
house with a drawing-knife, struck an Indian with it and
cut off his nose. Another Indian fired at Ralston, but missed
and the young man escaped. The Indians killed three of
Kinnan's children, but two others, Lewis and Joseph, escaped
with the assistance of Mrs. Ward, through a rear window.
Mr. Kinnan's brother, Lewis, was sleeping in a rear room and
escaped through the window. Mrs. Kinnan was taken prisoner and remained with the Indians several months in the
western country until General Wayne conquered the Indians
at the battle of Fallen Timbers. Andrew and Joseph Crouch
living a few miles below on the river, were notified next day.
They took their families to the home of James Warwick who
lived near where the Brick Church was built in later years,
and with some neighbors hurried to the rescue of the settlers
up the valley. While they were absent the Indians visited
the Warwick home where there were three white women,
several children and a colored man and his wife. An Indian
climbed to the roof of one of the buildings after nightfall and
set it on fire. The colored man put the fire out. Then the
stable was fired. The colored man went out and seeing an
Indian by the light of the burning building, shot at him and
let the horses out and returned in safety to the fort. When
the barn burned down and darkness returned the colored
woman left the fort and gave the alarm to the settlers down
the river. Next day the inmates of the fort were rescued.
This party also proceeded to the scene of the Kinnan massacre
and buried Mr. Kinnan and his children. The settlers believed that the Indians had withdrawn from the valley. However, they were lurking in the community and before leaving
killed Frank Riffle and William Currence and burned two
houses belonging to James Lackey. Riffle and Currence were
killed on the divide between Becca's Creek and Riffle's Creek,
near the later location of the Brick Church.

An inventory of the Joseph Kinnan estate was placed on
record in Randolph County Clerk's Office, June 21, 1793
with Edward Hart as administrator. The personal property

was valued at $517, a list of which is given below: "9 horses, wheat and rye, two curtains, 2 pairs pillows and cases, 1 towel, 1 fine shirt, 1 lawn apron, 1 black apron, 1 cambrick apron, fine trumpery, 1 silk-gause apron, 2 handkerchiefs, children's clothing, 1 coat, 1 jacket, 5 long gowns, 1 pair of shoes and silver buckles, 3 petty-coats, 2 check aprons, 4 short gowns, 2 beds and bed-clothing, 1 pair of pockets, 4 platters, 6 basins, 2 plates, 2 kegs, 1 pail, 1 pot tramble, 1 iron kettle, 2 scythes, 1 set of hangings, 1 gun, 1 pan, 2 bridles, 36 hogs, 16 cattle, 3 sheep, 1 grubbing hoe, two pairs plow irons and clevices, 2 pots, 1 jug, 1 candlestick, 2 flat irons, 1 pair of shears, 9 spoons, steelyards, 1 brush, 2 collars, 1 ax."

Tradition says that the Indians twice visited the Wilmoth settlement on Cheat. On one incursion they killed James Wilmoth and on another raid all were absent from the house except Mrs. Wilmoth. They searched the house and premises for the men, occasionally throwing their tomahawks into the logs of the cabin, at the same time giving vent to savage exclamations of threat and anger, as much as to say what they would do if the men could be found. In the meantime Mrs. Wilmoth had prepared a pot of corn meal mush, putting it in a sugar trough with milk and maple syrup, giving each Indian a spoon. The half famished savages partook of the repast with evident signs of delight and gratification. When one of the company would violate a rule of Indian table etiquette, he was punished by a stroke on the head with a spoon, accompanied by words of admonition with violent gesticulations, not to repeat the indecorum. After finishing their meal, the Indains fastened their eyes on Mrs. Wilmoth in a studious and penetrating gaze for several moments, evidently debating in their own minds what should be her fate, then giving a warwhoop they continued on their marauding expedition. Mrs. Wilmoth's diplomacy saved her life and established the fact that things more material and prosaic than music hath charms to soothe the savage breast.

The family of William Leavitt, who settled, in 1780, on the lands now owned by Drs. J. L. and Perry Bosworth, two miles north of Daily Station, was attacked by the Indians and the entire family, father, mother, and several children were tomahawked and scalped. The mother, though left for dead, revived, was rescued by her neighbors and completely recovered. The dead were enshrouded in deer skins and buried at the Currence graveyard, on the lands now owned by John D. Weese. The date of the tragedy is uncertain, but it was subsequent to 1780.

Then Indians at another time visited that community. The date is not definite, but the facts are direct from the lips of Isaac White, who was a member of the party, to persons now living. The cabin in this incident was situated near where the Troutwine Run crosses the county road on the Bosworth farm. The men were harvesting in the field in the bottom below. The community was apprehensive and several families were congregated at the cabin. The women usually accompanied the men to the field but on this particular day had remained at the cabin for a few minutes to attend to household duties following the mid-day meal. The Indians, who were lurking near by, thought the time opportune for an attack, but as they approached the house they were discovered by the women. Realizing that their lives depended upon reaching the men in the field, they took to flight and in crossing the fence to the field, raised their hands above their heads and shouted, "Indians!" The hand of one of the women was piereced by a bullet, as a result of a volley from the Indians. All others escaped injury. The men seized their rifles and started in pursuit. The savages fled to the adjacent forests and soon eluded their pursuers.

The Murder of the Bozart Family.

In the summer of 1795 the trail of a large party of Indians was discovered, leading toward the settlements on West Fork of the Monongahela, Tygarts Valley or on the Buckhannon, near where the town of Buckhannon is now situated. The trail was discovered in what is now Lewis County. Messengers were sent immediately to these settlements warning them of possible danger. John Bozart lived on the Buckhannon River, near the present town of Buckhannon, but at the time of the massacre of his family in 1795, the Buckhannon settlement was within the territory of Randolph.

Mr. Bozart and his two sons, John and George, were engaged in hauling grain to the barn near the house. They were alarmed by the shrieks of the family at the house and hastened to ascertain the cause. George approached the house a few paces in advance of his father, but the latter saw an Indian raise his gun to shoot the son, and shouted, "SEE George, an Indian is going to shoot you." The young man was too near the Indian to escape by flight, but watched closely the movements of the Indian and when he pressed the trigger young Bozart fell. The ruse was a success and the Indian, believing the young man dead passed on in pursuit of the father. The old gentleman proved a good runner and was leaving the Indian, when the savage in despair threw his tomahawk at him which passed harmlessly by and he made his escape. When George Bozart fell, as though dead, he lay upon the ground expecting to be scalped, determined to seize the Indian by the leg as he would bend over him and endeavor to bring his antagonist to the ground, where he hoped to successfully grapple with him. The Indian passing him in pursuit of his father, the young man arose and fled. He overtook a younger brother hobbling along on a sore foot. George gave him every assistance he could until he observed another savage closely pursuing them. Although much adverse to leaving his brother, he knew that remaining with him meant death to both. Taking to rapid flight, he soon came up with his father in the woods. Mr. Bozart, believing that his son was dead and hearing some one approaching, supposed he was being pursued by an Indian and seizing a heavy stick, turned to face his antagonist. He was greatly surprised to see his son and exclaimed, "WHY GEORGE, I thought you were dead." In his mistake he evinced a joyful moment in an awful tragedy.

At the house two or three children were massacred and Mrs. Bozart and two boys were spared and taken to the Indian towns west of the Ohio. They were surrendered to General Wayne at Greenville on September 9, 1795 by a party of Shawnees, numbering sixty or seventy. Puck-se-kaw, in delivering the prisoners spoke as follows: "My Father: I have been in the woods a long time. I was not acquainted with the good works which were transacting at this place by you and all our great chiefs. Last spring when we were hunting peaceably, our camp on the Sciota was robbed. We are very poor and the mischief that has since been done was in retaliation for the injuries then received. As soon as I received this belt, which you sent me by Blue Jacket, one of our great chiefs, and as soon as I was informed by him that the good work of peace was finished, I arose to come to see you and brought with me these four prisoners. I now surrender them to you, my father, and promise you that we will do you no more mischief.

"I hope for the future we shall be permitted to live and hunt in peace and quietness. We were poor and ignorant children, astray in the woods, who knew not that our nation and all other tribes of Indians had come in and made peace with you. I thank the Great Spirit for at last opening our eyes. Father, we beg you will forgive and receive your repentant children. These people whom I now deliver to you must plead our forgiveness and vouch for our conduct for the future."

The Last Indian Raids in Randolph.

The last Indian raids in Randolph were between the middle of June and the last of July, 1792. In that year they made three incursions in Randolph, but confined their depredations to stealing horses. On their return, they were attacked by a party of scouts on the Ohio and one Indian was wounded and the horses recovered. Although this was the last visit of the savages to Randolph, alarms were frequent until the victory of General Wayne over them at Fallen Timbers in 1794 and the treaty in the subsequent year. Scouts and militia were kept in constant service until after captives were returned after the Treaty of Peace at Greenville in August, 1795. At different times after 1792 Indian trails were discovered leading toward the valley, but the vigilance of scouts and militia prevented them penetrating the frontier farther than the Buckhannon settlement, which they visited in 1795, taking captive Mrs. Bozart and three children, and killing two or three of the smaller ones.

The following tribes subscribed to the Greenville treaty: Wyandottes, Ottawas, Miamas, Kicapoos, Delawares, Chippewas, Eel Rivers, Paneshaws, Shawnees, Pottowotamies, Weas, and Kaskaskies.

Treaty of Lancaster.

By the treaty of Lancaster, Pa., 1744, the Indians relinquished their claim to all the lands between the Blue Ridge Mountains and the Ohio River. This was the first conveyance to title to lands in this vast region. The consideration was £400—one-half in gold and one-half in goods. In the negotiations the Indian chiefs stated that the acquisition of the territory by conquest had cost them many lives. The treaty was as follows:

To all people to whom these presents shall come: Conasatngo, Joneeat, Caxhayion, Torachdadon, Nenrranarkto, Sachemsor, Chiefs of the nations of the Onondagors; Saqurhsonyunt, Gasroddodon, Huarasaly-akon, Rowamthalyhisso, Occoghquah, Seyenties, Sachems or Chiefs of ye nations of ye Cahugoes; Suadany alias Shirketiney, Onishudagony, Ononthkallydoroy alias Walrattuah, Tohosnorororow, Arrighahhorvand, Tiorhoosoy, Sachems or Chiefs of the Tuscaroras; Tansanegoesand, Tonikuunitus, Sachems or Chiefs of ye nations of ye Senekers, send greeting:

Whereas, the six united nations of Indians laying claim to some lands in the Colony of Virginia, signified their willingness to enter into a treaty concerning the same. Whereupon, Thomas Lee, Esq., a member of the Ordinary of his Majesty's Honorable Council of the State and one of the Judges of the Supreme Court of Judicature in the Colony, and William Beverly, Esq., Colonel and County Lieutenant of the County of Orange and one of the representatives of the people in the House of Burgesses of that Colony, were deputed by the Governor of the said Colony as Commissioners to treat with the said Six Nations or their Deputies, Sachems or Chiefs, as well of and concerning their said claim as to renew their covenant chain between the said Colony and the said Six Nations, and the said Commissioners, having met at Lancaster, in Lancaster County and province of Pennsylvania, and as a foundation for a stricter amity and peace in this juncture agreed with the said Sachems or Chiefs of the said Six Nations for a Disclaimer and Renunciation of their Claim or pretense of Right whatsoever of the said Six Nations and an acknowledgement of Right of our Sovereign, King of Great Britain to all the land in the said County of Virginia.

Now Know Ye, in and for the sum of four hundred pounds current money of Pennsylvania, paid and delivered to the above named Sachems or Chiefs, partly in goods and partly in Gold Money by the said Commissioners, they the said Sachems or Chiefs on behalf of the said Six Nations do hereby renounce and disclaim not only all the right of the said Six Nations, but also recognize and acknowledge the right and title of our Sovereign, the King of Great Britain to all the land within the said Colony as it now or may hereafter be peopled and bounded by his said Majesty, our Sovereign Lord, the King, his Heirs and Successors.

In Witness Whereof, the said Sachems or Chiefs, for themselves and in behalf of the people of the Six Nations aforesaid have herewith set their hands and seals this second day of July in the 18th year of the reign of our Sovereign Lord George the Second King of Great Britain and in the year of our Lord 1744.

Signed by all the above named Chiefs.

Signed, Sealed and Delivered in the presence of Edward Jennings at a General Court held at the Capital, October 25, 1744.

This Deed Poll was proved by ye oaths of Edward Jennings, Esq., Phillip Ludwell Lee, Esq., and William Black, three witnesses thereto and by the Court ordered to be recorded.

Teste: (Signed)

BEN. WALTER, Cl. Ct.

Early Customs.

It was some time after the first settlement of the county before the pioneers had the convenience of grist-mills. In the meantime various substitutes were devised. First, was the hominy block, then followed the hand mill. However, the settlers, later, availed themselves of the excellent water power furnished by the numerous streams in the county and tub mills were built in many localities. The hominy block was made by burning a large cavity like a druggists mortar in a block of elm wood. This was made to hold about a peck of grain. After soaking the grain in tepid water, it was pulverized by a wooden pestle. The coarse and fine particles were separated by a seive made by stretching a perforated

The Joe White Tub Mill, Dry Fork.

deer skin over a hoop. The fine meal was used for bread and the coarse for hominy.

The log house was necessarily the only kind of house built. The first houses were unhewn. The floor was made of puncheons. The roof was made of clapboards held on with weight poles. The stairway was a ladder of pegs fastened in the side wall. Some cabins were built with fire places so large that practically an entire tree could be used as a back-log. There was a door at each end of the fire place, which extended nearly across the cabin, and a horse would be driven in, dragging the log by the chain. Then the chain would be unhooked and the horse would be loosened and go out the other door. The log would then be rolled into the fire place.

The first settlers were under the necessity of making, with their own hands, or at least having made in the immediate neighborhood all the things essential in the home and on the farm. Every well ordered household had a loom, spinning wheel, little and big, a flax breaker, sheep shears and wool carders. All the processes that converted the wool or flax

A Pioneer Kitchen.

into clothing were deftly done at home with their own tools, by the mothers and daughters. The apparel worn by both sexes was made from linen and woolen fabrics, which had been woven on the loom in the farm house and dyed with coperas in combination with various barks. Buckskin pants were often worn, and vests from fawn skins and caps from coon skins were in vogue in some communities until the Civil War. In the winter, moccasins were worn. They were made from deer skin, came up around the ankles and were tied with "buck-skin" strings.

Stoves did not come into use until a comparatively recent period. All cooking was done over the fire place or in the bake oven. Kettles were suspended from a hook and trammel, which was fastened to an iron bar, secured in the chimney above. Matches not being in use, fires were kept as much as possible by covering live coals, or burning embers with ashes. When the fires went out however, a "chunk" was brought from a neighbor's supply, or resort was had to flint and steel with punk and tow. Kerosene lamps, being a later day in-

A Pioneer Barn.

novation, candles, pine knots or the ordinary dip light was improvised. The "dip" was made by immersing a twisted thread or cotton string in hog's lard or bear's oil and lighting the free end.

The practice of agriculture was rude and the most primitive tools were used. The plow was made entirely of wood and oxen drew them, as a rule, instead of horses. Harrows were made of wooden pegs in a wooden frame. Sometimes crab bushes or thorn bushes were substituted. The harvest was gathered with a sickle. Forks were made from forked dogwood saplings. Threshing was done, usually, with a flail and fifteen bushels was considered one day's work. Newly shod horses were sometimes used to tramp out the grain. Two or three pairs of horses would tramp out fifty bushels in one day. The grain was separated from the chaff by throwing both in the air and letting the wind separate them. Then came the hand wind mill and later the horse power thresher.

In pioneer days a wedding was an event of great social importance. No effort was spared to celebrate the event in such a way as to make the event a memorable one. It was a time of much mirth and pleasure. The wedding party started in a double file from the home of the groom, when within a mile of the home of the bride, an Indian warhoop was given and all raced at full speed. The one reaching the house first was given a bottle that was awaiting the victor. All were then expected to participate, men and women, in the refreshing and stimulating contents of the bottle, when it was returned to the winner. A feast followed the wedding ceremony, which was duplicated at the infare at the groom's home. Horn and puter spoons and hunting knives not infrequently adorned the table on these occasions. After supper the young people enjoyed themselves in the misty mazes of the dance. In pioneer parlance, it was the "hoe down." Occasionally the violinist was not an expert in his art and if his music failed to ascend in lofty and inspiring strains or fall in soft and sweet cadences, it was then that some rustic and unappreciative youth would likely compare his strident strains to "choking the goose." Other occasional festivities were corn huskings, log rollings, and house raisings. In the fall months, on a moonlight night the pioneer would ask in his neighbors, and from dark until 11 or 12 o'clock there would be a joyous combination of work and sport. There would be a contest between individuals and groups as to which would finish their work first, or which would find the most red ears of corn. All hands would occasionally take a rest to draw fresh inspiration from the pitcher of cider or the jug of "apple jack." The log rolling and the house raising were also affairs of festivities as well as of hard work. These undertakings were impossible undertakings alone, but with the combined assistance of friends and neighbors the task was easy. Then it afforded an opportunity to cultivate the social amenities. While father and son were busy with the throng at the rolling or raising, the mother and daughter were having a season of mirth and enjoyment at the house, cooking and quilting.

Wild Animals.

The mountains and valleys of what is now Randolph county was the habitat of many wild animals. This was a blessing to the pioneer in many ways. They not only supplied his larder with meat, but their skins covered his nakedness and protected him from the elements. The hunt and the chase also furnished him with diversion and relieved the monotony of an isolated life. The elk, deer, buffalo, panther, bear, otter, beaver, raccoon, wolf and catamount were the principal wild animals found by the first white men. The panther and wolf perhaps yet remain in very limited numbers in the eastern part of the county. The elk and buffalo disappeared early. A few deer remain and the black bear is rather plentiful in the mountain districts in the eastern part of the county. The wild turkey, pheasant and owl were here in abundance. The eagle, though not so plentiful, made its home among the crags and cliffs of our mountain peaks. The wolf was very numerous and very troublesome to the pioneer. It was necessary to fasten sheep and calves in an enclosure every night to prevent their destruction. Wolves were soon decimated, not so much by the hunter's rifle as the prevalence of rabies among them. Many were infected, "went mad," and often attacked the settlers in their homes. Wolves exhibited great cunning in preying upon other animals. They hunted in packs. They followed the deer in company until they became tired, then one kept the deer going until it made a turn in the direction of another wolf, which was sniffing the wind for scent of its prey. The deer was thus pursued by fresh wolves until it became the victim of their ravenous appetites.

The black bear is a timid animal and is not inclined to attack man only in self defense or in defense of its young. It was an object of superstitious reverence to the Indians, who never killed it without apologizing and deploring the necessity which impelled them to do so.

CHAPTER IV.

AMONG THE RECORDS OF RANDOLPH.

RANDOLPH COUNTY was formed by an act of the Virginia Assembly, October, 1786, and the house of Benjamin Wilson in Tygarts Valley was designated as the place for holding the first court. The territory of the new county

Randolph's First Court House.
(From an old photograph.)

embraced all of the present county of Tucker, half of the present county of Barbour, half of Upshur and a large part of Webster.

We give below the proceedings of the first County Court held in Randolph County. We have endeavored to produce the record as it is found in the time worn book, using the original words, spelling and punctuation:

Be It Remembered that at the House of Benjamin Wilson on the 28 day of May 1787, a Commission of the Peace &c held a session of Oyer & Terminer for the said county directed and ordered that Jacob Westfall, Salathiel Goff, Patrick Hamilton, John Wilson, Cornelius Westfall, Edward Jackson, Robert Maxwell, Peter Cassity, Cornelius Bogard, John Jackson, George Westfall, Henry Runyan, John Hadden & Johnathan Parsons, Gent, was presented and read. Whereupon the Ooath of Allegiance to the Commonwealth was administered by the said Patrick Hamilton, to the said Salathiel Goff and also the Oath of Office as directed by law, and by the said Salathiel Goff to Patrick Hamilton, John Wilson, Cornelius Westfall, Edward Jackson, Robert Maxwell, Peter Cassity, Cornelius Bogard, John Jackson, Geo. Westfall, Henry Runyan, John Hadden, & Jonathan Parsons.

Jacob Westfall, Gent. produced a commission of Sheriff from his Excellency the Governor Baring Date the 17th day of April 1787 which was openly Read, whereupon the Said Jacob Westfall, Gent. after entering into the bond, with Edward Jackson &c Salathiel Goff his Securities took the Oath of Allegiance and the Oath of Office as directed by law. John Wilson was chosen Cleark of the Court of Randolph county and after giving bond with Jacob Westfall for Security for the due and faithful execution of his office took the Oath Allegiance to the Commonwealth and the Oath of Office prescribed by law.

Upon motion William McCleary admitted to practice as an Attorney in Randolph County and the necessary Oaths prescribed by law & paid the Tax Directed by Law.

That Wm. Mc Leary be allowed the sum of four pounds to be paid quarterly by the Court for one Year Should the Court think proper to continue for that time, who is now admitted Attorney for the Commonwealth. Edward Jackson & John Haymond candidates for the Prinsible Surveyors Office for Jackson 7 votes for Haymond 4 votes.

That Edward Jackson be recommended to the Governor as a proper person to fill the Office of Surveyor, he being of Probity & Good Character.

That Salathiel Goff and Cornelius Bogard be recommended to the Governor as proper persons to fill the Office of Coroner.

That Jacob Westfall be recommended to his Excellency, the Governor as a proper person to fill the office of Lieut. of this county.

Patrick Hamilton Col.

John Wilson Major.

That the Public Buildings be erected on the Lands of James Westfall in that space of ground bounded by James Westfall fenses on the lower end of his plantation and the River & by a line, drawn from the River at Right angles passing the old School house and Westfalls Land and by the County Road.

If any spot within the tract of this order delineated that Jacob Westfall and Cornelius Bogard may appoint who is hereby appointed to view and lay off a certain tract not exceeding One Acre, the Said James Westfall giving and Granting the said Tract of One Acre together with Public Buildings.

That John Hadden, John Jackson & Cornelius Bogard be appointed Commissioners of Taxable Property.

That the Court do now adjourn till tomorrow Nine O'clock.

Salathiel Goff.

The next day May 29, 1787 the Court resumed its session. Jacob Riffle, Michael Yokum, Joseph Cooper, Thomas Holder, and Chas. Falanash were appointed Constables. Hezekiah Rosencranse was appointed Surveyor of Roads from Eberman's Creek, (now Chenoweth's Creek) to Files Creek. The House of James Westfall was selected as the place of holding the next Court. A wagon road was ordered opened from Mudlick at the County Road to Cheat River at the Horse Shoe Bottom. A bridle road was ordered to be opened from Connelies Lick to the Top of the Alleghany. Wm. Smith was appointed Surveyor of Roads from James Friend's to Wm. England's Ford. Uriah Gandy was appointed Surveyor of Roads from Benj. Wilson's to top of Alleghany.

The first session of Court held in what is now the town of Beverly, convened at the house of James Westfall, May

29, 1787. This house was a log structure, and was situated on the West side of Main Street adjoining the S. N. Bosworth house on the north. This house remained a landmark of pioneer days until long after the civil war. The "worshipful Justices" who conducted this session of court were "Edward Jackson, Robert Maxwell, Peter Cassity, and Cornelius Bogard, Gent."

At the June term of the court, this body entered upon new duties and performed functions hitherto not exercised. No controversy over property rights had so far marred the tranquility of the pioneer period. However, at the August term, no less than seventeen cases were on the docket. The style of the first case demanding the attention of the court at the June term was Wm. Peterson, plaintiff, vs. James Lackey, defendant. Judgment was given in favor of the plaintiff in the sum of $11.65. The first order for recording a deed for the conveyance of real estate was also passed at this term of the court.

Ebenezer Petty conveyed by deed 200 acres to Gabriel Friend. James Westfall was granted permission to "lay out lots for the purpose of a town between the fence or lower end of his plantation, the river on the West, Benjamin Wilson's line on the North and the county road on the east & that he have town lots laid off & Exposed to sale the first Day of August Court." (1787). No name had been given the embryotic town at that time, but later it was called Edmonton, and retained this appellation until three years later when by an Act of the Virginia Assembly the town of Beverly was created. At this term of the court the county was divided into three assessment districts as follows:

John Hadden's District:—From Simeon Harris' and Aaron Richardson's up Tygarts Valley, a straight line to Roaring Creek to the head, thence up Middle Fork to the head, thence to the Greenbrier line, "the neardest direction" and from the said Harris' to the Rockingham line, "the neardest direction."

John Jackson's District:—From John Haddan's line on Roaring Creek to its junction with the Valley River, thence a straight line where the road leading to Clarksburg crosses Laurel Run, the old pack road called "Pringle's Road," thence with this road to the head of Clover Run, thence with the meanders of Laurel Hill to the county line.

Cornelius Bogard's District:—All of Randolph County not included in Hadden's and Jackson's districts.

In more than one sense the court at this session became a trail blazer and a pathfinder. Highways were ordered to be viewed that were destined to become roads of State and National importance. Commissioners were appointed to report to the court on the "convenience and inconvenience" that would attend the opening of a road from John Jackson's on Buckhannon River to the court house in Beverly. This road was located some years later. The Staunton and Parkersburg pike was constructed practically on the same route, and became part of a great thoroughfare from the east to the Ohio river. It was also used extensively in military operations during the civil war.

John Wilson was appointed Surveyor of Highways from Mudlick in Tygarts Valley to foot of mountain on Northeast side of Horseshoe Bottom.

The July term, 1787, marked the beginning of the supervision and control of the liquor trafic in Randolph County. Jacob Westfall was "admitted to retail liquor till the November court and no longer without license."

During these years of peace Indian hostilities may have been in abeyance, yet the records evidence the fact that the Red Man was busy appropriating the settlers horses. The court ordered that Charles Parsons be exempted from paying taxes on "three horse creatures that have been taken from him by the Indians since the 9, of March last past." A similar order was passed in regard to five horses lost by Henry Fink and several lost by John Warwick. At this term of the court Nathan Nelson was brought before the court on the charge of being a vagabond and gave bond for his good behavior. Among the cases tried at this term of the court were the following:

John Smith vs. Michael Isner. Judgment for 4 pounds.

Jacob Stalnaker vs. John Phillips. The case agreed.

Ralph Stewart vs. James Pringle. Continued.

John Alford vs. Joseph Parsons. In this case the plaintiff made oath that he was afraid that the defendant would do him a private injury. Accordingly Parsons was put under bond to "keep the peace of the world and especially John Alford."

At this term of the court Hugh Turner and William Wilson were appointed to draw plans for a county jail, let the contract for its erection to the lowest bidder and report the same to the next August court.

At the July (1787) term provision was made for the first election to be held in Randolph County. Overseers of the Poor were to be elected. All other county officers except Members of the Legislature were appointive. It seems strange that the more important and remunerative offices of Sheriff and Clerk of the Court would be appointed by the Justices and the insignificant office of Overseer of the Poor be made elective at so much trouble and expense to the people.

The county was laid off into four districts as follows:

District 1, west of Rich Mountain, down to the Valley River, down the west side of the river to the county line. The territory between that line and Harrison county was the district, and John Jackson was appointed to conduct the election.

District 2, that part of the county northeast of Rich Mountain and east of Valley River, including the Horse Shoe setlement from Wilmoth's settlement down. Salathiel Goff was appointed to conduct the election.

District 3. The remainder of the county was "divided by a line due east from Rich Mountain, passing by William Wamsley's." North of the line was the third district and Robert Maxwell was appointed to hold the election.

District 4 consisted of the remainder of the county, and Patrick Hamilton was appointed to hold the election. The Sheriff was ordered to oversee the elections and make returns at the September court. Returns were not made until November, and then in only two districts. In No. 2, William Westfall and David Minear were elected; in No. 3, Aaron Richardson, Thomas Philips and William Wilson.

At this court Hugh Turner was ordered to draw plans and specifications for a jail, and the Sheriff was ordered to advertise for bids for building the jail.

At the August court, 1787, the first grand jury was drawn. The names were: John Hamilton, Daniel Westfall, Valentine Stalnaker, Jacob Stalnaker, John Currence, Simeon Harris, Joseph Crouch, Charles Nelson, Solomon Ryan, Abraham Kittle, Thomas Phillips, William Wilson, Charles Myers, Michael Isner, Nicholas Petro, Nicholas Wolf and Andrew Skidmore.

At the August term (1787) Jacob Westfall made the following report in reference to the county jail: "Jacob Westfall, Gent. came into court and reported that he struck off the building of the Public Jail to a certain Edward Hart, to be finished by the next March court." No reference was made as to the price at which the contract was given. Joseph Crouch was appointed Surveyor of Roads from Geo. Westfall's Mill up to John Alexander's plantation. Alexander Addison applied for a recommendation from the court to obtain a licence to practice law. He was given one year in which to obtain such license. At the expiration of this time the order of the court was to become void if he had not obtained law license in the meantime. A similar order was made in regard to Wm. McLeary.

At the September court (1787) John Wilson was allowed 200 pounds of tobacco "for service in regard to the tax law." This allowance was in all probability for the collection of the land tax, and was equivalent to $6.65.

The first reference to the insane is found in the records of that term of the court. Philip and David Minear informed the court that their brother John Minear "was crazy and had eloped from their charge and strayed into Monongalia County." They were given authority to take charge of him and his property.

The records of the October term (1787) reveal that John Jackson was appointed Captain of the Buckhannon Company and Edward Jackson Colonel of this county. Edward Jackson was grandfather of Thomas Jonathan (Stonewall) Jackson. Colonel Edward Jackson, though his military record was humble and obscure, may have possessed, for aught we know, the military genius of his illustrious grandson. He may have been one of those "gems of purest ray serene the dark unfathomed caves of oceans bear" and Stonewall may have inherited those qualities of a soldier that gave him imperishable renown from his paternal grandfather.

Two indictments were found at the November (1787) term for illegally retailing liquor. These indictments, as the record states, were found on the information of two members of the Grand Jury. At the same term of the court we find many orders similar to this one: Ordered that the killing of one old wolf by John Hadden be liquidated. Evidently the killing of wolves was an important infant industry. Meagre and indefinite information is found in the records of the following cases tried at this term of the court:

Cornelius Bogard vs. Wm. Short. Refused to be taken.

John Hamilton vs. Pat. Hamilton. Refused to be taken.

Benjamin Hornbeck vs. Joseph Summerfield. Not found.

At the January term (1788) Benjamin Hornbeck was "admitted to retail liquor for the term of the present day." The reason for the brevity of the life of his license is not clear. Perhaps he only wanted to dispense the ardent on the first day of court. In the earlier years of the county and even up to the second decade after the civil war the first day of court was largely in the nature of a social gathering. An event in which the monotony and isolation of pioneer life were broken by an exchange of greetings and experience of people similarly situated. Under these circumstances the wine not infrequently flowed with a spirit of good feeling and comradship. Hence the necessity of "admitting Mr. Hornbeck to retail liquor for the term of the present day."

At the same term of the court it was ordered that a certificate be issued to the Governor in favor of Wm. Blair for an increase in his pension for a wound received while rendering military service for the commonwealth under Colonel Charles Lewis at the battle of Point Pleasant, October 10, 1774.

Tavern rates were regulated at that term of the court as follows:

Maderia wine, per half pint		25		cents
Other wines, " " "		20	5-6	"
West India rum " " "		16	2-3	"
Other rums " " "		12	1-2	"
Peach brandy " " "		11	1-9	"
Good whiskey " " "		11	1-9	"
Dinner		16	2-3	"
Breakfast		12	1-2	"
Supper		12	1-2	"
Lodging, in clean sheets each night		8	1-3	"
Corn and oats, per gallon		11	1-9	"
Horse at hay, every 12 hours		11	1-9	"
Pasture, every 24 hours		8	1-2	"

Mr. McLeary was recommended to the Judges of the Court of Appeals as a suitable person to fill the office of Clerk of their court in Monongalia County.

At the May term (1788) the court ordered that the Sheriff collect $26.66 "for E. Hart to carry on the publick's joal."

At the July term (1788) the following extraordinary order was recorded: "That a writ go forth to bring Garret Lambert before the next court to show cause why he does not betake himself to lawful employment & demean himself as required by the laws of the Commonwealth." The exercise of such jurisdiction by the courts today would no doubt be considered an unwarranted infringement of personal liberty.

On the 22nd day of September, 1788, the court took the initial steps to build the first court house for Randolph County. The Justices of the Peace had previously prepared plans and specifications for the temple of justice and it was ordered that they be given to the Sheriff, who was directed to advertise for contracts for its construction.

At the February term (1789) the bond of Jacob Westfall, Sheriff, was fixed at $53.333. At the same term of the court Edward Hart was allowed $85 for building the jail to be paid when completed and delivered. James Cunningham was allowed $2.66 for bringing Acts of Assembly of Virginia from Richmond. At that term of the court it was ordered that Hugh Turner be paid $200 for building the Court House. Wm. McLeary, Attorney for the Commonwealth, was allowed $40 as his salary for one year.

At the March term of the court (1789) the Sheriff's house was "appointed a jail until the next term of the court."

At the April term (1789) Robert Maxwell served notice that he intended petitioning the General Assembly setting forth the utility of a ferry on Leading Creek from the lands of Robert Maxwell to Jonas Friend's. At the same term of the court Gabriel Dowell was ordered to appear at the next term and give security for the maintenance of himself and wife or be subject to the vagrant act. Dowell evidently gave no heed to the action of the court as that body at the next term ordered that both he and his wife be "taken by Constable William Hadden to Constable David Minear and he convey them into Washington County, Maryland, and there leave them."

At the July term of the court (1789) it was ordered that the roads from the county seat to Roaring Creek and from Jonas Friend's to Pringle's Ford and from Connalie's Lick to the top of Alleghany and from Wilson's Mill to the top of Alleghany at the Pendleton line be worked once a year and then cleared for a good bridle path eight feet wide. This order gives an insight into the status of the roads of that day. The roads mentioned above were among the important highways of the county at that time and no effort was made to keep them in a state of repair surpassing the bridal path standard.

The Grand Jury at the August term (1789) found only one indictment. There was one indictment for retailing apple brandy above the legal rate. The indictment was made on the information of five members of the Grand Jury. The importance and emoluments of the office of Commonwealth's Attorney had been keeping pace with the growth of the county. At this same term Wm. McLeary's allowance was raised to $33.33 per annum if there were two terms of the court and $50.00 if there were four terms. At the same term the Justices of the Peace took the oath of office as "required by Congress to support the Constitution of the United States." The constitution had been recently ratified and this was the first record of reference to the constitution.

At the September court (1789) Moses Ware was given a certificate for a land warrant for 400 acres of land for services as Sergeant in Colonel Gipson's regiment. The certificate explains that the warrant was taken from him when he was "captivated by the Indians." It does not say when or where. The court issued the certificate to Moses Ward, but at a subsequent term corrected its error by substituting Ware instead of Ward. The court at that term passed an order exempting Jacob Springstone from working the highway until he "be in a better state of health, he now being unsane."

Peace and pleasantness evidently did not prevail among the "worshipful" Justices at the March term (1790). Edward Jackson went before the Grand Jury and indicted his colleague, Robert Maxwell, for being drunk, whereupon Maxwell gave information to the Grand Jury that resulted in Jackson being indicted for the same offense. Jackson confessed, but Maxwell stood trial and was acquitted.

At the April term (1790) the court ordered that Hugh Turner be paid $200 to enable him to carry on the building of the court house, and that $200 be paid him subsequently, making the entire cost of the court house $400. At the same term the jail was accepted from Edward Hart, the contractor. Prisoners, who had been boarding with the Sheriff, could henceforth be domiciled at a home especially provided for them.

The Sheriff was ordered, at the June term (1790), to pay Wm. Blair $33.33, his pension for that year. Mr. Blair was wounded at the battle of Point Pleasant, October 10, 1774, while serving under Colonel Charles Lewis.

The town of Edmonton was destined to have a brief official life. Only once in the records was there any reference to Edmonton. At the October term (1790) a road was ordered opened from the town of Edmonton to Roaring Creek. In August of the next year, Beverly made its official bow to the public in the court records, when Edward Hart was licensed to keep an ordinary in the town of Beverly.

At the November term (1790) Maxwell Armstrong was the third attorney to be admitted to practice law in Randolph.

Thomas Wilson succeeded Wm. McCleary as Commonwealth's Attorney at the March term (1791) of the court. No reason was given for retiring Mr. McLeary.

At the May term (1791) Jacob Lewis was appointed ad-

ministrator of the estate of Joseph Kinnan. Mr. Lewis was
a brother of the widow Kinnan, whose husband was killed by
the Indians May 11th of that year, only a few weeks previous.
It will be seen by reference to another chapter that Mr. Lewis
made his escape from the Indians by way of a window in a
rear room where he was sleeping when the Kinnan house was
attacked by the Indians. Withers' "Border Warfare" is in
error as to the name and date. Withers has the name Caanan
and the date of the occurrence·in the latter part of the summer of 1794.

The records of the September term (1791) reveal that
Edward Hart, who built the jail was licensed to keep an
ordinary, also conducted a cooper's shop by the spring. The
adjacent forests with their retention of moisture made, probable, the existence of springs in the town of Beverly.

The cooper's trade in that day was a useful and important one. All tubs, casks, kegs, and barrels were made by
hand. The order referring to these subjects and prescribing
prison bounds reads as follows: Beginning at the corner of
Ed. Hart's lot on the Front street opposite to the lot next
above the lot whereon the court house is, thence down to
the lot Hart's cooper shop is on by the spring, thence down
with the lower line of the town to the lower end thereof,
thence up to the front street and thence to the beginning.
Imprisonment for debt was a legal proceeding and it is
probable that the boundaries here given applied particularly
to that class of prisoners. Creditors were compelled to pay
the expense of imprisoned debtors.

The sympathies of the court for those who were compelled to travel the long and lonesome mountain roads, without the company and consolation of something to revive and
cheer their drooping spirits, assumed a practical turn at the
June term (1792) when that body passed the following order:
"That Thomas Summerfield be permitted to retail liquor on
the road that leads from Tygarts Valley to the North Fork,
without payment of license, for the benefit of travelers on
such a long and lonesome road." At this same term of court
dollars and cents appeared for the first time on the records
of the county. Pounds, shillings and pence were used in the

transaction of the county for two or three years later, but gradually went out of use. Tobacco was the legal currency of Virginia until 1794. Official fees and county levies were frequently computed in pounds of tobacco. At this same session of the court a committe was appointed to examine the falls of the Tygarts Valley river, in the present county of Taylor, and report on the probable expense of putting them in condition for fish to ascend the river. At the July term additional action was taken and the cooperation was asked of the Harrison County Court with the expression of the hope that it would meet with "your worships approbation." However, nothing has been done to this day, though there has been perennial agitation of the project.

The first reference to a saw mill in the records of Randolph is found in the proceedings of 1794, when Jacob Westfall was permitted to erect a saw mill near the town of Beverly. Prior to this time the slab and the puncheon and the product of the cross-cut answered every purpose. The first steam saw mill is said to have been brought into this county from Virginia in 1878.

It is surprising that in so short a time, the most of our timber, our greatest natural wealth, the result of the provident process of the ages, should be without thought or consideration for the future, used, wasted and destroyed.

Indictments in most cases in the years of 1795-96 were for assault and battery. Although presentments for Sabbath breaking, "profane swearing" selling liquor "by the small," and against overseers of the highway for neglect of duty were by no means infrequent. In that day the individual's ability to take care of himself in conflict with savages and wild animals was considered a very desirable characteristic and the man who exceeded his fellows in strength and agility was looked upon as a hero in his community. An influence and environment of this sort necessarily resulted in personal encounters which terminated in the courts.

Randolph was still without a court house in 1795, though its construction had been undertaken seven years previous. At the August term (1795) the court ordered suit to be instituted against Edward Hart for failure to complete it.

The court at the September term (1795) gives us an index to the rate of daily wages in that day, when it allowed 50 cents a day to guards for prisoners at the jail for their services.

The records of the December term (1795) indicate that there was an Indian scare in the valley in that year. At that term of the court an allowance for patrolling Leading Creek was made to Thomas Phillips, Jacob Kittle, Samuel Ball, John Phillips and Moses Shuter. Although the Indians had not visited the valley since May, 1791, the settlers evidently believed that a raid was iminent.

There was a smallpox scare in Randolph in May, 1798. The court met in special session but did nothing except summon all the Justices in the county to attend the next session and to take action to prevent the spread of the disease. The records of the court are silent as to any further efforts to stop the contagion.

The limited income of the pioneer, together with the necessities of incessant toil, incident to the conversion of the wilderness into cleared and cultivated fields, with the distance and inconvenience of travel to good schools made anything but a rudimentary education for their children beyond their hope or ambition. The will of Raphael Warthen when admitted to record in 1798, is interesting for the reason that it shows the extent of the average and expected education of the youth of that period. One provision of his will provided that "as much of my estate as will be sufficient to educate my children to read properly, to write plainly and to have a knowledge of arithmetic as far as the rule commonly called the simple rule of three."

From the fact that the sickle was the tool commonly used in cutting grain and the flail and the winnowing sheet the usual method of threshing grain, made anything except limited crops in the early period of the settlement of this county, impossible. The inventory of the estate of Nicholas Wolfe gives information of the kind and quantity of the crops raised by the farmers in 1800, the year the appraisement of his estate was admitted to record. It was as follows: 5 acres of rye,

3 acres of wheat, 8 acres of corn, 5 acres of meadow, and 4 acres of oats.

Neither dude nor dullard ever became a pioneer. Discontent presupposes intelligence and contemplation. The first settlers of Randolph evidently were dissatisfied with conditions in their native land. They left home and friends to seek free homes in a free country for themselves and their children. It required hope, courage, decision and determination to undergo the isolation, hardships, and the inconveniences incident to the life of the pioneer. They may, or may not have had the advantages of a liberal education, yet they possessed excellent judgment and good common sense. It would be interesting to know the books they read and the nature and extent of their libraries. In the records of the county there are only vague hints on this subject. In the list of articles of the estate of Nicholas Wolf, sold at vendue in 1800, we find that three "Dutch books and one English Almanac" brought 50 cents. In the inventory of the estate of Jacob Westfall, there is listed the following books; 6 volumes Doddridge on the New Testament, 4 volumes Goldsmith, 2 volumes Pope's Homer, 2 volumes Flower's History, 2 Spectator, 2 Parcels old books, 2 volumes Blair's Lectures, 1 Book Washington's Reports, 1 Clark's Magazine.

From the report of the Commissioners appointed to pass upon disputed land entries, their report as recorded in this county, shows that Peter Poffenberger and John Bush settled on Radcliff's Run, on the Buckhannon River in 1774, and that John Fink settled on Fink's Run in the same year.

In the appraisement of the estate of Nicholas Wolf (1803) poplar boards were rated at $10 per thousand feet. Among the items of the expenses attending the sale of his personal estate we find this one: "one other gallon of liquor, 75 cents." In the sale of the personal effects of St. Leger Stout about the same time, some of the articles commanded the following prices: One pair dog irons $2.00; two pot trambles and fire shovel, $4.00; fifteen pewter spoons, $5.85. Dog irons and trambles, once articles of universal use, are practically unknown and discarded today. Dog irons or fire dogs were used to support the fore stick in an open fireplace.

Trammels were pendent hooks for suspending pots, kettles, etc., over an open fireplace. Chimneys were not in use prior to the early part of the 14th century and cooking and heating stoves are comparatively modern innovations. In 1741 Benjamin Franklin invented what he called a Pennsylvania fireplace, which consisted of several plates of cast iron with a shutter to regulate the draught and a register to distribute the heat. From this rude construction the modern stove has evolved. Previous to 1825 the use of stoves, generally of the box pattern, and of very rude pattern, was confined to stores, halls, hotels, barrooms, school houses, and churches, in the cities and larger towns. Not until the building of the B. & O. railroad, making possible the transportation of heavy goods, did the use of stoves come into general use in this county.

In the records of the court for the year 1803 we find the following item, in the report of an Administrator: "burial expenses, coffin, shirt and liquor and accommodations at the sale, $24.00."

In will book No. 1, page 23, there is recorded a list of the personal property of Joseph Kinnan, sold at vendue by Edward Hart, Administrator, and admitted to record, June 26, 1793. Mr. Hart(in his final settlement a few years later, among the necessary expenses incurred) mentions five gallons of whiskey. It was the custom in the pioneer period to treat or give free drinks to those in attendance upon a public auction. Perhaps the object was to promote a liberal attendance, as well as a condition of mental opulence among the prospective purchasers. The list is interesting from the fact that it gives an insight into the possessions of the average pioneer as well as the prices these articles commanded in that day. Mr. Kinnan, it will be remembered, was killed by the Indians, at his home near the mouth of Elkwater. The list is as follows:

Two pair shears	$ .50
One pot tramble	3.33
One keg	.40
One keg	.35
Two rockers	.90
Pewter	.80
One mattock	1.15
One cleavis	.35

Shoes and brush.. 2.00
Plow and irons.. 2.00
One kettle 1.85
One scythe 1.70
One ax 1.60
One horse 21.60
One ox 4.00
One heifer 7.50
Two yearling steers... 11.00
Two yearling calves... 12.00
One scythe 1.00
One jug .... .18
One bucket .... .35
One frying pan.. .70
One musket .... .90
One cow and calf... 17.25
One cow 11.25
One horse 7.25
One mare 12.50
One mare and bell.. 15.50
Hogs 40.00
Three sheep 6.50
Grain, upper place... 6.65
Two stacks of hay.. 1.65
Flax, growing .... .50
Corn on Sylvester Ward's loft.................................... 10.65
One brown horse.. 55.95
One bay colt... 18.95

Wills Recorded in Randolph County.

A list of wills recorded in Randolph County prior to 1836 is given below, with the name of the testator and the date of record:

Andrew McMullen	1788	Adam Stalnaker	1814
George Ward	1791	Jacob Helmick	1815
David Haddan	1791	John Phillips	1815
Jacob Stalnaker	1791	Isaac Kittle	181
John Miller	1794	Ebenezer Kelley	1816
Jeremiah Channell	1797	Isaac Bond	1816
Raphael Warthen	1798	Hezekiah Rosencrantz	1819
Catherine Carlick	1801	Martin C. Poling	1819
Thomas White	1802	Martin Poling	1820
Josiah Westfall	1802	James McLean	1820
John Haddan	1803	George Mitchell	1822
Vincent Marsh	1804	Robert Phares	1823
St.Leger Stout	1806	Elias Alexander	1825
Thomas Phillips	1806	Boston Stalnaker	1826
Henry Mace	1807	Jacob Weese	1826
Mary Ann Marteny	1809	Samuel Bonnifield	1826
Thomas Holder	1810	Benjamin Hornbeck	1827
Edward Hart	1811	Joseph Summerfield	1828
Charles Myers	1812	Frederick Troutwine	1829
Abraham Kittle	1813	William Parsons	1829

Joseph Pennell	1831	James McClung	1833
John Rush	1831	Valentine Stalnaker	1833
Rinehart Dumire	1831	Henry Petro	1834
Richard Kittle	1831	John Light	1834
John Chenoweth	1832	Richard Ware	1834
Joseph Pitman	1832	Isaac Poling	1834
Sarah Bond	1832	Gilbert Boyle	1835
Jacob Weese	1832	Solomon Collett	1836
Jacob Stagle	1832	Mathew Whitman	1836

First Will Recorded in Randolph.

Below is given a copy of the first will recorded in Ran-dolph County. It is evident fro mits freedom from legal phraseology that it was a product of his own mind. The document is characterized by simplicity and attention to de-tails and left no room for doubts or different construction of meaning. It is as follows:

"In the name of God, Amen, I, Andrew McMullen, of the County of Harrison and State of Virginia, being weak of body but of perfect mind and memory, do make this my last will and testament in manner and form following: That is to say that it is my desire, after my decease, that I be decently buried agreeable to my circumstances, out of what little I have behind; and as my affairs are in a very scattered condi-tion at present, owing to my past troubles, I therefore nomi-nate and appoint Robert Maxwell as my executor to see into and examine what trifles are mine, and goods likewise. When I was at Uriah Gandy's I lent him two pounds, five shillings cash, and gave him an order for a great coat of mine at Thomas Goff's a tailor, and a dollar to pay for the making of it; and I gave him my note, as I got his gun by way of loan. But at the time I was at his house I was not in my head as I ought to have been, and I know not what way the note or anything was; but I hope I will do justice as a Christian. And his gun he can have again; and what service he did for me, I hope he will be paid out of what he owes me. And for what orders I gave or sent Mr. James Cunningham, about getting my traps and other things, I hope they give them up to Robert Maxwell as I have appointed him to settle my affairs. And do acknowledge this and no other to be my last will and testament; as witness my hand and seal this 21, day of June, 1786.

ANDREW McMULLEN.

"Witness; James Taffee and Joseph Friend."

The first deed admitted to record in Randolph is given below:

At a Court held for the County of Randolph the 25th day of June, 1787, the following Deed of Bargain & Sale of 200 Acres of Land from Ebenezer Petty & Elizabeth, his wife to Gabriel Friend was acknowledged and ordered to be Recorded.

This Indenture Executed this Twenty-fifth day of June, in the year of our Lord One Thousand Seven Hundred and Eighty-seven, between Ebenezer Petty and Elizabeth his wife, of Randolph County, and Commonwealth of Virginia, of the one part, and Gabriel Friend, of the County of Washington and State of Maryland, of the other part. Witnesseth, That they the said Ebenezer Petty & Elizabeth his wife, their heirs and assigns for in and consideration of One Hundred and Twenty-five pounds, to them in hand paid, the receipt of which they hereby acknowledge, and themselves fully satisfye. Have bargained and sold and transferred unto the said Gabriel Friend a certain Tract of land lying and being in the said County of Randolph, on the west side of Tigers Valley River, adjoining the lands of John Harness and John Crouch, junior, and boundede as followeth, towit: Beginning at a Maple thence south Ten Degrees East Ninety-six Poles to a Beach, South Twelve degrees west Sixty-eight Poles to two Syca- more, South Eighteen degrees West Thirty-two Poles to a Sycamore & Elm, South nine degrees East Thirty Poles to a Sycamore and Walnut, North Eighty-six degrees, East Thirty poles to two walnuts, South Seventy degrees, East fifty-two poles to an Elm and Walnut, North forty-two Degrees East Seventy-four Poles to two White oaks, East fifty-eight poles to a Sycamore, North Seventy-one degrees East thirty-three poles to two Cherries John Harnesses Cor- ner North thirty-eight degrees west one hundred & forty poles to a Spanish Oak near two Pines his Corner North thirty-three degrees West Eighty poles to a white oak, his Corner South Eighty-seven degrees west. Ninety-six poles to the Beginning. Containing two hundred acres and appurtenances to have and to hold the said Tract or parcel of Land with its appurtenances to the said Gabriel Friend his Heirs and assigns forever.

In witness of the presents we have hereunto set our hands and affixed our Seals this Day and Date above written.

EBENEZER PETTY   [Seal]

her

ELIZABETH C. (X) PETTY, [Seal]

mark

Recorded and Examined

Teste: JOHN WILSON, C R C

The Price of a Slave.

In deed book No. 10, page 378 of the county of Randolph, can be found a document, bearing date of October 30, 1830, recording the sale of a slave, Henrietta Crown, to Geo. Buckey of Beverly. Henrietta gained the favor of her master and his family and remained with them to the time of her death, some thirty years subsequent to the time of obtaining her freedom. Mr. Buckey was opposed to the institution of slavery, though it meant to him financial loss and was a Union sympathizer in the war between the states. Below is a copy of the instrument of writing in that transaction:

Know all men by these presents, that I, George Washington Hilleary, of Prince George County, State of Maryland, for and in consideration of the sum of Two Hundred and Forty Dollars, to me in hand paid by George Buckey, of the town of Beverly, county of Randolph, and state of Virginia, to and before the sealing and delivery of these presents, the receipt whereof I do hereby acknowledge, have bargained, sold, granted and confirmed, and by these presents do bargain, sell, grant and confirm to the said George Buckey a certain female slave named Henny, to have and to hold said female negro slave and her future increase to the only proper use and behalf of the said George Buckey, his executors, administrators, and assigns forever, and I, the said George Washington Hilleary for myself, my executor and administrators, the said female negro slave with her future increase to the said George Buckey, his executors, administrators and assigns, and against all and every other person or persons whatsoever shall warrant and forever defend by these presents.

In witness whereof I have hereunto set my hand and affixed my hand and seal this 27th day of October in the year 1830.

GEORGE WASHINGTON HILLEARY,

(Seal)
Teste: Squire Bosworth,
Randolph County Court,
February Term A. D. 1831.

This bill of sale from Geo. W. Buckey appeared to have been acknowledged before the Deputy Clerk of the Court is ordered to be recorded.

Teste: A. EARLE, C. R. C.

The following names appear in the records of Randolph County prior to the year 1800:

Arnold, Alexander, Armstrong, Allison.

Bogard, Blair, Bodkins, Buffington, Barker, Breeding, Bell, Brigs, Badgely, Beard, Booth, Brown, Ball, Bird, Bishop, Beebe, Bond, Booth, Buckey, Boyles, Berry, Blue, Beaty.

Currence, Crouch, Cassity, Crow, Cooper, Conley, Christy, Clark, Chenoweth, Cook, Claypoole, Carper, Channell, Canfield, Cutright.

Davisson, Donohoe, Deener, Dent, Dawson, Dougherty, Daniels.

Elliott, Eberman, England.

Fink, Fisher, Friend, Ford, Ferguson.

Goff, Good, Gibson, Gandy, Green, Gallatin.

Hamilton, Haddan, Holder, Harness, Haddix, Hough, Hunt,

Hart, Heath, Harris, Howell, Hanna, Henderson, Hickman, Harper, Hacker.

Isner.

Jackson, Jones, Joseph, Jenkins, Jack.

Kittle, Kinnan, Kizer, Kuhn, Kykendale, Kerper.

Lin, Lackey, Lambert, Lowny, Long, Lamberton, Light.

McLeary, McMullen, McClung, Minear, McLean, Mitchell, Maxwell, Marteny, Mace, Myers, Middlebrook, Marstiller, McVicker, Moore, Morris, Miller, Mason.

Nelson, Neale, Neston.

Osburn.

Peterson, Parsons, Post, Petty, Peatro, Pendell, Phillips, Pamcake, Pryor, Patterson, Peter, Price, Patten, Pringle, Pleasants.

Reed, Rose, Rennix, Reeder, Rooney, Ryan, Robert, Riffle, Rosencranse, Rankins, Robinson, Riddle.

Scott, Smith, Stalnaker, Stewart, Summerfield, See, St. Clair, Stout, Steel, Strawder, Seymour, Seitz.

Taffee, Taft, Tolly, Truby, Thompson, Teter, Talbott, Thomas.

Vanscoy, Vandevander.

Westfall, Wilson, Whitman, Warwick, Ward, Wilmoth, Wiseman, Weese, Warthen, Wamsley, Wolfe, White.

Yokum, Yeager, Yenner.

Marriage Licenses.

Below will be found a list of Marriage Licenses issued from 1784 to 1817. Licenses issued prior to 1787 were issued by Harrison County, but the contracting parties lived in what is now Randolph.

1784

MAN'S NAME	WOMAN'S NAME	DAUGHTER OF	BY WHOM MARRIED
John Wamsley	Mary Robinson		
Henry Runyann	Mary Hagel		
Simon Harris	Christian Westfall		
James Bodkin	Mary Westfall		

1785

Man's Name	Woman's Name	Daughter of	By Whom Married
William Briggs	Sarah Westfall		
John Kittle	Elizabeth Wells		
John Haddan	Isabell Elliott		
Alexander Blair	Elizabeth Breeding		
Isaac McHenry	Margaret Blair		
Richard Kittle	Margaret Stalnaker		
David Crouch	Elizabeth Cassety		
John Phillips	Catherine Isner		

1786

David Henderson	Ingra Kittle		
John Jackson, Jr.	Rebecca Haddon		
Thomas Isner	Magelene Miller		

1787

William Low	Eliza Westfall		
David Thomas	Rachael Brooks		

1788

John Cutright	Rebecca Truby		
Zachariah Westfall	Hannah Wolf		
Henry Mace	Ann Currence		
James Holder	Diana Westfall		
William Gibson	Mary W. Henry		
Samuel Stalnaker	Susannah Batchiff		
George Harper	Mary Baxter		
Solomon Ware	Sarah Day	Leonard Day	J. W. Loofborough
Cottrill Tolbert	Elizabeth Reger	Jacob Reger	Isaac Edwards
Philip Reger	Sarah Jackson	John Jackson	Isaac Edwards
Moses Kade	Elizabeth Anglin	William Anglin	Isaac Edwards

1789

Nicholas Wilmoth	Susney Currence		J. W. Loofborough

1790

George Rennix	Judith Westfall	William Westfall	Isaac Edwards

1791

William Crow	Elizabeth Herrin		A. G. Thompson
Isaac Newell	Abagail Vanscoy	Aaron Vanscoy	J. W. Loofborough

1792

Samuel Ball	Elizabeth Maxwell	Robert Maxwell	J. W. Loofborough

1793

Isaac Phillip	Elizabeth Kittle	Jacob Kittle	J. W. Loofborough
John Phillips	Bathia Wells	Phineas Wells	J. W. Loofborough

1794

Robert Clark	Mary Friend	Jonas Friend	Valentine Power
Andrew Friend	Elenor McCall	Peter McCall	J. W. Loofborough
John Donoho	Mary Wilmoth	Thomas Wilmoth	J. W. Loofborough
Benjamin Baggley	Sarah Westfall	George Westfall	Valentine Power
Thomas Shaw	Margaret McCall		J. W. Loofborough
William Currence	Mary Ward	Sylvester Ward	J. W. Loofborough
Samuel Bringham	Sarah Neilson	John Neilson	Valentine Power

1795

Man's Name	Woman's Name	Daughter of	By Whom Married
Aaron Richardson	Jenney Bringham	Widow Bringham	Valentine Power
Samuel Currence	Elizabeth Bogard	Cornelius Bogard	Robert Maxwell
Hez. Rosekrans	Nancy Simpson	John Simpson	Robert Maxwell
George Baker	Susannah Cutright	Benjamin Cutright	Robert Maxwell
Jacob Riffle	Elizabeth Boarer	Jacob Boarer	Robert Maxwell
Aaron McHenry	Ann Gibson	William Gibson	Robert Maxwell
Philip Kunce	Barbara Barnhouse	John Barnhouse	Robert Maxwell
William Daniels	Catharine Stalnaker	Jacob Stalnaker	Robert Maxwell
John Sayler	Mary Ann Minear		Robert Maxwell

1796

Cornelius Westfall	Elizabeth Helmick	Jacob Helmick	Phineas Wells
John Hacker	Susannah Smith	David Smith	Joseph Cheaverout
Robert Clark	Gean Hudkins	Bennett Hudkins	Robert Maxwell
Jacob Shaver	Rachel Davis		Robert Maxwell
John Wilson	Mary Warthen	John Warthen	Matthew Ryan
Jacob White	Elizabeth Pickett	Heehcoat Pickett	Robert Maxwell
Moses Slutter	Nancy Parsons	Joseph Parsons	Phineas Wells
George Stalnaker	Susannah Hart	Edward Hart	Robert Maxwell

1797

James Booth	Phoebe Osborn	Terah Osborn	Robert Maxwell
Martin Miller	Margaret Lochrea	John Lochrea	Robert Maxwell
Abraham Springston	Mary Innis	William Innis	Robert Maxwell
Francis Riffle	Eva Mace	John Mace	Robert Maxwell
Joseph Donoho	Elizabeth Wilmoth	Thomas Wilmoth	Robert Maxwell
Thomas Gough	Rachel Burns	Patrick Burns	Phineahas Wells
Thos. Summerfield	Elizabeth Roy	Joseph Roy	Robert Maxwell
Samuel Keller	Anna Springston	Elizabeth Springston	Robert Maxwell
William Wright	Anna Marsh		Phineahas Wells
Garrett Johnson	Mary England	James England	Robert Maxwell
Henry Paine	Elizabeth Smith	William Smith	Robert Maxwell

1798

Joel Westfall	Elizabeth White	William White	Robert Maxwell
Isaac White	Margaret Haddan	David Haddan	Robert Maxwell
John M. Nail	Christian Riffle	Jacob Riffle	Robert Maxwell
Chris Burgess	Elizabeth Shaw	William Shaw	Robert Maxwell
Thomas Wilmoth	Amy Schoonover	Benj. Schoonover	Robert Maxwell
William Kelly	Gean Kittle	Jacob Kittle	Phineahas Wells
William Clark	Barbara Helmick	Jacob Helmick	Robert Maxwell
James Riddle	Anna Grayson		Phineahas Wells
John Clark	Mary Ryan	Solomon Ryan	Robert Maxwell
James C. Goff	Elizabeth Howell	William Howell	Robert Maxwell

1799

Wm. McCorkle	Juda McHenry	Samuel McHenry	Phinahas Wells
Benjamin Marsh	Sarah Minear	John Minear	Robert Maxwell
Alexander Goff	Elizabeth Riddle	James Riddle	Robert Maxwell
John Cutright	Deborah Osborn	George Osborn	Robert Maxwell
David Whitman	Nancy Daniels		Robert Maxwell
Barney McCall	Ann Buck	Tabitha Buck	Robert Maxwell
James Ferguson	Elizabeth Donoho		Robert Maxwell
Jacob Wees	Sarah Isner	Catharine Philips	Robert Maxwell
John Wilmoth	Mary Cunningham	James Cunningham	Robert Maxwell
Joseph Lyons	Elizabeth Mace	John Mace	Robert Maxwell

MAN'S NAME	WOMAN'S NAME	DAUGHTER OF	BY WHOM MARRIED
Aaron Vanscoy	Gean Taffe	Nancy Grimes	Robert Maxwell
Leonard Hire	Dolly Phyman		Robert Maxwell

1800

Jacob Baker	Nancy Showter		Robert Maxwell
Samuel Harris	Ann Mace	John Mace	Robert Maxwell
Jacob Parker	Elizabeth Burns	Patrick Burns	Phineahas Wells
John Hartley	Mary Roy	Joseph Roy	Robert Maxwell
David White	Eliz. Summerfield	Joseph Summerfield	Robert Maxwell
Levin Nicholas	Margaret Mace	John Mace	Robert Maxwell

1801

David Schoonover	Susanna Wilmoth	Thomas Wilmoth	Robert Maxwell
Richard Reeder	Urie Butcher	Samuel Butcher	Robert Maxwell
Jonathan Buffington	Madaline Helmick	Jacob Helmick	Robert Maxwell
Henry Schoonover	Mary Campfield	Daniel Campfield	Robert Maxwell

1802

Jonathan Daniels	Mary Channel	Joseph Channel	Robert Maxwell
Chris. Lamberton	Sidney Westfall		Robert Maxwell
Daniel Clark	Mary Ware		Robert Maxwell
Jacob Ward	Elizabeth Whitman	Mathew Whitman	Robert Maxwell
Asahel Heath	Eliza Currence	John Currence	Robert Maxwell
Robert Chenoweth	Rachel Stalnaker	John Stalnaker	Robert Maxwell
Peter Conrad	Ann Currence	John Currence	Robert Maxwell
George Kittle	Elizabeth Weese	Jacob Weese	Robert Maxwell
William Bonner	Jemima Carr	John Carr	Robert Maxwell
John Heater	Mary Higgins		Robert Maxwell
George Riffle	Margaret Helmick	Jacob Helmick	Robert Maxwell

1803

Jacob Lorentz	Rebecca Stalnaker	Val. Stalnaker	Robert Maxwell
Jacob Stalnaker	Nancy Channel	Joseph Channel	Robert Maxwell
Samuel Degarmo	Elizabeth Grimes	Mark Grimes	Robert Maxwell
Jacob Crouch	Jane Smith	Jonathan Smith	Robert Maxwell
J. W. Stalnaker	Mary Chenowith	John Chenowith	Robert Maxwell
William Booth	Deborah Hart	Edward Hart	Robert Maxwell
Enoch Osborn	Mary Tidricks		Robert Maxwell
Michael Westfall	Mary Helmick	Adam Helmick	Robert Maxwell
Jos. Summerfield	Abigail White		Robert Maxwell
Gaulaudat Oliver	Mary Ann Bogard	Cornelius Bogard	Robert Maxwell

1804

Barton Hoskins	Naomi Ingram	Abraham Ingram	Robert Maxwell
Samuel Channel	Sarah Hornbeck	Benjamin Hornbeck	Robert Maxwell
John Stalnaker	Elizabeth Haddan		Robert Maxwell
William Yokum	Sarah Ryan	Solomon Ryan	Robert Maxwell
John White	Jemima Heath	Asahel Heath	Robert Maxwell
Richard Ware	Polly Wilson	George Wilson	Robert Maxwell
Abraham Skidmore	Elizabeth Vance	John Vance	Robert Maxwell
Silas Smith	Sarah Shaw	William Shaw	Robert Maxwell
Timothy Vanscoy	Phoebe Wilmoth	Thomas Wilmoth	Robert Maxwell
Christian Bickle	Hannah Spillman	John Spillman	Robert Maxwell
Eli Butcher	Elizabeth Hart	Edward Hart	Robert Maxwell
Richard Hoskins	Elizabeth Ingram	Abraham Ingram	Robert Maxwell

1805

Benjamin Riddle	Nancy Goff	Salathiel Goff	Robert Maxwell

Man's Name	Woman's Name	Daughter of	By Whom Married
James Tyger	Elizabeth Parsons	William Parsons	Robert Maxwell
James Skidmore	Sarah Kittle	Jacob Kittle	Robert Maxwell
John Helmick	Joan Ryan	Solomon Ryan	Robert Maxwell
Jacob Wilson	Mary Helmick	Jacob Helmick	Robert Maxwell
John Spillman	Elizabeth Bickle	Jacob Bickle	Robert Maxwell
Abraham Kittle	Mary Scott		Robert Maxwell
Henry Mace	Mary Davis		Robert Maxwell
John Helmick	Rebecca Carle		Robert Maxwell
James McClean	Rachel Channel	Joseph Channel	Robert Maxwell
Isaac Riffle	Elizabeth Wash	John Wash	Robert Maxwell

1806

Samuel Wamsley	Elizabeth Crouch		Robert Maxwell
William Hoff	Rebecca Johnson	Robert Johnson	Robert Maxwell
Robert Darling	Sarah Vanscoy	Aaron Vanscoy	Robert Maxwell
Val. Stanaker	Lucretia Jenkins		Robert Maxwell
Robert Shanwlin	Mary Marstiller	Nicholas Marstiller	Robert Maxwell
Joseph Wamsley	Patty Jameson		Robert Maxwell
John Johnson	Elizabeth Poland	Peter Poland	Robert Maxwell
Isaac Westfall	Catharine Shreery	Joseph Shreery	Robert Maxwell
John Forrest	Lyhua Carpenter	Jere. Carpenter	John Skidmore
George Bickle	Mary Skidmore	John Skidmore	John Skidmore

1807

William Lynch	Nancy Hill		John Skidmore
Jeremiah Mace	Rhoda Williams	Sarah Williams	John Skidmore
John McLaughlin	Barbara Bickle	Jacob Bickle	John Skidmore
Robert Ferguson	Deborah Wilmoth	Thomas Wilmoth	Robert Maxwell
John Gibson	Nancy Harris		Robert Maxwell
John Conrad	Betsey Currence	John Currence	Robert Maxwell
Thomas Butcher	Susanna Petro	Henry Petro	Robert Maxwell
Andrew Skidmore	Margaret Hoskins	Bennett Hoskins	Robert Maxwell
Jacob Westfall	Dolly Wilson		Robert Maxwell
Abner McClain	Phoeba Daniels		Robert Maxwell
John Wilson	Betsey Vanscoy	Aaron Vanscoy	Robert Maxwell
Wm. Stalnaker	Elizabeth Goff		Robert Maxwell

1808

Basil Hudkins	Nancy Skidmore	Andrew Skidmore	Robert Maxwell
James Turner	Mary Corrick	John Corrick	Robert Maxwell
Isaac Newell	Luciana Wilson	Thomas Wilson	Robert Maxwell
John Brady	Susanna Ware		Robert Maxwell
Henry Hardman	Prudence Scott		Robert Maxwell
John Myers	Mary Stalnaker	Jacob Stalnaker	Robert Maxwell
John Holder	Mary Lewis	John Lewis	Robert Maxwell
George Harnick	Levina Royce	Joseph Royce	Robert Maxwell
Thomas Holder	Margaret Gandy	widow Jno. Gandy	Robert Maxwell
Abraham Kittle	Elizabeth Esters		Robert Maxwell

1809

Ulery Conrad	Sarah Currence	John Currence	Robert Maxwell
John R. Beall	Patty Holbert	Aaron Holbert	Robert Maxwell
John Wees	Mary Phillips		Robert Maxwell
George Helmick	Elizabeth Isner	Henry Isner	Robert Maxwell
William Burns	Susanna Chilcott	Robinson L. Chilcott	Robert Maxwell
Wm. Louchary	Margaret Johnson	Edward Johnson	Robert Maxwell
John Hardwick	Elizabeth Channel		Robert Maxwell

MAN'S NAME	WOMAN'S NAME	DAUGHTER OF	BY WHOM MARRIED
S. Cunningham	Mary Shagel	Jacob Shagle	Robert Maxwell
Jacob Borer	Sarah Helmick	Jacob Helmick	Robert Maxwell
Jacob Wilson	Mary Donoho	William Donoho	Robert Maxwell
Jonathan Vanscoy	Sarah Lochary	John Lochary	Robert Maxwell
Adam Chiner	Elizabeth Fields	John Fields	Robert Maxwell
Wm. F. Wilson	Jane Booth	Daniel Booth	Robert Maxwell
George Keener	Peggy Miller	John Miller	John Skidmore
Henry Wilfong	Christiana Wees	Jacob Wees	John Carney
Sol. Carpenter	Catharine Hill	John Hill	Simeon Harris
Isaac Hedley	Elizabeth Wilson	William Wilson	Simeon Harris
William Yeager	Elizabeth Thorn	Frederick Thorn	Simeon Harris
George Nestor	Millie Poland	Martin Poland	Simeon Harris
Robt. W. Collins	Mary Gibson	Nicholas Gibson	John Rowan
Uriah Ingrim	Hannah Holder	James Holder	John Rowan
Daniel Decker	Mary A. Yokum	Michael Yokum	John Rowan
Jacob Stanley	Nancy Chapman	Val. Chapman	Phineahas Wells
Abel Kelley	Jemima Kittle	Jacob Kittle	Phineahas Wells
Jacob Teter	Nancy Cade	Moses Cade	Phineahas Wells
Joshua Morgan	Hannah Gould	Aaron Gould	Henry Camdem

1810

Martin Poland	Mary Wilson	William Wilson	Simeon Harris
James Carr	Ann Hornbeck	Benj. Hornbeck	John Rowan
George Corrick	Jemima Chilcott	R. L. Chilcott	John Rowan
Eben Schoonover	Sarah Reck	George Reck	John Rowan
Simon Maloney	Sarah Hornick	Aug. Hornbeck	John Rowan
Benj. Phillips	Phoebe Walker		John Rowan
John Wilmoth	Ann Kittle	Richard Kittle	John Rowan
Geo. Barnhose	Susanna Pitman		Simeon Harris
Hezekiah Bussey	Fannie Knotts		Simeon Harris
James Ryan	Elzabeth Bennett	Sarah Bennett	Simeon Harris
John Black	Mary Bussey	John Bussey	Simeon Harris
Henry Hudkins	Mary Isner	Thomas Isner	Robert Maxwell
Andrew Crouch	Elizabeth Hutton	Jonathan Hutton	Robert Maxwell
Thomas Scott	Nancy Skidmore	And. Skidmore	Robert Maxwell
John Chenoweth	Mary Skidmore	And. Skidmore	Robert Maxwell
Solomon Parsons	Hannah Parsons	William Parsons	Robert Maxwell
Martin Miller	Nancy Day		Robert Maxwell
Peyton Butcher	Elizabeth Renix	George Renix	Robert Maxwell

1811

William Moore	Rachel Phillips	Henry Phillips	Simeon Harris
John Bussey	Susanna Warthen	John Warthen	Simeon Harris
Samuel Morrow	Isabella Barr	John Barr	Robert Maxwell
Joseph Royce	Sarah Summerfield	Jos. Summerfield	Robert Maxwell
Jacob Yokum	Jane Wamsley	Mathew Wamsley	John Rowan
Jeremiah Reddle	Margaret Hardman	Elizabeth Hardman	John Rowan
Thomas Wamsley	Jemima Channel	Jeremiah Channel	John Rowan
Ruben Holbert	Betty Brannon	John Brannon	John Rowan
John Hill	Nancy Warthen	John Warthen	Simeon Harris
Jonathan Yeager	Elizabeth Miller	Andrew Miller	Simeon Harris
Rod. Bonnifield	Nancy Minear	David Minear	Simeon Harris
Benjamin Helms	Rachel Moore	David Moore	Simeon Harris
Solomon Yeager	Mary Teeter	Jacob Teeter	Simeon Harris

1812

Dan Howdershell	Catherin Foreman	Jacob Foreman	Simeon Harris

Man's Name	Woman's Name	Daughter of	By Whom Married
Joseph Bennett	Mary Phillips	Henry Phillips	Simeon Harris
George Hill	Rebecca Scott	Henry Scott	John Rowan
Nicholas Mace	Elizabeth Riffle	Jacob Riffle	John Rowan
Thomas Parsons	Elizabeth Brannon		John Rowan
James Warner	Barbara Robbinet		John Rowan
Levi Ward	Cathe'e Whitman	Mat. Whitman	John Rowan
Edmond Jones	Melinda Carr		John Rowan
Archibald Earle	Mary Buckey	Peter Buckey	John Rowan
Ezekiel Paxton	C. Coykendall	J. Coykendall	John Rowan
Jacob Isner	Peggy Schoonover	Benj. Schoonover	John Rowan
And. Stalnaker	Clarissa Danbury		John Rowan
Ezekiel Hart	Peggy Hart	Daniel Hart	John Rowan
David Nutter	Elizabeth Cox	Henry Cox	Simeon Harris
Samuel Skidmore	Elizabeth Pitman	Joseph Pitman	Simeon Harris
George Beall	Mary Parsons	Isaac Parsons	Simeon Harris

1813

Man's Name	Woman's Name	Daughter of	By Whom Married
Benjamin Johnston	Catherine Hall		Simeon Harris
Henry England	Mary Alexander	Elias Alexander	Simeon Harris
John Gainer	Susanna Easter	Jacob Easter	Simeon Harris
John Shaver	Polly Nester	Jacob Nester	Simeon Harris
Jesse Hall	Sally Braidut	Luke Braidut	John Gill Watts
Samuel Love	Sarah Newall	Isaac Newall	William Munrow
Charles Scott	Agnes Kittle	Richard Kittle	John Rowan
Benjamin Scott	Jane Currence	William Currence	John Rowan
William Smith	Easter Pitman	Joseph Pitman	John Rowan
Frederick Corrick	Parmel' Checvate	Rb. L. Checvate	John Rowan
Jonathan Hornbeck	Kitty Wilt		John Rowan
Jacob Westfall	Sarah Hinckle	Justice Hinckle	John Rowan
Edwin S. Duncan	Prudence Wilson	Wm. B. Wilson	John Rowan
Chas. Marstiller	Peggy McLain	James McLain	John Rowan
Jehu Chenoweth	Elender Skidmore	Andrew Skidmore	John Rowan
Willis Taylor	Sarah Clark		John Rowan
John Petro	Tasa Butcher	Samuel Butcher	John Rowan

1814

Man's Name	Woman's Name	Daughter of	By Whom Married
Nathan Minear	Elizabeth Bonnifield		John Rowan
Amos Canfield	N. Schoonover	Benj. Schoonover	John Rowan
Abraham Wolf	R. McLaughlin		John Rowan
Elijah Skidmore	M. Cunningham	John Cunningham	John Rowan
Andrew Crouch	Eliz. Stalnaker	Bostain Stalnaker	John Rowan
Joseph Bennett	Catherine Paine	Henry Paine	John Rowan
Richard Moore	Mary A. Phillips	Joseph Phillips	Simeon Harris
Francis Vansy	Mary Gainer	George Gainer	Simeon Harris
Henry Smith	Catherine Lesher	Jacob Lesher	Simeon Harris

1815

Man's Name	Woman's Name	Daughter of	By Whom Married
Isaac Wamsley	Susanna Yeager	George Yeager	Simeon Harris
William J. Davis	Lydia Gould	Aaron Gould	Simeon Harris
Thomas Goff	Sarah Robison	John Robison	Simeon Harris
Solomon Westfall	Mary Moore	Daniel Moore	Simeon Harris
Henry Sturm	Eliz. Stalnaker	Wm. Stalnaker	Simeon Harris
Jonas Poling	Phoebe Headley	Cary Headley	Simeon Harris
John Phillips	Rachel Phillips	John Phillips	Simeon Harris
Solomon Collett	Sarah Petro	Henry Petro	John Rowan
Thomas Phillips	Peggy Westfall	Jacob Westfall	John Rowan
John Flanagan	Susan Donoho	William Donoho	John Rowan

MAN'S NAME	WOMAN'S NAME	DAUGHTER OF	BY WHOM MARRIED
Alex. McQuain	Elizabeth Scott		John Rowan
Aseal Isnear	Sarah Canfield	Daniel Canfield	John Rowan
Job Parsons	Jemima Ward	Jacob Ward	John Rowan
Wm. Schoonover	Char'e Marstiller	Nich. Marstiller	John Rowan
James Shreeve	Lydia Smith	Jonathan Smith	John Rowan
John Ryan	Susanna Briggs	William Briggs	John Rowan
John S. Hart	Jemima Stagle	Jacob Stagle	John Rowan
John McLain	Delilah Currence	John Currence	John Rowan
Henry Walter	Phoebe Wood	John Wood	John Rowan
Gabriel Chenoweth	Eliz. Currence	Wm. Currence	John Rowan
Edward Hart	Catherine Phillips	John Phillips	Asbery Pool
John Shreeve	Susanna Wamsley	James Wamsley	Asbery Pool

1816

Joseph Phillips	Margaret Kittle	Jacob Kittle	John J. Waldo
Squire Bosworth	Hannah Buckey	Peter Buckey	William Monroe
Joseph Cross	Mary Westfall		Simeon Harris
John Skidmore	Juda Pitman	Joseph Pitman	Simeon Harris
Joseph Moore	Mary Cross	Barbara Cross	Simeon Harris
John Fling	Elizabeth Gainer		Simeon Harris
John Stout	Barbara Cosner	Vandal Cosner	Simeon Harris
Daniel Boyle	Catherine Wilson	William Wilson	Simeon Harris
Andrew Foreman	Rachel Poland		Simeon Harris
Samuel Poling	Elizabeth Marks		Simeon Harris
William Ryan	Rebecca Bennett		Simeon Harris
George Goff	Nancy Robinson		Simeon Harris
Benjamin Arnold	S. W. Wamsley	Wm. Wamsley	Simeon Harris
John Norman	N. Montgomery		Simeon Harris
Martin Poling	Anna Right	William Right	Simeon Harris
Moses Kittle	Nancy Bennett	Jacob Bennett	Simeon Harris
James Skidmore	Elizabeth Monday		John Rowan
David Holder	Ellender Kittle	Abraham Kittle	John Rowan
Daniel Hardway	Hannah Helmick		John Rowan
Thomas Skidmore	Mary Kittle	Abraham Kittle	John Rowan
J. Cunningham	Mary Jordan	John Jordan	John Rowan
Maxwell Renix	Sarah Wilmoth	Nicholas Wilmoth	John Rowan
Andrew Snider	M. Summerfield		John Rowan

The following table shows the number of claims allowed for wolf scalps from 1787 to 1897. The high water mark was reached in 1822 when 56 claims were presented:

1787—2	1798—15	1809—43	1820—32	1831—21	1842—8	1853—3
1788—13	1799—17	1810—44	1821—32	1832—27	1843—15	1854—3
1789—8	1800—13	1811—38	1822—56	1833—14	1844—7	1855—8
1790—15	1801—3	1812—25	1823—42	1834—28	1845—3	1856—1
1791—30	1802—22	1813—30	1824—51	1835—24	1846—16	1860—3
1792—18	1803—23	1814—23	1825—23	1836—21	1847—5	1861—2
1793—20	1804—21	1815—47	1826—27	1837—18	1848—24	1897—1
1794—22	1805—30	1816—51	1827—33	1838—22	1849—7	
1795—12	1806—24	1817—47	1828—40	1839—17	1850—1	
1796—16	1807—29	1818—10	1829—43	1840—11	1851—2	
1797—20	1808—11	1819—36	1830—37	1841—15	1852—3	

The following table shows the record of panthers and wild cats killed in Randolph so far as preserved:

	1852	1853	1854	1855	1856	1857	1858	1859	1860	1861
Panthers	5	11	5	10	14	11	11	6	0	0
Wild cats	0	0	55	66	49	106	58	80	3	12

Sheriffs of Randolph.

[The year given is the date of assuming office.]

Jacob Westfall	1787	Levi Ward	1841
Cornelius Westfall	1789	Peter Conrad	1847
Edward Jackson	1792	Jacob W. See	1848
Uriah Gandy	1793	George McLean	1850
Cornelius Bogard	1796	W. C. Chenoweth	1856
John Wilson	1798	Solomon C. Caplinger	1857
Matthew Whitman	1800	Hoy McLean	1858
Asahel Heath	1803	Jacob Phares	1860
John Currence	1806	Jesse F. Phares	1862
Samuel Bonnifield	1806	John M. Phares	1864
George Rennix	1808	Archibald Harper	1864
John Chenoweth	1810	F. M. White	1870
Isaac Booth	1813	L. D. White	1872
John Crouch	1815	J. F. Harding	1876
Benjamin Hornbeck	1815	Jacob G. Ward	1880
William Daniels	1818	Z. T. Chenoweth	1884
Andrew Crawford	1820	Warwick Hutton	1888
Ely Butcher	1822	A. J. Long	1892
Robert Chenoweth	1827	A. W. Hart	1896
John M. Hart	1829	P. W. Marshall	1901
William Marteney	1830	Floyd McDonald	1905
George Stalnaker	1833	Thadeus Pritt	1910
David Holder	1829	A. J. Crickard	1915

County Clerks of Randolph.

County Clerks were appointed by the County Court until the adoption of the constitution of 1852.

John Wilson	1787	John B. Morrison	1870
Jacob Westfall	1793	James D. Wilson	1872
Archibald Earle	1810	Floyd Triplett	1890
D. W. Shurtliff	1838	Lee Crouch	1896
John W. Crawford	1845	S. A. Rowan	1905
Squire Bosworth	1858	F. A. Rowan	1910
William Bennett	1861	Thadeus Pritt	1915
John B. Earle	1868		

Circuit Clerks.

John Wilson	1809	L. D. White	1866
Archibald Earle	1812	Leland Kittle	1872
E. D. Wilson	1842	John B. Morrison	1879
Bernard L. Brown	1849	W. H. Wilson	1885
John B. Earle	1861	G. N. Wilson	1897

County Surveyors.

Edward Jackson	1787	Cyrus Kittle	1865
Henry Jackson	1793	Nicholas Marstiller	1868
Robert S. Shanklin	1809	C. M. Marstiller	1892
Thos. O. Williams	1819	Frank Parsons	1900
Bernard L. Brown	1849	E. E. Taylor	1904
Nicholas Marstiller	1852	A. J. Crickard	1908
Milton Hart	1858	A. W. Schoonover	1912

Signatures of Randolph's Early Sheriffs. (From Maxwell's History of Randolph County.)

Signatures of Early Justices of the Peace. (From Maxwell's History of Randolph County.)

Commissioners of the Revenue and Assessors.

The officers whose duty it has been to fix the valuation of property in Randolph County for purposes of taxation, have not been called by the same name at all times, nor have their duties been always the same. In early years they were known as Commissioners of Revenue, and of late years Assessors. A list follows of those who have filled the office in this county:

John Haddan	1787	John Harris	1832
John Jackson	1787	George Nestor	1833
Cornelius Bogard	1787	Andrew Crawford	1834
John Wilson	1788	Peter Conrad	1835
Peter Cassity	1789	Brown Jenks	1836
Abraham Claypool	1789	William Shaw	1837
William Wamsley	1790	John Moore	1838
Edward Jackson	1791	William Marteney	1839
Robert Clark	1792	Lair D. Morrell	1841
William Wilson	1795	Jacob W. See	1842
James Bruff	1796	Bushrod W. Crawford	1843
George Rennix	1796	George McLean	1844
Simon Reeder	1797	Ely Baxter Butcher	1845
St. Leger Stout	1800	George Wyatt	1846
Asahel Heath	1801	John Taylor	1848
Nicholas Gibson	1809	Absalom Crawford	1849
Isaac White	1809	Charles C. See	1850
William Wilson	1810	Jacob Ward	1851
John Crouch	1813	Parkison Collett	1856
John M. Hart	1814	John B. Morrison	1858
Ely Butcher	1815	Jacob Phares	1860
Robert S. Shanklin	1816	Squire B. Daniels	1861
Robert Chenoweth	1816	Archibald E. Harper	1861
John Currence	1817	J. M. Curtis	1876
Andrew Crawford	1818	Jasper W. Triplett	1880
George Wees	1819	H. H. Taylor	1880
Adam Myers	1821	Abel W. Hart	1884
George Stalnaker	1822	French H. Kittle	1881
Jacob Teter	1823	Sheffey Taylor	1892
Daniel Hart	1824	William O. Triplett	1892
Daniel Booth	1825	Thadeus Pritt	1900
Isaac Taylor	1826	J. C. Goddin	1902
Henry Martin	1827	L. W. McQuain	1902
Levi Ward	1828	A. W. Zinn	1910
Michael See	1830	J. N. Phares	1913
Matthew Whitman	1831		

Justices of the Peace.

From the organization of Randolph until the adoption of the Constitution of 1852 Justices of the Peace were appointed by the Governor, and held office for life if they chose to do so. After 1852 they were elected. The following list shows the names of the Justices and the year when they first appeared on the records:

1787—Jacob Westfall, Salathial Goff, Patrick Hamilton, John Hamilton, John Wilson, Cornelius Westfall, Edward Jackson, Robert Maxwell, Peter Cassity, Cornelius Bogard, John Jackson, George Westfall, Henry Runyan, John Haddan, Jonathan Parsons, Uriah Gandy.

1789—John Elliott, Abraham Claypool.

1790—Jacob Westfall.

1791—Abraham Kittle, Matthew Whitman, Terah Osborn, William Wilson, Jacob Polsley.

1794—William Parsons.

1795—Asahel Heath, John Pancake, John Currence, Jacob Kittle, Samuel Bonnifield.

1797—William Seymour, William B. Wilson.

1799—Simon Reeder, John Chenoweth, Nicholas Marstiller.

1801—Isaac Booth.

1802—Andrew Miller.

1803—Joseph Long, Daniel Clark, Barthan Hoskins, John Hartley, John Sanders, John Barnhouse, Joseph Joseph.

1804—Ebenezer Flanagan, Gilbert Boyles.

1806—John Crouch, John Lamberton, Benjamin Hornbeck, Nicholas Gibson, Isaac Booth.

1808—William Daniels, Jonathan Hutton, John Hart.

1809—Isaac White, Andrew Cawford, George Parsons, Samuel Ball.

1810—Matthew Hines, John Skidmore.

1811—Nicholas Storm, Daniel Booth, Benjamin Riddle.

1813—Zedekiah Morgan, Andrew Cross, George Wees, Jonathan Wamsley.

1814—Isaac Greggory, Adam Myers, Andrew Friend, George Stalnaker, Robert S. Shanklin, Jacob Sprigstone, Levi Ward.

1815—Hiram Goff, Robert Young, James Tygart.

1817—Ebenezer Leonard, Frederick Troutwine, Jacob Teter.

1820—Michael See, Isaac Taylor, William S. Wilson.

1824—Jonas Crane, Godfrey Hiller, Jonas Harman, John Harris.

1825—David Wiles, Robert McCrum.

1830—Brown Jenks, David Goff, Joseph Hart, William Shaw, John Walker, William Huff, John Moore, Peter Conrad, George Nestor.

1831—George See, Henry Sturm, Jacob See.

1832—William McLain, Squire Bosworth, Jacob Keller, Ely Butcher, Andrew Miller, Robert N. Ball, John Wyatt, Joseph Roy, William F. Wilson, Joseph Teter, Adam See.

1835—Jacob Harper, John Phares, William Rowan, Adonijah B. Ward, Valentine Stalnaker, Lorentz Mitchell, Daniel W. Shurtliff, Jarrett Johnson, Abraham Harding, Samuel Keller Arnold Bonnifield, Isaac Roy, Thomas S. White, John Arbogast, Andrew M. Wamsley.

1838—Lemuel Chenoweth, Job Parsons, Samuel Stalnaker, Samuel Elliott, Michael H. Neville, John W. Crawford.

1839—Charles C. See, Francis D. Talbott.

1841—John A. Hutton.

1842—Noah E. Corley, George Buckey, William Phares, John Kelley, William Johnson, John W. Moore, John Taylor.

1845—David Gilmore, Christian Simmons, Lenox M. Camden, Elijah Kittle, Archibald Chenoweth, Benjamin W. Kittle, Jacob Crouch, Abraham Crouch.

1848—Whitman Ward, Adam D. Caplinger, John W. Haigler, Harrison W. Campbell, James W. Parsons, William Talbott, James Shreve, William G. Greggory, Harman Snyder, Thompson Elza.

1852—Peter L. Lightner, Isaac G. Dodrill, William Hamilton, George W. Mills, Hezekiah Kittle, Henry Harper, William C. Chenoweth, Jacob Vanscoy, William R. Parsons, George H. Long, Nathaniel J. Lambert, Joseph White, James Vance, Jeremiah Lanham, James D. Simon, Absalom Stalnaker.

1854—Jacob H. Long, Henry C. Moore.

1856—Jacob W. Marshall, Thomas B. Scott, Hamilton Stalnaker, Abraham Hutton, John A. Rowan, Edwin S. Talbott, Eli Kittle, Aaron Coberly, Arnold Wilmoth, Samuel Dinkle, Noah H. Harman, James Wilmoth.

1859—Asa Harman, Mathias C. Potts, Joseph J. Simmons.

1860—Jacob Conrad, S. Salisbury, W. Wilson, Washington G. Ward, George Phillips, Wilson Osborn, Michael Yokum, William F. Corley, William Raines, James H. Lambert, William Jordan, Elijah J. Nelson.

1861—Jacob Daniels, Everett Chenoweth.

1862—Henry H. Leigh, D. G. Adams.

1867—Solomon S. Warner, James W. Dunnington, Charles Crouch, William Bennett, Patrick Durkin, Peleg C. Barlow.

1869—Sampson Snyder, Reuben S. Butcher, John A. Vance, John A. King.

1873—Jesse W. Goddin, J. Wood Price, Riley Pritt, George H. Phillip, Jacob C. Collett, Adam C. Currence, Emanuel White, Patrick Crickard, Leonard H. Schoonover.

1876—George W. Yokum, Holman Pritt, Miles King, Joseph Bunner, J. W. Summerfield.

1877—Alfred Hutton.

1880—George Beatty, John Bunner, William H. Wilson, Z. T. Chenoweth, J. W. Tyre, Jacob C. Harper, Randolph Triplett.

1882—Adam H. Wamsley, Peter Crickard.

1884—J. H. Dewitt, Melvin Currence, James L. Coff, John A. Hamilton, D. E. Coberly.

1886—James Shannon.

1888—William H. Goss, Adam C. Rowan, William M. Boyd, H. N. Brunner, Adam L. Findley.

1890—Caleb White.

1892—John R. Crickard, D. P. Harper, Job. W. Parsons, William Hamilton, James Coberly, J. J. Zickafoose, Lew Fahrion.

1895—G. F. Sims.

1896—B. Y. Cunningham, Floyd McDonald, W. A. Hornbeck, N. W. Talbott, A. Brandley, Page C. Marstiller, Peter Madden, W. Scott Woodford, W. S. Kelley, John W. Hartman, Elias Zickafoose.

Prosecuting Attorneys.

The prosecuting attorney, in former times, was appointed, and did not necessarily live in the county where he served. The same man sometimes was prosecutor in two or more counties at one time. Following are the names of the commonwealth's attorneys of Randolph:

William McCleary	1787	John S. Huffman	1841
Thomas Wilson	1791	Samuel Crane	1852
Maxwell Armstrong	1795	Joseph Hart	1862
Adam See	1798	Nathan H. Taft	1862
William Tingle	1809	Spencer Dayton	1863
Noah Linsley	1809	Gustavus Cresap	1867
Edwin S. Duncan	1814	Thomas J. Arnold	1868
Oliver Phelps	1817	Bernard L. Butcher	1876
Phineas Chapin	1818	Cyrus H. Scott	1880
John J. Allen	1820	Jared L. Wamsley	1888
William McCord	1829	C. W. Harding	1901-09
Gideon D. Camden	1837	H. G. Kump	1909-15
David Goff	1835		

County Coroners.

Salathiel Goff	1787	William B. Wilson	1807
Cornelius Bogard	1787	Charles Myers	1809
Robert Maxwell	1789	John Stalnaker	1820
Abraham Kittle	1792	Jacob Myers	1827
Simon Reeder	1796	William Rowan	1854
John Chenoweth	1803	Lemuel Chenoweth	1855
Adam Stalnaker	1805	William C. Chenoweth	1873

County Commissioners.

Solomon C. Caplinger	1880	C. S. Armentrout	1888
William M. Phares	1880	Jesse F. Phares	1882
Jacob S. Wamsley	1880	Jesse W. Goddin	1892
Omar Conrad	1880	P. Crickard	1896
Jacob Vanscoy	1884	John Heavener	1902
B. W. Crawford	1884	R. M. Harper	1904
G. W. Yokum	1886	K. B. Crawfird	1908
Patrick Crickard	1886	A. W. Hart	1912

Judges Circuit Court.

Hugh Nelson	1809	Thos. W. Harrison	1867
Daniel Smith	1811	John Brannon	1872
Edwin S. Duncan	1831	William T. Ice	1881
Geo. H. Lee	1848	Joeph T. Hoke..	1889
Gideon D. Camden	1851	John Holt	1897
William A. Harrison	1861	Warren B. Kittle	1912
Robert Irvine	1863		

Constables.

1787—Jacob Riffle, Michael Yokum, Thomas Holder, Jeremiah York, Jeremiah Cooper, Charles Falnash.

1788—William Haddix, David Minear, Valentine Stalnaker, Jacob Shook.

1794—William Clark, Henry Carr, Jacob Ward.

1796—Jacob Springston, Henry Phillips.

1797—John Runkins, Nicholas Smith, George Long, Matthew Wamsley.

1798—John Phillips, Thomas Cade, Joseph Joseph, John Sanders.

1799—Richard Ware, Daniel Canfield, Gilbert Bayles.

1800—Peter Buckey, John Cutright, John Hart, John Triplett.

1803—William Daniels, Samuel Pierce, Richard Ware.

1804—George Whitman, William Booth, William McCorkle.

1805—Barthan Hoskins, John Hartley, John Spillman, John Beall.

1809—George Stalnaker, John Chenoweth, William Steers, Edward Hart, William F. Wilson, William Stalnaker, James Holder, Alexander Morrison.

1810—Adonijah Ward, Samuel Burrett.

1811—John Clark, John Miller, Joseph Roy, Nicholas Weatherholtz.

1813—Jonathan Yeager, Levi Skidmore, John W. Stalnaker, William Kelley, Isaac Wamsley, Samuel Oliver, Isaac Stalnaker.

1815—David Holder, Wilby Taylor, John Snyder, Jesse Cunningham, John Lynch, Abraham Bryant.

1817—David Evans, Solomon Parsons, Isaac Post, Adam Lough, John Walker.

1818—Thomas Wamsley, Jonas Harman, Samuel Wyatt, Moses Phillips.

1819—Solomon Yeager, James Teter, Jesse Bennett, John Long, Joseph Walker.

1821—Robert N. Ball, Henry Sturm, Henry Cunning, Thomas W. Holder.

1823—William H. Crawford, Jesse Coberly, Enoch Minear, Abraham Wolford, Hugh Dailey, James Turner, Noah E. Corley.

1825—Elisha Poling, George Harris, Benjamin Johnson, Isaac B. Marsh.

1827—Absalom Wilmoth, William Wamsley, Jacob Kelley, Benjamin P. Marsh, John Taylor, William G. Gilmore.

1829—John W. Crawford, Eli Walker, Jacob Teter, Abraham Bowman, Edmund S. Wyatt, Thomas Byrd, Washington Taylor, Joshua Glascock.

1831—Burwell Butcher, Oliver E. Domire, Joseph Shaw, William Marsh, John Stout, William Rowan, William Pickens, Absalom Hinkle.

1832—John Conrad, John Phares, Samuel Keller.

1833—Edward Stalnaker, Daniel W. Shurtliff, James W. Corley, John P. Gray, Jesse Day, Levi Jenks, Arnold Bonnifield.

1836—Andrew M. Wamsley, William Wamsley, Thomas Phillips, John Sargent.

1837—Lair D. Morrell, Garrett Johnson, Absalom Harden, David Gilmore, James Vance, Thomas S. White, Joseph J. Simmons, John M. Crouch.

1838—Adam H. Bowman, William Simpson, Bushrod W. Crawford, Archibald Coyner.

1839—Isaac White, Elias Alexander, Lewis Gilmore, John C. Wamsley.

1841—William Wilmoth, Garretson Stalnaker, Francis J. Holder, John Tygart, Jesse Roy, John Arbogast, Jacob Conrad, Abraham Crouch.

1842—William W. Parsons, Samuel Wamsley, John M. Phares, Israel Coffman, Flavius J. Holder, Francis O. Shurtliff, James R. Parsons, Benjamin Kittle, Henry V. Bowman.

1845—Matthew W. Brady, Milton Hart, Michael Yokum, John Q. Wilson.

1847—William Currence, Michael Walters, Samuel P. Wallace, Job Parsons, Jr., James Long, Elias Wyatt, Washington Roy.

1848—Thomas James, George W. Mills, Cyrus Kittle.

1849—Allen J. Currence, John W. Adams, Solomon C.

Caplinger, W. H. Coberly, Samuel P. Wilson, Aaron Bell.

1851—Peter H. Ward, William Raines.

1852—Hugh S. Hart, Melvine Currence, Moses J. Phillips, Samuel P. Dinkle, Isaac Roy, Samuel Bonnifield.

1854—Jacob Currence, Isaac Wilmoth, Parkinson Collett, Jesse Parsons, David O. Wilson.

1855—Alfred Taylor, Washington Stalnaker, George W. Rowan.

1856—Michael Magee, Patrick Crickard, Powhatan A. Tolly.

1858—Levi White, Squire Daniels.

1860—Thomas J. Powers, Henry J. White, Patrick Durkin, Edward Grim, O. C. Stalnaker.

1867—Sampson F. Shiflett, William O. Ferguson, William H. Quick, Andrew J. Wilmoth, James A. Hicks, W. K. Herren, John Snider, John King.

1869—Daniel Cooper, Granger Lamb, Montgomery G. Mathews, James Hicks.

1870—John McGillivany.

[There is a gap of six years in the records which show the election of constables.]

1876—S. Tyre, E. O. Goddin, George W. Phares, John Pritt, Jasper Bolton, W. D. Currence, A. J. Wilmoth, Caleb White, A. J. Bennett, James S. Hutton.

1884—French H. Kittle, Lee Yokum, James R. McCallum, P. B. Conrad, A. B. Mouse, J. A. Cunningham, John J. Nallen, John W. Hartman.

1885—Creed L. Earle, R. L. Pritt.

1888—Page C. Daniels, R. G. Thorn, Charles W. Channell, Gideon M. Cutright, Hamilton Markley, Hyre A. Stalnaker, A. H. Summerfield, George W. Stalnaker.

1892—Lloyd D. Collett, J. H. Currence, Elam E. Taylor, W. D. Currence, C. C. Crickard, L. W. McQuain, William Snyder, Patrick Phillips.

1894—R. T. Hedges, Page C. Marstiller.

1896—R. C. Sassi, Daniel Cooper, Frank Shoemaker, James Brady, Oliver Daniels, A. B. Coberly, E. E. Taylor, N. B. Hutton.

Colonels of Militia.

Patrick Hamilton 1787
William Lowther 1796
Archibald Earle 1822
Robert N. Ball................1827
Solomon Wyatt 1831
Jacob Keller 1837

David Goff 1844
John W. Crawford................1850
Hoy McLean 1853
Melvin Currence 1860
Cyrus Kittle 1862

Captains of Militia.

Edward Jackson 1787
James Westfall 1787
Peter Cassity 1787
William Wilson 1787
George Westfall 1787
Jonathan Parsons 1787
John Jackson 1789
Jacob Kittle 1794
John Chenoweth 1794
John Haddan 1795
William Parsons 1796
George Rennix 1798
Adam See 1800
Matthew Whitman 1800
Samuel Ball 1802
Benjamin Vannoy 1805
John Crouch 1805
John Currence 1805
Nicholas Gibson 1806
John Forrest 1807
William Booth 1807
Anthony Huff 1807
Andrew Friend 1807
John Wood 1808
Thomas Butcher 1810
William Stalnaker 1810
Solomon Collett 1812
George Anderson 1816
Solomon Yeager 1817
Samuel Oliver 1818
Adonijah Ward 1818
Thomas W. Holder................1823
George McLean 1827
Charles C. See................1828
Solomon Parsons 1828
Arnold Bonnifield 1829
Solomon Wyatt 1829
William McCord 1830

Thompson Elza 1844
Benjamin Kittle 1844
Bushrod W. Crawford................1844
Jacob Conrad 1844
Daniel W. Shurtliff................1844
Elijah M. Hart................1844
John M. Crouch................1844
Wyatt Ferguson 1844
Hamilton Skidmore 1845
Andrew Stalnaker 1845
Hoy McLean 1846
Henry Rader 1846
George W. Berlin................1848
George Kuykendall 1848
Jesse L. Roy................1850
Cyrus Chenoweth 1850
Cyrus Kittle 1851
Washington Salsberry 1851
William C. Chenoweth................1851
Michael Yokum 1851
James L. Hathaway................1851
Heckman Chenoweth 1851
Abraham Hinkle 1852
Aaron Bell 1852
Allen Taylor 1852
Jacob Shafer 1852
Charles Crouch 1852
Jacob Currence 1860
William E. Logan................1860
Sampson Elza 1860
George W. Mills................1860
L. Phillips 1860
William Westfall 1860
George A. Hesler................1860
Arnold Phillips 1860
J. S. Collett................1860
John Rice 1860

Lieutenants of Militia.

Jacob Westfall	1787	Conrad Currence	1852
John Jackson	1787	Nathaniel Moss	1852
John Haddan	1787	George W. Long	1852
James Kittle	1787	Hull Ward	1853
Matthew Whitman	1787	Jacob Long	1853
Daniel Booth	1787	William E. Long	1853
William Parsons	1787	Simeon Philips	1853
George Rennix	1797	Robert Philips	1853
Asahel Heath	1799	Thomas T. Talbott	1853
John Crouch	1800	James W. Miller	1853
Nicholas Gibson	1805	John M. Stalnaker	1853
John Baker	1805	Hugh S. Hart	1853
James Frame	1807	George Little	1853
William Johnson	1807	Randolph Coberly	1853
William Currence	1807	Dolbeare Kelly	1853
Thomas Skidmore	1810	Ezra P. Hart	1853
Robert W. Collins	1810	Arnold Wilmoth	1853
William Bennett	1813	John Wyatt	1853
Robert Chenoweth	1814	Jacob Currence	1853
Jesse Phillips	1815	Charles Channel	1853
James Wells	1818	William E. Logan	1853
Arnold Bonnifield	1828	Sampson Salsberry	1853
Nathan Minear	1829	Samuel Channel	1853
Solomon Wyatt	1829	L. Denton	1860
Isaac Canfield	1843	L. Phillips	1860
Jesse Roy	1843	William M. Westfall	1860
Jacob Flanagan	1843	Abraham Smith	1860
Levi Stalnaker	1844	John W. Bradley	1862
Levi D. Ward	1844	Andrew C. Currence	1862
William G. Wilson	1844	James Scott	1862
John Bright	1844	Patrick King	1862
Jacob W. Manthus	1844	William Bennett	1862
Jeremiah D. Channel	1844	Jacob W. Fortney	1862
Isaac C. Stalnaker	1844	Alvin Osburn	1862
Vincent Pennington	1844	J. M. Westfall	1862
Cyrus Kittle	1844	Solomon P. Stalnaker	1806
Samuel Smith	1844	Squire B. Daniels	1862
Everet Chenoweth	1844	Harrison Moore	1862
Samuel P. Wilson	1844	Archibald E. Harper	1862
Elam B. Bosworth	1844	John G. Bradley	1862
George W. Rennix	1846	William S. Phares	1862
Washington Stalnaker	1848	Alfred Stalnaker	1862
John Phares	1849	Aaron Workman	1866
Cyrus Chenoweth	1850	Riley Pritt	1866

Majors of Militia.

John Wilson	1787	David Holder	1820
James Westfall	1794	Henry Sturm	1831
William Wilson	1794	John C. Wamsley	1843
John Haddan	1800	Benjamin Kittle	1849
Isaac Booth	1805	Patrick Crickard	1860
Matthew Whitman	1805	Archibald Earle	1860
John Crouch	1805	John M. Crouch	1862

Ensigns of Militia.

John Cutright	1787	James Tygart	1806
Jacob Westfall	1787	John J. Harrison	1807
Anthony Smith	1787	William Huff	1807
George Rennix	1787	Thomas Skidmore	1807
Job Westfall	1787	Jacob Pickle	1807
Jeremiah Cooper	1787	Solomon Yeager	1815
William Seymour	1796	Aaron Gould	1818
Samuel Ball	1796	Job Parsons	1818
George Kittle	1796	Nathan Minear	1828
James Booth	1798	Isaac D. Neville	1829
Barthan Hoskins	1802	William W. Chapman	1829
John Stalnaker	1805	Jesse Vannoy	1830
Thomas Williams	1805		

In the early records of Randolph frequent reference was made to Samuel Pringle, who deserted Fort Pitt in 1761 and located in what is now Upshur County in 1765. He was a witness in the court at Beverly in 1803 and was allowed for traveling 30 miles. This is the distance from Beverly to the former home of the Pringles near the present town of Buckhannon. Pringle's name is mentioned for the last time in the Randolph records in the year 1803.

It seems that the refusal to exercise the elective franchise was an indictable offense in pioneer days. At the May term of the court, 1803, a number of indictments were found against individuals who "for not giving or offering to give their votes for a member of Congress and two members of the General Assembly of the State."

CHAPTER V.

HARRISON COUNTY COURT PROCEEDINGS.

A T a court held at the residence of George Jackson on the Buckhannon River, July 20, 1784, the oath of office was administered to the following Justices of the Peace: Benjamin Wilson, John P. Duval, Wm. Lowther, James Anderson, Henry Delay, Nicholas Carpenter, John Powers, Thos. Chane, Jacob Westfall, Salathiel Goff and Patrick Hamilton.

At the same term of the court Jacob Westfall and Patrick Hamilton were authorized to celebrate the rites of matrimony.

Cornelius Westfall, Geo. Jackson, Edward Jackson, John Wilson and Robert Maxwell were recommended to the Governor as suitable persons to hold the office of Justice of the Peace.

Jacob Riffle, John Currence and Matthew Whitman were appointed Constables.

At a court held at Clarksburg, September, 1784, Patrick Hamilton, Jacob Westfall, John Wilson, were appointed Captains of Militia. Peter Cassity, Cornelius Bogard, and George Westfall were appointed Lieutenants of Militia.

Abram Kittle, Thos, Phillips, Geo. Westfall, Sr. and Benjamin Hornbeck were appointed Viewers of a road from Jacob Westfall's Mill to a bridge opposite Geo. Westfall's Mill.

Ebenezer Petty, John Yokum, Peter Cassity and Jacob Stalnaker, Sr., were appointed Viewers of a road from the bridge opposite Geo. Westfall's Mill to Darby Conly's Place.

At a Court held at Clarksburg, September 22, 1784, Jonas Friend was appointed a Surveyor of a Public Highway from his own house to Eberman's Creek. He was to collect tithables on Leading Creek, both side of the Valley River, up Eberman's Creek and across the river to Hezekiah Rosecrances, and to keep same in lawful repair.

At a term of the Harrison County Court held at Clarksburg, September, 1784, Henry Petro was appointed Surveyor of a highway from Ebermans Creek to Jacob Westfall's Mill and tithables from said Creek upwards to Files Creek and William Smith's.

Most of the litigation in the Harrison county court seemed to be between parties then living in that part of Harrison, now embraced in Randolph. The case of Cornelius Westfall vs. Joseph Donohue and Westfall & Crouch vs. Donohue, both cases of debt were at the September term 1784, dismissed as generally agreed.

At the same term of the Court the following cases involving people living in the valley were disposed of:

John Warwick, plaintiff, vs. Joseph Friend, defendant. Upon motion of the defendant that the plaintiff be nonsuited for failing to file his declaration, the court ordered the same to be nonsuited.

Case of John Westfall vs. Benjamin Hornbeck, trespass, continued.

Johnathan Smith vs. James Taffe, attachment. The attachment was dissolved and Thos. Wilmoth entered special bail for defendant and the common proceedings of law to issue. Declaration and plea of payment filed and rule for trial at March term.

David Bradford took oath as directed by law and was admitted to practice as an attorney. He was thus the first attorney to qualify in what is now Randolph County.

At Court held at Clarksburg, Va., November, 1784 Jacob Stalnaker was appointed Surveyor of Roads from Jacob Westfall's Mill to Alexander Maxwell's Old Place and to collect tithables for same. It is signficant that at this early date that a farm be designated as an Old Place.

On motion of Jacob Crouch, Thomas Lackey was fined 350 pounds of tobacco for contempt of Court for failing to answer summons as witness. He was summoned to appear at the next term of the Court to show cause why execution should not issue for said judgment.

The rate of liquor license, victuals, horse forage, etc., for

Ordinary Keepers was fixed as follows for the year 1784:

	S	P
Wine, per pint	1	6
Jamaica spirits, per pint	1½	
Peach and apple brandy, per pint		6
Rye whiskey, per pint		6
Beer, per quart		6
Cider, per quart		6
Mead, per quart		6
Warm breakfast		9
Cold breakfast		8
Warm supper		9
Cold supper		4
Bed for night, clean sheets		4
If not clean, nothing		0
Horse and hay for night		7½
Corn and oats per gallon		7½
Pasturage, 24 hours		4

The following Justices composed that Court: James Anderson, John Powers, John McCally, John Sleeth, and Edward Jackson.

In 1784 there were 337 tithables in Harrison County. Two-thirds, or 225 tithables, were in what is now Randolph, Tucker and Upshur counties.

At a court held at Clarksburg in August, 1785, Cornelius Bogard was appointed Surveyor of a highway from Wilson's Mill to Rockingham County line. The tithables in Tygarts Valley from Joseph Crouch's down, and including Leading Creek, Wilmoth's settlement and Dry Fork of Cheat settlements were by their labor to keep this highway in good repair.

At the term of the Court held at Clarksburg, Va., February 1, 1786, it was ordered that a path be opened from Conoly's Lick to the top of Allegheny Mountain. John Warwick was appointed Overseer. The petitioners for this road were James Lackey, Jr., David Henderson, James Lackey, Sr., Francis McDonald, Jacob Riffle, Geo. Wilson, Geo. Johnson, John Warwick, Geo. Parsons, Benjamin Abbott, John Alfred, David Haddan, Thos. Lackey, John Hamilton, James Moore, William Hamilton, James McLean, Pat. Hamilton, John Alexander and Robert Henderson.

At a Court held at Clarksburg, September, 1786, Wm. Wilson, Cornelius Westfall, Andrew Skidmore and Nicholas Petro were ordered to view a road from Tygarts Valley road

by way of Mud Lick to Cheat River at Phillip Menear's in
Horse Shoe Settlement.

An Early Inventory.

An inventory of the personal estate of John Crouch was
filed in the county court of Harrison County, September 4,
1786 by Charles Formelson, John Wilson and Patrick Hamilton. This indicates the usual articles possessed by the average citizen of that period as well as their valuation.

	L	S	d
One black mare	10		
One sorrel yearling horse colt	3		
One bay horse colt	15		
One saddle and bridle	1	2	
One rifle gun and shot bag	4		
One yearling bay horse colt	11		
One pair leather breeches	1	4	
One iron pot and dutch oven with bails	1	4	
One cow	3		
One jacket with scarlet fore shirt	1	5	
One pr. silver knee buckles and stork buck		18	
One straight coat	1	16	
One straight coat without lining	1		
One furred hat		10	
One Great coat	1	4	
One old jacket and old leggins		6	
One shirt		10	
One pair old leather breeches		6	
One sieve		8	
Cash and one Johannas	4	16	

Johannes, above mentioned, was a Portuguese coin of the
value of eight dollars; often contracted into joe; half-joe.
It is named from the figure of King John which it bears.

Residents in Randolph, 1785.

At the June term of the Harrison County Court, 1785, a
list of all the white inhabitants of Harrison County, subject
to the payment of taxes, was ordered taken. Assessors were
appointed and the county divided into districts. The names
of women who owned property are given.

H. Delay's District from Petty's Ford to Joseph Crouch.

Anthony Chevalear
George Westfall
John Crouch, Jr.
John Currenc
Charles Parsons
Henry Delay

Johnathan Crouch
Ebenezer Petty
John Crouch, Sr.
Liddia Currence
William Currence

Ed. Jackson's District—Buckhannon River Settlement.

Charles Foranash
Henry Fink, Sr.
John Cutrite, Jr.
John Bush
John Jackson
David Casto
Henry Fink, Jr.

Joseph Hall
Edward Jackson
John Bosart
Henry Runyan
John Cutrite, Sr.
John Jackson, Jr.

Jacob Westfall's District from Leading Creek up to
Petty's Ford. Both Sides of River.

Aaron Richardson
Abraham Kittle
Anthony Smith
Benjamin Wilson
Benjamin Cutright
Benjamin Jones
Cornelius Bogard
Daniel Westfall
David Cassity
David Henderson
David Phillips
Elizabeth Springstone
George Bredin
Henry Petro
John Trubies
John Pauly
John Wilson
Isaac McHenry
Johnathan Smith
Jacob Wolf
Joseph Donahue
Thomas Holder
George Breeding

Nicholas Petro
Nicholas Wolf
Peter Bredin
Peter Cassity
Phineas Wells
Phillip Clem
Richard Kittle
Solomon Ryan
Jonas Friend
Benjamin Hornbeck
Andrew Skidmore
Samuel McHenry
Samuel Quick
Thomas Phillips
Thomas Bore
Valentine Stalnaker
William Cassity
William Smith
William Levitt
William Blair, Sr.
William Briggs
William Blair, Jr.
Zacharia Wstfall

Jacob Stalnaker, Sr.
Jacob Stalnaker, Jr.
Jacob Westfall, Sr.
Jacob Westfall, Jr.
John Johnson
John Yoakum
John Kittle
John Cassity
Mathias Whitman
Michael Toner
Nicholas Smith

William Anglin
George Teter
Jacob Shook
Samuel Eberman
Alexander Blair
Elizabeth Shaver
Hezekiah Rosecronts
Jacob Shaver
Jacob Brinkle
Joseph Friend
James Bodkin

Cornelius Westfall's District from Leading Creek Down to
the County Line, Between the East Side of the
River and Cheat Mountain.

Cornelius Westfall
John Westfall
Robert Maxwell
William Westfall
Daniel Booth
Phillip Washburn

Samuel Cole
William Wilson
George Westfall
Hannah Wire
William Haddix
William Clark

Patrick Hamilton's District from Jacob Crouche's up to
the County Line.

George Alford
John Alexander
Judy Crouch
Robert Henderson
John Hadden
James Leckey, Sr.
Franceys McDonald
Charles Nilson
Elmer Riffle
Christopher Truby
Benjamin Abbott
Margaret Bare
Richard Elliott
William Hamilton
David Hadden
Thomas Leckey

James Moor
James Prathor
Daniel Simerman
John Warwick
Peter Shavers
John Alford
Joseph Crouch
Patrick Hamilton
John Hamilton
James Leckey, Jr.
James McClain
Joseph Milton
Jacob Riffle
George Shavers
George Wilson

CHAPTER VI.

EARLY MILITARY MATTERS.

JACOB CONRAD was a private in Uriah Springer's company in 1781 when the present area of Randolph was a part of Monongalia County. He was in service at Pittsburg.

There were three invalid pensioners in Randolph in 1835. They were William Shreves, Abram Burner and Fortunatius Snyder. Each received an annual stipend of $96.00. Others who were not invalids, but on the pension list for that year were: Henry Fansler, Virginia, Continental, aged 73; Jacob Kittle, New Jersey Militia, aged 77; Marney Rarvan, Virginia Continental, aged 83; Ambrose Lipscomb, Virginia Militia, aged 82; David Minear, Virginia Militia, aged 79; John Neville, Virginia State Troops, aged 69; John Ryan, Virginia Continental, aged 75; James Tenney, Virginia, aged 68; John Woolford, Virginia Militia, aged 80; Matthew Whitman, Virginia Militia, aged 74; Henry Whiteman, Pennsylvania Militia, aged 75.

The following pensioners of the Revolutionary war were living in Randolph in 1840: Mary Chenoweth, widow of John Chenoweth, aged 78; John Neville, Sr., aged 74; Henry Fansler, aged 79, residing with Andrew Fansler; Jacob Kittle, aged 84; Nancy Ann Hart, widow of Edward Hart, aged 83.

The following pensions were suspended awaiting further proof: Thomas Isner, service subsequent to the Revolution; Johnathan Smith, services not of a military character; Michael Boyles, awaiting further proof; Catherine Parsons, period, length and mode of service and name of company and field officers wanting.

Governor Beverly Randolph ordered into service in 1790 the following scouts for the protection of the settlements in Randolph County. They were in service two months from March 1, 1790 to May 1, 1790. The following facts have been obtained concerning them: Valentine Stalnaker, aged 30, size

5 feet 9 inches, nationality, Virginia; Phineas Wells, aged 30, size 5 feet 9 inches, nationality, New York; James Stewart Elliott, aged 22, size 5 feet 10 inches, nationality Virginia; James Westfall, aged 22, size 5 feet 11 inches, nationality Virginia; James Schoolcraft, aged 20, size 5 feet 8 inches, nationality Virginia; Jacob Reger, aged 23, size 6 feet, nationality Virginia.

In 1792 Governor Henry Lee, apprehending an Indian incursion into the valley ordered into service the following scouts in Randolph: Valentine Stalnaker, Charles Parsons, Geo. Westfall, John Jackson, William Gibson, William Westfall, and Thomas Carney.

The following persons from Randolph were officers in the war of 1812: Isaac Booth, Colonel, date of commission, Dec. 10, 1807; John Crouch, Major, date of commission, Aug. 30, 1806; Hiram Goff, Major, date of commission, Dec. 10, 1807; Solomon, Collett Captain, served at Norfolk and other places on Atlantic seaboard in 1812.

Randolph County paid $5,465.50 in direct taxes to aid the United States in prosecuting the war of 1812.

The following correspondence from Colonel Benjamin Wilson to Governor Harrison, dated December 9, 1782, reveals the dangers to which the early settlers were subject, during the first two decades of the occupation of the county. Many other facts of interest are disclosed. Flints which at that time were necessary munitions of war were furnished by the General Government. The number of men in the county subject to military duty is also gleaned from the reports.

Sir:—At this time duty obliges me to lay before youi Honor this letter which contains a narrative of the present state of the County of Monongalia together with my humble request.

Notwithstanding your parental care of my county, last Spring before aid came to its relief, the settlement of Buckhannon broke up and moved into the interior parts of the county, which unhappy event caused about fourteen or fifteen families of the settlement of Tygarts Valley to leave the county. At this time Tygarts Valley is a frontier, also Horse

Shoe, West Fork, Dunkard Bottom and about fifteen miles of Cheat River settlement, the county as now inhabited is about one hundred and ten computed miles from North to South.

There are about sixty-eight effective men in Tygarts Valley, eighteen at the Horse Shoe, eighty at West Fork, twenty-five at Dunkard Bottom and about one hundred and sixty at forks of Cheat River and Sandy Creek Glades, so that from the scattered condition of the country the damages the people have already sustained by the frequent incursions of the Indians since the commencement of this war, will, I believe (and from the voice of the people) cause the firse four mentioned settlements to break up and leave the country, should the Indians pursue the war with the vigor they did last Spring, unless timely relieved by your excellency's interposition.

I here insert the different incursions made by the Indians in my county this year until the eleventh day of October: first incursion made February 7th, next 10th day, next 12th day, next 20th day of March, next 22nd day, next 7th day of April, next 12th, next 24th, next 29th day of May, next 12th day of August. I await your answer.

Sir, from your most obedient and very humble servant,

BENJAMIN WILSON.

Memorial to the Governor by Delegates from Randolph County.

On October 27, 1790, Abraham Claypool and Cornelius Bogard, delegates to the Assembly from Randolph County, addressed a memorial to the Governor of Virginia praying that the four scouts from Randolph be allowed their claims for services rendered during the year, 1789. These delegates also petitioned Governor Beverly Randolph, Nov. 1, 1790, stating the defenseless condition of the counties for 400 miles along the Ohio river exposed to the hostile invasion of the Indians and destitute of every support, is truly alarming. The Governor was asked to relieve the people from the threatened danger or lay their complaints before the proper tribunal for redress.

John P. Duvall, County Lieutenant of Harrison County to Governor Henry Lee, December 20, 1791.

Sir :—I could wish to have about twenty of the men to be raised for the defense of Harrison County, stationed on the Ohio, ten at Neal's Station, the Little Kanawha, and ten at or near the mouth of the Muskingum.

I could also wish your excellency to appoint some person to employ a person to prepare the arms belonging to the State in the counties of Ohio, Monongalia, Harrison and Randolph, as they are much out of repair, and also wish you to appoint Colonel Benjamin Wilson to muster the men for the counties of Harrison and Randolph.

And am Sir, Your Excellency's most obedient, humble servant,

JOHN P. DUVALL.

In 1792 the Governor of Virginia authorized the distribution of a number of scouts to protect the frontier from the apprehended invasion of the Indians from the territory West of the Ohio River. William Lowther, of Harrison County, wrote to Gen. James Woods informing him of the following distribution of men at his disposal: Two scouts at the mouth of the Little Kanawha, two scouts on the frontier of the West Fork settlements. In Randolph he stated he had under his command a Lieutenant, two Sergeants, two Corporals and twenty-five privates which the Randolph officers distributed as follows: Lieutenant, fifteen privates, Sergeant and Corporal in the upper end of the valley. Eleven men and a Sergeant were sent to the Buckhannon settlement

The Governor of Virginia Sends Flints to the Settlers.

With the modern inventions of the weapons of warfare, it seems incredible that as late as 1792 the Governor of Virginia would send flints to the settlers of the frontier as munitions of war in their defense against the invasion of Indians from tribes West of the Ohio River. However, Colonel Benj. Wilson, writing to General James Woods, from Morgantown,

June 7, 1792, informs him that powder, lead, and flints had been received and distributed to the Captains of Militia in Randolph, Harrison and Monongalia counties.

Philadelphia War Department, 7th April, 1792.

Colonel Benjamin Wilson,

Sir:—I am directed by the President of the United States to acknowledge the receipt of yours to him of the 29th of February, 1792, and inform you that his excellency, the Governor of Virginia, was authorized in behalf of the President of the United States to add as many scouts as he should judge expedient, at the general expense to any part of the exposed not exceeding eight in number in any one county.

It is the disposition of the President of the United States that the most entire protection should be afforded the exposed counties that the nature of the case may require. The executive of Virginia must be presumed to be competent to judge of this matter, and they have made an arrangement upon this subject, but as some inconvenience may result from waiting for an application from the Governor of Virginia, the counties of Randolph and Monongalia will be permitted the four scouts requested by your letter of the 27th February, together with such a sufficient number of rangers upon the continental establishment as a temporary arrangement as shall be deemed indispensably necessary, not exceeding the Company mentioned in your letter, until the executive of Virginia may make an application confirmative of the same for the season.

I am your humble servant,

H. KNOX.

Strength of Militia in Randolph.

The County Lieutenants reported to James Woods, Lieutenant Governor of Virginia, June 7, 1792, the following as the strength of the militia in the counties of Harrison, Randolph and Monongalia: Benjamin Wilson reports strength of Harrison County militia at 400; Jacob Westfall reports strength of Randolph County militia at 174 or 200; John

Evans reports strength of Monongalia County militia at 730.

Colonel Benjamin Wilson Appeals to President of United States.

Harrison County, Va., February 29, 1792.

Sir:—It would be intruding on you for me to call your attention to the disposition of the Indians when fired with conquest, on their dastardly way of war. Particularly their lying in wait about houses to take advantage of defenseless women and children, their ambuscading roads, robberies, etc. It may suffice only to mention the situation of the exposed frontier and the present fears of the people.

Ohio County covers a part of Monongalia County and Harrison a part of Randolph County, and my observation since the year 1774, Ohio and Harrison have stood on a similar footing in point of danger. The lamentable catastrophe that befell the Federal Army last fall has with fear so impressed the minds of the exposed people that it is pitiable to hear their complaints, and sure I am that many of them would move from the exterior settlements was not their consolation a full confidence in your granting extensive temporary relief, as well as to pursue the reduction of the Indians upon a more extensive scale than has been heretofore done. I wish not to trespass upon your time or patience, but conceive it my duty to mention my adjoining counties, viz: That Randolph may be favored with an addition of four scouts, and Monongalia with four, Ohio I learn is by your excellency provided for, with an additional number of those allowed by this State.

Sir, I am your humble and devoted servant,

BENJ. WILSON.

Sir:—If you condescend to answer the above, the way by Winchester is the swiftest and surest conveyance.

B. W.

Captain Cornelius Bogard of Randolph to Governor.

Randolph County, August 16, 1794.

On receiving your orders I raised a company of volunteers for the defense of the Monongalia District. On the 17th March last I received orders from Captain William Lowther to station the troops raised in this county at the head of the Tygarts Valley and Buckhannon Rivers. I acted agreeably to his instructions and kept the troops stationed at these points until I received another letter from Captain Lowther with orders to march them under my care to the mouth ot the Great Hock Hocking, or a little settlement about four miles above Hock Hocking. I received said orders on tne 8th of July. On consideration of the distance I had to march I thought it would be impracticable to march before the first Monday in August, but on the 29th I had an express from Buckhannon, giving the intelligence that the Indians had taken a young woman prisoner from the West Fork. I immediately marched a part of my company to the place where the mischief was done, but did not overtake the enemy. I got back to the Valley the 10th of August where I found the people much alarmed. I think it my duty to try to detect the enemy if they be in the settlement before I march to the Ohio. The vacancy on the Ohio between Belleville and the mouth of the Big Kanawha is the worst inlet to the Indians.

CHAPTER VII.

EARLY LAND PATENTS.

THE General Assembly of Virginia in 1777, passed an Act, providing that all persons, who settled on the Western Waters prior to the 24, day of June, 1776, should be given 400 acres of land for every family. In 1779 that law was changed to require one year's residence and the raising one crop of corn, to entitle him to 400 acres. In 1781 a commission was appointed to grant certificates to those who were entitled to lands in the counties of Monongalia, Ohio and Yohogania. These certificates are of the greatest historical value as fixing the date and place of occupancy of the pioneers.

Appended are certificates granted to settlers in this section of the District. The first one is copied in full, followed by extracts from others.

We, the commissioners for adjusting claims to unpatented lands in the counties of Monongalia, Yohogania and Ohio, do certify that William Isner is entitled to 400 acres of land in Monongahela County, on Tygarts Valley River to include his settlement made in 1775, adjoining lands of Benjamin Wilson.

Given under our hands at Colonel John Evan's this 7, day of March in the fifth year of the Commonwealth 1781.

> JOHN P. DUVALL,
> JAMES NEAL,
> WILL HAYMOND.

This certificate cannot be entered with the surveyor after the 26, of October, 1781.

> Wm. McCleary, Clk. Com.

Ent'd, 9th. April 1781.

Thos. Wilmoth is entitled to 400 acres of land on Cheat River to include settlement made in 1776.

Thos. Wilmoth, assignee of Geo. Shaver, 400 acres on Cheat River near to lands of settlement of 1776.

John Wilmoth 200 acres on Cheat River to include settlement made in 1776 and adjoining lands of Thos. Wilmoth.

John Haddin, 200 acres on Haddin's Mill Run to include settlement of 1774.

Jacob White 100 acres on Laurel Run to include settlement made in 1773.   Preemption.

Richard Jackson, 400 acres on South Fork of Ten Mile Creek, including his settlement made in 1775.

Geo. Walker, 200 acres, adjoining lands of John Wilmoth, including settlement of 1777.

John Yeoakum, 400 acres on Barker's Creek to include settlement made 1773.

Michael Yeoakum, 400 acres on Sugar Creek to include settlement of 1772.

Noah Hadden, 1000 acres 2 miles from mouth of Elk Creek and Haddin's Cabbin.

Daniel Fink, 1000 acres on Fink's Run to include his settlement, made in 1772.

David Wilson, 400 acres on Buckhannon River to include settlement of 1772, adjoining lands of Henry Fink.

John Fink, preemption 1000 acres on Buckhannon River to include settlement of 1777.

Phillip Menear, 400 acres on Cheat River.

William Westfall, 1000 acres on Teter's Creek, including settlement of 1772.

John Jackson, Junior, 400 acres Turkey Run on Buckhannon River, adjoining lands of John Jackson, Senior, to include his settlement made in 1773.

Benjamin Wilson, 400 acres on Leading Creek, right of residence and including improvements made in 1773.   Adjoining lands of Thos. Skidmore.

Jacob Conrad and Benjamin Wilson, tenants in common, 400 acres at Bulltown, on Kanawha River, including settlement made in 1775.

John Jackson, 400 acres on Buckhannon, including settlement made 1776.

Isaac Brooks, assignee of Samuel Pringle, 400 acres on Buckhannon River including settlements made in 1772.

Timothy Dorman, 400 acres on Buckhannon River including improvements of 1773.

John Reger, 400 acres on Buckhannon River to include settlement made 1773.

Salathiel Goff, 400 acres Cheat River to include settlement made in 1774.

Thomas Parkeson, 1000 acres by right of preemption at the Tygarts Valley Falls to include improvements made 1773.

John Wilson and Martin Shobe, assignee, of James Knotts, as tenants in common, 400 acres on Dry Fork of Cheat to include settlement made at Horse Camp in 1776.

Edward Jackson and John Fink, as tenants in common, assignees to George Parsons, 400 acres in Parsons right ot residing and raising a crop of corn, to include an improvement made by the said Parsons on the Head of Little Elk, adjoining lands claimed by Timothy Dorman in 1775.

David Minear, 200 acres Clay Lick Run, a branch of Cheat River in right of residence to include improvements of 1776.

Salathiel Goff, assignee of William Wilson, 400 acres at the mouth of Pleasant Creek, opposite to lands claimed by Thos. Parsons, to include settlement of 1776.

Salathiel Goff, assignee of Thomas Pence, 200 acres on Cheat River nearly opposite Horse Shoe Bottom, to include settlement of 1776.

John Reger, 400 acres on each side of Buckhannon river nearby joining lands of Timothy Dorman to include his settlement made 1773.

Edward Jackson, 400 acres Finks Run to include settlement of 1774.

Geo. Peck, assignee of Edward Tanner 400 acres on Buckhannon River, adjoining lands of George Jackson to include settlement 1774.

Christopher Strader, 400 acres in the right of raising corn crop before 1778 on Buckhannon Fork.

Charles Fornash, assignee of Alexander Sleath, 400 acres on the Buckhannon River, to include his settlement of 1772.

Jeremiah Prather, assignee of John Davis, who was assignee of Daniel Hagle, 200 acres in Tygarts Valley on the West side of the river, adjoining lands of Peter Cassity and Benjamin Jones, to include his settlement of 1771.

James Parson, 400 acres in the Horse Shoe Bottom, Cheat River, to include his settlement made in 1769.

John Heagle, 400 acres on Buckhannon to include his settlement made in 1776.

John Haddin, 200 acres on Haddin's Mill Run, a branch of the Tygarts Valley River, to include his settlement made in 1774.

Geo. Teter, 400 acres on Tygarts Valley River, adjoining said river, to include his settlement made in 1772.

William Anglin, 400 acres on Tygarts Valley River at Pringle's Ford, including his settlement made in 1773.

Geo. Jackson, assignee Alexander Sleeth, 400 acres on Buckhannon River including his settlement made in 1769.

Isaac Brooks, assignee of Samuel Pringle, 400 acres on Buckhannon River, to include settlement of 1776.

John Jackson, assignee of William White, 400 acres on Buckhannon River to include settlement made in 1772.

Old Land Entries.

Joseph Friend entered 100 acres on the East side of Cheat River to include improvements made in 1783.

Andrew Skidmore, assignee of William Wamsley, entered 5000 acres to include Salt Black Lick, 1783.

John Harness, 600 acres on Black Water, a branch of Cheat River, adjoining lands of Ruby Shobe and Isaac Hornbeck, 1783.

John Crouch, assignee, Geo. Harness, 70 acres adjoining lands he now lives on Tygarts Valley River, 1783.

William Westfall, 24 acres, West side Tygarts Valley River, 3 miles to the left hand of Geo. Westfall's Mill to include the Coper Banks, April, 1783.

Uriah Gandy, 200 acres on Dry Fork of Cheat to include land he formerly lived on, 1783.

Phineas Wells, assignee of Ben. Wilson, 100 acres, below and adjoining lands of Abraham Kittle, 1781.

David Lilly, 600 acres East of Tygarts Valley River, adjoining lands of William Westfall, 1783.

From the entry of William Westfall as given above, the "Coper Banks" were evidently a place of local celebrity in the vicinity of Beverly in 1783.

Real Estate Conveyances, 1787-92.

200 Acres. Ebenezer Petty to Gabriel Friend, adjoining lands of John Crouch and John Harness in Tygarts Valley.

10 Acres. John Warwick to Sylvester Ward, East side of Valley River.

900 Acres. James Arnold to Jacob McEnry, Cave Run, a branch of Tygarts Valley River.

5400 Acres. Samuel Hanaway to Mathias Halstead, Elk River.

600 Acres. John Hagel to Henry Runyan, Buckhannon River.

130 Acres. Jacob Shaver to Wm. Briggs, Kings Run.

200 Acres. Joseph Friend to Henry Smith, Mud Lick Run.

1000 Acres. James Hanaway to Benjamin Hall, Davis Run and Hawe's Run.

540 Acres. James Arnold to Ignatius Hayden, Tygarts Valley River.

600 Acres. James Arnold to Robert Price, Sandy Creek.

300 Acres. Charles Tomilson to James Lackey, Tygarts Valley River.

170 Acres. James Lackey to Charles Tomilson, Tygarts Valley River.

103 Acres. John Lackey to John Hadden, Tygarts Valley River.

170 Acres. Joseph Crouch to Geo. See. Tygarts Valley River.

400 Acres. Wm. Gibson to Charles Myers, Sugar Creek.

131 Acres. Simean Harris to David Lilly, Tygarts Valley.

225 Acres. James Arnold to Thomas Martin.

2000 Acres. Edward Jackson to Henry Arkeport, adjoining lands of John Jackson and James Arnold.

1000 Acres. Richard Mason to Wm. W. Cary, Middle Fork.

250 Acres. William Wilson to John Shenick, West side Cheat River.

400 Acres. John Hardin to Hector Hardin, Cove Run.

1000 Acres. Brooks Beal to William Wilson, East side Tygarts Valley River.

6¼ Acres. Henry Petro to Richard Kittle, Wilson Creek.

197 Acres. Aaron Richardson to Charles Myers, West side Tygarts Valley River.

186 Acres. Sylvester Ward to Geo. See, John Warwick land.

213 Acres. Cornelius Bogard to Jacob Stalnaker, Files Creek.

135 Acres. John Crouch to John Pancake, West of Tygarts Valley River, adjoining lands of Ebenezer Petty.

20 Acres. Abram Kittle to Phineas Wells, East side of Valley River.

210 Acres. John Alexander to Jacob Poseley, East side of Valley River.

130 Acres. Jacob Shaver to Wm. Biggs, Trout Run.

197 Acres. Elizabeth Shaver to Boston Stalnaker, adjoining lands of Alexander Maxwell and Wm. Currence.

500 Acres. John Jackson, Jr. to Wm. Waters, Turkey Run.

200 Acres. Daniel Westfall to Henry Fink, East side Tygarts Valley River.

112 Acres. Nicholas Smith to Wm. Smith, West side Tygarts Valley River, adjoining lands of Isaac White.

120 Acres. Benjamin Jones to John Currence, West side Tygarts Valley River.

190 Acres. Daniel Henderson to Wm. Clark, Tygarts Valley River.

300 Acres. John Cassity to Wm. Wamsley, West side of Valley River, adjoining lands of Peter Cassity above and Wm. Levett below.

166 Acres. Cornelius Bogard to Daniel Richardson, Files Creek.

96 Acres. Jeremiah Cooper to Patrick Burns, Cheat River.

3000 Acres. Hugh Thompson to Joseph Gibson, Elk River.

396 Acres. David Conley to Jacob Kuhnrod (Conrad), adjoining lands of Wm. Hamilton.

330 Acres. Wm. Wilson to John Beall, Mouth of Roaring Creek.

260 Acres. Jacob Eberman to John Smith, Tygarts Valley River.

9322 Acres. Thomas Pennell to Stephen Sherwood, Elk River.

5000 Acres. Joseph Pennell to Stephen Middlebrook, Elk River.

1434 Acres. Thomas Pennell to Stephen Sherwood, Elk River.

57 Acres. Henry Mace to John Bogard, Cheat River.

190 Acres. Geo. Reed to John Currence, West side Valley River.

77 Acres. Thomas Wilmoth to James Thompson, Cheat River.

77 Acres. James Thompson to Uriah Gandy, Cheat River.

200 Acres. Philip Kizer to Cornelius Bogard, Shavers Run.

337 Acres. Peter Cassity to Benjamin Hornbeck, adjoining land of Wm. Wamsley, West side Valley River.

300 Acres. Sylvester Ward to John Pancake, East side Valley River.

135 Acres. Wm. Briggs to Jacob Weese, Kings Run.

150 Acres. Jacob Westfall to Sylvester Ward, East side Valley River.

200 Acres. Geo. Breeding to Abraham Claypool, East side Tygarts Valley River, between the two tracts of Geo. See.

190 Acres. Michael Isner to David Henderson, both sides of the river, adjoining lands of Abram Kittle and Henry Peatro.

195 Acres. Nicholas Petro to Henry Petro, adjoining land of Benjamin Wilson, Daniel Westfall, Abram Kittle, John Kittle and Jacob White.

402 Acres. Cornelius Bogard to Jacob C. Harper, East side Tygarts Valley River.

The consideration in the sale of the 402 acre tract of land of Cornelius Bogard to Jacob C. Harper was $1,458.00. In the sale of 337 acres of land of Peter Cassity to Benjamin Hornbeck, the consideration was $972.00. This tract was north of the present railway station of Daily, in Valley Bend District, and the descendants of Benjamin Hornbeck own and reside upon a portion of the tract at the present time.

Old Surveys.

The following surveys were made in what is now Randolph County before separation from Harrison:

August 3, 1785, Geo. Harness, adjustor for both sides, surveyed a tract on both sides of Dry Fork of Cheat River above Buffalo Lick.

Surveyed in 1785, on Westfalls Mill Run for Jacob Westfall, Jr. and Geo. Westfall, Sr., 322 acres.

Surveyed 1785, for Benjamin Wilson, assignee of Henry Banks, 200 acres East side of Valley River, adjoining lands of John Truby. Chain Carriers, Wm. Cassidy, Jacob Westfall and Cornelius Bogard.

Surveyed, August 1785, for John Jackson, assignee of Geo. Harness, 148 acres of land in Harrison County, on Black Water Creek, a branch of Cheat River.

Surveyed August, 1785, by Geo. Harness for Wm. Haymond, a tract of land on Black Water Creek. Chain carriers, Henry Mace and John Jackson.

Surveyed June, 1785, for Isaac Westfall, assignee of Cornelius Westfall, assignee of Joseph Friend, assignee of Andrew Woodrow, 152 acres of land in Harrison County on both sides of left hand fork of Isners Run, adjoining lands of Thos. Isner.

John Wilson, adjustor, surveyed in 1785, for Henry and Nicholas Petro, 200 acres adjoining the land they then lived on and lands of Daniel Westfall and William Wilson, assignee of Benjamin Wilson, assignee of Henry Banks.

Surveyed by Edward Jackson, adjuster, 1735, for Wm. Haymond, Sheriff of Harrison County, lands of Christopher Strader on Buckhannon River, including mouth of Little Sand Run.

Surveyed 1785, for Jacob Riffle, 50 acres on waters of Tygarts Valley River, adjoining lands of John Alexander, Geo. Harness, surveyor. Chain carriers, James Lackey and Geo. Wilson.

Surveyed, August 1786, for James Taffee, assignee of Israel Brown and Robert Chanee, 698 acres on both sides of river that empties into Tygarts Valley River below Roaring Creek.

Surveyed February 1786, for James Taffee, assignee of Israel Brown, assignee of Robert Chanee, 875 acres on West side of the waters that empty into Roaring Creek. Chain carriers, Jonas Friend and John Westfall.

Surveyed by Daniel Pugh for James Taffee, 1000 acres of land on King's Creek, a branch of Tygarts Valley River and adjoining lands of John Wilson, Benjamin Wilson and Henry Petro.

CHAPTER VIII.

EARLY ROADS IN RANDOLPH.

"One day through the primeval wood,
A calf walked home, as all calves should;
But made a trail all bent askew,
A crooked trail as all calves do.

"And then the wise bell weather sheep,
Pursued the trail o'er vale and steep
And drew the flock behind him, too
As good bell-weathers always do.

"This forest path became a lane,
That bent and turned and turned again;
This crooked path became a road,
Where many a poor horse with a load,
Toiled on beneath the burning sun,
And traveled some three miles in one.
And thus a century and a half
Trod in the footsteps of that calf."

THE roads of a country are an index to its culture and civilization. The status of any people, historic or contemporaneous, may be determined by a knowledge of its facilities for intercommunication. The civilization of the classic ancients reached its limitations in stone highways. The carts, wheelbarrows, canals and junks are parallelled by the civilization of the Celestial Empire. Civilization today is moving forward on railroads, steamships and magnetic telegraphs, while the possibilities of aerial navigation are challenging man's inventive genius.

Of course good roads were an impossibility in Randolph for many years because of the sparsely settled condition of the county.

In 1774, when Pendleton was still a part of Augusta, a road was ordered to be surveyed up Seneca and over the Alleghany divide in order to connect the infant settlements on Cheat and Tygarts Valley with the communities east of the mountains. Whether this road was ever surveyed and improved is uncertain. Road making in that day, however, consisted largely in cutting out the brush and removing the logs along the proposed highway. A new order for a road over the same route was ordered by the Court of Pendleton County in 1787. Regardless of the condition of the trail, this was the main route traversed by the pioneer in reaching his new abode West of the mountains.

Among the important early road surveys were the following:

In 1787 a road from the county seat by Wm. Smith's to Middle Fork.

Same year a road from the county seat to Sandy Creek.

Same year a road from Salt Lick on Leading Creek to Mud Lick.

In 1788 a road from the Tygarts Valley Road to Crab Apple Bottom in Highland County.

In 1789 a road from Peter Cassity's to the Clarksburg road at the mouth of Leading Creek.

In 1790 a road from Michael Isner's in Tygarts Valley to the Hardy County line.

Same year a road from Connolly's Lick to the top of the Alleghanies at the Augusta County line.

In 1792 a road from Beverly to the upper ford of Cheat.

In 1793 a road along Currences Blazes square across the Valley.

Same year a road from Beverly to the Carpenter settlement on Elk.

In 1795 a road from Beverly to Jacob Westfall's Saw Mill on Files Creek, so as to intersect the Big Road.

In 1798 a road from Beverly to Wolf's at the foot of Rich Mountain toward Buckhannon.

The travel in an early day between the valley and settlements to the Westward was probably across the mountains South of Huttonsville.

In 1814 a road was ordered to be made that would be passable for pack horse from Beverly to Buckhannon.

The Staunton and Parkersburg Pike was built about 1840. Evidently the Board of Public Works intended to cross the mountains South of Huttonsville. This would have left Beverly ten or twelve miles to the north. To induce the

Board to make Beverly a point on the road, several thousand dollars was subscribed by citizens of Beverly to be used in the construction of the road.

In 1784 Henry Petro was appointed surveyor of a road from Eberman's Creek to Jacob Westfall's Mill.

In 1785 Cornelius Bogard was appointed surveyor of a road from Wilson's Mill on Wilson's Creek to the Rockingham County line. This was practically a continuation of the Seneca Trail by which most of the settlers had entered the valley from the East. It crossed over Cheat Mountain at the Kelly settlement to Cheat River, thence up the river to the mouth of Taylor Run, ascending Shaver Mountain by a dividing ridge just South of Taylor Run, passing down on the east side of the mountain about one-half mile north of the Coberly farm, uniting with the road as presently located at or near Laurel Fork.

At a court held at Clarksburg, September, 1784, Abram Kittle, Thos. Phillips, Geo. Westfall, Sr., and Benjamin Hornbeck were appointed viewers of a road from Jacob Westfall's Mill to a bridge opposite Geo. Westfall's Mill. Geo. Westfall's Mill was located, perhaps, in the vicinity of the old Baker Mill at Beverly, while Jacob Westfall's Mill was probably located on the Buckey Mill site, about one mile east of Beverly, on the same stream.

At the same term of the court, Ebenezer Petty, Jacob Yokum, Peter Cassity, and Jacob Stalnaker, Sr., were appointed viewers of a road from a bridge opposite Geo. Westfall's Mill to Darby Conoly's place. This road, perhaps, the most travelled road in the first half century in the history of the county, crossed the river about one mile south of Beverly at what is known as the slaty ford on the Coberly farm, then skirted the base of the old river terraces up the river, passing about 100 yards to the west of the old Isaac White house on the brow of the hill, thence up the river at the base of the foot-hills, crossing over the bluff near the site of the old Methodist church a quarter of a mile west of the residence of J. A. Crawford, thence on up the valley largely on the west side to Conley Run.

Jonas Friend was made overseer of a road by the Harrison County Court in 1784, from his home near the mouth of Leading Creek to Eberman's Creek, now Chenoweth's Creek.

CHAPTER IX.

ANNALS OF EDUCATION.

THE education of the youth of Randolph, in the first decade of its history, because of the sparsely settled condition of the country, must have been limited to the home and fireside. While the achievement that mostly concerned the pioneer was the conversion of the wilderness into homes and farms, yet a people with the courage and intelligence to take advantage of the opportunities afforded by a frontier community with the laudable ambition to improve their condition, would not long neglect the education of their children. Accordingly, private schools were early established by two or more families uniting and employing a teacher. The next step in the way of elementary education was in the direction of subscription schools, open to all who were able to pay the tuition fees. Often the teacher of these schools was a roving individual, whose qualifications were limited to his ability to teach the most rudimentary branches, such as reading writing and arithmetic and his physical ability to maintain discipline. As a rule these teachers received a meagre salary and boarded around with the patrons of the school. However, not a few of the early teachers of Randolph were men of classical scholarship, and the impress and influence of their teaching is not only manifest today, but will extend to future generations. Such men were James H. Logan, Dr. Squire Bosworth, Rev. Thomas and Jacob I. Hill.

Education was a subject the early lawmakers of Virginia considered worthy of their consideration and Randolph Academy was established by act of the Virginia assembly of December 1, 1787. In the following November, among the additional trustees appointed, were the following from Randolph County: John Haddan, Abraham Claypoole, James Westfall, and Henry Fink. The trustees selected Clarksburg as the most eligible location for the proposed institution of learning. A copy of the act founding Randolph Academy is appended:

WHEREAS, The inhabitants of the counties of Harrison, Monongalia, Randolph and Ohio, are from their remote stiuation, deprived of the advantages arising from the establishment of public seminaries within the state; and it is just and reasonable that the one-sixth of the fees of the surveyors of the said counties, which are now applied toward the support of the William and Mary College, should be applied to the establishment of a public seminary within one of the said counties.

BE IT THEREFORE ENACTED BY THE GENERAL ASSEMBLY, That his excellency Edmund Randolph, Benjamin Harrison, Patrick Henry, Joseph Prentiss, James Wood, George Mason, George Nicholas, John Harvey, Thomas Mathews, William Ronald, Henry Banks, William McLeary, John Evans, William John, Francis Worman, John Pearce Duvall, George Jackson, Benjamin Wilson, Nicholas Carpenter, John Powers, Archibald Woods, Moses Chapline, Ebenezer Zane, David Chambers, John Wilson, Jacob Westfall, junior, Robert Maxwell and John Jackson, junior, gentlemen, shall be and they are hereby constituted a body politic and corporate, to be known by the name of "The trustees of the Randolph Academy," and by that name shall have perpetual succession and a common seal.

The said trustees shall hold their first session in Morgantown in Monongalia County, on the second Monday in May next; they shall then or as soon after as conveniently may be, fix upon some healthy and convenient place within one of the counties of Harrison, Monongalia, Randolph, or Ohio, for the purpose of erecting thereon the necessary buildings for the said academy.

After defining the powers and duties of the trustees of the academy the act concludes in the following sections, indicating the source from which the financial support of the institution should come:

The surveyors of the said counties of Monongalia, Harrison, Randolph, and Ohio, shall not be accountable to the president and masters of William and Mary College, for any part of the fees which shall accrue to them after the first day of January, one thousand seven hundred and eighty eight: And the bond as given by them for the yearly payment of one-sixth of their fees to the president and masters of the said college, shall be and are hereby declared to be null and void, so far as relates to the fees which shall become due to them after the said first day of January, in the year last mentioned.

Each of the surveyors of the said counties shall, within one month after he shall be required by the board of trustees, give bond with sufficient security in a reasonable sum, for the yearly payment of one-sixth part of the fees which shall become due to him after the said first day of January, to the said trustees; and in case any one of the said surveyors shall fail or refuse to give such bond and security he shall forfeit and pay to the said trustees the sum of one hundred pounds, to be recovered by motion in the court of the county of such surveyor, upon giving him ten days previous notice of such motion: and each of the said surveyors shall annually forfeit and pay the like sum to the said trustees, to be recovered in the same manner, until he shall give such bond and security.

Free School System.

In order to understand the causes that resulted in the foundation of the free school system, it is necessary to give a cursory review of the origin and progress of popular education in the mother state. Thomas Jefferson, in 1779, prepared and had submitted to the Virginia Assembly a bill "For the Better Diffusion of Knowledge." This was the first movement to establish a system of Free Schools in Virginia. The object of Mr. Jefferson's Free School bill, in conjunction with his other bills for religious freedom and the abolition of entails and the rights of primogeniture, was to form "a system by which every fiber would be eradicated of ancient or future aristocracy, and a foundation laid for a government truly republican."

Mr. Jefferson's Free School bill was not even considered

by the General Assembly, but it greatly influenced public sentiment and laid the foundation for all subsequent legislation on public education in Virginia. It proposed a system embracing three classes of schools, namely:

1. Elementary schools, free to all and supported by public expense.

2. General schools, academies and colleges, to be maintained partly by public expense, and partly by tuition fees.

3. A State University, at the head of the system.

In his "Notes on Virginia" Mr. Jefferson gives the following particulars of the system:

"The bill proposes to lay off every county into small districts of five or six miles square, called hundreds, and each of them to establish a school for teaching reading, writing and arithmetic. The teacher to be supported by the hundred and every person in it entitled to send his children three years gratis, and as much longer as he pleases, paying for it. These schools to be under a visitor, who is annually to choose a boy of best genius in the school, of those whose parents are too poor to give them further education, and to send him forward to one of the grammar schools, of which twenty are proposed to be erected in different parts of the country, for teaching Greek, Latin, geography and the higher branches of numerical arithmetic. Of the boys thus sent in one year, trial is to be made at the grammar schoods one or two years, and the best genius of the whole selected, and continued six years, and the residue dismissed. By this means twenty of the best geniuses will be annually instructed at public expense, so far as the grammar schools."

"At the end of six years' instruction, one-half are to be discontinued, from among whom the grammar schools are to be supplied with future masters, and the other half who are to be chosen for the superiority of their parts and dispositions, are to be sent and continued three years in the study of such services, as they may choose at William and Mary College, the plan of which is to be enlarged, as will hereafter be explained, and extended to all the useful sciences."

        *   *   *   *   *   *   *   *   *   *   *

The general objects of the law are to provide an education adapted to the years, to the capacity, and the condition of every one, and directed to their freedom and happiness."

In 1796, December 22, an act to establish public schools was passed which embodied the provision of Mr. Jefferson's bill for elementary schools, being the first grade of the system.

This act contained the general plan of an efficient free school system. The entire management of the proposed system was placed in the hands of three county officers, styled aldermen, who were empowered to divide the county into school districts, employ teachers, determine the amount of money necessary to build school houses, to pay teachers' salaries and to make a levy upon the property of the inhabitants of each county for this purpose. A fatal proviso, however, was added to the act: "That the court of each county, at which a majority of the acting magistrates thereof shall be present, shall first determine the year in which the first election of aldermen shall be made, and until they so determine no such election shall be made." Concerning the failure of his law, Mr. Jefferson said: "The justices, being generally of the more wealthy class, were unwilling to incur the burden, so that it was not suffered to commence in a single county." Although ths law was never repealed, there is no record showing that this act was ever put in operation.

The Literary Fund.

The opportunity was again presented for the agitation of the public school question in 1810 when the Literary Fund was created.

"It was enacted on the 2d of February, 1810, that all escheats, confiscations, fines, penalties and forfeitures, and all rights in personal property accruing to the Commonwealth, as directed, showing no rightful proprietor, shall be appropriated to the encouragement of learning; and the auditor was directed to open an account to be designated as the Literary Fund."

The following year an act was passed protesting against any other application of the revenues of this fund by any other General Assembly, to any other object than the education of the poor. This was the beginning of what was called the "Pauper System" which continued in force up to 1861 and was in operation in every county except those in which a free school system had been established and in such counties their just quota of the Literary Fund went into the county school fund.

Various amendments were made to the Literary Fund bill from time to time, however, under laws most friendly to free schools, it required the endorsement of two-thirds of the legal voters of the county, before a single public school be established. This, coupled with the property qualification of voters, gave a vast advantage to the enemies of public education.

The constitution, which was adopted by the state of West Virginia in 1861, made provision "for a thorough and efficient system of free schools." The legislature on the 10th day of December, 1863, passed an act, establishing our present system of free schools. However, some slight amendments were made under the new constitution adopted in 1873.

School Commissioners for Randolph County.

At a session of the County Court, held on the 27th day of October, 1856, by Joseph Hart, Thos. B. Scott, and Jacob Vanscoy as members of the court, the following School Commissioners were appointed for Randolph County:

District No. 1—John W. Moore.
District No. 2—Harmon Snyder.
District No. 3—John M. Crouch.
District No. 4—E. B. Bosworth.
District No. 5—Wm. P. Brady.
District No. 6—Squire Bosworth.
District No. 7—John I. Chenoweth.
District No. 8—Levy Moore.
District No. 9—Wm. M. Phares.
District No. 10—Washington Taylor.
District No. 11—Samuel Dinkle.
District No. 12—Cyrus Kittle.
District No. 13—Alexander Grim.
District No. 14—Alph Taylor.
District No. 15—Jesse M. Roy.

School Statistics of Randolph County for 1866.

Amount of School Fund	$2,157.00
School Houses in 1865	2
School Houses in 1866	12
Average value of School House, 1866	$140.00
Enumeration	1736
Enrollment	761
Daily Attendance	615
Teachers—Male	21
Teachers—Female	9
Average Salary—Men	$24.00
Average Salary—Female	$15.00
Average length of term	2.8 months

Statistics 1910.

Names of Magisterial and Independent Districts	No. School in District	No. White Pupils Enumerated	No. Colored Pupils Enumerated	Total Amount of Building Fund	Total Amount of Teachers' Fund
Beverly	20	643	46	$ 2,898.32	$ 7,375.74
Dry Fork	41	1365		5,940.81	13,316.35
Huttonsville	15	666	13	1,951.75	4,965.11
Leadsville	20	716		2,053.19	5,901.38
Mingo	14	361		2,599.33	4,709.03
Middle Fork	25	627		2,801.04	7,039.81
New Interest	13	425		1,113.22	3,648.35
Roaring Creek	16	516		3,987.92	4,805.57
Valley Bend	8	253		1,728.12	2,335.23
Elkins Independent	33	1584	65	65,572.31	20,831.73
Total	205	7143	128	$90,646.01	$74,929.20

Public Schools of Randolph in 1882.

A. S. Bosworth was County Superintendent that year and from his report we learn the following facts: There was an enrollment of 1758 pupils in the county; there was but one graded school in the county and this was at Beverly; there were 24 log buildings and 34 frame buildings for school purposes in the county; the average value of school buildings was $211. Fifty-three teachers were licensed that year with grades as follows: 20 first grade, 25 second grade, and 8 third grade. The following teachers were licensed: H. L. Stalnaker, G. W. Cunningham, C. S. Moore, Teresa Cain, A. M. Bradley, D. B. Curtis, Anna McLean, Maud Chenoweth, Nannie Daniels, John L. Bosworth, James B. Litle, B. W. Taylor, P. C. Webley, Lee Marstiller, J. B. Canfield, W. Marstiller, Agnes Marstiller, Angelia Scott, Alice Scott, F. M. Canfield, C. M. Marstiller, M. A. Durkin, Ella Wilmoth, F. J. Triplett, Sylvester Wilmoth, Arnold Wilmoth, L. B. Triplett, D. E. Coberly, E. R. Skidmore, D. A. Denton, M. E. Lawson, Lemuel C. Rice, Delpha Marstiller, Celia Wilmoth, Flora Channel, B. B. Herron, T. L. Daniels, Sheffey Taylor, Thomas Madden, Mary King, W. P. Madden, John F. Ward, F. H. Kittle, John Hutton, Martin Madden, Mollie L. Thomas, Henry Simmons, W. O. Grim, H. B. Morgan, J. H. Wamsley, J. L. Wamsley.

Superintendents of Schools.

David Goff	1853	C. S. Moore	1888
W. F. Corley	1865	D. A. Hamrick	1890
S. B. Hart	1867	S. L. Hogan	1892
Jacob I. Hill	1869	W. T. Woodyard	1895
J. W. Price	1872	A. J. Crickard	1899
A. F. Wilmoth	1875	E. A. Poe	1903
A. S. Bosworth	1882	W. J. Long	1905
B. W. Taylor	1884	Troy Wilmoth	1915
F. P. Madden	1886		

The Davis and Elkins College.

The founding of the Davis and Elkins College marked a new era in the educational history of Randolph. The first session opened in 1904 and has steadily grown in power, patronage and usefulness. Until 1908, the college was under Lexington and Winchester Presbyteries. The Presbyterian church of the State is now united in its support. The College received an endowment of $100,000 under the will of the late Senator Davis. The College is open to both sexes and compares favorably with the best institutions of learning in this country.

CHAPTER X.

CIVIL WAR PERIOD.

O N December 20, 1860, South Carolina adopted an ordinance of secession declaring that the Union existing between South Carolina and the other States was dissolved. The spirit of secession spread with great rapidity, and by the first of February, 1861, five other states—Mississippi, Florida, Alabama, Georgia and Louisiana—all had taken similar action. On February 4, 1861, delegates from six of the seceded states met at Montgomery, Alabama, and formed a new government called the Confederate States of America. February 8th, the same year, Jefferson Davis was elected President, and Alexander Stevens, Vice-President. Virginia was not only the oldest but, in many respects, the most influential among the slave holding States. She was soon to become the principal theatre in which the great Civil War drama was to be enacted. The public mind at this time was much agitated and the impending crisis cast its shadows before. Under these circumstances Governor Fletcher called the General Assembly in extra session on Monday, January 7, 1861, and an act was passed providing for a State Convention and the election of delegates thereto. The object of this convention was to determine the position Virginia should take in regard to secession. The election was held February 4, 1861, and the convention was to be held February 13th following. John N. Hughes was elected to represent Randolph County in that convention. The public mind was further inflamed by the bombardment of Fort Sumpter by the forces of South Carolina on April 13, 1861. On April 17, 1861, this convention passed an ordinance of secession by a vote of yeas 88 and nays 55.

The Civil War was precipitated in Western Virginia by an effort on the part of Virginia, aided by the other seceding states, to prevent a division of the state. In the counties west of the Alleghanies the preponderance of sentiment was in favor of maintaining the Union. However, in some counties, as Randolph, secession sympathizers were in the majority. Robert E. Lee was appointed Commander in Chief of the military and naval forces of Virginia, April 23, 1861. He at once began the organization in the counties west of the Alleghanies of an army of volunteers.

On May 4, 1861, Colonel A. Porterfield was ordered to Grafton by General Lee to take charge of the volunteer troops of that section. About the middle of May, 1861, General Lee ordered Colonel Heck to transport 1,000 muskets from Staunton to Beverly for the use of volunteer companies. General Lee being disappointed in the enlistment of volunteers, sent General Garnett across the mountains with troops from Virginia, Georgia and Tennessee. While the Confederacy was organizing an army in Northwestern Virginia, the general government was not idle. Two thousand stands of arms were shipped to the Northwestern Panhandle on May 7, 1861. Colonel Benjamin F. Kelley organized a force of Federal volunteers at Wheeling, May 26, 1861, and was commanded to obey the orders of General McLellan, who was then at Cincinnati. The next day Colonel Kelley was ordered to Grafton to engage Colonel Porterfield. On reaching Grafton Colonel Kelley learned that Colonel Porterfield had abandoned Grafton for Philippi. Colonel Kelley with a much superior force surprised and routed Colonel Porterfield at Philippi on the morning of June 3, 1861. Colonel Porterfield retreated to Huttonsville where he met and was relieved of his command by General Garnett, who with the combined forces of Porterfield and his own men commanded an army of about 6,000 soldiers. Against this force General McLellan was approaching with an army of 20,000 men. General Garnett sent Colonel Pegram to fortify the western base of Rich Mountain with 1,300 men. General Garnett marched with the main body of his army of between 4,500 and 5,000 to the northern base of Laurel Hill near Belington. General Morris was ordered to advance from Philippi and make a demonstration as though the principal attack was to be made on the Confederate forces at Laurel Hill, while McLellan, designed to route Pegram's forces at Rich Mountain and cut off Garnett's retreat at Beverly.

On June 22, 1861, General McLellan crossed the Ohio River at Parkersburg. By way of the B. & O. Railroad he reached Grafton next day. He marched to Buckhannon by way of Clarksburg and Weston, leaving fortified posts at Webster, Grafton, Clarksburg and Parkersburg. He reached Buckhannon, July 2, 1861. Under date of July 5, 1861, Buckhannon, Va., General McLellan informed Colonel E. D. Townsend, Washington, D. C.:

"I expect to find the enemy in position on Rich Mountain, just this side of Beverly. I shall, if possible, turn the position to the south, and thus occupy the Beverly road in the rear. Assure the General that no prospects of brilliant victory shall induce me to depart from my intention of gaining success by maneuvering rather than by fighting. I will not throw these men of mine in the teeth of artillery and intrenchments, if possible to avoid it. From all that I can learn the enemy is still uncertain as to where the main attack is to be made, and is committing the error of dividing his army in the face of superior forces."

Colonel Pegram, the Confederate commander, had a picket post at Middle Fork Bridge to keep watch on the Federal advance. A scouting party from McLellan's army ran into these pickets on July 6th, and were repulsed with one killed and five wounded. This was the first armed conflict between the Federals and Confederates in Randolph County. General McLellan in his report to the Federal Government says that seven Confederates were killed. This statement was erroneous as the Confederates had three wounded and none killed. On July 7, General R. L. McCook drove the Confederates from Middle Fork bridge. General McLellan occupied the bridge next day, July 8th, and on the evening of July 9th, moved to the Hillery farm on Roaring Creek, within two miles of Pegram's fortifications at the base of Rich Mountain. On July 10, 1861, the Confederates under Colonel Pegram, and the Federals under General McLellan were facing each other at the western base of Rich Mountain. Simultaneously General Morris was feigning preparations for an attack on the forces of General Garnett at the northern base of Laurel Hill, acting under orders from General McLellan to withhold his attack until he was in a position to intercept General Garnett's retreat at Beverly. Colonel Scott was encamped at Beverly on the night of July 10th, on his way from Staunton to Laurel Hill to reinforce General Garnett. It was apparent that a battle was impending. General McLellan, conscious of his superior force and equipment, was confident of victory. In his report to Colonel Townsend from Buckhannon, July 6th, he said: "By the 8th or 9th, at least, I expect to occupy Beverly, fighting a battle in the meanwhile. I propose to drive the enemy over the mountain toward Staunton. General Garnett was discouraged by the prospect of meeting a force much larger than his own, as well as disappointed by the meager number of volunteers and the lack of support and co-operation on the part of the people. In his report of June 25th, from Laurel Hill, to the Confederate government at Richmond, Va., among other things he said: "I have been, so far, wholly unable to get anything like accurate information as to the numbers, movements, or intentions of the enemy and begin to believe it almost an impossible thing. The Union men are greatly in the ascendency here and are much more zealous and active in their cause than the secessionists. The enemy are kept fully advised of our movements, even to the strength of our scouts and pickets, by the country people, while we are compelled to grope in the dark as much as if we were invading a foreign and hostile country." Instead of large additions to his forces as he expected, only eight men had joined his army prior to July 1st, and only fifteen had joined Colonel Heck's camp to that date. That General Garnett realized his inability to cope with the superior forces of the Union army was evidenced by his report from Laurel Hill dated July 6, 1861, in which he said: "I do not suppose this force can ever obtain a strength relative to that of the enemy, which would warrant us in giving him battle. The only certain result we can calculate upon is that our presence here will occupy a considerable force of the enemy, and relieve other points of the state where they might be employed against us." Colonel Pegram seemed to be the only officer on either side who had no adequate idea of the comparative strength of the opposing armies. The day before the Rich Mountain battle he asked permission of General Garnett to attack McLellan's army, intimating his belief that his forces were adequate for such an engagement. General Garnett very wisely refused him permission.

Colonel Pegram was under the impression that the Federal army would endeavor to attack him from the rear by sending a detachment across the mountain by an abandoned road to the north of the pike and which entered that road one and one-half miles west of Beverly. Colonel Pegram accordingly sent a message to Colonel Scott on the morning of July 11th, stating: "I think it almost certain that the enemy are working their way around my right flank to come into the turnpike one and one-half miles this side of Beverly." This message reached Colonel Scott when his regiment had reached a point four miles north of Beverly. Colonel Scott immediately retraced his march to Beverly and thence to the position where the old road intersects the turnpike at the eastern base of Rich Mountain. While Colonel Pegram was industriously trying to circumvent the opposing forces from reaching his rear from the north, General Rosencranse was without molestation moving approximately 2,000 men to Pegram's rear by way of a circuitous route through the woods a mile or more to the south of the Pike, being piloted by David B. Hart, son of Joseph Hart, who resided on the crest of the mountain, where the pike crosses, a mile and a half to the rear of Pegram's camp. Young Hart visited McLellan's camp about 10 o'clock on July 10th, and volunteered his services in piloting the Federal troop to his father's farm on the top of the mountain from which point Pegram's forces could be attacked from the rear. Generals McLellan and Rosencranse discussed the plan and concluded to accept Hart's services. Rosencranse was given a detachment of 1917 men, and on the morning of July 11th, at 5 o'clock with rations for one day, they started to execute the movement. Rosencranse says: "The column formed and moved forward in the following order and strength:

Eighth Indiana, under Benton	242	strong
Tenth Indiana, under Manson	425	"
Thirteenth Indiana, under Sullivan	650	"
Nineteenth Ohio, under Beatty	525	"

Total infantry	1,842
Burdsal's cavalry	75

Aggregate	1,917

"Colonel Lander, accompanied by the guide, led the way through a pathless forest, over rocks and ravines, keeping far down on the south eastern declivities of the mountain spurs, and using no ax, to avoid discovery by the enemy, whom we supposed would be on the alert, by reason of the appearance of unusual stir in our camp, and the lateness of the hour. A rain set in about 6 A. M. and lasted until about 11 o'clock A. M. with intermissions, during which the column pushed cautiously and steadily forward, and arrived at last and halted in rear of the crest on the top of Rich Mountain. Hungry and weary with an eight hours' march over a most unkindly road, they laid down to rest, while Colonel Lander and the General examined the country. It was found that the guide was too much scared to be with us longer, and we had another valley to cross, another hill to climb, another descent beyond that to make, before we could reach the Beverly road at the top of the mountain. On this road we started at 2 o'clock, and reached the top of the mountain after the loss of an hour's time by mistake in the direction.

"Shortly after passing over the crest of the hill, the head of the column ordered to be covered by a company deployed as skirmishers, was fired on by the enemy's pickets, killing Sergeant James A. Taggart and dangerously wounding Captain Christopher Miller, of the Tenth.

"The column then advanced through dense brushwood, emerging into rather more open brushwood and trees. when the rebels opened a fire of both musketry and 6-pounders, firing some case shot and a few shells. * * * * * * *

"We formed about three o'clock under cover of our skirmishers, guarding well against a flank attack from the direction of the rebels' position, and after a brisk fire, which threw the rebels into confusion, carried their position by a charge, driving them from behind some log breastworks, and pursued them into the thickets on the mountain. We captured twenty-one prisoners, two brass 6-pounders, fifty stand of arms, and some corn and provisions. Our loss was 12 killed and 49 wounded.

"The rebels had some 20 wounded on the field. The number of the killed we could not ascertain, but subsequently the number of burials reported to this date is 135—many found scattered over the mountain. Our troops, informed that there were one or two regiments of rebels toward Beverly, and finding the hour late, bivouacked on their arms amid a cold, drenching rain, to await daylight, when they moved forward on the enemy's intrenched position, which was found abandoned by all except 63 men, who were taken prisoners. We took possession of two brass 6-pounders, four caissons, and one hundred rounds ammunition, two kegs and one barrel powder, 19,000 buck and ball catridges, two stands of colors, and a large lot of equipment and clothing, consisting of 204 tents, 427 pairs pants, 124 axes, 98 picks, 134 spades and shovels, all their train, consisting of 29 wagons, 75 horses, 4 mules, and 60 pairs harness.

"The enemy finding their position turned, abandoned intrenchments, which, taken by the front, would have cost us a thousand lives, and dispersed through the mountains, some attempting to escape by the way of Laurel Hill and others aiming for Huttonsville."

Rosencranse and his army reached the mountain crest, at the lone tree. This point is a little more than a mile from Hart's house, where the battle was fought. The valley to cross and the hills to climb were comparatively small depressions and elevations, as the crest of the mountain from the lone tree to Hart's house is a descent of nearly 600 feet. The Confederate pickets were stationed about a half mile south of Hart's house, and upon approach of Federal forces, fired and fell back, joining the Confederate detachment at the Hart farm.

The Confederates were informed of the flank movement about noon by a messenger sent from Rosencranse to McLellan. This messenger lost his way and was captured by the

Confederates. Acting upon this information Pegram sent 350 men and one 6-pound cannon to the top of the mountain. The Confederates opened fire on the first approach of the Federals, although the Federals outnumbered the Confederates, about six to one, the battle lasted three hours, and was stubbornly contested. Hart's house was occupied by the Confederates, who fired from the windows and from the chinks between the logs. The Federals finally drove them out, killing one Confederate who was settling himself in a far corner of an upstairs room. Many dead and wounded were carried into the house, and blood stains are still visible on the floors and stairways, having penetrated the wood beyond the effect of the scouring brush.

Colonel Pegram's report is much more complete than Rosencranse's, and is here appended. It was written while he was a prisoner at the residence of Johathan Arnold in Beverly. He says:

"Not knowing where a communication will find General Garnett, I submit the following report of the fight at Rich Mountain. The battlefield was immediately around the house of one Hart, situated at the highest point of the turnpike over the mountain, and two miles in the rear of my main line of trenches, the latter being at the foot of the western slope of the mountain. The intricacies of the surrounding country seemed scarcely to demand the placing of any force at Hart's, yet I had that morning placed Captain DeLagnel there with 310 men and one piece of artillery, with instructions to defend it to the last extremity against whatever force might be brought to the attack by the enemy, but also to give me timely notice of his need for reinforcements. These orders had not been given two hours before General Rosencranse, who had been conducted up a distant ridge on my left flank and then along the top of the mountain by a man, attacked the small handful of troops under Captain DeLagnel, with 3,000 men. When, from my camp, I heard the firing becoming very rapid, without waiting to hear from Captain DeLagnel, I ordered up reinforcements, and hurried on myself to the scene of action. When I arrived the piece of artillery was entirely unmanned, Captain DeLagnel having been severely wounded, after which his men had left their piece. The limber and caisson were no longer visible the horse having run away with them down the mountain, in doing which they met and upset the second piece of artillery, which had been ordered up to their assistance. Seeing the infantry deserting the slight breatsworks hastily thrown up that morning by Captain DeLagnel, I used all personal exertion to make them stand to their work until I saw that the place was hopelessly lost. On my way back to my camp I found the reinforcing force under command of Captain Anderson, of the artillery, in great confusion, they having fired upon their retreating comrades. I hurried on to camp and ordered the remaining companies of my own regiment in camp to join them. This left my right front and right flank entirely unmanned. I then went back up the mountain where I found the whole force drawn up in line in ambuscade near the road, under Major Nat Tyler. I called their attention and said a few encouraging words to the men, asking them if they would follow their officers to the attack, to which they responded by a cheer. I was here interrupted by Captain Anderson, who said to me, 'Colonel Pegram, these men are completely demoralized, and will need you to lead them.'

"I took my place at the head of the column, which I marched in single file through laurel thickets and other almost impassable brushwood up a ridge to the top of the mountain. This placed me about one-fourth of a mile to the right flank of the enemy, and which was exactly the point I had been making for. I had just gotten all the men up together and was about making my dispositions for the attack when Major Tyler came up and reported that during the march up the ridge one of the men in his fright had turned around and shot the first sergeant of one of the rear companies, which had caused nearly the whole of the company to run to the rear. He then said that the men were so intensely demoralized that he considered it madness to attempt to do anything with them by leading them on to the attack. A mere glance at the frightened countenances around me convinced me that this distressing news was but too true, and it was confirmed by the opinion of three or four company commanders around me.

They all agreed with me that there was nothing left to do but to send the command under Major Tyler to effect a junction with either General Garnett at Laurel Hill, or Colonel William C. Scott, who was supposed to be with his regiment near Beverly. It was now half past six in the evening, when I retraced my steps with much difficulty back to the camp, losing myself frequently on the way, and arriving there after 11 o'clock at night. I immediately assembled a council of war, composed of the field officers and company commanders remaining, when it was unanimously agreed that, after spiking the two remaining pieces of artillery, we should attempt to join General Garnett by a march through the mountains to our right. This act was imperative, not only from our reduced numbers, now being about 600, and our being placed between two large attacking armies, but also because at least three-fourths of my command had no rations left; the other one-fourth not having flour enough for one meal. Having left directions for Sergeant Walker, and giving directions to Assistant Surgeon Taylor to take charge of the sick and wounded in camp, and to show a white flag at daylight, I called the companies together and started at one o'clock A. M., without a guide, to make my way, if possible, over the mountains, where there was not the sign of a path, toward General Garnett's camp. As I remained in camp to see the last company in column, by the time I reached the head of the column, which was nearly a mile long, Captain Lilly's company had disappeared and has not since been heard from. * * * *

"The difficulties attending my march it would be impossible to exaggerate. We arrived at Tygart's Valley River at 7 P. M., having made the distance of twelve miles in about eighteen hours. Here we were met by several country people, who appeared to be our friends, and who informed us that at Leadsville Church, distant three miles, there was a small camp, composed of a portion of Garnett's command. Leaving Colonel Heck with instructions to bring the command forward rapidly, I hired a horse and proceeded forward until in sight of Leadsville Church, when I stopped at a farmhouse where were assembled a dozen men and women. They informed me that General Garnett had retreated that afternoon up the Leading Creek road, into Tucker County, and that he was being pursued by three thousand of the enemy, who had come from the direction of Laurel Hill as far as Leadsville Church, when they turned up the Leading Creek road in pursuit. This, of course, rendered all chance of joining General Garnett, or escaping in that direction, utterly impossible. Hurrying back to my command, I found them in much confusion, firing random shots in the dark, under the impression that the enemy were surrounding them. Reforming them, I hurried back to the point where we first struck the river, and persuaded a few of the country people to cook all the provisions they had, hoping that it might go a little way toward satisfying the hunger of my almost famishing men.

"I now found, on examining the men of the house, that there was, if any, only one possible means of escape, and that by a road which, passing within three miles of the enemy's camp at Beverly, led over precipitous mountains into Pendleton County. Along this road there were represented to me to be but a few miserable habitations, where it would be utterly impossible for even a company of men to get food; and as it was now 11 o'clock P. M., it would be necessary to leave at once, without allowing them to get a mouthful where they were. I called a council of war, when it was agreed almost unanimously (only two members voting in the negative) that there was left to us nothing but the sad determination of surrendering ourselves prisoners of war to the enemy at Beverly. I was perfectly convinced that an attempt on our part to escape would sacrifice by starvation a large number of the lives of the command."

Colonel Pegram sent a note to the commanding officer of the United States forces at Beverly, and dispatched it about 12 o'clock on the night of July 12th. The messenger returned next morning with Colonel Key, one of General McLellan's staff officers. After a conference between Colonels Pegram and Key, the former's officers and men, numbering 555 marched to Beverly and stacked their arms. They were kept at Beverly until July 17th, when all but Colonel Pegram were released on parole, Pegram being refused his parole because he had not resigned as an officer in the United States Army.

Lieutenant Charles W. Statham, in his report, gives interesting additional details of the battle of Rich Mountain. He says:

"I have to report that on the 11th instant, by your order, I moved with one gun and a detachment of twenty-one men to occupy this pass in Rich Mountain. We took our position about 1 o'clock P. M. In less than two hours the enemy made their appearance in large column, six regiments strong, immediately on the hill south of the pass. We reversed our gun, which was pointed down the pass, and prepared to receive the enemy in the direction in which he was approaching. In a few minutes the sharpshooters of the enemy commenced a fire upon us from behind trees and rocks at a distance ranging from two to three hundred yards, the body of the enemy being still farther. We opened upon the main body with spherical shot, which I cut at first one second and a quarter, and could distinctly see them burst in their midst. I knew we did good execution, as I could distinctly hear their officers give vehement commands to close up ranks. After firing this way some little time at the rate of near four shots per minute we forced the enemy to retire.

In about twenty minutes the enemy reappeared in a column of three regiments, advanced briskly upon us, when we moved our gun a little higher up the opposite hill and again opened upon them, and with our spherical shot cut as low as one second down to three-quarters. After firing rapidly for some time the enemy again beat a hasty retreat, when my men, including the infantry not yet in action, rent the air with their shouts, confidently believing that we had gained the day. But in a short time the enemy again formed and renewed the attack with more swiftness than before, and soon played havoc with our horses. These, with the caisson, ran down the mountain with drivers and all, leaving us with only the small amount of ammunition in our limber-box. We then limbered and moved our gun near a small log stable, behind which we placed our horses for protection. By this time our men were falling fast. Sergeant Turner, of the gun, had both legs broken and shot through the body; Mays had his left arm splintered with a musket ball; Isaiah Ryder shot through the head, and died instantly; John A. Taylor had his thigh broken; E. H. Kersey, shot in the ankle; Lewis Going, wounded in the arm; William W. Stewart, badly wounded in the head and breast. This left me but few to man the gun. Captain DeLagnel, who was the commander of the post, having his horse shot under him and seeing our crippled condition, gallantly came and volunteered his valuable aid, and helped load and fire three or four times, when he was shot in the side, and I think, in the hand. He then ordered us to make our escape, if we could, but the enemy was too close, and his fire too severe, to admit of safe retreat to many of us. I was shot through the right hand and am now a prisoner."

Colonel W. Scott with the 44th Virginia Infantry was stationed at the western base of Rich Mountain, during the battle on Rich Mountain. Scott heard the muskets and artillery, but supposed that the fighting was at the fort six miles distant. Scott obeyed orders and remained guarding the old road at its junction with the pike. However, becoming suspicious and impatient, Scott sent Jno. N. Hughes, a lawyer who lived in Beverly, to Pegram's headquarters for information. Hughes never returned. When at the turn of the road, a few hundred yards east of Hart's house, he was fired on by mistake by the Confederates and killed. Hughes was a brilliant lawyer, but was addicted to drink, and it has been charged that he was intoxicated when he undertook to discharge this dangerous service. Colonel Scott denies that Hughes was drinking the day he lost his life.

Lieutenant James Cochrane, of the Churchville Cavalry, in a report to Colonel Scott, of the exciting and interesting events in which he participated on the day of the Rich Mountain fight, says:

"I was sent out with a squad of six men by Captain DeLagnel, who commanded our forces engaged in the fight, to bring up some cavalry that he had fired on through mistake. In going down the turnpike I unexpectedly met with your regiment drawn up in the road about a mile and a half from Beverly. I told you your regiment was needed at the battle which was then going on; that the enemy to the number of four or five thousand had gotten around Colonel Pegram's left flank, and were engaged with a few hundred of our men about a mile and a half in the rear of Colonel Pegram's camp; that the enemy were on the left, and our men in and on the right of the turnpike as you would approach the camp; that our men had but one piece of artillery. You asked me if I would go with you and act as guide. I consented. You instantly put your regiment in motion in double-quick time. I remonstrated; told you we had to go between four and five miles up the mountain before we could reach the battlefield, and if the men traveled at that rate they would not be fit to fight when they got there. You then brought them down to quick time.

"In going up the mountain we met with several men on horseback who had been in the battle; one I recollect, of my company, who had been shot through the foot, and another whose coat had been shot across the shoulders. The latter told us that he was aid to Colonel Pegram, and that Colonel Pegram had been killed. Some of these men turned back and went with us part of the way up the mountain, but they all disappeared before your regiment stopped. On our way up I informed you of the death of Hughes, and you requested me not to mention it to your men, as it might dampen their spirit. When we arrived within about a mile of the battle the firing ceased, and in a few moments a loud huzza was heard coming from the position our forces had occupied when I left them. You asked me what that huzza meant. I told you that I was fearful the Yankees had driven our men from the field and captured our artillery, for the shout came from about the place where our artillery and fortifications stood. You continued your march to within half a mile of the battleground, when I informed you that it was unsafe to go farther, that you could not with one regiment encounter successfully four or five thousand of the enemy, with the advantage of position, fortifications, and a piece of artillery. You halted your regiment, you and I dismouted and in company with some of your officers passed around a turn in the road that we might see, if possible, how things stood at the pass on top of the mountain, when we did see more men, as I told you at the time, exulting and shouting, than Colonel Pegram had in his entire command. You were yet unwilling to go back, but requested me either to go myself or to send some of my men to reconnoiter. I told you I would not go, nor should any of my men go, for I was perfectly satisfied as to how things stood. A young man named Lipford, of your regiment, stepped forward and proposed to go if he could get a pistol and horse. Thus equipped, he went off up the road, but in a very short time we heard the shout from many voices, "Halt, shoot him," and the firing of several guns, and then another loud huzza. It being now plain that the enemy had either killed or taken Lipford prisoner, you were satisfied that I was right, and that the enemy did have possession of the field. You appearing still unwilling to go back, some of your officers suggested that as the enemy's pickets could plainly be seen around the fields on each side of the road in which we stood, if you went forward the enemy would receive you in ambuscade, whereas if you went back they would probably follow, and then you could take them in ambuscade. This suggestion being approved by all of us who expressed any opinion, you marched your regiment down the mountain, leaving men in the rear to give you information of the approach of the enemy. In going down, information was brought you that the enemy were in pursuit, when you put your men in position to receive them. After remaining there some time, and the alarm proving false, and all being quiet on the mountain, you returned to Beverly."

Lipford, referred to above, was not killed but was captuerd by the Federals. Colonel Scott correctly conjecturing the true state of affairs on the mountain top, retreated, setting an ambuscade on the way for the Federals, who were believed to be in pursuit. This proved to be a mistake and Scott returned to Beverly, reaching that place about dark. Colonel Scott held a conference with Confederate sympathizers in Beverly, and concluded to march that night to Laurel Hill, but on going into the street, where he had left his regiment, he found that his Lieutenant Colonel, acting on erroneous information, had gone in the direction of Huttonsville. Colonel Scott mounted his horse and dashed up the pike, overtaking his troop about two miles above Beverly. He turned his regiment in the direction of Laurel Hill, and on his return to Beverly, was informed that General Garnett was retreating. Accordingly, about 10 o'clock on the night of the 11th, Colonel Scott started from Beverly on his retreat by way of Huttonsville, across Cheat Mountain. On the night of July 11th, General Garnett sent a message to Colonel Scott to hold the Federals in check on the pike west of Beverly, until daylight next morning. The message was not received by Colonel Scott until the morning of the 12th, when he had reached a point seven miles south of Beverly. The victorious Federals did not seem eager to follow the retreating Confederates, as the forces under Rosencranse camped on the field of battle on the night of the 11th, and did not occupy the abandoned Confederate fortifications at the western base of the mountains until July 12th. The Federal forces entered Beverly July 12th, about one o'clock. General Garnett had ample time to retreat south by way of Beverly and Huttonsville, but a messenger, whom he sent to Beverly on the evening of the 12th, mistaking Colonel Scott's regiment for Federals, reported to him that McLellan's army was occupying Beverly.

While the Federal troops were entering the town and crossing the wooden bridge over the Tygarts Valley River, Captain Richards, a Conferedate, rode up Main Street, and when opposite the bridge, fired into the approaching Federals. The Federal cavalry pursued him for about a mile south of Beverly, when Captain Richards entered a by-road and escaped. The day following the Rich Mountain fight, many of the sympathizers in Beverly left their homes and refugeed to Eastern Virginia.

Garnett's Retreat.

General Garnett heard the artillery on Rich Mountain on the afternoon of July 11th, and interpreted its meaning. He received intelligence that evening that McLellan had reached Pegram's rear; however, he incorrectly believed that the Federal troops had gained Pegram's rear by a road north of the turnpike. It was then he sent a message to Colonel Scott to hold the Federals in check west of Beverly until he could retreat up the valley, but as stated elsewhere, this order did not reach Colonel Scott until he was some miles south of Beverly on his retreat across Cheat Mountain. Garnett left Laurel Hill and retreated up the valley within about 3½ miles of Beverly, when he was falsely informed that McLellan's army occupied Beverly. He then turned back and retreated to Cheat River, by way of Leading Creek and Pleasant Run. General Morris, who had been feigning preparations for an attack on General Garnett's army at Laurel Hill, moved forward and took possession of the deserted camp on the 12th, but on account of shortage of supplies, was not in position to make effective pursuit. The Federal forces advanced to Leadsville on the evening of the 12th, and encamped there until next morning, when with a detachment of 3,000 men, General Morris pursued the retreating Confederates into Tucker County. At 6:10 A. M. Captain Benham, sent a message to Major Williams that the Federals had reached a point 1½ miles east of New Interest (now Kerens) and that the Confederates were supposed to be about six miles ahead. The Federal army was compelled to subsist largely on beef, procured in the vicinity, without bread or salt. Captain H. W. Benham, in his report of the pursuit of Garnett, and action at Carrick Ford, says:

"At about noon we reached Kaler's, or the first ford of the Shaver Branch or Main Cheat River, having within the previous two or three miles, fired at and driven in several pickets of the enemy protecting those who were forming the barricades, and at one place we broke up a camp where the meals were being cooked. At the ford near Kaler's and about one-half of the distance to another ford, which we afterwards met with about one mile farther on, we saw the baggage train of the enemy, apparently at rest. This I proposed to attack as soon as strengthened by the arrival of Steedman's second battalion, with Dumont's regiment, when the thoughtless firing of a musket at our ford set the train rapidly in motion, and long lines of infantry were formed in order of battle to protect it. In a few minutes, however, the arrival of Barnett's artillery, with Dumont close upon it, enabled the command to push forward in its original order, but the train and its guard had retired, leaving only a few skirmishers to meet us at the second ford, where, however, quite a rapid firing was kept up by the advance regiment, and the artillery opened for some minutes to clear the adjacent woods the more completely of the enemy.

"We then continued our march rapidly to the ford, and as we approached it we came upon their train, the last half of it just crossing the river. The enemy was found to have taken a strong position, with his infantry and artillery upon a precipitous bank of some fifty to eighty feet in height upon the opposite side of the river, while our own ground was upon the low land, nearly level with the river. Steedman's regiment, in the advance, opened its fire most gallantly upon them, which was immediatly returned by their strong force of infantry and by their cannon, upon which Barnett's artillery was ordered up and opened upon them with excellent effect.

"As I soon perceived a position by which their left could be turned, six companies of Colonel Dumont's regiment were ordered to cross the river about three hundred yards above them, to pass up the hill obliquely from our right to their left, and take them in rear. By some mistake, possibly in the transmission of the order, this command crossed at about double this distance and turned at first to their right, which delayed the effect of the movement. After some fifteen minutes, however, this error was rectified, and, the hill being reported as impracticable, this command, now increased to the whole regiment, were ordered down to the ford, under close cover of this hill on their side, and there to take them directly in front at the road.

"The firing of Steedman's regiment and of Milroy's, now well up and in action, with repeated and rapid discharge of the artillery during this movement, decided the action at once. As Dumont reached the road, having passed along and under their whole front, the firing ceased, and the enemy fled in great confusion, Dumont's regiment pursuing them for about one mile farther, having a brisk skirmishing with their rear for the first half of that distance, during which General Garnett was killed. The enemy would still have been followed up most closely, and probably to the capture of a large portion of their scattered army, but this was absolutely impossible with our fatigued and exhausted troops, who had already marched some eighteen miles or more, in an almost incessant, violent rain, and the greater part of them without food since the evening, and a portion of them even from the noon of the yesterday, so warm had been the pursuit on their hasty retreat from Laurel Mountain, twenty-six miles distant. The troops were, therefore, halted for food and rest at about 2 P. M.

"The result of the action proves to be the capture of about forty loaded wagons and teams, being nearly all their baggage train, as we learn, and including a large portion of new clothing, camp equipage, and other stores; their headquarter papers and military chest; also two stands of colors and one fine rifled piece of artillery; while the commanding general, Robert S. Garnett, is killed, his body being now cared for by us, and fifteen or twenty more of the enemy are killed and nearly fifty prisoners are taken. Our loss is two killed and six or seven wounded; one dangerously."

We have fuller details of Garnett's retreat and battle of Carrick's Ford in the report of Colonel W. B. Taliaferro of the Confederate 23rd, Virginia Infantry. He says:

"On the evening of the 12th of July, General Garnett bivouacked at Kaler's Ford, on Cheat River, the rear of his command being about two miles back on Pleasant Run. On the morning of the 13th July the command was put in motion about 8 o'clock, the Thirty-seventh Virginia and Colonel Jackson's regiment and Lieutenant-Colonel Hansborough's battalion, with a section of artillery, under Captain Shumaker, and a squadron of cavalry under Captain Smith, forming the advance; then the baggage train, and then Colonel Ramsey's First Georgia and the Twenty-third Virginia Regiment, constituting, with Lieutenant Lanier's section of artillery and a cavalry force under Captain Jackson, the rear of the command. Before the wagon train (which was very much impeded by the condition of the county road over which it had to pass, rendered very bad by the heavy rains of the preceding night) had crossed the first ford half a mile above Kaler's, the cavalry scouts reported that the enemy were close upon our rear with a very large force of infantry, well supported by cavalry and artillery. The First Georgia Regiment was immediately ordered to take position across the meadow on the river side and hold the enemy in check until the train had passed the river, and then retreat behind the Twenty-third Virginia Regiment, which was ordered to take position and defend the train until the Georgia troops had formed again in some defensible position.

"By the time the Georgians had crossed the river, and before some of the companies of that regiment were thrown out to ambuscade the enemy could be brought over, the enemy appeared in sight of our troops, and immediately commenced firing upon them. This was briskly returned by the Georgia regiment, who after some rounds retired, in obedience to the orders received. The Twenty-third Virginia and the artillery were halted about three-quarters of a mile below the crossing, and were ordered to occupy a hill commanding the valley through which the enemy would have to approach and a wood which commanded the road. This position they held until the Georgia regiment was formed some distance in advance of the Virginians, then the former command retired and again reformed in advance of the Georgians. This system of retiring upon eligible positions for defense admirably selected by Captain Corley, adjutant-general to General Garnet, was pursued without loss on either side, a few random shots only reaching us, until we reached Carrick's Ford, three and a half miles from Kaler's. This is a deep ford, rendered deeper than usual by the rains, and here some of the wagons became stalled in the river and had to be abandoned.

"The enemy were now close upon the rear, which consisted of the Twenty-third Regiment and the artillery; and as soon as this command had crossed Captain Corley ordered me to occupy the high bank on the right of the ford with my regiment and the artillery. On the right this position was protected by a fence, on the left only by low bushes. but the hill commanded the ford and the approach to it by the road, and was admirably selected for defense. In a few minutes the skirmishers of the enemy were seen running along the opposite bank, which was low and skirted by a few trees, and were at first taken for the Georgians, who were known to have been cut off; but we were soon undeceived, and a hearty cheer for President Davis having been given by Lieutenant Washington, C. S. Army, reiterated with a simultaneous shout by the whole command, we opened upon the enemy. The enemy replied to us with a heavy fire from their infantry and artillery. We could discover that a large force was brought up to attack us, but our continued and well-directed firing kept them from crossing the river, and twice we succeeded in driving them back some distance from the ford. They again, however, came up with a heavy force and renewed the fight. The fire of their artillery was entirely ineffective, although their shot and shell were thrown very rapidly, but they flew over our heads without any damage, except bringing the limbs of trees down upon us. The working of our three guns under Lieutenants Lanier, Washington, and Brown was admirable, and the effect upon the enemy very destructive. We could witness the telling effect of almost every shot.

"After continuing the fight until nearly every cartridge had been expended, and until the artillery had been withdrawn by General Garnett's orders, and as no part of his command was within sight or supporting distance, as far as I could discover, nor, as I afterwards ascertained, within four miles of me, I ordered the regiment to retire. I was induced, moreover, to do this, as I believed the enemy were making an effort to turn our flank, and without support it would have been impossible to have held the position, and as already nearly thirty of my men had been killed and wounded. The dead and severely wounded we had to leave upon the field, but retired in perfect order, the officers and men manifesting decided reluctance as being withdrawn. After marching half a mile I was met by Colonel Starke, General Garnett's aide, who directed me to move on with my regiment to the next ford, a short distance in advance, where I would overtake General Garnett.

"On the farther side of this ford I met General Garnett, who directed me to halt my regiment around the turn of the road, some hundred and fifty yards off, and to detail for him ten good riflemen, remarking to me, "This is a good place behind this driftwood to post skirmishers." I halted the regiment as ordered, but from the difficulty on determining who were the best shots, I ordered Captain Tompkins to report to the general with his whole company. The general, however, would not permit them to remain, but after selecting ten men, under Lieutenant Depriest, ordered the company back to the regiment.

"By General Garnett's orders, conveyed by Colonel Starke, I posted with that officer three of my companies on a high bluff overlooking the river, but, finding the undergrowth so thick that the approach of the enemy could not be well observed, they were withdrawn. A few minutes after these companies rejoined the regiment, Colonel Starke rode up and said that General Garnett directed me to march as rapidly as I could and overtake the main body. In a few minutes afterwards Lieutenant Depriest reported to me that General Garnett had been killed. He fell just as he gave the order to the skirmishers to retire, and one of them was killed by his side.

"It gives me pleasure to bear testimony to the coolness and spirit displayed by officers and men in this affair. Lieutenant-Colonel Crenshaw and Major Pendleton set an example of courage and gallantry to the command, and the company officers behaved admirably, doing their whole duty. It would be invidious, when all behaved so well, to distinguish between them. The gallantry of Lieutenant Washington was conspicuous. After the 6-pounder rifled piece had been disabled and it was discovered it had to be abandoned, he spiked it under a heavy fire.

"It is not my province, perhaps, in this report to speak of officers outside of my own command, but I trust I shall be pardoned for bearing testimony to the coolness and judgment that characterized the conduct of Colonel Starke and Captain Corley during the whole of this day and afterwards on the march. These officers, but more particularly the latter, selected every position at which our troops made a stand, and we were never driven from one of them.

"The loss to the enemy in this section must have been

very great, as they had from their own account three regiments engaged, and the people in the neighborhood whom I have seen since report a heavy loss, which they state the enemy endeavored to conceal by transporting the dead and wounded back to Belington in covered wagons, permitting no one to approach them.

"After receiving the order of General Garnett I marched my regiment four miles farther on to Parson's Ford, a half mile beyond which I overtook the main body of our troops, who had been halted there by General Garnett, and which had been drawn up to receive the enemy.

"The enemy did not advance to this ford, and after halting for some time our whole command moved forward, and marching all night on the road leading up to the line of Horseshoe Run, reached about daylight the Red House, in Maryland, a point on the Northwestern turnpike near West Union. At this last place a large force of the enemy under General Hill was concentrated. This body did not attack us, and we moved the same day into Virginia as far as Greenland, in Hardy County."

General Morris did not pursue the Confederates further after the battle of Carrick's Ford, but returned by way of St. George and Clover Run, reaching Belington July 15th. His army was practically without rations, and had been marching and fighting without food for twenty hours. General Garnett's army had a narrow escape from capture at the Red House on the Northwestern pike. Federal troops to the number of 6,000 concentrated at that point to intercept the Confederate retreat, but they arrived there about one hour after Garnett's army had passed. The Confederate army retreated to Monterey, Va. without further molestation. At the battle of Carrick's Ford the Confederates lost 13 killed and 15 wounded. The Federals lost 2 killed and 7 wounded. At Laurel Hill the Confederates lost 2 killed and 2 wounded. The Federals lost 4 killed and 6 wounded. At Rich Mountain the Confederates lost 45 killed and 20 wounded. The Federals had 12 killed and 49 wounded.

It is an undisputed fact that both Federals and Confederates made serious blunders in the campaign in western

Virginia. However, the result could not have been different with the great disproportion in the size of the two armies. General McLellan, though regarded by many as the greatest General on the Union side in the Civil War, betrayed in the West Virginia campaign a weakness in not vigorously pursuing an advantage, that was later manifested at Malvern Hill and Antietam. That General McLellan was a man of great civic and military attainments is universally conceded, yet it is interesting to know how he underestimated the military resources of the Confederacy. On July 7th, 1861, he wrote to General Scott that with 10,000 troops in eastern Tennessee, in addition to his West Virginia army, he could "crush the backbone of secession." However, in January, 1862, when made Chief Commander of the army, he estimated that 273,000 men would be necessary for the main army operations, aside from those needed for the defense of Washington.

Both in his proclamation to the Union men of West Virginia and in his reports to the general government, he showed a strong devotion to the Union, but an equally strong opposition to the abolition of slavery. In his instructions to Colonels Irvine, Kelly, Steedman and others, he invariably closed his admonitions with, "see that the rights and property of the people are respected, and repress all attempts at negro insurrection." In his proclamation to the people of West Virginia, he said:

"Notwithstanding all that has been said by the traitors to induce you to believe that our advent among you will be signalized by interference with your slaves, understand one thing clearly—not only will we abstain from all such interference, but we will, on the contrary, with an iron hand, crush any attempt at insurrection on their part."

Woodley's Reminescence of Rich Mountain.

Willis H. Woodley, then a lad in his teens, joined a company of Upshur County Confederates, known as the Upshur County Grays, and was a participant in the battle of Rich Mountain. We are indebted to him for the following interesting narrative:

"In compliance with your request I am giving you my personal recollections of the events immediately preceding and those occuring in the battle of Rich Mountain. After our stampede at Philippi we returned to Huttonsville, and in the course of a week or ten days we were reinforced by troops from Virginia, Infantry and Cavalry, and under the command of Colonel Heck, we came back to the western foot of Rich Mountain and went into camp near Alexander Hart's, where we began to fortify and commenced a systematic course of drilling, in the meantime completing a line of breastworks from the top of one ridge down across the pike and small ravine to the top of a parallel ridge to the north. There were very few tents in the command of about 2,500 men. We, the Upshur Grays, Co. B. 25th Va. Infantry, known at that time as Reger's Batallion, which was afterwards united to Hansbury's Batallion, forming the 25th Va. Infantry, made our tents of brush under which we managed to sleep the best we could, with water dripping on our faces.

"A few days before the battle at the top of the hill, we, the Upshur Grays, under command of Captain John Higgenbotham, were ordered to go to Middlefork Bridge on a reconnoitering expedition. Below Fords, the half-way house, we ran into the advanced pickets of the enemy, drove them in, and also drove in a second outpost, when we discovered that we were confronting McLellan's army, who were encamped at the bridge. Bugles blowing, the long roll beating, warned us of our danger. We immediately began a hasty retreat which we accomplished without being pursued. The next evening General McLellan advanced and camped at the Hilleary place, known as Fisher, and made his headquarters in the old log house, known at that time as the Hilleary House and is still standing, and was about two miles from our fortification. Next morning our videttes wounded and captured a Federal Sergeant and brought him in on a stretcher, the first person in blue that any of us had ever seen and he was quite a curiosity. The night before the battle on top of the mountain at S. B. Hart's house and farm, the Upshur Grays, under Captain Higginbotham, were ordered to do picket duty on the middle ridge immediately above Colonel Pegram's headquarters, who had recently superceded Colonel Heck in command. All through the night we distinctly heard the sound of axes to our left and Captain Higgenbotham sent twice to notify Colonel Pegram of the fact, and receiving the curt reply from Colonel Pegram 'to mind his own business,' which of course ended all communications between Colonel and Captain for the remainder of the night.

"It it worthy of mention and fixed indelibly on my mind, the most beautiful comet, the head extending to the southern horizon, the tail reaching across the entire heavens, was clearly visible the whole night and presented the most beautiful appearance, surrounded by myriads of constellations and stars, so peaceful, so sublime, so glorious, a sad commentary of the brutality of man to man to be enacted on the morrow.

"Diverging slightly from a continuation of the narative to inject a few personal interrogations. Why did Colonel Heck select the foot instead of the top of the mountain? When Hanibal in the Carthagenian wars with Rome, demonstrated the fact that where one man can go 100,000 or more can go also, and Napoleon Bonaparte confirmed the fact when he scaled the Alps under almost the same identical conditions.

"Resuming the incidents as occurred early next morning, the Upshur Grays were ordered to the top of the mountain, and when we had passed the O'Donnell turn, Colonel Pegram overtook us and asked Captain Higgenbotham if he thought the boys—for we were all boys—would stand fire. Immediately the reply came from the boys themselves, 'try us, try us.' When we reached the top we were halted right at the very summit, and for a few moments we were exposed to a volley from an unseen foe, whose numbers were entirely unknown, realizing to the fullest extent the danger of being shot down under such conditions without having a ghost of a show to retaliate, made me weak kneed for sure, but as soon as we fronted and marched into the woods and were told to conceal ourselves by any natural or artificial object, all fear seemed to go out, and as soon as I placed myself behind a good sized tree, almost immediately thereafter the racket commenced in earnest by vollies fired by Federal companies, the bullets pattering against the trees way above us. We, of course returned the fire, aiming for the most part at the smoke arising from the edge of the woods. This desultory firing was kept up for an hour, neither side knowing the strength of the other. DeLagniel with his one 6 pound cannon certainly must have produced consternation in our foes, for they at once began to reconnoiter with the most satisfactory results to them, for availing themselves of a temporary cessation of firing occasioned by quite a shower coming up, to send one body of men to flank the cannon, and another to cut us off from our camp at the foot of the mountain, and when the shower was over the enemy had a clear insight as to position and numbers confronting them, and they advanced with the certainty of victory. The firing in front was renewed with increased activity, while the flanking parties were getting in their work. The party that gained the pike between us and the camp, came up crying reinforcements, at almost the same time another flanking party rushed the one cannon and took it. At about the same time a boy the same age as myself, from Buckingham Lee Guards, with their Captain Irving commanding, stepped up behind me and said, 'do you care if I stand behind you?' We fired several shots almost at random, when he called my attention to a group of officers who had come out of the woods and were in plain view, about two or three hundred yards in the open field above Hart's house, and said watch one fall.' We had both loaded, my musket being held against the tree, as he sidestepped to take deliberate aim, I watching on the other side of the tree. He never fired the gun. The flanking party that had come up the pike, calling out "reinforcements," had deployed along the pike and three men had crept behind a big rock, one of the three had put a bullet through the head of my comrade, and for the first time in my life I heard the "thud" of a bullet against flesh. In turning from looking at my fallen comrade I caught a glimpse of three men in blue with brown hats tiptoeing and gazing at the boy in gray whom they had just shot to death. Instantly I jumped to the opposite side of the tree from the three men, at the same time bringing my Springfield musket to bear on the middle man. I saw him scringe and all three heads dissappeared behind the rock at my shot.

Trepidation seized me and I ran up the hill, and every bullet that passed me knocked up the leaves around me which only accelerated my speed. In fact there is no telling how fast a fellow can go with bullets pattering around his feet. I have always attributed my life to the fact of having on a blue U. S. Army overcoat which my oldest brother obtained while a station agent in Kansas in '58 and '59, in the employ of Russel Magor & Wadell, who had the government contract of transporting supplies to Albert Sydney Johnson who was in Utah quelling the depredations of the Mormans. Running about 100 yards I concealed myself behind a large chestnut tree, got my nerve, loaded and let slip a bullet at random, where the Federals were yelling over the capture of DeLagnel's gun. I at once resumed my retreat up the hill and overtook several of the Upshur Grays including Captain Higgenbotham, John Fuchert, Third Lieutenant, Bill McFadden, Orderly Sergeant, and Ben Patterson, and others numbering twelve of the same company. We spent the remainder of the evening in an aimless wandering on Rich Mountain until finally we arrived in the Valley at Caplinger settlement, when we took possession of an old log stable and went to sleep on the floor which was covered with hay. Some time during the night I was awakened by the regular tramp of marching men. I nudged my companion when we held a subdued conversation and concluded it was the Federals. The next morning we were at sea. We did not know which way to turn, when fortunately one of the Caplingers came by and said the way was clear to Beverly, as the enemy had not advanced. We at once took up our line of march for Beverly, where Mrs. Leonard, the kindly disposed matron of the Old Valley House, gave us our breakfast. We proceded up the valley and reached Mrs. Bradley's at now Valley Bend, who kindly gave us our dinner. Lying at full length on the green sod after dinner, along came a solitary cavalry man who said 'boys, get out of this, the Yankee Cavalry are in Beverly.' We lost no time in getting a move on us, and when we reached Huttonsvillle, Scott's 44th Va. Regiment were just pulling out for Cheat Mountain. They left us some hard-tack and bacon, and as soon as we had fried it on the smouldering fire, left by the 44th, we too headed for

Cheat Mountain, and the first clear field we came to on the mountain side about five miles from Huttonsville, we laid down under the canopy of Heaven and slept the sleep of utter exhaustion, disturbed once by the yell of a wild cat or panther. Next morning we resumed our weary way, and upon reaching the top found the 44th on the move again; they kindly left us something to eat. We were actually the rear guard without knowing it. After resting and eating our breakfast, we pulled out again, twelve of us, and upon arriving in the valley between what it now Durbin and Travellers' Repose, we blundered into the camp of the 12th Georgia, who had come so far and had orders to fall back to McDowell. They left us beef and hard-tack, which we proceeded to cook and devour. After a good long rest we followed across the Alleghenies, Crabbottom, Monterey and finally reached McDowell, where we found the 1st Georgia, 3rd Arkansas, 12th Georgia, 44th Virginia, two batteries and a lot of cavalry. We moved to Monterey, and daily stragglers came in bunches, the most woe begone, foot sore, demoralized set of men it is impossible to describe. During our stay at Monterey and McDowell we were reviewed by General Lee, and my impression of him as he sat on a bay stallion, with his dark mustache and hair, his whole bearing of calm repose, with a pent up reserved force, communicated to us by some invisible magnetic force that instantly gave us renewed energy and faith, and there was not one of us West Virginia snakes who would not have followed him to death at a moment's notice.

"One more incident. George King, a little awkward Upshur County boy, was so unfortunate as to get a flint-lock musket, that of necessity, he had to keep. My father came on from Staunton and joined us at Monterey, when the stragglers were coming in, father jokingly said to George, 'Well, George did you kill a Yankee at Rich Mountain?' 'No,' said George, I didn't.' 'Why?' said my father. 'Because,' George replied, 'I could not get my gun off.' The rain wet the powder in the pan, and poor, brave simple George had stood during the whole engagement, flashing powder in the pan of his old flintlock without being able to fire a single shot. If there ever was a hero, George deserves to be ranked with the bravest of the brave."

General Lee at Elkwater.

On July 22, 1861, General McLellan was called to Washington to take charge of the military forces there. General Reynolds succeeded him as Commander of the Federal forces in northwestern Virginia, with headquarters at Beverly. The Federal forces had been reduced by the expiration of enlistments and by sending detachments to other fields. In the course of a few months General Reynolds moved to Huttonsville and remained in undisputed possession of that section until September. However, the Union army and especially its scouts were in the meantime greatly annoyed by Confederate irregulars, who used their superior knowledge of the country to fire upon the Federals from ambush and then make their escape into the mountain fastnesses. Union sympathizers resorted to the same tactics when opportnuity afforded.

The Confederate government planned to retrieve their fortunes and regain the territory of northwest Virginia. Early in September, 1861, General Loring established himself at Huntersville, in Pocahontas County with 8,500 men. General H. R. Jackson with 6,000 men was stationed on the Greenbrier River, where the Staunton and Parkersburg pike crosses that stream in Pocahontas County. General Robert E. Lee was commanded to take charge of these forces by the Confederate government and drive the Union army out of northwestern Virginia. Accordingly General Lee concentrated his forces, which now numbered 14,500, at Big Springs, Pocahontas County. General Lee planned to drive Reynolds from the valley and march northward to the B. & O. railroad at Grafton. General Reynolds' army in the valley numbered about 9,000 men and he prepared to resist the approach of Lee by fortifying two advanced positions at Elkwater and Cheat Mountain. These positions were 18 miles apart by way of Huttonsville, but General Reynolds established communication between the two fortifications by a bridal path seven miles distant. General Lee advanced to the valley and skirmishing between the opposing armies began. The Confederates occupied a position between Elkwater and Cheat Mountain and also the pike leading toward Huttonsville.

In the three days skirmishing, which followed, the Union
army lost 9 killed, 15 wounded and 60 prisoners. Among the
killed of the Confederate army was General John A. Washington, a relative of General Lee and President Washington.
The Washington and Lee families were closely related.
Under a flag of truce General Washington's body was conveyed to the Confederate lines. General Lee decided to attack the Federal forces at Elkwater and Cheat Mountain
simultaneously, on the morning of September 12. Loring
and Jackson were to attack the Federals on the Huttonsville
side of the mountain and Rust was to open the attack from
the rear, which he had gained by crossing Cheat Mountain
and descending Cheat River. Loring and Jackson in front
and Lee at Elkwater were to await the signal of Colonel Rust's
artillery, when they would also assault the Federal forces.
With loaded guns and fixed bayonets, Colonel Rust was ready
to make the assault, when a captured picket made him believe
that 5,000 Federal troops awaited his attack. This ruse of
the picket with the approach of dawn and the sight of the
strong fortifications so terrified Colonel Rust that the intended signal to the other detachments of the Confederate
army was never sounded. With the want of concert of ac-
ton of Colonel Rust and his own army hungry and without
rations General Lee did not make the proposed attack at Elkwater. General Lee, in order to be nearer base for supplies,
withdrew to the Greenbrier river in Pocahontas County.

General Lee was greatly disappointed by the failure of
his campaign in northwestern Virginia. In writing to his
wife he said: "I cannot tell you my regret and mortification
at the untoward events that caused the failure of the plan.
I had taken every precaution to insure success and counted
on it, but the Ruler of the Universe willed otherwise and sent
a storm to disconcert the plan."

General Lee, perhaps, referred to the rain storm that on
the previous day destroyed the provisions of his army. It
will be observed that the operations of Lee himself were successful, but there was no communication between the detachments of his army, which rendered a favorable termina-
tion from concerted action improbable.

Raids into Randolph.

General John D. Imboden, of the Confederate army, made a raid through Pendleton, Tucker, and Randolph counties in August, 1862. His object was to destroy the B. & O. railroad bridge at Rowlesburg in Preston County. With 300 men he set out from Franklin, Pendleton County, August 14, 1862. He followed the Seneca Trail to Dry Fork, and thence down that stream to the Abram Parsons Mill, where the town of Parsons now stands. He expected to surprise and capture a squad of forty Federals, who were stationed at that place. However, Miss Jane Snyder, daughter of John Snyder, of Dry Fork, had divined their intention as they passed down the Fork and mounting her horse and taking a by-path hastily rode to Parson's Mill and gave warning to the Federals, who retreated to Rowlesburg. Imboden, realizing that the plans and destination of his raid had become known to the Federal army, retreated through the forests and mountains to the south and in three days reached Slaven's Cabin on the Staunton and Parkersburg Pike in Pocahontas County.

General Imboden made a second raid into Randolph in November, 1862. Rowlesburg was again his objective point. However, he ventured no farther than St. George. With 310 men he marched in a severe snowstorm on the night of November 7, 1862, down Red Creek to its junction with Dry Fork and thence down that stream and Cheat to St. George, where he surprised and captured forty Federals. Believing that further operations against Rowlesburg would be futile, he again retreated southward this time by way of Glady Fork and the Sinks and thence into Pendleton and Hardy counties. He was compelled to subsist upon the resources of the country through which he passed, obtained by force or otherwise. To compensate the Union sympathizers for their losses and to avoid surprises in the future by Confederate invaders Captain Kellogg, issued very stringent orders of assessment and notification directed to numerous southern sympathizers. The assessments largely exceeded the losses sustained by the Union sympathizers and ranged from $7 to $800. As a sample of the general order we give below the one directed to Adam Harper:

St. George, Tucker County, Va., Nov. 28, 1862.

Mr. Adam Harper, Sir: In consequence of certain rober-
ies which have been committed upon Union citizens of this
county by Bands of Gurilies you are hereby assessed to the
amount of ($285.00) Two Hundred and Eighty-five Dollars
to make good their losses. And upon your failure to make
good this assessment by the 8th day of December, the following order has been issued to me by Brigadier General
R. H. Milroy:

"You are to burn their houses, seize their property and
shoot them. You will be sure that you strictly carry out
this order. You will require of the inhabitants for ten or
fifteen miles around your camp on all the roads approaching
the town upon which the enemy may approach that they
must dash in and give you notice and that upon any one failing to do so you will burn their houses and shoot the men."

By order of

BRIG. GEN. R. H. MILROY.

Captain Kellogg Commanding 123 Ohio.

Raid Under Jenkins.

General A. G. Jenkins, with a Confederate cavalry force
of 550 men, made a raid across West Virginia into Ohio in
August and September, 1862. He passed through Randolph
above Huttonsville and planned an attack on Beverly, with
the co-operation of General Imboden. The Federal forces at
Beverly consisted of 450 men, but on being informed that
General Kelley had reinforced the Beverly garrison with 1,500
men, General Jenkins abandoned his intended attack upon that
place and moved to Buckhannon by crossing from the valley
to head of the Buckhannon River, and thence over to French
Creek and down that stream to the town of Buckhannon,
which he surprised and captured. He also captured Weston,
Glenville, Spencer and Ripley on the Ohio River. At Buckhannon he destroyed considerable military stores. A Federal
scout by the name of Gibson, who refused to surrender to
Jenkin's troops was killed above Huttonsville.

In his report General Jenkins says that the population
along French Creek was among the most disloyal in Western
Virginia and that his forces emerged so suddenly from the
mountains that the inhabitants could scarcely comprehend
that they were Southern troops. The truth of this statement
is easily accounted for when we reflect that the French Creek
settlement consisted, largely, of emigrants from New England, who, no doubt, believed that their situation west of the
mountains protected them from Conferedate invasion.

Imboden's Raid of '63.

In the spring of 1863 a Union force of 878 men, with two
canon were garrisoned at Beverly. Colonel George R. Latham
was in charge. General Jones and Imboden to execute a
policy planned and outlined by General Lee, were to invade
West Virginia. General Jones was to march through Hardy
County to Oakland, thence to Grafton, where he was to form
a junction with General Imboden, who was to cross Cheat
Mountain by way of the Staunton and Parkersburg Pike,
thence by way of Philippi to Grafton, whence their combined
forces would move west. General Imboden commanded 3,365
and General Jones 1,300 men. General Imboden, after a four
day's march in a drenching rain, entered Tygarts Valley above
Huttonsville, on April 23. He had crossed Cheat Mountain
by way of the Staunton and Parkersburg Pike. He planned
to surprise and capture the Federal garrison at Beverly. However, when he reached Huttonsville he found that the Federal
pickets had been withdrawn and believed that the forces at
Beverly had received intelligence of his approach. Believing
that he had lost his opportunity to surprise the Federals at
Beverly, Imboden camped for the night at Huttonsville. The
next day he resumed his march and when about six miles
above Beverly, the advance guard of Imboden's army attempted to halt Jesse F. Phares, Sheriff of Randolph County.
Mr. Phares refusing to surrender, was fired upon and shot
through the lungs. He succeeded in reaching Beverly, recovered from what at the time was thought to be a mortal
wound and lived many years after the war. It developed that
Sheriff Phares was the first man to give intelligence to the

federal army of Imboden's approach. The skirmishing continued during the day when the Federal army retreated toward Philippi.

The object of these raids was to destroy the B. & O. railroad, which was an important means of transportation for Federal troops, destruction of military stores and to gain Confederate recruits west of the Alleghenies.

Jackson's Raid.

In July, 1863, General W. L. Jackson, with a force of 1,200 men entered Randolph County by way of Valley Head and Cheat Mountain with the object of surprising and capturing General Harris and a garrison of 800 Federals at Beverly. General Jackson, with the main body of his men came down the Valley by way of Huttonsville. Major J. E. Lady with a detachment of 200 men by way of the back road reached and guarded the Buckhannon Pike west of Beverly. Colonel Dun detoured to the east of Beverly with a detachment with the object of reaching the Philippi pike in the rear of the Federals. At a signal of the firing of a cannon by General Jackson the Federal forces were to be attacked simultaneously by the three detachments. Skirmishing began when the main body of the Confederates reached a point about two miles south of Beverly. General Jackson advanced to an eminence on the M. J. Coberly farm, one and one-half miles southwest of Beverly. At 2 o'clock General Jackson fired the gun that was to be the signal for a uniform attack but Colonel Dun failed to appear and General Jackson delayed the intended assault. In the meantime, a lively artillery duel was in progress. The Federals occupied Mt. Izer, where the Confederate monument now stands. The Confederate projectiles did not reach the Federal fortifications, but exploded in Beverly and the Leonard Hotel as well as some other houses were damaged. The Federals moved their artillery to the D. R. Baker bluff, south of Beverly, after which their cannonading was more effectual. On the morning of July 3, General Jackson, in observing the pike north of Beverly for the approach of Colonel Dun, discovered the advance of General Averill with a brigade of Union soldiers from Philippi to reinforce General Harris. General Jackson at once re-treated up the valley and over the mountains into Virginia. The Confederates lost four killed and five wounded. The Federals lost fifty-five prisoners. Colonel Dun finally reached Beverly, but not until after General Averill had come to the rescue of General Harris. Colonel Dun's delay had been attributed to the fact that a mountain still was on the line of his march, which he and his men were loth to leave as long as there remained a sparkling drop of the mountain dew.

The writer, at the age of four years, was an involuntary participant in General Jackson's retreat. As the General re-turned up the valley the main body of his army passed where the writer's parents resided in Valley Bend District. As the Confederates slowly and unheedingly passed the house, the Federal cannon balls flew over our heads and exploded against the hillside to the west. One projectile became so uncom-fortably familiar and informal as to cut the branches from a chestnut tree under which the writer, with James Morrison and a few other Confederate soldiers were standing. Captain J. W. Marshall is held in grateful remembrance for appearing on the scene at the time of the most spirited cannonading and directing the family and assembled neighbors to a place of comparative safety. The cannon of which there has been so much controversy is distinctly remembered and the appear-ance of the ordnance as well as the statements of the cannon-eers was to the effect that the axel of the cannon had been broken not by a shell from the Federal batteries but in recoil when the instrument was discharged.

Hill's Raid.

At 5 o'clock A. M. on the morning of October 29, 1864, Major Benjamin Hill with 300 men made an attack on about an equal number of Federals stationed at Beverly, under the command of Colonel Robert Youart. Major Hill had flanked the pickets and approached to within 150 yards of the Fed-eral camp, when upon a challenge from a picket, the Confed-erates raised a yell and charged the Federals. The attack had been delayed too long and instead of finding the Fed-erals asleep they were in rank for reveille roll call. The Confederates succeeded in reaching the Federal quarters. In the darkness friend and foe could not be distinguished. At the break of day the Federals organized and drove the Confederates from the field. The Federal loss was eight killed, twenty-three wounded and thirteen captured. The Confederate loss was four drowned in crossing the river, twenty-five wounded and ninety-two captured.

Rosser's Raid.

In the early morning before the break of day, January 11, 1865, General Rosser with 300 Confederates surprised the Federal garrison at Beverly, consisting of about 1,000 men, taking 580 prisoners, killing six and wounding twenty-six. About 400 Federals escaped capture and marched to Philippi. Rosser's loss was slight. It was one of the most remarkable military feats of the war. The Federal forces were commanded by General Robert Youart. It was in mid-winter and the high waters and severe weather lulled the Federals into a feeling of security. There was a ball in the town on the evening previous, largely attended by the officers, who remained until a late hour. The Federals had pickets posted during the day at Russell's, a mile below town, at the Burnt Bridge, two miles above town, and at the bridge in Beverly on the Buckhannon Pike, a corporal and three men. At dark the pickets were withdrawn from Russell's and the Burnt Bridge and in their stead single sentinels were posted. Rosser crossed Cheat Mountain by way of the Staunton and Parkersburg Pike, came down the Valley on the east side of the river, made a detour around Beverly and formed their line of battle in a hollow within 450 yards of the Federal camp. The sentinel saw the Confederates and challenged them, "Who comes there?" The reply, "Friends" threw the sentinel off his guard, who moved toward the Confederates and was captured. The Federals were awakened by having the doors of their quarters forced open and they were asked to surrender. Many of the officers were quartered in the town and Colonel Youart was asleep in Alfred Buckey's Hotel in Beverly when the attack was made. Many of the prisoners marched from Beverly to Staunton barefoot in the snow and suffered greatly from hunger and cold.

Burnt House Incident.

Captain David Poe, of Buckhannon, in his "Personal Reminiscences of the Civil War" relates his experience in capturing a squad of Federals, who were stationed at the John Taylor Burnt House on Cheat River, about a mile above the present village of Bowden. He says: "After we left the Upper Sinks and got down Shavers Mountain near the Glady Fork of Cheat we were informed that there was a company of Federal soldiers encamped over on the Main Cheat River at the Taylor Burnt House. So we got together and held a council of war. The strength of the enemy at the Burnt House was one question to be settled. I was made guide and we took up the line of march, crossing the mountain between Glady Fork and Cheat River through the woods. The rain was falling in torrents, so fast that a red deer, when scared up, came near running over Ed. Boor of Marion County. We crossed up toward the top of the mountain, on the opposite side of the Burnt House. It was then nearly night. It had been so rainy that day I think the blue coats felt no fear of danger. We had no dinner and for supper ate hard sweet apples that chanced to be on a tree in a nearby field. We all remained on the mountain until 2 o'clock in the morning, when the moon rose and we moved down to the bank of the creek, near their camp. I went down into the creek and standing in the shade of some timber on the bank, counted the horses, finding only twenty in camp. They had ten pickets. I went back and told the men all about it, eighteen of us and twenty-two of them. All said we could take them. I suggested to the officers that we cross the creek near the tents and wait until day light came; that I could pilot them across without being seen by the enemy, but that when we got to the bank of the creek we would have to crawl along the ground opposite the tents in the grass and weeds. When daylight was sufficient to tell blue from gray I was to raise up and give the order to remove the tents, which were what we called fly tents for cavalry. The sentinel was walking the beat. The order was for no firing unless the blue coats commenced it. At the proper time I arose and gave the order, which was promptly obeyed. Lem Tenant was next the sentinel; he was a tall slim man and by the time he got straightened up the sentinel fired his gun, but the bullet went wild. The tents were removed at once and the boys in blue in confusion. Some seized their guns, others surrendered at once. I took one tent from two boys; one surrendered, but the other pointed his carbine square at me. I knocked it away so that the bullet missed me, but he tried to shoot me until I fired my revolver close enough to his body to burn him, and then he surrendered. He was but a boy about fourteen years old and as pretty as a girl. The Captain had not yet surrendered, but was contending with two of the boys, Buck Carter of Barbour and Tom Alton of Marion County. He was trying to mount his horse and when he threw his belt around to put it on his pistol slipped off the belt. He drew his sabre and cut the hitch strap of his horse when the boys seized him and demanded his surrender. Buck Carter's patience wore out and he drew his spencer rifle and stepped back and said, 'I will make you surrender.' Just then I caught his gun and pushed his muzzle down so the ball went into the ground. I slapped the Captain on the shoulder and said, Captain, you had better surrender; and he did. Tom Alton took charge of him and the fight was over. Two or three of the boys in blue were wounded and two horses were wounded. We piled the tents, bent the guns and set fire to them. We took Captain Farrow of Miami County, Ohio and another man with us as pisoners and sent them to Richmond and paroled the rest. I asked my little boy why he was in the army, and he replied that his mother was a widow and that he could make more money for her in the army than anywhere else. I told him I was going to set him free and told him he had better go home to his mother and keep out of the army. He said he did not know about that. I will put you on parole; you will go home until you are exchanged, I said. 'I may do that' he said. I do not know what he did, as I did not get his name, only that he lived in Miami County, not far from Dayton, Ohio. We got breakfast and some rations to last us through to Crabbottom. We were all well mounted. I got a very good horse and kept him seven years. The man who rode him while he served the blue, while he was getting his wife's and child's pictures from the saddlepockets, said I had a good tough horse, which I found to be true."

Captain Poe does not give the date of this exploit, but it was in the latter part of the summer of 1864.

Confederate Soldiers.

Below is a list of Confederate soldiers from Randolph. This list was compiled by George W. Printz for Maxwell's History of Randolph:

James Anthony, Joseph H. Anthony, killed at Fort Steadman; Jackson Apperson, Jefferson Arbogast, killed at the "Bloody Angle," Spottsylvania Court House; Moses Bennett, John W. Bosworth Lieutenant, S. N. Bosworth Sergeant, Joseph Chenoweth Major, killed at Port Republic; Z. T. Chenoweth, Eli Currence, Emmett Crawford, Burns Crawford, died of wounds, 1863; Jacob Currence Captain, N. S. Channell, Cyrus Crouch, killed at Fredericksburg; Milton Crouch, killed at Cold Harbor; Garland Cox, died in prison; Peter Cowger, Henson Douglass, killed at the "Bloody Angle," Spottsylvania Court House; William Daft, Edward Daft, Adam E. Folks Corporal, John Folks, killed at the Wilderness; George Gainor, Eugene Hutton, killed at Bunker Hill, Va.; George E. Hogan, Levi Hevener, Adam Hevener, killed at Spottsylvania; Andrew Hevener, scout for Lee, killed at Elkwater; J. F. Harding Captain, after Major of Cavalry, Marion Harding, killed at Elkwater, October, 1862; George Harding, died in camp; Thomas Herron, Edward Kittle, killed at "Bloody Angle," Spottsylvania Court House; Marshall Kittle, killed in Beverly at the Hill Raid 1864; Asa Kelly, died of wounds at McDowell; Charles Kelley, John Logan, G. W. Louk, John Louk, Claude Louk, Dudley Long, Third Lieutenant, killed at Petersburg; J. H. Long Corporal, killed at Port Republic; Thomas Long, died in hospital; O. H. P. Lewis, Lieutenant, Walter Lewis, died in hospital; Thomas Lewis, killed at Fort Steadman; Stephen D. Lewis, John Lewis Jr., killed at Cedar Mountain; John Lewis Sr., William Lemon, died of wounds at McDowell; Jacob Lemon, died in hospital; James W. Lemon, John D. Moore, died in hospital; Andrew C. Mace, Elisha McCloud, John B. Pritt, Newton Potts, John Quick, died from wounds; Claude Rader, George W. Rowan, Corporal, Jacob Riggleman, Washington Riggleman, Joshua Ramsay, died from wounds; Thomas Ramsay, Branch Robinson, George Salsbury, Lieutenant, Hiram Smith, Chesley Simmons, David Simmons, Joseph Simmons, Franklin Stalnaker, died in hospital; Absalom Shifflett, D. H. Summers, John C. Swecker, John M. Swecker, Thomas Shelton, David Shelton, Joseph Stipes, killed at "Bloody Angle" Spottsylvania Court House; William Stipes, Joseph Vandevander, Adam Vandevander, William H. Wilson, Lieutenant, David O. Wilson, James R. Wilson, James D. Wilson, Corporal, James W. Wilson, W. H. Wamsley, Enoch Wamsley, L. D. Westfall, John M. Wood, Joseph Wood, Randolph Wise, lost arm at Chantilly.

Dudley Long, J. H. Long and Thomas Long, mentioned above were brothers, all losing their lives in the Southern cause.

In the above list John W. Lewis Sr. was the father and O. H. Lewis, Walter Lewis, Thomas Lewis, Stephen D. Lewis and John Lewis Jr. were sons.

There were five Kittle brothers in the Conferedate service: George Kittle, Marshall Kittle, Ira Kittle, Edward Kittle, and Squire B. Kittle.

Eighteenth Virginia Cavalry.—J. D. Adams, John Bennett, Jacob Chenoweth, Judson Goddin, Sergeant, Charles Myers, L. G. Potts, William Powers, George Powers, Thomas Powers (killed), Adam C. Stalnaker, Eli Taylor, Judson Taylor, Haymond Taylor (killed at Winchester, I, 1864), Elam Taylor, Lieutenant, H. H. Taylor, F. M. Taylor, Perry Taylor, J. W. Triplett, Oliver Triplett, Frank Triplett (killed at the Sinks), James D. Wilson, George Ward, Perry Weese, Duncan Weese, Haymond Weese, Lafayette Ward.

Twentieth Virginia Cavalry.—J. N. C. Bell, William H. Coberly, A. C. Crouch, John H. Dewitt, Claude Goff, Elihu Hutton, Colonel, John Herron, Eugenus Isner, Morgan Kittle, John Killingsworth, M. P. H. Potts, Jacob Salisbury (killed at Winchester), Sheldon Salisbury, Adam Stalnaker, Harrison Westfall, Fred White.

Nineteenth Virginia Cavalry.—John Baker, J. H. Currence, Archibald Earle, Simon Fowler, Nathan Fowler, Ira Kittle, John Kinney, Thomas G. Lindsey, James A. Logan, Thomas Logan, David H. Lilly, John Manley, James Morrison (killed at Droop Mountain), Adam Propst Jr., Jesse W. Simmons, Jonas Simmons, Nimrod Shifflett, J. S. Wamsley, Captain, Randolph Wamsley, Samuel B. Wamsley, Adam H. Wamsley, George F. Wamsley, George Ware, John Ware, Allen Ware, Elihu B. Ward, Jacob G. Ward, Lieutenant, R. S. Ward, L. M. Ward, Jacob Wilmoth, David J. Wilmoth.

M'Clanahan's Battery.—Andrew Chenoweth, Adam C. Caplinger, C. L. Caplinger, John Caplinger, Parkison C. Collett, Lieutenant, Andrew J. Collett, Sergeant, Hoy Clark, James Daniels, Bugler, Harper Daniels, Calvin C. Clark, C. B. Clark, John Marstiller (died at Bridgewater), David B. Marstiller, Blackman Rummell (died in prison), Jacob Weese, Andrew C. Weese.

Sixty-seventh Virginia Infantry.—A. Canfield, S. B. Kittle, William Keasy, Cyrus Myers, Randolph Phillips, Moses Phillips, George Phillips.

Churchville Cavalry.—Andrew C. Goddin, Lieutenant.

Twenty-fifth Virginia Infantry.—Jacob Heator, Dock Heator, Herbert Murphy, Jacob Mathews, Captain, Charles Mathews, James Shannon, Michael Shannon, Martin Shannon, Curtis Taylor, W. T. Ware, Sturms Gainer, Andrew J. Murphy.

Scouts.—William Nelson (killed on Dry Fork), and Thomas Wood.

Remarkable Recoveries.

On the night of March 20, 1864, a squad of Confederate scouts, consisting of Adam C. Stalnaker, Jasper Triplett, Oliver Triplett, Anthony Triplett, Taylor Chenoweth, James

D. Wilson, Jacob Wilmoth, Luther Parsons, Lafe Ward and Dow Adams were fired upon by thirty-three Home Guards, known as Swamps, while they were sleeping before a camp-fire at the Sinks on the head of Dry Fork. Oliver Triplett was killed instantly. Anthony Triplett and Adams were so severely wounded that they were thought to be dead. However, upon the removal of their boots they showed signs of

Rich Mountain Battle Field.

life and were clubbed with muskets and left for dead. Later they regained consciousness and Adams, in a dazed condition, fell into the fire and was severely burned. Mr. Teter, who lived near, found the wounded men next day and cared for them at his home. Adams had been hit by eighteen missiles, yet both he and Triplett recovered. Those escaping injury fled to the adjacent woods. Messrs. James D. Wilson and Adam C. Stalnaker, having departed the camp without their shoes, wrapped their feet in the capes of their coats, tied them on with their handkerchiefs, and waded through the snow several feet deep to Hightown, eight miles distant. Messrs. Perry Weese, John and Eli Taylor were with the Confederate scouts, but Mr. Weese stopped for the night with a Mr. Teter, who lived near. He was surprised and captured before the soldiers at the camp were fired upon, but was help-less to warn his comrades. Messrs. John and Eli Taylor, fear-ing a night attack, did not remain with the main body of the scouts, but were passing the night about a half mile distant, when the discharge of muskets warned them of their danger. They made their escape. Mr. Weese was turned over to the Federal authorities and sent to Camp Chase, where he remain-ed until the close of the war. These Confederates were re-turning from a visit to their homes in this section. They also designed to surprise and capture the Federal wagon train of supplies on its way from Webster Station to Beverly. Prepar-ration was made for the attack a few miles below Beverly, but when the train appeared the guard was too strong for their small force and their object was abandoned.

CHAPTER XI.

LAWS ANCIENT AND OBSOLETE.

"The world advances and in time outgrows
The laws that in our father's days were best,
And doubtless after us some purer scheme
Will be shaped by wiser men than we."

RANDOLPH COUNTY was governed by the constitution and statutes of Virginia from the time of its settlement to 1861. From 1863 to the present time the constitution and statutes of West Virginia have been the laws of the land. The study of the laws of an epoch or a country is interesting and instructive from the fact that they reflect the customs, usages, intelligence and civilization of a people. Blackstone defines statute law as, "A rule of action, prescribed by the supreme power of a state, commanding what is right and prohibiting what is wrong. Accepting this definition, we can determine from the laws of a country what its people regard as right and wrong. The consideration of the laws of the past is also interesting in throwing light upon the advancement of society. As mankind progresses in civilization there decreases the necessity for harsh, punitive and deterrent laws. A comparison of the laws of today with the statutes of a century ago is sufficient to convince the most skeptical and pessimistic that there has been real progress. The fact that laws were not repealed, is not evidence that they were not distasteful to a majority of the people. They often remain on the statute books long after they ceased to be enforced.

The laws that governed Randolph County, as a part of Virginia, during the first half century of its existence, were framed or inspired by the most distinguished statesmen our country has produced. They were largely responsible for the laws, whether good or bad. These men not only provided the State of Virginia with its code of laws, but dominated the policies of the general government as well. Among this galaxy of statesmen may be mentioned Patrick Henry, George Washington, John Randolph, John Marshall, James Madison, James Monroe, William Wirt and Thomas Jefferson. If some of the laws of their day seemed incompatible with their learning and wisdom, as we view them today, we must remember that they were intended for a people more primitive. A people steeped and inured in king-craft, with many laws and usages venerable with age. The laws may have been inharmonious with the spirit of the age, but they were hallowed by the usages and traditions of their ancestors and they were loth to alter or change them. If these laws, the product of the brain of these sages and statesmen, fall below our expectations, it may serve the purpose of removing the glamour and illusion that often attaches to the lives and teachings of those who have preceded us and leave us free to fashion our own destiny in the light of present day conditions.

In 1792 a law was enacted in the interests of good morals and the suppression of vice and provided a penalty of eighty-three cents for swearing, or getting drunk and in default of payment, the offender was to receive ten lashes on the bare back.

For working on the Sabbath the fine was one dollar and sixty-seven cents. In the early records of Randolph there is frequent reference to the violation of the Sunday law; in most instances for going to mill on the Sabbath. However, mitigating circumstances set the offender free in most instances.

For stealing a hogshead or cask of tobacco, found lying by the highway, the punishment was death.

By act of the Virginia Assembly of December 19, 1792, it was a crime punishable with death for any one to be found guilty of forgery. The same penalty was attached to the crime of eracing, defacing or changing the inspector's stamp on hemp or flour. A similar penalty was attached to the crime of stealing land warrants.

The individual, who made, passed, or possessed counterfeit money with knowledge that it was counterfeit, was to be put to death without benefit of clergy.

In the early days of Virginia laws were often classed as

"clergible" and "unclergible." Benefit of clergy was a privilege which arose from the pious regard paid by Christian princes to the church in its infant state. Clergymen were exempt from criminal processes before the secular judge in a few particular cases. This exemption of the clergy, as they increased in wealth, power and honor was extended to every subordinate officer belonging to the church or clergy. For a time the clergy could have his clerks or subordinates remitted out of the courts as they were indicted. This privilege was later changed so that the prisoner could only claim benefit of clergy after conviction in arrest of judgment. Before the general dissemination of learning the fact that the individual could read was competent evidence that he was a clerk or clericus and entitled to the benefit of clergy. Therefore, in the early history of our county, when the offender was found guilty and sentenced to expiate his crime with his life without benefit of clergy, it did not mean that the tribunal was essaying to extend its jurisdiction beyond earthly courts, but that the prisoner should not plead benefit of clergy in arrest of judgment. The principal argument upon which the clergy of that day claimed exemption of the law, was founded upon that text of Scripture, "Touch not mine annointed and do my prophets no harm."

In 1789, an act was passed by the Assembly of Virginia, making arson, burglary, the burning of a courthouse or prison, church, robbing a house in the presence of its occupants, breaking into and robbing a dwelling house by day, after putting its owner in fear, murder in the first degree, punishable with death without benefit of clergy.

By a law put on the statute books in 1792, gossip was discouraged in the following terms:

Whereas, many idle and busy headed people, do forge and divulge false rumors and reports, be it

Resolved: By the General Assembly, That what person or persons whomsoever shall forge or divulge any such false report tending to the trouble of the country, he shall be by the next Justice of the Peace, sent for and bound over, to the county court, where if he produce not his author, he shall be fined forty dollars or less if the court sees fit to lessen it, and besides give bond for his good behaviour, if it appear to the court that he did maliciously publish or invent it."

Hog stealing was a very grave crime in the eyes of the early Virginia law makers. Special penalties were provided, perhaps for the reason of the opportunities and temptations for appropriating another's swine. Hogs, more than other stock, were inclined to roam farther from the settler's cabin and clearing and remain for months or years without the care or attention of their owners. They were marked and turned loose to live, fatten and multiply upon the nuts and roots of the forest. A law enacted in 1792, provided that a person stealing a hog, shoat or pig should receive thirty-five lashes on the bare back, or pay a fine of thirty dollars and in either event he should pay the owner eight dollars for each animal stolen. For the second offense he should stand in the pilories with both ears nailed to the pilories on a court day. For the third offense the culprit was to be put to death without the benefit of clergy. The laws of marks and brands made the possession of a hog without ears sufficient evidence that the possessor had stolen it. Indians, under the law, were prohibited from selling the settler hogs unless the ears were produced to indicate the ownership.

Slaves whether regarded as property, or as men, severe laws were passed for their restraint and regulation. Historians differ as to the precise date of the introduction of slaves into Virginia. Smith, the first historian of Virginia thus expresses himself: "About the last of August came in a Dutch man of warre that brought us twenty Negars."

Prior to 1788 it was no punishable offense for the owner to accidentally kill his slave, by stroke or blow, intended for their correction. This law was repealed by act of the Assembly, November 21, 1788.

The assemblage of slaves at any school for teaching them reading or writing either in the day or night, was demed an unlawful assembly and the offenders were subject to corporal punishment, not to exceed twenty lashes.

Prior to 1806 an emancipated slave remaining in the State more than one year forfeited his or her freedom. No free negro or mulatto was permitted to migrate into the State under the penalty of receiving thirty-nine lashes for every week while he should remain in the State.

The General Assembly of Virginia in 1785, in order to prevent the further introduction of slaves into the State, passed an act that slaves brought into the Commonwealth and kept therein one year should be free.

It was unlawful for a slave to leave the premises of his master without a permit. No person was allowed to sell to or purchase from a slave any commodity without the master's consent.

In the same year the General Assembly declared all persons to be mulattoes, whose grandfathers or grandmothers shall have been negro, although all his other progenitors shall have been white persons. Also, every person, who shall have one-fourth part or more negro blood should be deemed a negro.

The early laws of Virginia recognized another species of servitude; that of servants. The legal status between servant and master was clearly defined by statute. Many poor persons in the mother country contracted for service on Virginia plantations in consideration of transportation. Then the mother country from motives of economy of gibbets and jail room at home transported a number of individuals who had not displayed a proper ethical consideration for the rights and properties of others in England. This class of individuals were sold to the American planter. In a new environment, with the inspiration of the opportunities of a new and growing country, removed from the scenes of their crimes, these exported convicts, as a rule, became upright and exempulary citizens.

No negro, mulatto or Indian could purchase any servant other than their own complexion.

By act of the Assembly of 1792, the servant could not be compelled to perform a contract exceeding seven years. Infants under fourteen years of age, with consent of parents or guardian could serve until of age. Servants, whose compensation was limited to transportation, food, lodging and clothing were to receive at the end of their service a suit of clothes, suited to the season: to-wit, a coat, waist coat, pair of breeches, and shoes, two pair of stockings, two shirts, a hat and a blanket.

A Justice of the Peace could convict a servant for laziness and have him corrected with stripes. No servant was permitted to sell or receive any commodity.

In offenses by free persons punishable by fines, servants were punished by lashes. Every servant upon the expiration of his or her time, was upon proof, to receive a certificate from the cleark of the court where he or she last served.

The Virginia Assembly passed an act November 13, 1788, to prevent the importation of convicts into Virginia, as follows:

"Whereas, it has been represented to this general assembly by the United States in congress, that a practice has prevailed for some time past of importing felon convicts into this state, under various pretences, which said felons convict so imported and sold and dispersed among the people of this state, whereby much injury hath been done to the moral, as well as the health of our fellow citizens: for remedy whereof,

"Be it enacted, that from and after the first day of January next, no captain or master of any sailing vessel, or any other person, coming into this commonwealth, by land or water, shall import or bring with him, any person who shall have been a felon, convict, or under sentence of death, or any other legal disability incurred by a criminal prosecution, or who shall be delivered to him from any prison or place of confinement, in any place out of the United States."

Religious Freedom.

Virginia had originally an established church with some of the intolerance of the mother church of England, but under the leadership of Thomas Jefferson, who is justly venerated as the father of religious liberty in Virginia, the legislature incorporated the liberal views of this distinguished statesman in the statutes of the state. In 1776 a committee had been appointed to revise the statutes of the state and the most important of these bills were enacted into law in 1785 and 1786. Among the bills recommended was one for establishing religious freedom, which became a law in October 1785. Patrick

Henry was at that time Governor of Virginia. The preamble and act was as follows:

"Whereas, Almighty God hath created the mind free; that all attempts to influence it by temporal punishments or burdens, or by civil incapacitations, tend only to beget habits of hypocricy and meanness, and are a departure from the plan of the Holy author of our religion who being Lord both of body and mind, yet choose not to propogate it by coercion on either, as was in his almighty power to do; that the impious presumption of legislators and rulers civil as well as ecclesiastical, who being themselves but fallible and uninspired men, have assumed dominion over the faith of others, setting up their own opinions and modes of thinking as the only true and infallible, and as such endeavoring to impose them on others, hath established and maintained false religions over the greatest part of the world, and through all time; that to compel a man to furnish contributions of money for the propogation of opinions which he disbelieves, is sinful and tyranical; that even the forcing him to support this or that teacher of his own religious persuasion, is depriving him of the comfortable liberty of giving his contributions to the particular pastor, whose morals he would make his pattern, and whose powers he feels most persuasive to righteousness, and is withdrawing from the ministry those temporary rewards, which proceeding from an approbation of their personal conduct, are an additional incitement to earnest and unremitting labours for the instruction of mankind; that our civil rights have no dependence on our religious opinions, any more than our opinions in physics or geometry; that therefore the proscribing any citizen as unworthy the public confidence by laying upon him incapacity of being called to offices of trust and emolument, unless he profess or renounce this or that religious belief, is depriving him injuriously of these privileges and advantages to which in common with his fellow citizens he has a natural right; that it tends only to corrupt the principles of the religion that it is meant to encourage, by bribing with a monopoly of worldly honors and emoluments, those who will externally profess and conform to it; that though indeed these are criminal who do not withstand such temptation, yet neither are those innocent who lay the bait in their way; that to suffer the civil magistrate to intrude his powers into the field of opinion, and to restrain the profession or propogation of principles on supposition of their ill tendency, is dangerous fallacy, which at once destroys all religious liberty, because he being of course judge of that tendency will make his opinions the rule of judgment, and approve or condem the sentiments of others only as they shall square with or differ from his own; that it is time enough for the rightful purposes of civil government, for its officers to interfere when principles break out into overt acts against peace and good order; and finally, that truth is great and will prevail if left to herself, that she is the proper antagonist to error, and has nothing to fear from the conflict unless by human interposition disarmed of her natural weapons, free argument and debate, errors ceasing to be dangerous when it is permitted freely to contradict them:

Be it Enacted by the General Assembly, That no man shall be compelled to frequent or support any religious worship, place or ministry whatsoever, or shall be enforced, restrained, molested or burthened in his goods, nor shall otherwise suffer on account of his religious opinions or belief; but that all men shall be free to profess, and by argument to maintain, their opinion in matters of religion, and that the same shall in no wise diminish, enlarge, or affect their civil capacities.

And though we well know that this assembly elected by the people for the ordinary purposes of legislation only, have no power to restrain the acts of succeeding assemblies, constituted with powers equal to our own, and that therefore to declare this act irrevocable would be of no effect in law; yet we are free to declare, that the rights hereby asserted are of the natural rights of mankind, and that if any act shall be hereafter passed to repeal the present, or to narrow its operation, such an act will be an infringement of natural right."

The military spirit prevailed in the early history of this county, to a much greater extent than today. The long contest with the Indians and French had imbued the people with a military spirit and inured them to the hardships of war. After the revolution the masses of the people gladly returned to the pursuits of peace, but the thunder and mutterings of the war god in Europe, echoed in the New World and the drill and efficiency of the militia was the constant care and patronage of the state. Musters for military drills were gala days in the pioneer period. In that day, when physical prowess was at a premium from an environment of danger and hardship, it was not an unusual occurrence for the participants of the muster, to test their physical skill and endurance in a fistic encounter.

The law under which musters were held was passed October 17, 1785. Patrick Henry was at that time Governor of Virginia. Several salient sections of the law are produced below:

"That all free male persons between the ages of eighteen and fifty years, except the members of council of state, judges, millers, ministers of the gospel, etc., shall be inrolled or formed into companies, of three serjeants, three corporals, a drummer and a fifer, and not less than forty and not more than sixty-five rank and file; and these companies shall again be formed into regiments of not more than one thousand, nor less than five hundred men, if there be so many in the county. Each company shall be commanded by a captain, lieutenant, and an ensign; each regiment by a colonel, and a major; and the whole by a county lieutenant. There shall be a private muster of every company once in two months, except December and January, at such convenient time and place as the captain or next commanding officer shall appoint: a muster of each regiment on some day in the month of March or April in every year, and a general muster of the whole on some day in the month of October or November, in every year, to be appointed by the county lieutenant.

"Every officer and soldier shall appear at his respective muster field on the day appointed, by eleven o'clock in the forenoon, armed, equipped and accoutered as follows: The county lieutenants, colonels, lieutenant colonels, and majors, with a sword, the captains, lieutenants, and ensigns, with a sword and espontoon, every non-commissioned officer and private, with a good clean musket, carrying an ounce ball and three feet eight inches long in barrel, with a good bayonet and iron ramrod well fitted thereto, a cartridge box properly made, to contain and secure twenty cartridges fitted to his musket, a good knapsack and canteen, and moreover, each non-commissioned officer and private shall have at every muster one pound of good powder, and four pounds of lead, including twenty blind cartridges; and each serjeant shall have a pair of moulds fit to cast balls for their respective companies, to be purchased by the commanding officer out of the monies arising on delinquencies.

"Provided, that the militia of the counties westward of the Blue Ridge, and the counties below adjoining thereto, shall not be obliged to be armed with muskets, but may have good rifles with proper accouterments, in lieu thereof.

"And whereas it will be of great utility and advantage in establishing a well disciplined militia, to annex to each regiment a light company to be formed of young men, from eighteen to twenty-five years old, whose activity and domestic circumstances will admit of a frequency of training and strictness of discipline, not practical for the militia in general, and returning to the main body, on their arrival at the latter period, will be constantly giving thereto a military pride and experience, from which the best of consequences will result.

"If any non-commissioned officer or soldier shall behave himself disobediently or mutinously when on duty, on, or before any court or board directed by this act to be held, the commanding officer, court or board, may either confine him for the day, or cause him to be bound neck and heels for any time not exceeding five minutes. If any by-stander shall interrupt, molest or insult any officer or soldier while on duty at any muster, or shall be guilty of the like conduct before any court or board, as aforesaid, the commanding officer, or such court, or board may cause him to be confined for the day.

And when any militia shall be in actual service, they shall be allowed pay and rations as follows: A brigadier general, one hundred dollars per month, and twelve rations of provisions and five rations of forage for himself and family, per day; an aid-de-camp, thirty dollars per month; a colonel,

seventy-five dollars per month and six rations of provisions
and two rations of forage per day; a brigade major, thirty
dollars per month, four rations of provisions and two rations
of forage per day; a brigade quartermaster, thirty dollars per
month, and three rations of provisions and one ration of forage
per day; a lieutenant colonel, sixty dollars per month, and five
rations of provisions and two rations of forage per day; a
major, fifty dollars per month and two rations of forage per
day; a captain, forty dollars per month and three rations of
provisions per day; a lieutenant, twenty-seven and two-thirds
dollars per month and two rations of provisions per day; an
ensign, twenty dollars per month and two rations of provisions
per day; a surgeon, sixty dollars per month and three rations
of provisions and two rations of forage per day; a quartermaster, twenty dollars per month and two rations of provisions and one ration of forage per day; a paymaster, forty
dollars per month and two rations of provisions and one ration
of forage per day; an adjutant, twenty-four dollars per month
and two rations of provisions and one ration of forage per day;
a quartermaster sergeant, eight dollars per month and one
ration per day; a sergeant, eight dollars per month and one
ration per day; a corporal, seven dollars per month and one
ration per day; a private, five and one-half dollars per month,
and one ration per day. A ration shall consist of one pound
of fresh beef or pork, or three-quarters of a pound of salt
pork, one pound of wheat bread or flour, or one pound and a
quarter of corn meal, one gill of rum, when to be had, and one
quart of salt, one quart of vinegar, two pounds of soap, and
one pounds of candles, to every hundred rations; but in case
salt meat be issued, the salt to be withheld; and a ration of
forage, of ten quarts of corn or oats, and fourteen pounds of
hay or fodder.

The pioneer depended, much more than people of the
present day, upon the local grist mill for converting his corn
and wheat into meal and flour, whereof was obtained the
"staff of life." The miller was an important and conspicuous
personage in the community and an object of much consideration by the law making bodies. Unless the mill was established by court, the owner could collect no toll nor receive

any compensation for grinding grain. The law, in part, governing the operation of grist mills was as follows:

"All millers shall well and sufficiently grind the grain, brought to their mills for the usual consumption of all persons bringing the same and their families: and in due turn as the same shall be brought and may take for the toll, one-eighth part and no more, of all grain of which the remaining part shall be ground into meal and one-sixteenth part and no more of all grain of which the remaining part shall be ground into hominy or malt.

"And every miller or occupier of a mill, who shall not well and sufficiently grind as aforesaid, or not in turn as the same shall be brought, or take or exact more toll, shall, (whether such mill be established by law or not) forfeit and pay to the party injured, five dollars for each and every offense, recoverable with costs before any justice of the peace of the county where such offense shall be committed. And where the miller shall be a slave free or mulatto, he shall, upon the first conviction for such offense, receive ten lashes, and on the second conviction twenty lashes, on his or her bare back, well laid on, in lieu of the forfeit aforesaid; but upon a third conviction, the master of such slave, where the party is a slave, or his overseer or agent, shall be liable to pay to the party injured, five dollars, recoverable as aforesaid, and so for every offense by such slave afterward committed; provided that every owner, or occupier of a mill, shall have a right at any time to grind his or her own grain for the consumption of his or her family; And provided, That no miller shall be obliged to run more than one pair of stones, for the purpose of grinding grain brought to his mill for the consumption of the persons bring the same and their families.

"Every owner or occupier of a mill established, or grinding for toll, as aforesaid, shall keep therein sealed measures, of half bushel and peck, and toll dish sealed, and shall measure all grain by strike measure under the penalty of paying two dollars and fifty cents for every such failure, recoverable with costs, before a justice of the peace for the county wherein such mill shall be, to the use of the informer, and if the miller be a slave or servant, his master or owner shall be liable to the penalty."

According to the code of Virginia of 1819, in case of trespass by horses and cattle upon the lands of another, for the third offense the "party injured may kill the beast without being liable to an action."

In the question of the lawfulness of a fence, in case of trespass the justice was compelled to issue his order for "three honest and disinterested house keepers," to view the fence and their testimony was good evidence to the jury.

Persons injuring trespassing live stock, when their fence was not up to the legal standard, were mulcted in double damages. The statute read as follows: "If any person damified for want of such sufficient fence shall injure or cause to be injured, in any manner, any of the kind of animals above mentioned, he shall pay to the owner double damages, with costs recoverable as aforesaid."

The penalty for making a fence across a public road was one dollar and sixty cents for every twenty-four hours the fence remained.

On November 7, 1787, an act was passed by the Virginia Assembly of considerable historic interest. John Fitch, of Pennsylvania was granted exclusive privilege to navigate steamboats upon all waters within the jurisdiction of the state for a term of fourteen years. This act was to become void if he did not have his boats or crafts in use at the expiration of three years from the passage of the act. The preamble of the bill cited that John Fitch "hath constructed an easy and expeditious method of propelling boats through the water by force of fire or steam." Several years previous, while sailing on the great western rivers, the idea occurred to him that they might be navigated by steam. He applied for pecuniary assistance to several states without success. However in 1786, he succeeded in forming a company for the prosecution of his enterprise, and a steam packet was launched on the Delaware. The undertaking proved a losing one and Mr. Fitch, in poverty and disappointment, committed suicide in 1798. James Rumsey disputed Fitche's claim to be the inventor of steam navigation, but, he as well as Robert Fulton, who in 1806, succeeded in propelling a boat through the water by the use of steam, perhaps, appropriated the ideas conceived and suggested by Fitch several years previous.

District courts were established by act of the Virginia Assembly December 22, 1788. Randolph, Harrison, Monongalia, and Ohio composed one of the circuits. Court for this district was to be held at Monongalia court house on the 3rd day of May, and the 20th day of September of each year. Judges were elcted by joint ballot of the both houses of the Assembly. There were to be two judges for each circuit. Where the charge was of such a nature as to subject the party to capital punishment or burning in the hand, two judges were required to try the issue, whether in law or fact. Their jurisdiction obtained in civil causes, only, where the matter in controversy amounted to 3000 pounds, or more, of tobacco.

On November 20, 1788, the Virginia Assembly apportioned the state into ten Congressionad districts and passed an act for the election of representatives pursuant to the constitution of the United States, which had been ratified by Virginia in June of the same year. Randolph county was linked with Harrison, Hampshire, Berkeley, Frederick, Shenandoah, Ohio, Monongalia and Hardy in the formation of one congressional district. This congressional district, with a few variations, remains much the same today.

On December 9, 1795, the General Assembly of Virginia passed an act for removing the obstructions for the passage of fish in the Tygarts Valley river. There is no record or tradition that anything was ever accomplished and the agitation for this project, though hoary with the frosts of many winters, today shows the vitality of vigorous youth. The falls referred to exist a few miles below the city of Grafton. The narrows, near Cornelius Westfall's, has reference to the passage of the Valley river through the mountains, a few miles below Elkins. A copy of the act is produced below:

"Be it enacted by the General Assembly, That Robert Maxwell, Abram Kittle, John Pancake, Abram Springstone, Jacob Stornaker, Benjamin Hornbeck, Simon Reader, Hezekiah Roincrantz, and Jonas Friend, gentlemen, shall be and are hereby constituted and appointed commissioners, for taking and receiving subscriptions for the purpose of defraying the expense of removing the obstructions to the passage of fish, in the Tygarts Valley River between the falls and the narrows near Cornelius Westfall's.

"If any person shall neglect or refuse, when required to pay the money by him subscribed, it shall be lawful for the said commissioners or the survivors of them, to recover the same by motion in the court of the county where the subscriber resides: Provide, the party has ten days previous notice of such motion, and the clerk shall endorse on every execution issued by virtue of this act, 'No security to be taken.'

"The commissioners, or a majority of them, shall have power to contract and agree with one or more fit person or persons for removing the obstruction to the passage of fish in Tyger's Valley river between the falls thereof and the narrows near Cornelius Westfall's and take a bond or bonds with sufficient security for the due and faithful performance of the undertaking: and of the money arising from the subscription as aforesaid, to pay the expense thereof.

"This act shall commence and be in force from and after the passing thereof."

The Virginia Assembly on December 10, 1793 passed an act authorizing the county of Randolph to open a wagon road from the court house at Beverly to the State Road at David Minear's on Cheat River. Under this act the surveyors of the different precincts of the county were to compel all persons in their precincts, who were subject to the road law, to assist in the construction of this road. The road law at that time compelled "all male labouring persons, of the age of sixteen years or more, except such as are masters of two or more male labouring slaves of the age of sixteen years or more to work on some public road." The penalty for the violation of this statute was seven shillings and six pense for each day's offense. The following is a copy of the act referred to above:

"Whereas it has been represented to the present general assembly that the inhabitants of Randolph County have long laboured under many disadvantages for the want of a wagon

road from the court house thereof to the state road at David
Manear's on Cheat River, which can not be effected by the
ordinary mode of prescribed by law:

"Be it therefore enacted by the general assembly, That it
shall and may be lawful for the court of the said county of
Randolph to order the attendance and services of the several
surveyors of highways in Tyger's Valley, Leading Creek and
Cheat River, with the hands assigned to work thereon, to
open and complete a wagon road from Thomas Skidmore's, in
Tyger's Valley, to David Manear's on Cheat River, where the
state road crosses the same.

"And be it further enacted, That any person failing to
comply with the requisitions of this act, shall be subject to
the same fines and penalties as are inflicted by the act entitled,
'An act concerning public roads.'

"This act shall commence and be in force from and after
the passing thereof."

Tavern keepers were for many years in the early history
of the state licensed by the Governor, but from the time of
the formation of this county the licenseing power was vested
in the county court. A special penalty, forfeiture of license,
was attached to the offense of permitting "any person to
tipple or drink more than is necessary on the Lord's day or
any day set apart by public authority for religious worship."
Prices to be charged by the innkeeper for diet, lodging, liquors,
and horse feed were left to the discretion of the county court.

The culture of tobacco was for many years the principal
pursuit in the early history of Virginia and it was the only
staple commodity to which the first settlers could be induced
to turn their attention. Various laws were, at first enacted by
the legislature, wth a view to improve its quality and lessen
the quantity, the distance at which the plants should be set
apart, the number of plants to be attended by each labourer,
and the number of leaves to be gathered from a plant, were
all prescribed by act of Assembly. At one period a law was
in force, declaring that no tobacco should be planted after a
certain day in the year; at another there was a total suspen-
sion from planting for a year, which was called a cessation or
stint. The size of a hogshead of tobacco was, for a number

of years, three hundred and fifty pounds weight. Before any warehouses were stablished, the inspection of tobacco was performed by an order from a commander of plantations, two men in the neighborhood, who were to view it and if of bad quality to burn it.

Postage Rates. Laws of the United States of April 9, 1816: For every letter, of a single sheet, conveyed not exceeding thirty miles, 6 cents; over thirty and not exceeding eighty miles, 10 cents; over eighty and not exceeding one hundred and fifty miles, 12½ cents; over one hundred and fifty and not not exceeding four hundred miles, 18¾ cents; over four hundred miles, 25 cents. For every double letter, or one composed of two pieces of paper, double those rates; for a triple letter, or one composed of three pieces of paper, triple those rates. One newspaper could be sent by each printer to every other printer free of charge. The postage of newspapers was one cent for any distance not more than one hundred miles and one and one-half cents for any greater distance. The postage of magazines and pamphlets was one cent a sheet for any distance not exceeding fifty miles, one and one-half cents for any distance over fifty.

We give below the Act of the General Assembly creating Randolph County, That portion of Harrison County embraced in the territory west and east of the lines given, hounded on the west by Pendleton, south by Greenbrier, constituted the county at the time of its formation.

Be It Enacted by the Geenral Assembly of Virginia: That from and after the first day of May, 1787, the county of Harrison, shall be divided into two distinct counties, that is to say, so much of the said county, lying southeast of the following lines, beginning at the mouth of Sandy Creek, thence up Tyger's Valley River to the mouth of Buckhannon River, thence up said river including all the waters thereof, thence down Elk River, including the waters thereof to the Greenbrier line, shall be one distinct county and called and be known by Randolph and the residue of said county shall retain the name of Harrison. A court for the said county of Randolph shall be held by the Justices thereof on the fourth

Monday of every month after the said division shall take place, in such manner as is provided by law for other counties, and shall be by their Commissioners directed. The Justices so named shall meet at the house of Benjamin Wilson in Tyger's Valley in said county, upon the first court day after the said division shall take place, and having taken the oaths prescribed by law and administered the oaths of office to, and taken bond of the Sheriff according to law, proceed to appoint and qualify a Clerk, and fix upon a place for holding court in the said county at or near the center thereof as the situation and convenience will admit of, and thenceforth the said court shall proceed to erect the necessary public buildings at such place and until such public buildings are completed, appoint any place for holding courts as they may think proper. * * * * * * *   In all elections of a senator, the said county of Randolph shall be of the same district as the said county of Harrison.

When a new county was organized the Governor commissioned a number of men to act as "Worshipful Justices." They were not only Justices of the Peace, but were also a board of County Commissioners. They held office for life, except that the Governor might remove them for cause. Vacancies were filled by new men recommended by the Court, and commissioned by the Governor. The Court was therefore self perpetuating.

This was the law of the land until 1852. The senior Justice in point of service became Sheriff. The Justices were selected from the influential and land owning class; they alone were entitled to the title of "Squire" or "gentlemen." The office often descended from father to son. To be eligible to vote or hold office in that day, it was necessary to own a plat of ground of 25 acres and have a house thereon of the dimensions of 12 x 12 feet or in lieu thereof, a plat of fifty acres of unimproved land.

From the formation of the government of Virginia until 1794, tobacco was the legal currency of the state, one hundred pounds being equivalent to one pound in coin. One pound was the equivalent of 3⅓ cents.

By an act of 1788, the county court was for the trial of all presentments and criminal prosecutions, suits at common law and in chancery, where the sum exceeded five pounds or 500 pounds of tobacco, depending therein and continuing for the space of six days unless the business should be sooner determined. It had general police and probate jurisdiction, control of levies, of roads, actions at law, and suits in chancery. The Justices served without pay, and their number was not limited by law. A quorum consisted of four. The grand jury of twenty-four members, sworn for an "inquest on the body of the county" was selected by the Sheriff from the freeholders.

CHAPTER XII.

RANDOLPH COUNTY LAWYERS.

THE members of the legal profession have ever left a marked impress upon the times in which they lived. They
were, not only the principal factor in framing laws, but were
largely influential in moulding public sentiment, which found
expression in the statutes of the state. Since the organization of the county, Randolph has had a bar that would bear
favorable comparison with that of any other county in the
state. Many of the lawyers that became prominent at the
Randolph county bar received their legal training and tute-
lage from such learned and eminent jurists as Tucker, Minor,
and Brockenborough. More than 200 lawyers have been admitted to practice in Randolph county, a list of whom is given
below, with the date when the name of each first appeared
on the record:

William McCleary	1787	Edwin S. Duncan	1811
Alexander Addison	1787	Jonathan Jackson	1813
Maxwell Armstrong	1790	James Gilmore	1813
Adam See	1793	William Colwell	1814
Francis Brook	1793	Thomas Wilson	1815
Isaac White Williams	1794	James McCally	1815
Gilbert Christie	1795	Marmaduke Evans	1915
Patrick Hendrin	1797	James McGee	1815
Nathaniel Davisson	1798	John Brown	1817
Christopher Lamberton	1801	Phineas Chapin	1818
John G. Jackson	1801	Thomas C. Gordon	1820
Isaac Morris	1802	John J. Allen	1820
James Wilson	1803	Jefferson Phelps	1822
James Evans	1803	Lewis Maxwell	1822
John M. Smith	1804	John Ramsell	1823
William Tingle	1805	Daniel G. Morrell	1823
George C. Davisson	1807	George C. Baxter	1823
Samuel McMeechen	1809	William L. Jackson	1824
Nathaniel Pendleton	1809	Edgar C. Wilson	1825
Noah Lindsey	1809	George J. Wilson	1826
Philip Doddridge	1809	Joseph Lovell	1827
William G. Payne	1809	Solomon Wyatt	1827
George I. Davisson	1809	Blake B. Woodson	1827
William Parinlaw	1810	Reuben W. Short	1827
Oliver Phelps	1810	Gideon D. Camden	1827
Lemuel E. Davisson	1910	Augustine L. Smith	1828

W. W. Chapman	1828	Thomas B. Rummell	1858
W. G. Brown	1829	John W. Barton	1858
W. G. Naylor	1829	William H. Gibson	1858
James H. Craven	1829	John W. Crawford	1859
William C. Haymond	1830	Charles W. Cooper	1859
William R. Crane	1830	William Ewin	1859
Frederick M. Wilson	1830	John Kearanans	1860
William A. Harrison	1832	Spencer Dayton	1863
George H. Lee	1832	Thomas J. Arnold	1863
Beverly H. Lurty	1832	C. J. P. Cresap	1863
Charles McClure	1832	Charles J. Pindall	1863
Robert Wallace	1832	Joseph Thompson	1863
Leroy E. Gaston	1833	Fontain Smith	1864
Burton A. Despard	1834	James W. Dunnington	1866
John G. Stringer	1834	W. C. Carper	1866
Cabell Tavener	1834	Cyrus Kittle	1866
David Goff	1834	Willis J. Drummond	1866
Thomas Brown	1835	Charles S. Lewis	1866
William McKinley	1836	James M. Seig	1867
Hyre Jackson	1836	Alexander M. Poundstone	1867
Joseph Hart	1837	John S. Hoffman	1870
Wesley C. Kemp	1838	Lorenzo D. Strader	1870
John S. Carlisle	1840	Thomas P. R. Brown	1873
Matthew Edmiston	1840	A. G. Reger	1873
Bernard L. Brown	1840	E. T. Jones	1873
John L. Duncan	1841	Stark W. Arnold	1873
Richard M. Whiting	1841	Gustavus Cresap	1873
James M. Jackson	1841	Adonijah B. Parsons	1873
Edgar M. Davisson	1842	J. L. Hall	1873
John D. Stephenson	1842	W. G. L. Totten	1873
Charles A. Harper	1843	C. C. Higginbotham	1873
Alpheus F. Haymond	1843	Jasper N. Hall	1875
Uriel M. Turner	1843	Henry Brannon	1875
Preston W. Adams	1844	Bernard L. Butcher	1876
Edwin L. Hewitt	1844	William T. Ice	1876
Benjamin F. Myers	1845	W. B. Maxwell	1876
Samuel Crane	1847	Philetus Lipscomb	1877
Caleb Boggess	1847	Shelton Leake Reger	1877
Jonathan Koiner	1847	William L. Kee	1878
Phillip M. Morrill	1847	Alston G. Dayton	1879
Jonathan M. Bennett	1847	Cyrus H. Scott	1879
Joseph C. Spalding	1848	A. C. Bowman	1880
Nathan H. Taft	1848	Leland Kittle	1880
Benjamin Wilson	1850	H. C. Thurmond	1880
Philip Williams	1851	B. F. Martin	1881
Daniel A. Stofer	1852	William G. Brown	1881
John N. Hughes	1852	John W. Mason	1881
Edwin Maxwell	1852	W. W. Haden	1881
William H. Ferrill	1853	John E. Wood	1881
Thomas A. Bradford	1853	R. S. Turk	1881
Samuel Woods	1853	John Bayles Ward	1881
Charles Hooton	1853	A. S. Bosworth	1882
George W. Lurty	1854	L. S. Auvil	1883
James Bennett	1855	Frank Woods	1884
Edgar M. Williams	1855	William E. Clark	1884
Claudius Goff	1856	E. D. Talbott	1884
David M. Auvil	1856	James A. Bent	1884
David H. Lilly	1858	Jared L. Wamsley	1884

J. F. Harding	1885	G. H. A. Kunst	1902
S. M. Reynolds	1885	E. A. Bowers	1902
H. N. Ogden	1887	S. T. Spears	1903
A. Jay Valentine	1887	J. C. Canfield	1903
W. C. Clayton	1887	W. W. Brown	1903
Charles W. Russell	1888	E. Clark Ice	1903
Melville Peck	1888	S. H. McLean	1903
C. W. Dailey	1890	Roy See	1905
Charles W. Lynch	1890	W. G. Bennett	1905
L. H. Keenan	1892	Myron Clark	1905
W. G. Wilson	1893	Fred L. Cox	1905
Geo. B. Scott	1893	H. G. Kump	1905
Geo. M. Curtis	1893	E. F. Morgan	1905
A. M. Cunningham	1893	Thos. Horner	1906
W. T. Woodyard	1893	H. H. Rose	1906
Andrew Price	1894	W. J. Strader	1906
Henry C. Ferry	1895	D. W. Bauske	1907
W. H. Baker	1895	D. E. Cuppett	1907
Lew Greynolds	1895	H. P. Camden	1907
C. O. Strieby	1896	Haymond Maxwell	1907
J. F. Strader	1896	L. M. McClintic	1907
W. E. Baker	1896	R. H. Waugh	1907
H. E. Wilmoth	1896	Tucker H. Ward	1907
W. B. Kittle	1896	C. N. Pew	1908
C. W. Harding	1897	H. S. Rucker	1908
Malcolm Jackson	1897	Geo. A. Vincent	1908
J. N. McMullen	1897	T. A. Bledsoe	1909
E. P. Durkin	1897	T. M. Beltzhoover	1909
Geo. B. Scott	1897	B. H. Hiner	1909
J. C. McWhorter	1897	P. R. Kump	1909
W. T. George	1897	Earl H. Maxwell	1909
C. P. Guard	1897	J. W. Robinson	1909
B. F. Bailey	1897	R. S. Spillman	1909
S. H. Summerville	1897	R. E. Swartz	1910
W. T. Ice, Jr.	1898	F. E. Tallman	1910
C. W. Maxwell	1898	John F. Brown	1911
F. A. Rowan	1898	W. A. Arnold	1912
B. W. Taylor	1898	Chas. Richie	1912
W. H. Cobb	1898	C. H. Marstiller	1912
Michael King	1899	Robert Irons	1913
C. M. Murphy	1899	Geo. W. McClintic	1913
J. B. Ware	1899	Cecil Crickard	1914
Russell Allen	1902	Neil Cunningham	1915
B. M. Hoover	1902		

Wm. McLeary, the first attorney to be admitted to practice in Randolph, was also the first Prosecuting Attorney of the county. Record or tradition gives little information in regard to him. He received the munificent sum of $13.33⅓ per annum "should the court think it proper to continue him for that term." In 1791 Mr. McLeary moved to Morgantown and became the Clerk of the District Court. He was succeeded as Prosecuting Attorney by Thomas Wilson.

Thomas Jackson, who was admitted to practice in 1813, was the father of General Stonewall Jackson and was a member of the Clarksburg bar. He was a son of Edward and Mary (Haddan) Jackson. His father Edward Jackson, was a member of the pioneer family of Randolph by that name.

William L. Jackson, who was admitted to the Beverly bar in 1824, became a General in the Confederate army and was repulsed in an attack upon the Federal forces at Beverly.

John S. Carlisle, admitted to the Randolph county bar in 1840, was a member of the Secession Convention at Richmond, Virginia, 1861, and was expelled for voting against the Ordinance of Secession. Mr. Carlisle and W. T. Wiley were the first representatives of the new state in the United States Senate.

Alpheus Haymond, admitted in 1843, Samuel Woods, admitted in 1853, and Henry Brannon, admitted in 1875, were at a later date, elevated to the Supreme bench of the state.

W. W. Hayden, for a time located in Beverly, and admitted to the Beverly bar in 1881, was a native of Fincastle, Virginia. He returned to his native town.

H. N. Ogden, admitted to the Randolph county bar in 1887, for a time practiced his profession in Beverly, but returned to his native town of Fairmont, where he achieved success and prominence.

Cyrus Kittle, admitted to the bar in 1866, was the grand father of W. B. Kittle, the present Judge of the Randolph-Barbour Circuit.

CHAPTER XIII.

PHYSICIANS AND SURGEONS OF RANDOLPH.

> When two single cells were joined in one embrace,
> Fraternity was born, time never could efface.
>
> Traced in the mammal's maternal instinct wild,
> She gave her substance for the welfare of her child.
>
> Man in his cave home first felt another's grief and pain;
> He then upward turned his course to God again.
>
> His love toward man He then deigned to reveal,
> Conformed man to His image with power to heal.

THAT period of the past, contemporaneous with the interval from the early settlement of Randolph to the present day, marked the transition of medicine from an empiric art to a precise science. Among the epoch making achievements embraced within that period, may be mentioned vaccination for small pox, the germ theory of disease, anesthetics and serum therapy. The physician of the present day deprived of these aids and instruments in his warfare against disease would be tempted, no doubt, to hoist the white flag of truce and abandon mankind to the fates. However, what the physicians of that period lacked in methods and equipment, was compensated by faith in his remedial agents and the benevolence with which he pursued his profession. The ethics of the time forbade the question of fee or reward, and whether amid the storms and snows of winter, the sultry heat of summer, in the glare of the noonday sun, or the midnight hour, when deep sleep falleth upon men, the calls of human need were obeyed with equal cheerfulness into the hut of the pauper or the palace of the prince. Then, as now, other men might by proxy, by reason of fortutitious circumstances, relieve the suffering and afflicted, but the physician must give the sweat of his own brow, the fatigue of his own body, the toil of his own intellect and the anxieties of his own soul.

The old-time physician, in a degree that cannot be conceived today, was regarded as a friend and advisor of the community. To the credit of his time, let it be said that he seldom was rewarded for his sacrifice and unselfish devotion to duty by criticism and ingratitude.

The dangers and hardships of the pioneer physician were augmented by the sparsely settled condition of the country, with poor roads and few bridges. A night call of thirty or forty miles, across mountains, following a bridal path, was not an infrequent occurrence. He shared with his horse the fame and affection of the community. So much depended upon the ability of the animal to carry its rider safely and swiftly through the forest, over mountain and stream, to the bedside of his patient. As a rule it was the most magnificent and stalwart specimen the community could produce: spirited, sure and fleet of foot, trained to swimming swollen streams, carrying its rider safely over, while elevated above high water mark, suspended from his own shoulders, were his shiny saddle bags.

Because of the distance from the physician, the early settler often had recourse to home remedies. To "draw out the fire" apple butter or a poultice of corn meal or scraped potatoes was applied to burns and scalds. The juice of roasted onions had the reputation of being a specific for croup. The Virginia snake root, Serpentaria, was the standard remedy to produce perspiration and abort a fever. Other remedies were boneset, horehound, chamomile, wild cherry and prickly ash. As late as 1777 the physicians in Rockingham County, Va., were authorized to inoculate persons living within three miles of a smallpox infected locality. Previous to the introduction of vaccination, the method of preventative treatment by what was known as inoculation had been employed. This consisted of introducing into the system—in a similar way to the method commonly employed in vaccination—the smallpox virus from a mild case with a view to introducing the disease also in a mild form in the person inoculated and thus offering him protection from a further attack. The testimony of physicians was to the effect that this practice made a marked impression upon the fatality of the disease. However, it was a prolific source of the spread of the contagion.

From the fact that a medical society did not exist in

Randolph until a recent period no records have been kept and perhaps several physicians, who should live in local history, by reason of the merit of their work and lives, have passed to oblivion. The sketches given are the result of the best information now obtainable, in some instances brief and fragmentary:

Robert Maxwell was the first man to locate in Randolph who made any pretense to the practice of medicine—perhaps. The early records of the county show that he did not bear the title of Doctor, yet in 1789 he was appointed Coroner and in the same year he was surgeon for the county militia. He was also a preacher and performed many marriage ceremonies in the pioneer period. Nothing is known of his education or parentage and that branch of the Maxwell family is now extinct in Randolph. He resided about one mile below the site of Elkins on Leading Creek. He died in 1818.

Dr. Benjamin Dolbeare was, perhaps, the first man in Randolph to pursue the practice of medicine as a profession. He was a man of education and superior ability in his profession. He came to Randolph from Connecticut, the precise date is not known. He was a brother-in-law to Lorenzo Dow and that eccentric genius made Dr. Dolebeare's home in Beverly a place of a few day's rest and recuperation in his annual pilgrimages as a missionary through the wilds of America. After practicing a few years at Beverly, perhaps from about 1810 to 1815, he removed to Clarksburg.

Dr. Squire Bosworth, student under and successor of Dr. Dolebeare, was born in Hampshire county, Massachusetts, in 1794. He was born in the same year and in the same county, and was a fellow student at Williams College of William Cullen Bryant. After his graduation at Williams College Dr. Bosworth came to Virginia as a volunteer soldier in the war of 1812. On reaching Parkersburg on his way to Norfolk, Virginia, the company to which he belonged was disbanded, peace having been declared. He remained in Parkersburg as a Deputy County Clerk under a Mr. Neal for two years. He then came to Randolph to assume the same duties for Mr. Archibald Earle, then Clerk of the Circuit Court of Randolph county. Soon thereafter, he married Hannah, daughter of

Peter Buckey of Beverly and with his bride returned to Parkersburg and opened an Academy. A few years later he again became a resident of Beverly and began the study of medicine under Dr. Dolbeare. At a later period he attended lectures in Richmond, Va. For many years he was the only physician in Randolph and a night trip to Tucker, Barbour, or Webster was not an unusual occurrence. There is an authentic tradition that Drs. Bosworth and Dolbeare successfully performed the operation of tracheotomy nearly a century ago. In his religious faith he was a Presbyterian and practiced the strict tenets of an early-day New England Puritan. He carried tracts of a religious nature for distribution in the communities in which he was called and, in remote districts, would call the settlers together and hold prayer meeting. He was Clerk of the Circuit Court two terms and represented Randolph and Tucker in the Virginia legislature of 1855 and 1856. He died in the year of 1870 in the 76th year of his age after more than half a century's active practice in the county.

Dr. Samuel H. Dold practiced his profession in Beverly from 1870 to 1873. He returned to Augusta county Virginia. He received his medical education as a student of his brother-in-law, Dr. J. W. Bosworth, at Philippi, and at the Jefferson Medical College, Philadelphia.

Daniel S. Haymond, M.D., born in Taylor County in 1838, graduated in the medical department of the University of New York in 1867. He began the practice of medicine at Simpson, Taylor County, and moved to Leadsville, Randolph County, in 1869. He was an active practitioner for a quarter of a century.

Eugene B. Wilmoth, M.D., son of Oliver and Louisa Taylor Wilmoth, was born in 1859, died 1895. He was educated in the public schools at Philippi, Grafton, and the Normal School at Fairmont. He received his education in medicine at the University of Maryland, where he graduated in 1888. He practiced at Meadowville, Harmon and then located at Elkins. Although a comparatively young practitioner at the time of his death, he attained an eminent place in the medical profession of Randolph.

Dr. George W. Yokum was born in Randolph County

December 19, 1831, and was the eldest of five children born to John and Melinda (Kuykendall) Yokum. The paternal grandfather, William Yokum, was a native of Virginia, On his father's farm in Randolph County Dr. Yokum spent his early life and received a limited education in the log schoolhouse of those days. In 1849 he began the study of medicine with Dr. William Briggs and in 1853 and 1854 attended lectures at Jefferson Medical College, Philadelphia. In May, 1854, he began to practice and in 1859 located in Beverly, where he practiced until the time of his death, ... He was well read and a very successful physician. In 1858 he married Miss Mary C. Ward, a native of this county and a daughter of George W. Ward. Although not a politician, because of his wide range of knowledge and strong mentality he was called upon to serve the people four years as President of the County Court and six years as Commissioner of the County Court. Dr. Yokum was honored by the party of which he was a member by being selected as a delegate to the National Democratic Convention which assembled in Chicago in 1892.

Dr. Oscar Butcher was the eldest son of Baliss G. and Patsy McNeil Butcher, and was born in Randolph County, December 24, 1820. He moved to Indiana with his father and studied medicine under Dr. Creigh, of Delphi, that state, and later attended medical lectures in Chicago. He returned to Virginia and commenced the practice of medicine at Falling Springs, Greenbrier County. He married Sarah J. Beard of that county May 16, 1849. In 1851, he moved to Green Bank, Pocahontas County, where he practiced until he moved to Huttonsville, this county, in 1860. He practiced at Huttonsville until the outbreak of the war, when he became identified with the Confederate army. He was with the advance on Elkwater and Cheat Mountain, also at Stewart Run and Camp Bartow and Allegheny Mountain. In declining health for several years, he died at Lockwillow, in Augusta County, December 21, 1861. Although always in delicate health he was energetic and a very successful physician.

Dr. George White located at Huttonville in the early forties. He was from eastern Virginia. After several years' practice in that locality he returned to his native county.

Dr. James Hamilton of Bath County, Virginia, located at Huttonsville, about 1850. He moved to Parkersburg prior to the outbreak of the civil war.

Dr. Jones located in Huttonsville about the commencement of the civil war. He returned to Virginia during the progress of that conflict.

Dr. Blair was located at Huttonsville for a short time subsequent to the war of the rebellion.

Dr. David W. Gibson was born in Pocahontas County in 1829 and was the son of David and Mary Gibson. He was married in 1861 to Martha, daughter of Ellen and Jacob Stalnaker. He studied in Richmond, practiced in Buckhannon a few years, then located near Elkwater, where he practiced until the time of his death.

Dr. Charles Rice, son of Rev. John and Susan (Denton) Rice, was born December 3, 1855. He was educated in the public schools and at the Fairmont Normal school. He received his medical education at the University of Maryland, where he graduated in 1884. He was married to Miss Georgie Brown of Louisville, Kentucky, May 9, 1888. He died of typhoid fever, October 14, 1888 From the time of his graduation until his death, Dr. Rice was engaged in the practice of his profession at Kerens, this county. During his short professional career he revealed a marked adaptability to his chosen profession and attained a success that gave promise of a useful and honorable career.

W. F. Snyder, M.D. was born in Charleston, Virginia, in 1859, son of David H. and Mary Snyder, was married to Isis, daughter of J. Harvey Woodford. He was educated at the Military Institute, Lexington, Virginia. After graduating from the medical department of the University of Maryland, he located at Huttonville, where he entered upon the practice of his profession in 1887. He received the Democratic nomination for House of Delegates in 1888, and died suddenly a few hours later of an affection of the heart. He had built up a large practice and was regarded as one of the foremost physicians of the country.

Dr. William B. Collett, son of Solomon and Edith Davisson Collet was born in 1832. Dr. Collett was perhaps, the first physician in Randolph County to receive a diploma from a medical school. When 23 years old in 1855, he graduated from the Winchester Medical College, a school then conducted by Dr. Hunter McGuire, who in later years became one of the noted surgeons of the country. After the war Dr. McGuire moved to Richmond, Virginia, and founded the College of Medicine. Dr. Collett was regarded as a very skillful and successful surgeon and performed operations before the days of asepsis and anaesthesia that would do credit to modern surgery. In 1885, he visited Brazil as a surgeon for a commercial company and contracted an illness which compelled him to return to his native country. However, he did not regain his health and died at Beverly in 1860.

Dr. John T. Huff practiced at Beverly, Huttonsville, and Valley Bend for several years in the eighties.

J. C. Irons, M.D., born in Monroe County, Virginia, 1853. He was educated in the public schools of Monroe County. Prior to studying medicine Dr. Irons taught school several terms. He graduated in medicine from the Central University of Louisville, Kentucky, in 1881. He has practiced his profession at Huttonsville and in Elkins and is at present physician for the Wildell Lumber Company at Wildell. He has been three times mayor of Elkins and was the first mayor of the city in 1890.

Dr. O. L. Perry, M.D. born in 1861, in Upshur County. He was educated in the public schools and graduated in medicine from the College of Physicians and Surgeons, Baltimore in 1891. He has practiced his profession at Belington and Elkins.

A. M. Fredlock, M.D. was born 1866, in Maryland; was educated in Roanoke College, Virginia, and State University at Morgantown. Dr. Fredlock took his degree in medicine from the University of Maryland. He was one of the first residents of the city of Elkins and was a member of the first city council. Dr. Fredlock is serving his fourth term as mayor of the city.

Perry Bosworth, M.D., son of G. W. and Mary (Currence) Bosworth, born in 1867. He was educated in the public schools. He graduated in medicine in 1892 from the Baltimore Medical College and has since practiced his profession at Huttonsville. He is also a licensed pharmacist.

J. L. Bosworth, M.D., son of G. W. and Mary (Currence) Bosworth was born in 1856. He was educated in the public schools, West Virginia College and graduated from the Fairmont Normal School in 1881. He graduated in medicine from the College of Physicians and Surgeons in Baltimore in 1889. He was health officer for Randolph County for several terms. Prior to studying medicine he was for seven years editor of the "Randolph Enterprise."

Dr. A. S. Bosworth, M.D., son of George W. and Mary (Currence) Bosworth, was born January 12, 1859. He was educated in the public schools and at the Fairmont Normal School, where he graduated in 1881 and was elected superintendent of the schools of Randolph County the same year. He studied law at the University of Virginia and has been admitted to practice in the Circuit and Supreme courts. He was eight years editor of Randolph Enterprise, and from 1884 to 1886 was in Nebraska where he was editor and owner of the Culbertson Sun and the Trenton Central. He graduated from the Baltimore Medical College in 1892 and has practiced at Beverly and Elkins. He is vice president of the State Medical Association and was elected delegate to the American Medical Association in 1910.

Dr. Thomas B. Crittenden was born in King and Queens County, Virginia, in 1862; was educated in the schools of that county and graduated from the medical department of Georgetown University, Georgetown, D. C. in 1895. Dr. Crittenden was attached to the clinical service of the Emergency Hospital for two years. Since 1897, he has been physician for the Parsons Pulp and Lumber Company at Horton.

Decatur Montony, M.D., was born in 1868, in Pendleton County. He was educated in common schools and at the Fairmont Normal School; graduated in medicine from the Baltimore Medical College in 1894. He has practiced his profession at Harmon since graduation.

C. H. Hall, M.D. was born at Boothsville, W. Va., in 1876. He was educated in the public schools and at the Fair-

mont Normal School. He graduated in medicine from the
University of Kentucky in 1904. Dr. Hall was a member of
the Elkins city council in 1912-15.

R. R. McIntosh, M.D. was born in Boston, Massachusetts
in 1875. He was educated in the Boston public schools. He
graduated in medicine from Tufts College in 1897. After taking his degree, Dr. McIntosh spent three months in Floaty
Hospital, Boston, one year in St. Johns Hospital, Lowell,
Mass., was two years in charge of eye clinic of Methodist
Hospital, Boston and has taken post graduate work in Eye
and Ear Hospital in New York City. Since 1908, Dr. Mc-
Intosh has been a specialist as occulist and aurist in Elkins.

William W. Golden, M.D. was born in Russia in 1866.
He was educated at Vilna and Bielostock. Dr. Golden gradu-
ated from the medical department of the University of the
City of New York in 1892. The same year he located in Elkins
and is surgeon of the Davis Memorial Hospital. He is an ex-
President of the State Medical Society and the State Board of
Health and is at present a member of the State Health Com-
mission.

S. G. Moore, A.B., M.D., was born in Barbour County in
1877. He received the degree of Bachelor of Arts from the
State University at Morgantown. Dr. Moore graduated from
the College of Physician and Surgeons in Baltimore in 1906,
and took a post graduate course in the Harvard Medical
School in 1914. He is Professor of Biology in the Davis-Elkins
College, Elkins, W. Va.

Humbolt Yokum, M.D., son of Dr. G. W. Yokum, was
born in 1860. He was educated in the public schools and at
the State University. In 1885 he graduated from the Jefferson Medical College, Philadelphia, Penna. He has been engaged in the practice of medicine at Beverly since his graduation. He has also been prominent in business circles and is
President of the Beverly Bank.

Dr. L. W. Talbott, son of William Woodford and Sarah
(Simon) Talbott was born in Barbour County in 1855. He
was educated in the public schools, West Virginia College
and Jefferson College. He graduated in medicine at the University of Maryland in 1883. Dr. Talbott took a post gradu-

ate course in New York City in 1894, and located in Elkins in 1896, where he has since practiced his profession.

William R. Dove, M.D. was born in Pendleton County in 1880. Dr. Dove was educated in the public schools and Normal School. Prior to studying medicine he was nine years a teacher. After graduating in medicine from the Medical College of Virginia at Richmond, in 1907, he located at Harmon, where he has since had a large and lucrative practice.

Dr. D. P. Buckey was born in 1871, son of Alpheus and Lizzie (Daniels) Buckey. Dr. Buckey's preliminary education was obtained in the Conference Seminary, Buckhannon and in the public schools. He graduated at the Baltimore Medical College in 1894 and entered upon the practice of medicine at Parsons. After remaining there about two years he located at Beverly, where he remained about two years and moved to Flemington, Taylor County, as surgeon for a mining company. After about two years' successful practice of his profession at Flemington he met an accidental death.

Dr. Stuckey practiced medicine at Helvetia in this county from 1872 to 1889, a period of seventeen years. He was a native of Switzerland and a graduate of the University of Berne. Before coming to America he was a student in a Paris hospital for one year. Dr. Stuckey had an extensive practice and his fame as a successful physician was not limited to the locality in which he practiced. He died in 1889 in the 72nd year of his age.

Otto W. Ladwig, M.D. was born at West Milford, W. Va., October 11, 1875. He was educated in the public schools and at the Fairmont Normal School, where he graduated in 1901. He taught school a number of years and was principal of one of the Clarksburg schools. Dr. Ladwig was graduated from the Louisville Medical College in 1905. He practiced for a short time in Harrison and Lewis counties and has been located at Evenwood, this county, since 1908.

Dr. G. C. Rodgers, son of Wm. G. and Rachel (Campbell) Rodgers, came to Randolph County in 1902. He was graduated from the University College of Medicine, Richmond, Va., in 1900. He has taken postgraduate courses in surgery in the hospitals of Philadelphia and has been surgeon at the City Hospital since 1907.

Dr. H. W. Daniels, son of Rev. Wm. P. and Minerva (McLean) Daniels, was educated in the public schools and at the Buckhannon Wesleyan College. He graduated in medicine at the Baltimore Medical College in 1894. He has been a member of the city council and health officer for the city of Elkins since 1905.

B. L. Liggett, M.D. was born in Braxton County, W. Va., in 1887. He was educated in the common schools and Wesleyan College at Buckhannon. He graduated at the Hanneman Medical College, Kansas City, Mo., in 1910 and in the medical department of the University of Maryland in 1914. Dr. Liggett was located at Fort Worth, Texas, three years and has practiced his profession at Mill Creek since 1914.

Thomas H. Chaney, M.D. was born in Marshall County, W. Va., November 21, 1871. He was educated in the West Virginia Conference Seminary, Buckhannon, W. Va. He graduated in medicine from the Starling Medical College, Columbus, Ohio, in 1896. He commenced practice at Littleton, W. Va. and has practiced at Montrose and Elkins.

Dentists.

Dr. David S. Strock, son of Jacob and Letitia Strock, was born April 16, 1871 in Champaign County, Ohio. Dr. Strock was educated in the public schools and at the Ohio Normal University. In 1899, he graduated from the Pennsylvania Dental College with the degree of D.D.S. Dr. Strock has been in active practice in Elkins for eleven years. Dr. Strock was married on April 23, 1895 to Edith Russell, daughter of Mahlon and Arabella Russell. Dr. and Mrs. Strock have one child, Richard Junior.

Dr. John U. Baker, son of Daniel Randolph and Margaret (Chenoweth) Baker, was born in 1879. He was educated at the Wesleyan College, Buckhannon. Dr. Baker married Lena Mae (Bedell) Schuyler. Phillip Schuyler, the ancestor of that family in America came from Amsterdam, Holland, and settled in New Amsterdam, New York, in 1683. Dr. Baker graduated from the Baltimore Dental College in 1906, since which time he has practiced his profession in Elkins. Dr. and Mrs. Baker have three children: Rosalind, Margaret Christina, and Daniel Randolph.

Dr. G. C. Baker, son of Eli and Margaret (Sexton) Baker was educated in the public schools and the Wesleyan College at Buckhannon, and was graduated from the Baltimore College of Dental Surgery in 1906. He practiced his profession at Gassaway from 1906 to 1908. He came to Elkins in 1909, since which date he has practiced dentistry in that city.

Dr. Nathaniel Barnard was born in Westernport, Maryland in 1887. He graduated from high school and attended the Davis and Elkins College at Elkins. He received the degree of D.D.S. from the University of Maryland in 1913. After practicing at Mill Creek for a short time he moved to Elkins where he has practiced about two years.

CHAPTER XIV.

PORTE CRAYON IN RANDOLPH.

"The rudiments of empire here
Are plastic yet and warm,
The chaos of a mighty world
Is rounding into form."

DAVID HUNTER STROTHER, author and artist, was born at Martinsburg, Va., September 26, 1816. He studied under Sam. F. B. Morse of New York and also spent five years as a student in Europe. From 1852 to 1861 he contributed to Harper's Magazine a series of illustrated articles chiefly on Virginia and the South, some of which appeared in book form under the title of "Blackwater and Virginia Illustrated." At the outbreak of the civil war he volunteered into the United States service and was appointed Captain, rising to Brigadier General in 1865. He served as Consul to Mexico from 1879 to 1885. He died in Charleston, W. Va., March 8, 1888. These sketches appeared in Harper's Magazine in 1852. Though often somewhat exaggerated, they reveal a people primitive in their habits and aspirations. This section, because of its mountainous isolation, long retained pioneer customs and characteristics. However, a half century and communication with the outside world by means of a railroad have wrought marvelous changes and Dry Fork district today rivals any other section of the county in all that goes to make up a moral, cultured and intelligent people.

Porte Crayon summarized the gratification of his visit to Dry Fork as follows: "It has been one of the supreme enjoyments of my life to wander among these wild communities, until I have become familiar with their occupations, instincts and aspirations as one 'to the manor born,' learning thereby to respect their unsophisticated manhood, and appreciate their simple virtues, and it has sometimes appeared to me there was a grace in the woodland blossoms, and a flavor in the crabbed fruit not to be found in the cultivated gardens of civilization."

The Country Store.

Adamson's Store.

Although Adamson's store was located at the mouth of Seneca in Pendleton County, it was for years the emporium for the section described in this chapter and the characters mentioned were mostly residents of Randolph. The incidents chronicled by Strothers, moreover, were so typical of the country store of an earlier period that we reproduce the narrative. Mr. Sylvester Rains, to whom reference is made, is spoken of by his former employer, Mr. George Adamson, who is now a resident of Elkins, as having been a faithful clerk and an honorable and upright gentleman. As the irony of fate would have it, Mr. Rains lived a life of single blessedness, heart whole and fancy free and has long since gone to his reward, an alien and stranger to the joys, charms and delights of "domestic bliss, the only source of paradise below that hath survived the fall."

"The junction of the North Fork Turnpike and the Pack Horse Road, across the Alleghanies from Beverly, has grown up a little settlement at this place, consisting of a half dozen families, with the conveniences of a store, postoffice, blacksmith shop, a schoolhouse, and I believe a meeting house and apple-jack distillery. There was no tavern or regular place of entertainment, but to atone for this deficiency, any of the householders were ready to take in travelers as a special favor.

"Having been recommended to Adamson, the proprietor of the merchantile establishment about a mile up the creek, we presented ourselves and were hospitably received. Here we dined and spent the afternoon lounging about the store and hooking a mess of trout from the Seneca. Adamson is an exotic, a Scotch Irishman, who had the reputation of being a shrewd and intelligent trader and a worthy and upright citizen. He has set up shop at this outpost to barter the knickknacks of civilization for the products of the mountains and to furnish clothes for one class of the natives in exchange for the coats which they strip from another class.

"The place retains many of the characteristics of those frontier trading posts, which we read of in the days when the United States had frontiers and they skinned the aboriginees as well as bears.

"All sorts of queer people congregated here, bringing in peltries, ginseng, venison, yarn stockings, maple sugar, homemade cloth, oats, corn, potatoes, butter and eggs to exchange for gay colored dry goods, crockery, tin and hardware, gunpowder, tobacco, snuff, infinitesimal packages of coffee, and corpulent jugs of whiskey. Some came on foot, others in sleds, most on horseback, and very few in wheeled vehicles, the country in general not being addicted to this mode of transportation. Adamson's fancy salesman is the model of a mountain beau, in his own conceit at least. Going to the desk to jot down some notes of our journey, I took up a scrap of paper with the following inscription legible, amidst a maze of inky smirks and flourishes: "Sylvanus Rains is my name and happy is the gal that gits me for a man." Thrice happy, Sylvester, may your delusions be perennial! They will help to keep you amiable and obliging, and enable the mountain belles to make better bargains in calicoes and ribbons. After this accidental insight I observed Sylvester more closely, and remarked that when a wrinkled dame, overladen with butter and eggs, or a sallow matron, encumbered with babies rode up, she was allowed to dismount as best she could, and might tumble off if she could do no better, but when a frisky lass, all bouncing and blooming, appeared coming up the lane, down went pen, yard stick and molasses jug and out rushed the gallant clerk all smiles and empressment. Although either Mahala Armentrout, Susie Mullenix, or Peg Teters could have jumped from the saddle, or meal bag, to the ground, without discommoding a flounce and after landing, shouldered Sylvester and carried him into the store, never-theless, he must drop everything, run out with a chair and hold the critter, carrying the basket in and then giving his roach, and shirt collar each a sly twig as he passed the fly-specked looking glass, take his stand behind the counter with, 'Well Miss Susan, what can I have the pleasure of show-ing you today?' Meanwhile Dame Wrinkle with her bundle stands waiting and grumbling. 'Take a seat on the tobacco box, I'll attend you presently, mum.'

"'Lookee here man; I can't stop here all day a foolin,' I can't, eh, I'm in a desput hurry, I am eh.'

"But here comes Mr. Adamson himself, and the impa-tient granny prefers to deal with him in person rather than wait for that fool feller that hain't no manners for old folks, but only for his likes. So she trucks off to the best advantage the contents of her basket and gets her measure of calico for her daughter's dress, two hats for her grandsons, a quarter of pound of coffee, not forgetting the complimentary paper of snuff—the invariable conclusion of all trades and pur-chases in these stores. Meanwhile Sylvester has denuded the shelves of gay prints, and the drawers of ribbon boxes. He and his fair customers, mutually inclining over the barrier of dry goods, continue to discuss business in a more quiet and rather indirect manner:

"'I say, Miss Susan, how's folks over on Dry Fork about these times?.'

" 'Well, all about our settlement is middlin' hearty, they are.'

" 'Have you been havin' any fun over there lately?'

" 'Ye--es indeed, we had a turrible good time at Zed. Kyle's last week, we had, eh. You see Zed had a wool pickin', he had, and all the gals and fellers was there, they was, and danced the holen joren night, we did.'

"Sylvester looked radiant at the thought and then with a sly leer asked in a lower tone, 'was Jess there?'

"Susan's face seemed to have caught the reflection from the box of pink ribbons which she was examining with sudden interest. 'Pshaw, Mr. Rains, what account was it to me if Jess was there? He mostly hunts with them Kyles and Armentrouts, he does, and I shouldn't wonder ef he mought have been there.'

" 'And he seen you home after the dance now didn't he?' whispered the clerk with a smart diplomatic wink.

" 'He done no sich thing' replied Susan, sharply, 'cause he only come as fur as the Fork with me and Marta and Dilly and Emily.'

" 'And I'll bet a new dress he carried you across.'

" 'And I'll take the dress jist now off this red and yaller piece, I will; for we all waded across, we did, eh, so we did.'

" 'Mr. Rains, Old Sam Bonner from over the mountain has just brought in a lot of bear skins. Go out and receive them. Miss Susan I can wait on you. Have you selected a dress yet?' "

Soldier White's.

Porte Crayon, in this chapter, narrates incidents and experiences of customs long since obsolete. Goose-picking or any form of labor which would be a tedious task for one person in that day, was interchanged and a frolic and a dance was the result. Soldier White, as well as most other characters referred to by Porte Crayon, have gone to their reward. Their lives were simple, moral and happy. The innocence and isolation of their primitive environment gave them a childish zest and appreciation of life that the modern man, striving

for the material rewards, in order to shine, dazzle and out-
strip his neighbor, can neither enjoy nor comprehend.

"At Soldier White's we found a regular two-storied log
house, containing half a dozen rooms, which serves as a place
of entertainment to drovers who come from below to sum-

SOLDIER WHITE.

mer their cattle on the Fork, and to the occasional traveler
who ventures to cross the wilderness by pack horse road from
Seneca to Beverly, the county seat of Randolph. Here is also
a tub mill, driven by a pretty stream of water, which has
been caught and utilized before being swallowed by the dry
river. This combination of circumstances makes Soldier
White's rather a notable place in the Dry Fork community,
and as the proprietor himself observed somewhat boastfully,
'ther's not a month passes but he sees a stranger of one sort
or another under his roof.' The soldier is personally a man

worthy of consideration. He is upward of sixty years old and for his peculiar opportunities for seeing the world, is more cosmopolitan in his speech and views than most of his neighbors. He wears shoes habitually, and his residence exhibits the grade of civilization pertaining to a pack horse road. His face, including his stack of hair, looks as if cast in bronze, while his square sinewy hands are of the type most frequently carved and painted by Michael Angelo. His tall, athletic figure is a model of strength and endurance. Its proportions are slightly modified at present, owing to an accident. About six weeks ago, at the saw mill, a log about three feet across the butt rolled over him, and flattened him out considerably; but he thinks he is drawing up to his natural shape again by degrees, and his ribs and backbone getting set back in their places. To assist Nature in her praisworthy efforts at reconstruction, he distends himself as much as possible by eating heartily, and greases his exterior with bear's fat.

"Having never been in the military service, he cannot explain how he got the sobriquet of 'Soldier,' but thinks it was simply a tribute to his youthful strength and activity, which were extraordinary. Being a justice of the peace for Randolph, he is now sometimes more properly addressed as Squire White, which title of dignity he prefers. The Squire has a partner who is worthy of him, and a daughter 'rising of sixteen' who assists in the house keeping.

"Martha White is entirely too pretty to be sketched as a type of the mountain maiden. A sparkling brunette, lithe and graceful as a fawn, she is also, from the habit of meeting strangers, more affable in her manners than most of her mountain cousins. On being asked if she understood cooking trout, she replied smartly, 'You'd better catch a mess first and try me,' indicating at the same time that there was good fishing just below the mill.

"The Major and myself took the hint, and soon hooked a pretty string of medium and small sized fish. There were, however, some magnates we saw moving about in the crystal water who could not be tempted by any bait we had to offer. They would glide out from beneath the cool shadows of the boulders, approach our traps with a certain majestic deliberation, sometimes even rubbing their noses against the hooks, then, as satisfied that it wasn't worth the risk, would retire contemptuously and let the minnows take a bite, tickled no doubt at seeing how rapidly the youngsters snapped and went up. While we were worrying with the sly old rogues, Martha came down armed with a hickory wand with a running noose of horse hair attached to the end. With an arch smile

Noosing Trout.

she requested us to hold off a while and let her try her hand. Creeping like a cat over the rocks, she marked a grand old voluptuary half dreaming among the shadows. Silently and gradually dropping her slender noose into the water, sh drew it toward him. As the enticing hair touched his fin, it suggested a slight suspicion of mischief, and he slowly retreated to a distance of about half of his length, then resuming his indifference again, lay balanced and immobile, very possibly felicitating himself on the superior wisdom which had enabled him to detect the gilt and feathered shams displayed to deceive the small fry of his race, and the lofty virtue which had taught him to resist the allurements of casual appetite. The next moment he was whipped from the water by an invisible noose of horse hair, and wriggling in Martha's cat-like clutches, and her plump cheeks pitted with rosy dimples. Quieting our applause with a gesture, she readjusted her trap, and presently lifted out another beauty, then another, and another, until she had captured four of the largest fish we had seen, one weighing two and a half pounds, and surpassing any we had taken with the hook. Having thus justified her own skill, she handed her angle to the Major, at the same time instructing him how to use it; but neither he nor I had the dainty glibness of hand to execute the trick successfully, and after several awkward failures each, we gave up and returned to the house. The trout at dinner were as brown as fritters, and verified another of the pretty maid's accomplishments.

"The afternoon was whiled away with smoking, sleeping, and discoursing with Squire White and his sprightly daughter. We were given to understand that if we could content ourselves to remain a couple of days we might participate in some fun at the house, as there was to be a goose-plucking, at which all the gay society of the Fork would be gathered. Mr. Rains, from Seneca, had sent word he would be over. Dilly Wyatt also would be there with her fiddle, and when she played it would set a cripple to dancing.

"And who was Dilly Wyatt?

"'Ye never heard of Dilley?' exclaimed the Squire, with an expression of gratified surprise as if he had discovered a defect in our education. 'She's our brag gal over here, she is, and strangers like to hear about her.'

"Then do tell us her story, to pass away the long evening.

"The Squire thrust his nervous square-cut fingers into the shock of iron wire which stood for his hair, and after a preliminary rustling and scratching proceeded to deliver the following narrative, which we will endeavor to translate into smoother English, at the risk of losing something of its original naivete and graphic point:

"Several years ago there was a young stranger from the lowlands who was in the habit of spending the greater part of the summer months roaming about the mountains. What brought him here was never clearly understood, nor could the limited fancies of the natives ever suggest a plausible motive for his frequent visits and long sojourning. Some supposed he might be a drover seeking a lost steer; others reckoned he was one of these 'inchimists' who could tell brass from gold, and was prospecting minerals; a third respectfully suggested that he must be an engineer locating a railroad—a nefarious contrivance to increase taxes and the price of land, which would scare all of the game out of the country. Shrewder gossips insinuated he was possibly a refugee from the oppressions of lowland law or society, whose vague terrors occasionally chilled the hearts of free-born mountaineers even in their most secluded retreats.

"But neither the stranger's appearance nor ways seemed to justify any of these surmises. He was a handsome youth, with a wild romantic eye and a contract of blonde hair falling over his shapely shoulders. Reticent of speech and shunning companionship, he seemed to take delight only in savage and solitary places. The hunters sometimes met him in the recesses of the forest, tearing through the laurel as if pursuing or pursued by some wild 'varmint.' Then he would lie for hours basking beside a sequestered brook, idly watching the gambols of the trout or the movements of the uncivilized creatures that came down to drink and prey upon each other. Again they would tell of his reckless activity in scaling frightful precipices, or how he stood upon the summit of inaccessible peaks looking down upon the eagles, always carrying rifle and haversack, he was so heedless of sport that he was never seen to bring in any game. With pencils and tablets in his pockets if he ever sketched or wrote, the world never heard of it. A worshiper of Nature, who sung no anthem to her praise, and laid no votive offering on her altars; an Alpine climber who kept no record of the nameless heights he scaled, or the lonely dangers he encountered, a romantic voluptuary, content to revel in beauty and sublimity without the courage or ambition to rehearse his emotions before a cynical and unappreciative world. A poet without verses, an artist without works, a dreamer, an idler, a genius, whose life was a bold defiance, or perhaps an unconscious protest against a society domineered by mercenary traders in stock; 'whose speech is of oxen' or of meaner speculators in stocks, whose voices are modulated by the rise and fall of gold. As time wore on he ceased to shun the friendly faces of the settlers, and was frequently seen warming himself at their hearths, sitting at their tables, and even sleeping in their beds. They were entertained with the novelty of his conversation, and amazed at the extent and variety of his conversation, while he found in their society gratification of his natural longings for human speech and presence without the risk of intrusion into the hallowed precincts of his ideal world.

"Dilly Wyatt was the only child of a widower, a stout herdsman and mighty hunter of the wild valley, whose cabin stood in one of the most savage and secluded passes. She was a tall, fine looking girl after the mountain pattern, beaming with health and good humor, and uncommonly smart in all the learning pertaining to her people. She could cook or keep house equal to any maid or wife on the Fork. She could shear a sheep, card and spin the wool, then knit a stocking or weave a gown with a promptness and skill that were beyond rivalry. Besides these feminine accomplishments, she could fish, shoot with a rifle, swim, or skin a bear, in a manner to challenge the supremacy of the other sex.

"Our wandering artist had frequently stopped at Old Wyatt's cabin, where, among other attractions, he found an ancient fiddle with which the proprietor had once amused his roistering youth. Being an expert on the instrument, he sometimes tuned it up and played for hours, to the great delight of father and daughter. When the men were gone Dilly took up the fiddle herself and being one of those who could turn a hand to any thing, she soon learned to play several airs upon it. Next time the visitor returned she surprised him with her new accomplishment, and he, perceiving that she had both taste and will to learn, undertook to initiate her regularly in the mysteries of the art. His time and teachings were not wasted, for she learned with surprising rapidity, and soon developed very decided talent.

"Thenceforth it might have been observed that the erratic stranger was less frequently heard of in the wilderness, and oftener seen in the vicinity of old Wyatt's sociable dwelling, while Dilly's acquaintances were annoyed with her increasing absent mindedness and continued humming of dancing tunes, both in and out of season. But it was natural enough, when wearied with his own lonesome ways, the teacher should find a solace in the company of so apt and willing a pupil, and that a mountain maiden, amidst her rude surroundings, should become enamored of her gentle and engaging art. Fortunately there were no meddlesome gossips at hand to suggest that it might be the artist instead of the art.

"One morning, after giving Dilly her musical instruction as usual, the artist stored his haversack with some cold victuals, and promising to return by evening, struck across the dry river and disappeared in the forest. The cottagers were so accustomed to his eccentric courses that his failure to appear at the appointed hour excited no surprise or uneasiness. Next day was stormy. A windy tempest swept the woods, and the rain came down like a water-spout. During the night that followed the storm swelled to a hurricane. Tree-tops were hurled through the murky air like thistle down, and the forest shrieked and howled for the downfall of the tallest chieftain. The Wyatts sat beside their lowly hearth glaring with pine knots, and occasionally enveloped in clouds of smoke and ashes, to which the father responded defiantly with counter-puffs from his root pipe, while Dilly concealed any vague uneasiness she might have felt behind her darling fiddle. Soon the old man removed his pipe, and pricking his ears as if to catch some special note of the tumultuous chahivari without, exclaimed, 'D'ye hear that, Dilly?'

"She answered, with a nervous start, 'What is it, daddy? Did you heary anybody?'

"He motioned silence, and her straining ears became presently aware of a low rushing sound distinguishable amidst the fitful voices of the tempest by its steadiness and continuity. As they listened there was a sudden swelling of the storm, followed by a crash so enormous and stunning that it seemed as if the whole magazine of thunder bolts had blown up at once. Old Wyatt started to his feet, staring wildly upward at the roof of his trembling cabin, while the daughter snatched a flaming brand and rushed out into the darkness. By the flash of her torch she saw near at hand a freshly upheaved wall of earth and roots higher than the chimney top, and stretching away across fences and cabbage patches lay the prostrate body of a mighty hemlock tree which had long overshadowed their humble dwelling.

" 'Come back gal,' cried the father, resuming his pipe and his stolidity at once. 'The Fork is up, and the big hemlock is down, so we might as well go to bed.'

"The second morning dawned through clouds and mists, which hung on hillsides and tree-tops like sloppy rags put out to dry. Æolus was quietly folding up his flaccid windbags, and Aquarius resting languidly on his empty watering pot, but the dry river was full from bank to bank, and careering like a mad bull. After breakfast the old man mounted his nag and rode away toward Soldier White's to gossip anent the storm and look after a grist he had carried there some days before. Dilly was left alone to tend her household affairs and nurse a vague uneasiness about her absent friend. The day passed wearily enough between spinning, fiddling, and strolling up and down the stream, vainly listening for some signal call, and straining her eyes into the depths of the opposite forest. Late in the afternoon she was startled by hearing a distant rifle shot, and hurrying up the stream a half mile or more she discerned through the midst the figure of a man emerging from the wood on the further shore. Flushed with the sight, she gave a ringing halloo which evidently struck the wanderer's ear, and was answered by a feebler shout, about like a cry for help. Then the figure tottered forward, sunk, and disappeared among boulders and thickets.

"Agitated with mingled hopes and fears, she repeated her calls again and again, awakening the echoes away up in the mountains, but no response from any living voice. Then, as if struck with a sudden thought, she hurried back to the house, and in a short time returned clad in a scanty linsey gown, bare armed and bare footed, with a stout package tied firmly on the top of her head. Her eyes sparkled, her lips compressed, and there was resolution expressed in every feature and in every movement. Scanning the savage torrent above and below, she hesitated for a few moments, as if instinctively calculating its force and speed, she nimbly descended to the stream, flung herself into the raging water. A few bold strokes brought her to the mid-current, which swept her away light as a feather in a whirlwind.

"The girl had evidently underrated the power of the stream, but she was a strong and confident swimmer, and in spite of the resistless downward sweep, continued to strike vigorously for the further shore, holding her head erect, as if intent on keeping her bundle dry at all hazards. Amidst the heaving and boiling of the mad current her downward course was so rapid that it was difficult to estimate her transverse progress; but as she approached a bend in the river, just at the head of a succession of falls, it might have been noted that the color forsook her cheek, and her efforts became more hurried and spasmodic. Suddenly, as if caught up in a water spout, she was heaved over a submerged boulder and dashed headlong into the foaming eddy below. For a moment she was lost to sight, then her head popped up through a bed of yellow froth, blinded and gasping. Clearing her eyes with a quick movement of her hand, she saw that the bend and current had helped her on her way, and she was almost in reach of shore. Another desperate effort and she succeeded in grasping a trailing root, by which she drew herself to land. Once more on firm footing she felt for the package on her head, and finding it still in place, hurried up the bank to search for the object of her solicitude.

"Nearly a quarter of a mile above her landing place she stumbled upon the body of a man lying prostrate among the bushes. Beside him was a rifle, dropped from the nerveless grasp; his clothes were drenched and torn in shreds; his upturned face, half hidden by the tangled hair and battered hat, was white and motionless as death. On the brave girl's face the dawning smile of recognition was suddenly quenched. With trembling hand she loosened the bundle from her head, and laying it on a rock, dropped on her knees beside the body.

A few moments after she started from the cold embrace with a countenance all radiant with joy, and quickly opened her precious package, displayed its contents on the sward—a cold corn pone partially soaked in muddy water, some greasy slices of fried venison, and a small flask of liquor.

"Dilly clapped her hands and laughed, 'Not dead yit, by a long sight, but only jist half starved. See what I've brung ye, my pretty boy!'

"But at the sight of the bread and meat the languid eyes closed again, as if in token of refusal. Then, tenderly encircling the youth's clammy head with her plump arm, she raised him to a half sitting posture, and in coaxing tones half whispered, 'Now this ye won't refuse, I'm sure.'

"Then followed the resonance of an osculatory smack, as his pallid lips met those of the devoted girl's brandy bottle. The timely stimulant assisted exhausted Nature across the narrow bridge which led from death to life. The patient opened his eyes, sat up alone, and consented to nibble a little at the corn bread and venison. In the meantime the indefatigable nurse had collected a heap of wood, and by means of the rifle kindled a blazing fire, and warmed a portion of the food to render it more savory and wholesome.

"Drink, food and fire had so far restored the wanderer that he was enabled to give a brief account of his absence. He had strolled many miles away toward the summit of the back-bone, where he was caught in the storm. Having eaten up his provisions, he undertook to return, fell from a ledge of rock and sprained his ankle, and thus crippled and half starved, he had spent two terrible days in endeavoring to drag himself back to the cabin. Now he required only shelter and rest; but the stream was still impassable, and from his sprained ankle and general exhaustion he was incapable of locomotion. To a city belle the situation might have appeared hopeless; but Dilly 'was not born in the woods to be scared by an owl.' In a marvelously short time, with moss and hemlock twigs she had made a bed which, under the circumstances, might have been esteemed luxurious. A canopy of evergreen boughs sheltered it from the sky, while a blazing fire dispelled unwholesome damps and diffused an air of cheerfulness around. The remnants of the meat and drink were placed beside it, and the hollowed surface of a convenient rock contained several gallons of fresh rain water to quench the invalid's thirst, if required. Regarding these arrangements with a smile of satisfaction, the mountain heroine cut short a grateful speech by ordering her patient to lie still and get a good night's sleep. 'By morning,' said she, 'the Fork will be down,

Goose-Plucking.

and dad'll fetch ye over to the house on his horse.' The stars were shining when she took leave, and walking some distance up the stream to find a longer sweep of unbroken current, she boldly took the water again, and reached the cabin in safety.

"Next morning the river bed was nearly dry, and by sunrise the invalid had been transferred to old Wyatt's cabin. He had slept profoundly, and was refreshed; but his ankle was fearfully swelled, and it took a fortnight's nursing to set him fairly on his feet again. When the time came for the stranger to leave he pressed a pretty sum of money into old Wyatt's hand, and thanked the daughter with a warmth and fullness of speech which ought to have been satisfactory; but there was at the same time a reserve and even stateliness of manner which rather wounded the warm-hearted girl. He went and returned no more."

" 'And did he go off and forget such a girl as that?' Exclaimed Dick indignantly. 'By thunder I'd have married her!' 'Very chivalric,' suggested the Major; 'but in your case that might be thought poor return for a heroic service.'

" 'Tomorrow she will be at the goose-plucking, and we will tarry to see the heroine, and dance to her music.'

"Next morning we were out early, trying to earn our breakfast before we ate. After breakfast while the materials for the frolic continued to arrive, I received a private invitation from Squire White to look in at the goose picking. As we slyly peeped between the logs of the barn the whole interior seemed to be a whirlwind of laughter, screeching, and flying feathers, so that it was hard to distinguish the pluckers from the plucked. Occasionally as the downy clouds subsided one might catch a momentary glimpse of groups of worthy of the antique scenes that may be carved and painted more elegantly and easily than described—and as such we commend them to the Praxitileses and Photogeneses of modern art; and for a more practical account of the subject we must refer our readers to those good old-fashioned folks who raise geese and sleep in feather beds.

"Dilly Wyatt at length arrived, carrying her fiddle in a muslin bag slung over her shoulders. She was a buxom lass with grand black eye and regular features; but we were disappointed in her appearance, as we usually are by the personal presence of famous people. Nevertheless our mountain heroine showed the ameliorating influences, in dress and manners, of her association with the Muses.

"After the midday dinner our party was swelled by a number of young bucks from the neighborhood, and the dancing commenced. The movements at first were rather shy and constrained, but a few rounds with the inspiring strains of Dilly's music warmed their blood and started the wheels of gayety to buzzing. We had all done our best in playing the agreeable to the ladies to avoid offending the jealous susceptibilities of their native beaux, and had nearly got through the afternoon without an accident.

"With his usual luck however, Cockney narrowly escaped getting us in a row. Delighted with the opportunity of showing off his strong points he had been exceedingly gay and prominent in the dance, but becoming wearied and disgusted with the succession of jigs, reels and square figures, he asked Miss Roy if she understood the round dances. That young lady signified her willingness to shake a foot to any tune that

The Dance.

could be started, and promptly took her place on the floor beside the gallant. Encircling her waist with his arm, Augustus politely requested the fiddler 'to please give us a polka.' The mystified musician was silent; and the equally mystified partner, red as a trout about the gills, delicately attempted to elude the embarassing embrace. He, entirely absorbed with the idea of electrifying the assembly with his graceful whirls, reiterated his call for a polka, mazourka, waltz or any round dance, and persisted in holding on to his retreating partner.

"At length a tall, iron-bound forester, who had been squirming with jealousy, forgot his hospitable politeness, and laying his heavy hand on Cockney's shoulder, exclaimed, 'Lookee here mister. Our gals won't stand huggin' on sich short acquaintance, they won't, eh.' Augustus was himself electrified, and the house buzzed with mingled laughter and indignation. The Major, prompt in all social engagements and emergencies, stepped forward and explained the situation. Cockney apologized to the lady and the company, and the big woodsman made amends for his rudeness by a grasp of the hand so friendly and penitent that it brought tears to the recipient's eyes."

Shooting Contest.

Shooting matches in which the prizes were usually turkeys, were frequent occurrences in the earlier history of the county. So much depended in those days on the skilful use of the rifle, not in the way of self-defense only, but in obtaining the necessities of life, also, that the skillful marksman was a hero in the community. Porte Crayon here relates his experience in a contest for markmanship with Tom Mullenix:

"Observing that Jess Teter had conceived an extravagant admiration for a neat little powder flask I carried, I took occasion to present it to him. In the fullness of his gratitude he took me aside, and in a whisper, informed me that he was the best rifle shot on the Fork. I had heard as much.

" 'Well, now, said he, wouldn't you like to learn the secret.'

" 'Then there is a secret?'

" 'Yes, I can learn it to you in a day, so that you can beat any of these fellers.'

"Jesse's proposition accorded so exactly with my humor that I eagerly accepted it. We got our guns, and privately slipped off together to the woods, where after exacting a promise not to reveal his trick, he proceded to put me through a course of instruction.

"Whether there was any virtue in his teaching, or whether the mountain air had cleared my eye and braced my nerves, it is true that from a very indifferent marksman I presently became very expert with my rifle and after driving the center three consecutive times at sixty yards, I expressed myself satisfied, and my tutor slapped me on the shoulder and said emphatically, 'You'll do.'

* * * * * * * * * * *

"After a most friendly leave taking, we mounted and rode down the valley toward Soldier White's. About two miles below we stopped at the cabin of Tom. Mullenix (commonly known as Hunter Tom.), hoping to have a chat with him on the subject of hunting in these mountains. He was barely civil but not at all communicative. He told us very frankly that he never missed killing game when he went out alone, but he never had any luck when these gentlemen hunters went along. They had too many patent fixings and talked too much. With his long flint-lock rifle, munitioned with an ounce of powder, and with from three to five bullets wrapped in greased buckskin patching, he could always kill more game than he could carry home. Some fellers pack so much ammunition and cold victuals that they broke down before they found any game, and couldn't hit anything if they happened to see it. For his part he couldn't see any sense in all these percussion traps. As the hunter made these disparaging remarks, he cast a contemptuous glance at my ornate German rifle, which being observed by my companion, drew a laugh at my expense.

" 'Mr. Mullenix,' said I, 'what do you value that bear skin at, which I see hanging upon the porch?"

"That skin,' replied Tom. 'mought be worth about four dollars over at Franklin.'

"Very well. Now I'll bet you five dollars in cash, against that bear skin that with this percussion grim-crack of mine, I can beat you shooting three best shots out of five, line measure, at any distance or in any way you may choose.

"Tom eyed me for a moment as he would probably have stared at a rabbit suddenly turning and trying to bite him. His astonishment presently resolved into a fit of contemptuous laughter; but as I had already put up my money in the Major's hand, and showed by my manner that I was in earnest. His cupidity got the better of his contempt.

" 'Well mister,' said he, taking down and proceeding to load his long gun. 'Hits not becoming of me to disappint a stranger in a little innocent sport, and if you kin beat me shootin', that bar skin's your'n!' and the hunter's face warmed with a smile of sinister benevolence.

" 'Laureate, said the Major, aside, 'I wouldn't give the churlish dog a chance to make five dollars so easily.'

"I answered, carelessly, there are always two sides to a question, and I've taken quite a fancy to that bear skin.

" 'Laureate,' whispered Dick, 'try to make a good chance shot, and if you beat him I'll give you my horse.'

"Dick's horse was a borrowed one, but his good-will was none the less appreciated. Meanwhile the preliminaries had been arranged—two best shots out of three, at sixty yards.

"The Major stepped off the distance and Dick placed the target against the tree. The mark was a circle of white paper about the size of an ancient half-dollar, tacked upon a blackened board. We were to shoot alternately, and tossed a copper for the first fire. The hunter won it, and took his position accordingly, observing as he did so, 'I reckon I'll have to shoot a little wild to give you a opening.'

"As Tom raised his rifle and leveled it at the mark all the slouchiness of his manner disappeared, and he settled into a pose of iron firmness. As his rifle cracked, the target fell forward on its face, and Dick ran at full speed, followed by the others at a more dignified pace, to verify the shot.

"The ball had cut the left edge of the paper with half its diameter. Mullinx chuckled. "There's a leetle wind," said he, 'and I forgot to allow for it; but ther's the opening I promised ye.'

"It was a good shot, however, and my friends looked blank enough as I took my stand. Their evident anxiety annoyed me, and for a moment a sense of responsibility unnerved me. Then I shut my eyes, recalled my lessons, and concentrated my mind on the work in hand. My shot parted, the target rattled and fell. The next moment Rattlebrain waved it triumphantly over his head, shouting, 'Centre!' It was impossible for Dick to be exact. It was not a centre shot, but the

whole ball was in the paper, beating Mullenix by half a diameter.

" 'Can you do that again?' whispered the major.

" 'I think I can do better.'

" 'Then we've got the rascal to a certainty,' said he, rubbing his hands with hopeful satisfaction.

"The gleam of benevolence had departed from Mullenix's
face, and he proceeded to load his piece with a precision quite
the reverse of his former half insolent carelessness.   He
waited for a lull in the almost imperceptible breeze, and when
he took aim the steadiness of his attitude was statuesque.

"Dick Rattlebrain looked as if he would burst during the
process, and the result of the hunter's shot did not relieve
his anxiety in the least.   The paper was perforated just beneath the central tack—so close that we wondered it had not
been knocked out.

"Tom looked vengefully benevolent again.

" 'I reckon, mister, I hain't left ye much of an opening
this time.'   He said this with a wicked chuckle.

"My friends looked grave again.   Dick desired to give
me some advice, but the Major restrained his zeal and persuaded him to keep quiet.

"On coming up for my second trial I had a more severe
struggle with my nervousness than at the first.   The opening was indeed a narrow one, and then my success had aroused
hopes which must not be disappointed.   I succeeded, however,
in attaining the requisite coolness, and fired.

"The board fell forward as usual.

"Dick Rattlebrain gave a convulsive start, and then step-
ping up to me said, 'By thunder, Larry, I haven't the heart
to look at it!'   But the Major presently approached with the
board in one hand and the paper in the other.   The tack was
gone, and there was a clean hole exactly through the center
of the mark.   Dick uttered a triumphant yell, and nearly suffo-
cated me in his rude embrace.

" 'Come Dick; having won, we must triumph like gentlemen.'

"Tom Mullenix eyed me like a basilisk.

" 'Well mister, the bar skin's your'n; you've won two, and

hit's not worth while to waste the third shot. Powder and lead is too scarce up here to waste on nothin'.'

"I sincerely sympathized with the mortified mountaineer; so that when he came formally to deliver the bear skin I politely attempted to decline it. But the flash of his eye and sternness of his manner quickly showed that I had made a mistake.

" 'Mister,' he said, 'I don't like any man to fool with me. The skin is fairly your'n and you must take it.'

A rousing swig from the Major's flask was more appreciated than my fanciful magnanimity, and we took leave with all due civility."

Killed a Wolf.

Porte Crayon here relates his experience in killing a wolf. His former rival in a shooting match, Hunter Tom Mullenix, showed feelings of umbrage and resentment by Porte Crayon's competition in the wolf industry. Crayon says:

"As I stood to gaze I saw something moving on a ledge thirty or forty feet above, and at length perceived two fiery eyes glaring downward, and my blood was stirred by a long-drawn savage howl.

"I again remembered Jesse's secret, and steadying my rifle against a hemlock tree, took aim and fired. With a brushing sound, followed by a crash, the body of a large wolf fell into the thicket nearly at my feet. Neither my shot nor the fall had quite killed the savage beast, which writhing and snarling in its death agony, bit frantically at its wounds, sticks, leaves and everything within its reach. Staining the rocks and moss with its life blood, its struggles gradually subsided, and at length, with a spasmodic shiver, it stretched itself out and died. Drawing my knife, I approached the body, and discovered that the creature was a female, and evidently had a young family somewhere up the cliff. But this was no time to be speculating about game, so I was contented to take the scalp as a trophy, and congratulating myself that I had probably broken up a whole family of robbers, proceeded to reload my piece.

"On the following morning, as had been agreed, we left Soldier White's and started down Dry Fork to visit Roy who lived at Red Creek and to seek such other sports and adventures as the country afforded. As we passed the mill we recognized several acquaintances among a group of mountaineers, and stopped to exchange civilities and take leave. The Major politely offered his flask and drinking cup which, notwithstanding the early hour, was honored duly as it passed from hand to hand with, 'well, here's good luck, men.' My quondam antagonist, Tom Mullenix, however, put aside the cup with a scowl and, to the surprise of everybody, retired sullenly into the mill. The bear skin I had won of him was thrown over my saddle, and it occurred to me that the sight of this trophy had again recalled the mortification of the shooting match. Anxious to leave good feeling behind us, I asked Jesse Hedrick to bring Tom out that we might drink and shake hands, burying all animosities before we parted.

"Jesse laughed at the suggestion of the shooting match and then looked grave.

" 'Hit's not that he minds; sure Tom's got too much sense for that. But he's mighty riled about somebody a killin' of his wolf, and he 'lows hit was one of you men as done hit, and he swears vengeance agin ye, he does.'

"At the mention of wolf I was electrified, and drawing Jesse aside, asked him earnestly if Tom had lost a pet wolf lately.

" 'Well not exactly that,' he replied, 'but ye see Tom makes his living pretty much by huntin', and there's a middlin' high bounty on wolf scalps; and so you see when he finds out where an old she has a den, instead of killin' of her he plays sharp and waits till she has young uns, and as they begin to come out and play around he kills them off and gits the premium on five or six scalps every season. So ye see when a feller finds the haunt of an old wolf he lays claim to her, and takes care of her, and she brings him a smart little income every year. And for any man to go and kill another man's wolf is a big spite, and a fightin' business, it is. And somebody killed Tom's wolf up here by the tunnel day before yesterday, they did; and he's dangerous mad about it, so he is.'

" 'And who does he blame?' I asked in breathless curiosity.

" 'Well,' said Jess, 'he lays it on that feller there—Mr. Rattlebrain—but he says he hain't sure of hit quite, or else there would a been trouble.'

"Now here were revelations and explanations and personal responsibilities which admitted of no shirking or hesitation.

"Taking Jesse by the arm, I entered the mill and cornered Mullenix so that he had to stand up and look me square in the face.

" 'Mullenix,' I said, 'somebody killed your wolf, I understand.'

" 'Yes, they did and took her scalp,' he replied grimly, 'the sneaking hounds, which is jest about equal to highway robbery; and durn him, I—I—'

" 'Well suppose the man who did it will tell you he meant no wrong, not being aware of your claim on the animal, and will give you up the scalp and a fair reimbursement for any further loss you may sustain in the matter?'

" 'Well, mister, that would look like the feller meant fair,' said Tom, 'and if he does that I'd bear him no grudge, I wouldn't.'

"I then handed Mullenix the scalp and put ten dollars into his hand, and ere he fairly recovered from his astonishment we mounted and rode off."

A Crowded House—Domestic Bliss.

The proverbial hospitality of an earlier period did not countenance the refusal of entertainment to any one. The rooms might be few and small, the table might be dearth of tempting viands, yet their all was shared with others with unstinted liberality. Porte Crayon herewith narrates amusing incidents of the entertainment of his party in houses of two rooms:

"As candles and kerosene lamps are reckoned among the

superfluities in these parts, we lit our cigars and pipes and repaired to the starlight of the front porch. Then bedtime was announced, and being ushered into the proprietor's chamber, a single bed of moderate dimensions was assigned for the accommodation of our party; we could arrange it to suit our convenience. 'As thick as three in a bed,' has become a by-word; four in a bed surpasses the limits of proberbial philosophy, and being naturally addicted to seclusion, I yielded my share of the couch and took the floor with a saddle for my pillow and a blanket for covering.

"Sleep, like a loving lass, needed but a brief wooing. Except in romances virtue is not always rewarded, and in spite of doctor's promises—fresh air, exercise, and a temperate supper—will not insure the coveted repose. Mine was interrupted by nightmare dreams of creeping through subteranean passages to escape from robbers, and finally plunging head foremost into an abyss of mud where I stuck, panting and suffocating. In my struggles I awoke, realizing the peculiar sensations which had doubtless suggested the dreams and which filled me with real alarm. There was a rumbling in my ear like the buzzing of a spinning wheel; my head and face were so hot and oppressively heavy that I could not rise from the saddle. Disengaging one hand from the blanket, I felt the upper side of my face and head covered with a squirming mass of soft, warm fur which, upon further exploration, developed into five kittens, cuddled in a loving heap and purring with contentment. I was far from satisfied with the arrangement and especially aggravated at having my rest disturbed, so I arose suddenly to a sitting posture, unceremoniously tumbling the happy family out of their bed. They clung together, mewing and striving to climb back to their comfortable position. In my wrath I seized one by the back of the neck and slung it vindictively at the bed occupied by the ancient couple. Considering the darkness, my aim was good, and the mauling missile struck the pillow with a rip which stopped the old man's snoring.

" 'Scat! scat! Wife, here's one of these darned kittens jumped on the bed.'

" 'Well, fling it out, can't ye!' she muttered impatiently.

Having found it in his fumbling, he dropped the animal quietly on the floor, whence it quietly trotted back to its fellows on my blanket. Meanwhile I directed another toward the same point.

" 'Scat! scat!' cried a shriller voice.

" 'You old fool, yev'e flung the nasty critter right in my face, ye hev now!' and giving the kitten a spiteful toss, she sent it over the bed where my three comrades lay. I heard a stifled snickering in that direction, and presently the shot was returned, flying with outspread claws, and tearing as it ricochetted across the coverlet. Then as the wrathful dame rose to grope for the offender, I let fly a plumper which carried away her nightcap.

By this time there was a general tumult of scatting, mauling, pounding on the wall, and calling for the lights. As the patriarch got up to unbar the door I pitched the rest of my amunition on his back, where the little wretches clung with all their claws.

" 'Wife! wife!' he exclaimed, as he danced and stumbled around the room, 'I believe the devil himself is got among these cats. Take 'em off! scat! take 'em off!'

"This suggestion of the presence of the evil one aroused the dame's superstitious fears, and redoubled her calls for Betsy and a light, declaring that she would not touch one of these creeters to save the old man's life.

"The door was at length unbarred and Betsy came to the rescue with a pine torch. The light revealed the stranger guests all sleeping the sleep of untroubled consciences, and the five tempest tossed kittens wandering around mewing in concert.

" 'Them's all our cat's kittens,' said Betsy, 'all white and tortoise shell; the pretty little dears.'

" 'Haint there a big black cat somewhere around?' asked the old woman in a tremulous voice. The favorite mask of the Arch Enemy was nowhere to be seen.

" 'Take 'em out! take 'em out!' growled the patriarch, 'the devilish things hev well nigh scratched the shirt off me back.'

"Betsy smiled audibly. 'Well daddy, ye've always achavin'

of somebody to scratch yer back, and maybe hits done ye good, haint hit?'

" 'Git out with you and yer cussed cats,' cried daddy. 'I'll drown the whole misbegotten litter tomorrow, so I will."

"At this direful threat Betsy snatched up her pets, and smothering her youthful felines in her apron, went out with the light, and there was peace until morning. At sunrise the door opened again, and a pleasant, manly voice called out, 'Men git up and rinse your countenances; folks is goin' to git up!'

"Breakfast went off very civilly, and on observing the clawed faces of the seniors I felt a twinge of remorse for my deeds of darkness. Dick Cockney and Betsy, however, had got up a triangular giggle which broke out at the slightest allusion to cats. At length the matron, with a severe and significant glance toward her junior guests, observing that she had never knowed them kittens to behave so before, and she had a suspicion there mought be wuss devils in the house than sich as come in the shape of black cats."

*   *   *   *   *   *   *   *   *   *   *

Another incident and experience of Porte Crayon's is here reproduced as explanatory of old time customs. Owing to their isolation, primitive ways were still in vogue at the time of Strother's visit:

"The cabin was so small and the flaring pine knots revealed such a multitude of good humored faces, that we began to entertain some doubts whether we should not have done better to have remained and enlivened the bachelor's lonely hall and helped him cook his solitary supper. Still everybody, young and old, seemed glad to see us, and there was no hint of crowding or inconvenience. The family consisted of husband and wife, four sons, two grown to manhood, and a daughter between ten and eleven years old, a grandson, and a hired boy. The other domestics were three hounds and a cat with kittens.

"The cabin was eighteen by fifteen feet in the clear, divided into two rooms. Although limited in space, all the sanitary arrangements in regard to ventilation had been especially attended to. The cabin built of logs, turkey pen fashion, were only partially chinked with moss and still more imperfectly tapestried with male and female garments, bunches of dried herbs, with deer and fox skins stretched on the outside. This open space did away with the necessity and expense of glass and had several other advantages, as we afterward ascertained. We could study the planets at ease, and tell the character of the weather without the inconvenience and awkwardness of getting up to look out of the window. Jess also informed us that of nights when he wasn't sleepy, he could chaw tobacco and spit through the cracks without siling the old man's floor, which was a pleasing indication of filial consideration. We experienced the fact that a family of nine persons with four guests could be comfortably fed, entertained ,and lodged in such apartments, but during our sojourn of several days, we never understood how it was done.

"The head of the family was a native of the mountains, about fifty years of age, with good features, light hair and complexion, broad chested and powerfully built. His countenance was amicable and his manner frank and obliging; consenting to everything that was said with the grace of a courtier, and closing every sentence with an echo and twang, a habit common to the whole region—ye-as; oh ye-as, I wouldn't wonder now, ah, ye-as indeed, as—at the same time confusing you with the universality of his admissions, coming back with opinions of his own which he sustained with true courtier like tenacity.

"Dick Rattlebrain attempted to pump him on the subject of politics, and to our astonishment, knew neither the names of the opposing political parties nor the names of their presidential candidates.

"'Oh,' exclaimed Dick somewhat airily, 'I see you do not read the papers up here.'

"'Mister, yer'e mistaken, I tell ye ye are, ah; we do git newspapers up here we do, ah. There was a feller fetched one up here last summer and my wife read it to me, she did, ah. Wife look if that newspaper haint in the chest under the head of the bed.'

"'No, it haint, for ye know ye lent it to Zed Kyle. Hits

three weeks today and he haint fetched it back yit. But he ort
to have fetched it back, he ort, fer I heerd of him having of hit
up to Teter's last Sunday a readin' of hit to them, and he
mought git hit tore, so he mought, and hit will be many a day
afore he sees another one.'

"Madam it seems can read, and the only book larnt member of the family. She showed me the only specimen of Guten-
berg's art, except the newspaper, in the settlement, an ex-
tremely aged and well thumbed copy of a Methodist hymn-
book. In this precious volume, she assured me, she had read
a hymn or two every Sunday for thirty years, and kept it up
regular for fear she mought forgit how.

"Having thus established a sort of literary fellowship with
the old woman, I seated myself on the chest while she was
getting dinner and continued the conversation. This was not
difficult for after the sluices were fairly opened, my share
consisted in listening. She opened on polemics and naming
all the religious sects and denominations she had ever heard
of, gave each a passing punch or two, quite intelligently delivered. As they all fared alike in her hands, I at length in-
quired what church she belonged to.

" 'None.'

"Here was something of an anomaly. A Christian of no
sect, pious on her own hook; unguided except by the traditions of her childhood and the greasy old hymn book, yet as
far as my observation extended her conscience and practice
were as near the purest Christian standard as if she had all
her life enjoyed the advantages of a five thousand dollar pew
under the ministry of the Rev. Dr. Plumpcushion in the great
and enlightened city of Hubadub. And so the worthy dame,
on hospitable deeds intent, brimming over with smiles and
amiability, went on baking, boiling and stewing and frying
her viands and her neighbors,until everything was done up
and dished up. By the time our meal was over, Jess then
announced that there was to be a yoking of a pair of steers
over at Nelson's that afternoon, and offered to introduce us to
the sport if we were so minded. Augustus requested him to
oblige us by describing the nature of the diversion.

" 'Oh,' said Jess, 'they have turrible times specially if

the steers happen to be fractious. They hook and kick and beller, run off and jump fences, and sometimes break a fel- ler's leg; they mostly cripple themselves or something else afore they are done with it. Then they hev a keg uv licker and there is some as thinks there is right smart fun in it.'

On the whole we thanked Jess for his civility and de- clined going. He did not appear much disappointed and care- lessly observed that he would slip over to Tom Mullenix's and proceed to put some extra touches on his toilet. Jess

A Flirtation.

was evidently the pet and pride of the family and it was amus- ing to observe the general solicitude in his toilet. The old woman picked at his waistcoat and shirt collar; the little sis- ter Jane tugged his coat tails straight; Job pulled the wrinkles out of his breeches legs, while the boy Harvey pulled them up again to make the red morocco boot tops show. Jess got off at length and soon after his father, excusing himself to us, followed in the same direction. About the middle of the after- noon the old man came back with an unusual solemn coun- tenance, shaking his head as he announced the doleful tidings:

"'Wa-al wife, they've had orful bad luck down to Mullenix's. That brindle cow of hisn had two desput fine calves this mornin', and they're both of 'em dead, yes, they are, ah. The old woman she just sot down and cried, she did, and Suze, she was afeard to milk her, ye-as she wuz-ah, till Jess he drew her up in a corner and hilt her by the horns, then Suze she milked her, she did, and they wuz two turrible fine calves, yes, indeed, they wuz, so they wuz, ah.

A Sylvan Golgotha.

A Sylvan Golgotha was Porte Crayon's apt and poetic description of a "deadening." The appellation applies today to the entire forested area of the country. The destruction of our forests has been an improvident blunder and an economic sin. Large areas have been denuded, suited neither for grazing nor agriculture. Porte Crayon gives this description of an "improvement" as it impresses his poetic imagination.

"Savage and lonely as are these vast tracts of primitive forests, there is yet a virgin freshness in their haunts; a variety and affluence of natural life which relieves their monotony and charms away their solitude. But on issuing from the pillared aisles and verdant archways of nature's temples into a mountain, 'improvement,' one feels as if approaching the lair of some obscure and horrible dragon. Death, desolation, and decay are visible on every hand. Skeleton forests, leafless, lifeless, weather-beaten, and fire blasted; heaps of withered branches, split rail fences, warped and rotten; in the midst of a space from whence every green thing and graceful form has been banished."

Trout Fishing.

"Thus am I teased, my vision pleased,
    Commingling sport with idle wishing,
Time moves as if his wheels were greased,
    While I half dreaming sit, half fishing.

Strothers and his party are now on Gandy, a tributary of the Dry Fork, and at that time teeming with the vermillion spotted, salmon tinted trout. The explosion of a stone beneath a fisherman's coffee pot and frying pan, while not on the program, when it does occur, adds zest and excitement to piscatorial pleasures and largely compensates for the loss sustained. In this case it supplied an interesting incident for Porte Crayon's pen and pencil. He gives the following narrative of the ludicrous incident:

"Pleased with the idea of cooking our own meal, we soon raised a fire whose smoke circled above the tree tops. I was detailed to make the coffee while the Major superintended the preparation of the fish. The Major discoursed with the assurance of an expert and sliced his middling with a certain affectation of nicety which impressed his assistants with the idea of his profound science. Laying a cut on one of the heating stones, he exclaimed, 'It is just in trim. Now boys bring your trout!' The scullions hastened to obey the order, each bearing a tin platter with a dozen selected fish. The chief picked them off with a forked stick and daintily arranged them side by side in the bubbling fat.

"A tall mountaineer, on an absurd little horse, who had stopped in the road to look at us, now approached with gaping countenance and outstretched neck, as if deeply interested in the proceedings.

" 'My friend, won't you 'light and take dinner with us?'

" 'No,' said the fellow bluntly, 'I don't want none of your victuals, but I'm cur'us to see ye cook them fish.'

" 'Just wait a moment then,' said the culinary director with a complacent wink, 'and you'll see something to surprise you.'

"At the word there was an explosion like that of a ten-pound shell; a fragment of a cooking stove whizzed by the spectator's head and a hot trout slapped him in the face. 'Heavens,' he shouted, 'I've seen enough!' and putting whip to his horse he started up the road at full speed. Then in quick succession there followed a whole battery of explosions, sending stones, fish, firebrands and tinware in every direction, some cutting through the branches of the adjacent trees, others sizzed into the stream; the horses broke loose and scampered away; the cook and attendants dodged behind trees or scampered after the horses. I deftly dropped behind a sycamore log, creeping under the opposite side where I remained during the bombardment. I had been watching the coffee, and after the firing ceased, ventured to raise my head above the log parapet to look after my charge. Its place was vacant, but I saw the pot overturned near the margin of the stream some twenty yards off.

"'Hello, Laureate! Are you all safe and do you think it's over?'

"I saw the Major peeping from behind a large maple with a queer expression as if he was undetermined whether to laugh or swear. As the fire was pretty well scattered and not a trace of our cooking visible, I thought we might leave cover and so we did.

"Searching land and water and branches of trees we recovered most of our tinware, dented and battered, but still available for all purposes. The actual loss consisted of two dozen trout and a boiler of coffee. Nevertheless, it behooved the Major to explain the result of his cooking arrangements, which he did in this wise: 'For the sake of shape and cleanliness we selected stones from the bed of the stream; they contained cells filled with water, which as they became heated, generated steam and blew everything to pieces.' Agustus plucked up:

"'I've seen flying fish in Barnum's museum, but scarcely expected to see flying fish in the mountains.'

"'Pepper away, pepper away, young gentlemen; but mind your work and don't let the dinner lag. Without accident you will find the receipt a good one.'

"Said I, 'It will appear in the cookery books as a "sauté" of trout with capers, furnished by an officer of the United States Artillery.'

"'Bravo, Laureate! excellent! Now,' said the annoyed chief, handing me a hot fish on a biscuit, 'put that under your ribs and then comment on my receipt.'

"The hot stones had been again heated and cooked our fish very quietly. Their flavor fully justified the Major's boasts, and we made a delightful meal, all the merrier because of the preliminary misadventure.

"Expanded by a dozen or more of his brownest specimens, a stiff toddy and an excellent cup of coffee, the culinary chief answered all our rallying good naturedly and even kept his temper when the Dry Forker stopped to gibe at us on his return.

" 'I say men, is them fish done yit?'

"Dick asked him how he liked the specimen he got.

" 'It was something hotter than I ginerally take 'em,' said he facetiously, 'and then instead of bread ye gim me a stone, which is agin scripter, haint hit?'

" 'Oh, you didn't quote scripture as you rode off a while ago,' rejoined Dick. 'But get down and we will give you the receipt for cooking the fish which you can teach to your wife.'

" 'Excuse me mister, my wife don't want none of your receipts for blowin' up things; she's got a way of her own which is more convenient.'

" 'Come neighbor, 'light and be sociable,' said the Major, holding up his flask in an insinuating manner.

" 'Now that's the kind of talk I understand,' said the native, dismounting and joining our party. 'Gentlemen, here's luck!' and when the drink was swallowed he seated himself upon the log and laughed long and loud. 'Well for all the world I'd like to know what was in them devlish stones.'

"The Major explained everything to his satisfaction, in return for which he told us his name was Roy. We engaged to visit him and said he, as he took leave, 'I'll show you how to cook 'em without blowin' your head off.' "

Poetic Pleasure.

Anyone who cast a line in "Gandy's amber waters" a half of a century ago will appreciate this stanza of Strother's:

> "On an afternoon in blooming June,
> I sit by Gandy's amber water
> 'Mid vernal bowers and scented flowers,
> And trout in plenty to be caught there.

Rhetorical Dry Fork.

Here is a poetic description of Dry Fork by Porte Crayon that merits preservation:

"Brawling brooks come tumbling down from the wooded hills, full of noisy confidence, like provincial capitalists rushing into Wall Street to find themselves 'sucked up' ere they can find a puddle deep enough to float a trout. Thoughtless little cascades, tripping and skipping through thorny bowers, jumping down from moss clad ledges, and are lost before they reach the channel. So they come, one after another, like joyous children with their dimpled faces and tinkling voices, sinking to death and silence in this cruel sepulchre. Oh remorseless grave, to whose dark prison the loveliness, the music, and the glories of earth are ever hastening, when shall thy ravening cease, or when thy mysteries be revealed?

"At certain points, by placing the ear close to the loose stones which form the river's bed, we may hear or imagine we hear, the whispering and moaning of the lost waters deep down below, as if the ogre stream was dragging its innocent captives through subterranean passages to some deeper, darker prison. Then again, the Dry Fork is not always a valley of dry bones, for sometimes during the season of melting snows or after one of those diluvial thunder showers common in this region, the silent, grinning skeleton awakens to life and comes down roaring and foaming like a maniac broke loose. For a day or two the stream is dangerous and impassable, then sinks again into its deathlike trance."

CHAPTER XV.

MISCELLANEOUS.

Trial by Fist and Skull.

IN the earlier history of the county the delays and intricacies of the law were not always invoked to settle disputes of title to land and other property. Near the Old Brick Church in Huttonsville District, James Warwick built a cabin and made a clearing, by virtue of which he claimed the contiguous bottom. John and William White claimed the land also. The White brothers proposed to settle the title by a resort to a fight, fist and skull. Mr. Warwick fearing the result traded lands with Andrew Crouch, who was to clear his title by accepting the challenge of the other claimants. Mr. Crouch met and vanquished William White who accepted the result with satisfaction and Mr. White and Mr. Crouch became close friends. John White was killed in the battle of Point Pleasant and William White fell a victim to Indian savagery in what is now Upshur County.

Major Andrew Crouch.

Price's History of Pocahontas County records the following interesting reminiscences of Major Andrew Crouch:

"In a visit to Major Andrew Crouch May, 1857, this aged man related a reminiscence of his boyhood.

"When he was six years old his father took him to the corn field and while the father worked the little boy sat on the fence. One of his uncles came up in great haste, bringing the news that Lewis Canan (Kinnan) and three children had just been killed by the Indians. The Crouches hurried their families to the home of James Warwick, not far from where the Old Brick Church stood. In their hurry the Crouch broth-

ers and Warwick seized their guns to go to help the families
exposed to the Indians farther up the river; they neglected to
barricade the fort, and so the little boy and the two little girls
went out to the branch. While the little boy was washing
the blood from his face, caused by his nose bleeding, the little
girls became frightened and without saying anything, ran
back into the fort and left him alone. When his bleeding
stopped he went back and found the fort barricaded. The
Crouch brothers had been met by some persons from the lower
fort, took them along, and so their wives and children were
left to themselves at Warwick's to make the best they could
of a perilous situation.

"When the boy, Andrew Crouch, came to the fort, he
heard his aunt in a loud voice giving orders as if there was
quite a number of men in the fort, when in fact the force consisted of three white women and one colored man and wife
and some little children. An Indian climbed to the roof of the
fort buildings after night and set it on fire. The colored man
put it out. Then the stable was fired. The black man said
they should not burn the horse. He went out and carefully
approached the place. Seeing an Indian by the light he shot
at him and let the horse out and safely returned to the fort.
He dared the Indians to come on and as there seemed to be
but two or three that showed themselves it seems they were
not disposed to storm the loud but little garrison.

"When the barn burned down and became dark the colored woman insisted on leaving the fort and giving the alarm
farther down. She was allowed to do so and the next day
the men came up and moved all farther down. Then the
little boy and eight of the others went to bury the dead, Lewis
Kinnan and the three children. He says no one wept nor
did any feel afraid while the funeral was going on.

"After the burial the men seeing no signs of Indians believed they had withdrawn and so they disbanded. But late
in the evening an Indian killed Frank Riffle near where the
Brick Church stood and burned two houses not far away belonging to James Lackey. Major Crouch remembers seeing
Lackey not long after the battle of Point Pleasant. He could
show the rock on which Lackey sat and sung a war song,

then very popular among the mountaineers, in commemoration of the battle of Point Pleasant, that eventful struggle.

"In subsequent years Mr. Warwick moved to Ohio and rewarded his faithful negro with his freedom for his gallantry in saving the fort and the property. This Mr. Warwick was the ancestor of the Ohio Congressman of that name who, represented McKinley's district a few years ago."

Lackey's war song was as follows:

Let us mind the tenth day of October,
Seventy four, which caused woe,
The Indian savages did cover
The pleasant banks of the Ohio.

The battle beginning in the morning,
Throughout the day it lasted sore
Until the evening shades were turning down
Upon the banks of the Ohio.

Judgment proceeds to execution,
Let fame through all ages go,
Our heroes fought with resolution
Upon the banks of the Ohio.

Seven score lay dead and wounded
Of champions that did face the foe,
By which the heathen were confounded
Upon the banks of the Ohio.

Elk Horns Found.

In 1913, Chas. Collett discovered Elk horns in a cave or sink on the Pritt farm, at the head of Files Creek, that measured eight feet from tip to tip. The horns and the skeleton of the animal were in a good state of preservation. The sink was about twenty feet deep and its sides almost perpendicular. The animal probably fell into the cave and perished from the fall or starvation.

The Formation of Randolph County.

Randolph County was formed from Harrison by act of the Virginia Assembly, October, 1786. The following is a copy of the act:

I. BE IT ENACTED BY THE GENERAL ASSEMBLY, That from and after the first day of May one thousand

seven hundred and eighty seven, the county of Harrison shall
be divided into two distinct counties, that is to say, so much
of the said county lying on the southeast of the following
lines, beginning at the mouth of Sandy Creek, thence up Tyger's Valley to mouth of Buchanan river, thence up the said
river including all the waters thereof to the Greenbrier line,
shall be one distinct county, and called and known by the name
of Randolph and the residue of said county shall retain the
name of Harrison. A court for the said county of Randolph,
shall be held by the justices thereof on the fourth Monday
in every month after the said division shall take place, in such
manner as is provided by law for other counties and shall be
by their commissioners directed. The justices to be named
in the commission of the peace for the said county of Randolph
shall meet at the house of Benjamin Wilson, in Tyger's Valley, in the said county, upon the first court day, after the said
division shall take place, and having taken the oath of office
to, and taken bond of the sheriff, according to law, proceed to
appoint and qualify a clerk, and fix upon a place for holding
courts in said county, at or as near the center thereof as the
situation and convenience will admit of; and thenceforth the
said court shall proceed to erect the necessary public buildings at such place, and until such buildings be completed to
appoint any place for holding courts as they may think proper.
Provided always, That the appointment of a place for holding
courts, and of a clerk, shall not be made unless a majority of
the justices of said county be present, where such, majority
shall have been prevented from attending by bad weather, or
their being at the time out of the county, in such case the
appointment shall be postponed until some court day when
a majority shall be present. The Governor with the advice of
the council, shall appoint a person to be first sheriff of the
said county, who shall continue in office during the term, and
upon the same conditions, as is by law appointed for other
sheriffs. It shall be lawful for the sheriff of the said county of
Harrison to collect and make distress for any public dues or
office fees, which shall remain unpaid by the inhabitants thereof at the time such division shall take place, and shall be ac-

countable for the same in like manner as if this act had not been made. The court of the said county of Harrison shall have jurisdiction of all actions and suits in law or equity, depending before them at the time of said division, and shall try and determine the same, issue, process, and award execution thereon.

II. AND BE IT FURTHER ENACTED, That the court of the said county of Harrison, shall account for and pay to the said county of Randolph, all such sums of money as shall or may be paid by the inhabitants of the said county of Randolph, toward defraying the expense of erecting a court house and other public buildings in the said county of Harrison. In all elections of a senator, the said county of Randolph, shall be of the same district with the said county of Harrison.

The Whiskey Insurrection.

In the year of 1794, there occurred in the Monongalia Valley and adjacent territory, a series of acts in resistance to the Federal Revenue Laws, known in history as the "Whiskey Insurrection." Upon the recommendation of Alexander Hamilton, Secretary of the Treasury, Congress passed an Act, taking effect June 30, 1791, that there should be paid on every gallon of spirits distilled in the United States, duties ranging from 9 to 25 cents. There was great dissatisfaction with this provision and Western Pennsylvania determined to resist its enforcement, and endeavored to secure the co-operation of Monongalia, Ohio, Harrison, and Randolph counties. This conflict between government officials and the distillers has found expression in violence and bloodshed in the mountain districts of the Southern States for more than a century. The incident is of historical interest as it was the first test of the efficiency of the general government in dealing with the opposition to the enforcement of Federal laws as well as indicating the trend of public sentiment toward the nullification of such laws by sections and states.

Governor Lee, of Virginia, sent a circular letter to Hon. Thomas Wilson of Morgantown. The following reply was borne to the Governor by an express rider. William McCleary or McCreery was the first prosecuting attorney of Randolph County and married Barbara, daughter of Michael See.

Colonel McCreery's letter to Governor Lee was as follows:

Morgan Town, Va.
28th of Aug. 1794.

Sirs:

Your express arrived here today with sundry letters addressed to the care of Thomas Wilson, who happened not to be at home; thinking it right (in this alarming time) I received the papers & Passed a receipt for them. Mr. Wilson will be at home tomorrow & no doubt will send them instantly forward to their address.

We are all in this, Harrison & Randolph counties in Peace & also Ohio with some exceptions; a state of neutrality is all we are able to support, and indeed, we are in this town much threatened now for lying still by our Powerful neighbors. However I trust we will support it until the Government takes steps to bring aboutPeace—the Commissioners who attended at Pittsburg, by order of the President of the United States, and also by the order of the Governor of Pennsylvania, but nothing has yet transpired that can be relied upon; a Committee of 12 men from the insurgents met them, and it is reported that no terms but the repeal of the Excise Law will be accepted by the People—however this is only report. I am in heast Sir.

Your Excellency's Obedient Servant,
William McCreery.

Mr. McCreery had become a citizen of Monongalia several years previous to this incident.

Randolph Representatives in the Assembly of Virginia, 1782-1865.

Below are given the names of the Representatives, Delegates and Senators from Randolph County in the General Assembly of Virginia from 1782 to 1865, a period of eighty-three years. The senatorial and delegate districts were often changed and the name is given of the Delegate or Senator of the district of which Randolph was a part. This, also, applies to the representatives from Monongalia at the time the present territory of Randolph formed a part of that county.

Senators.

Thomas Wilson 1793
John Haymond 1798
Thomas Wilson 1803
Phillip Dodridge 1806
James Pindall 1811
Noah Zane 1814
Geo. I. Davisson 1818
Edwin S. Duncan 1822
Chas. S. Morgan 1826
John J. Allen 1830
Chas. S. Morgan 1831
Richard Watts 1833
Francis Billingsley 1836
William J. Willey 1839
John S. Carlisle 1847
Albert G. Reger 1852
Lewis Steenrod 1854
Albert G. Reger 1856
John Brannon 1858

Delegates from District Including Randolph.

Benjamin Wilson 1782
Geo. Jackson 1786
Johnathan Parsons 1788
Johnathan Parsons and Cornelius Bogard 1789
Cornelius Bogard and Abraham Claypoole 1790
John Haddan and Cornelius Bogard 1792
John Haddan and Abraham Claypoole 1793
Robert Green and Cornelius Bogard 1795
Robert Green and John Chenoweth 1796
Adam See and John Haddan 1798
William B. Wilson and John Haddan 1799

Adam See and William B. Wilson 1801
John Haddan and William B. Wilson 1803
John Haddan and Mathew Whitman 1804
William Wilson and William Ball 1805
William Wilson and Jacob Kittle 1806
William Marteney and Nicholas Gibson 1807
Adam See and William Marteney 1810
William Marteney and James Booth 1811
Edwin S. Duncan and William Marteney 1813
John M. Hart and William Marteney 1814
Adam See and William Marteney 1815
Adam See and William Daniels 1816
Isaac Booth and William Marteney 1817
Samuel Ball and Isaac Booth 1820
Daniel Hart and William Marteney 1821
Isaac Booth and William Marteney 1822
Isaac Booth and Adam See 1823
William Daniels and William Marteney 1824
Robert Crum and William Marteney 1826
William Daniels and Isaac Booth 1827
Joseph Hart and William Daniels 1828
Benjamin Dolbear and Adam Myers 1829
Joseph Hart and Isaac Booth 1830
Joseph Hart 1831
Isaac Booth 1833
William Marteney 1835
William C. Haymond 1837
Henry Sturms 1838
Samuel Elliott 1841
Henry Sturms 1843
Washington J. Long 1846
Henry Sturms 1847
David Goff 1849
Chas. S. Hall 1850
Henry Sturms 1851
John Taylor 1852
John Phares 1854
Dr. Squire Bosworth 1856
Jacob Conrad 1858

Samuel Crane 1860
B. W. Crawford 1864

John and Benjamin Wilson represented Randolph County in the Constitutional Convention of 1788.

Adam See represented Randolph County in the Constitutional Convention of 1830.

John N. Hughes was a delegate from Randolph to the Constitutional Convention which met at Richmond, Va., in 1861. He was succeeded by Jacob W. Marshall, after his death on the Rich Mountain battle field.

Josiah Simmons represented Randolph County in the Constitutional Convention which convened at Wheeling, November 26, 1861. This was the convention to form a constitution for the new state.

First Auditor of West Virginia from Randolph.

Joseph Hart, Milton Hart and W. J. Drummond were the delegates from Randolph to the first State Convention of Union men, held at Parkersburg, W. Va., May 6, 1863. Samuel Crane, of Randolph County, A. I. Boreman, of Wood County, and Peter VanWinkle, also of Wood, were presented to the convention by their friends for the nomination for Governor. No nomination was made on first ballot as neither aspirant received a majority of the votes cast. Before the second ballot was taken, Mr. Crane withdrew his name and Mr. Boreman was nominated. Mr. Crane was then unanimously nominated for State Auditor.

Samuel Crane, the first Auditor of West Virginia was born in Richmond, Va. When a mere boy he moved to Tucker County, where he grew to manhood. He married a lady near Richmond, Va., and moved to Randolph County. He practiced law at Beverly until the breaking out of the Civil War, when he became active in politics. His wife died in Wheeling in 1863 and in 1866 he moved to Missouri to assume the management of the family and property of a deceased brother. Soon after going to Missouri he entered the ministry of the Methodist Episcopal church.

The Vote of Randolph for State Capitol.

On the first Tuesday in August, 1877, there was held throughout the state an election on the question of the permanent location of the state capitol. The places voted for were Martinsburg, Clarksburg and Charleston. In that contest Randolph cast 859 votes for Clarksburg, 31 for Charleston and 2 for Martinsburg. The vote of the state was: Charleston, 41,243; Clarksburg, 29,942, and Martinsburg, 8,046.

Elections.

The vote of Randolph County, March 26, 1863, to accept or reject the amended constitution of the new state was as follows: For ratification 167, Against ratification 13.

In the election for state officials held May 22, 1863, Randolph County cast 78 votes for F. H. Pierpoint for Governor, 76 for Daniel Posely for Lieutenant Governor, and 65 votes for James S. Wheat for Attorney General.

Members of the Legislature.

The following persons have represented Randolph County in the Legislature since the formation of the state:

Cyrus Kittle	1863
Jesse F. Phares	1865
Chas. W. Burke	1867
James W. Dunington	1868
John A. Hutton	1869
Lemuel Chenoweth	1871
John A. Hutton	1872
John Taylor	1873
Elihu Hutton	1877
C. J. P. Cresap	1881
A. B. Parsons	1883
Harmon Snyder	1885
J. F. Harding	1887
W. L. Kee	1889

J. B. Finley 1891
G. H. Daniels 1893
J. F. Harding 1895
T. P. R. Brown 1897
J. A. Cunningham 1899
W. G. Wilson 1901
Lew Greynolds 1903
Warwick Hutton 1905
J. F. Strader 1907
James W. Weir 1909
John T. Davis 1911
E. D. Talbott 1913
James W. Weir 1915

In the second Constitutional Convention held at Charleston in 1872, J. F. Harding was a delegate from Randolph and Tucker.

Beverly Threatened to Secede.

Prior to the adoption of the constitution of 1851, none but freeholders could participate in the elective franchise in Virginia. All offices were appointive except members of the Legislature, overseers of the poor and town trustees. It was claimed that the territory west of the mountains received very unfair treatment in the distribution of power. The proposed constitution of 1830 gave one hundred and three members of the House of Delegates to the counties east of the mountains and thirty-one to the territory west of them. Randolph was much opposed to the new constitution and a public meeting was held at Beverly, March 10, 1830. In the discussion of the merits of the proposed constitution at that meeting, it was stated that in one company of seventy-four soldiers from a county of Virginia in the war of 1812, only two had the right to vote. The Beverly mass-meeting adopted the following resolution:

Resolved, That we would sooner commit to the flames

the new constitution and vote for a division of the state than
to vote for its adoption.

The opposition west of the mountains availed nothing and
the constitution was ratified by a vote of 26,055 for and 15,563
against. However, the opposition of the people resulted twenty years later in the adoption of the constitution of 1851, which
granted the right of suffrage to all white males of the state
of more than 21 years of age, and made most offices elective
instead of appointive.

Fined Four Hundred Pounds of Tobacco.

The first superior court for the territory west of the
Alleghenies, under the Act of the Virginia Assembly of 1788,
was to be held at Morgantown, May 4, 1789. This district
embraced Randolph, Ohio, Harrison, and Monongalia Counties. No court was held on that date owing to the attendance
of an insufficient number of grand jurors. Robert Maxwell,
Cornelius Bogard, Peter Cassedy, Edward Jackson, and
George Jackson had been summoned from Randolph but failed
to attend. The court fined each four hundred pounds of tobacco. However, at the September term of the court these
fines were remitted.

Tory Camp Run.

Big and Little Tory Camp Runs are the only two objects
in Randolph that perpetuate memories of the Revolution. Little Tory Camp Run is a tributary of the Dry Fork on the east
side about a mile above the town of Harman. Big Tory Camp
Run is a tributary of the same stream on the same side about
two miles farther south and a short distance below the village
of Job.

Tory was a term that designated one who favored the
mother country. The revolutionist was called a Whig. The
feeling between these two classes of citizens was very bitter
during and for many years subsequent to the Revolution.
Midnight raids of neighbor against neighbor in which murder
and arson were the objects sought were frequent occurrences

in communities in which there was a division of sentiment.

Virginia enacted drastic laws against the Tories. Many left the country and sought protection under the flag of Great Brittain. A number from the counties of Hardy, Hampshire and Pendleton entered the wilderness and established camps in the eastern part of Randolph. A few years ago evidences of their encampments were still visible.

The First Settlement on Lower Middle Mountain.

The first man to make settlement on the lower Middle Mountain, below the Seneca Road, was Jacob W. Car. In 1874, he married Mary Ann Kerens and with his bride, for better or worse, to carve out their fortunes from the virgin forests, located many miles from human habitation. However, the fates favored their adventurous spirits and they have a large landed estate to transmit to their children in a community of churches, schools, stores and railroads. Twelve children have blessed their union, all living except one son, French, who died in his fifteenth year. Children living: James H., Albert L., Asa Martin, Enos, Jacob, Job, John, Hulda Jane, Barbara E., and Eliza Jane.

Neighbors in Pendleton and Randolph.

The ancestors of several prominent families in Randolph were friends and neighbors in Pendleton. The Caplingers and Harpers who were pioneers in Randolph were close neighbors in Pendleton before locating in this county. These two families have been on terms of neighborly intimacy in Randolph for a century. The same can be said of the Wards, the Colletts and the Phareses. Representatives of these families were constables appointed by the Governor in the organization of Pendleton in 1787. They were Gabriel Collett, Johnson Phares and William Ward.

Abraham Springstone.

Springstone Run, emptying into Leading Creek about a

mile northwest of Kerenes, is supposed to have received its
name from the fact that it has its source in the mountains,
where the springs flow from stony beds. However, this supposition is erroneous as it was named for Abraham Springstone, who settled on its banks in the pioneer period. Little
is known of his antecedents or decendants. He married Mary,
daughter of William Innis, in 1797.

Imprisonment for Debt.

Imprisonment for debt was a legal barbarity in vogue
during the earlier years of the history of Randolph. The
court records ran as follows:

Thereupon came A. B. and undertook for the said defendant in case he be cast in this suit, he shall pay and sat-
isfy the condemnation of the court, or render his body to
prison in execution for the same, or that he, the said A. B.
would do it for him.

Trustees of Moorefield.

Moses Hutton, Johnathan Heath and Geo. Rennock were
the trustees of the town of Moorefield in 1777. Moses Hutton
was, perhaps, the son of Abraham, who was the first of the
Hutton family to come to America. Geo. Rennix was sheriff
of Randolph in 1808 and captain of militia in 1798. Whether
it was the same Geo. Rennix is not known. Ashael Heath
was sheriff of Randolph in 1803 and lieutenant of militia in
1799. The name Rennock has been changed to Renix.

Early Church History.

In 1748, at Frederick, Md., a log church was built by the
settlers who were German reformers. Among the members of
this church were names of families identified with the settlement of Randolph County: Lingenfelders, Buckeys, Kuntzs,
Witmans, now Whitman and Weiss, now Weese.

A Lutheran church was built at Monocacy, Md., in 1747.
Among the members of this congregation were the Ebberts,

Jenkins, Myers, and Conradts, afterward spelled Conrad; Poes, Whites, Wilhides, Hedges, Wiers. William White moved from Monocacy, Md., to the Shenandoah Valley in 1734. Probably his decendants settled in the valley in the vicinity of Hadden's Fort.

Elkins Weather Bureau.

This station was established January 1, 1899. Albert Ashenberger was in charge from that date until October 31, 1903. Louis Dorman succeeded him and was in charge until June 1, 1911, when he was succeeded by Harry M. Howell, who remained in charge until November, 1914, when upon his own request he was transferred to the Philadelphia station and later to Washington, D. C. Mr. H. H. Jones, of Tennessee, has been in charge of the station since the transfer of Mr. Howell. Mr. Jones is ably assisted by Jesse Robinson, a Randolph County young man. Mr. Howell commenced as an assistant to Mr. Dorman and his promotion has been rapid. Besides his position as chief of the Elkins bureau and his present situation in Washington, D. C., he has held important positions in the service at Savannah, Georgia, and Louisville, Kentucky.

The Socialist Movement in Randolph.

The Socialist party was first organized in Randolph, March 5, 1908, when a few adherents of that economic philosophy met at the M. P. church in Elkins and organized a local. Dr. A. S. Bosworth was chairman of the meeting and W. G. Howell was secretary. An address was made by J. E. Kildow. Those who were present and became members of the local were: J. E. Kildow, Dr. A. S. Bosworth, A. R. Conoway, S. W. Hayden, Adam See, R. M. Stalnaker, W. G. Howell, Edward Tucker, and H. M. Howell.

Indian Ring.

On Conrad Street in the village of Mill Creek can be seen what is called an "Indian Ring." It is about 50 feet in diameter. The ring was more distinct before the land was culti-

vated.   Large trees originally grew on the spot, indicating
many years since the ring was the scene of occupancy by the
Red Man.   The soil forming the elevation was about one foot
high.   The ring is too large to have been a wigwam and is
in all probability the remains of an ancient palisade.   In the
adjoining county of Pendleton there is evidence of a ring en-
closing almost an acre of ground.

Indian mounds exist on the farm of Will Harper, in
Leadsville District and on the adjacent farm of Arch Lytle in
Beverly District.   From the mound on Lytle's farm stone
hatchets have been taken.   From the mound on the Currence
farm, a mile south of Daily, two stone pipes and parts of a
human skeleton were removed.

The Inter-Mountain.

The Inter-Mountain, the first Republican paper in Randolph County, was established in 1892, in the town of Elkins.
Professor N. G. Keim was its first editor under the management of a publishing company.   Professor Keim remained in
charge two years, when he was succeeded by M. S. Cornwell,
of Hampshire County.   Mr. Cornwell remained editor two
years or until 1896, when he resigned on account of failing
health.   William S. Ryan edited the paper for a few months
and was succeeded by Chas. E. Beans.   Mr. Herman Johnson
succeeded Mr. Beans in August, 1898.   Mr. Johnson is still editor and owner of the paper.   A daily edition has been published since October, 1907.

Randolph Men in the French and Indian War.

Quite a few of the early settlers of Randolph had been
soldiers in the French and Indian War of 1754-60.   The following is a partial list.   However, in a few instances the descendants of these men, only, became residents of Randolph.
Friend Jonas, Sergeant; Phares John, Corporal; Briggs Samuel, Conrad Ulrich, Coplinger George, Cunningham James,
Cunningham Robert, Cunningham William, Eberman Jacob,
Haigler Benjamin, Haigler Jacob, Harman George, Harper

Adam, Harper Phillip, Hevener Michael, Kile George, Kile
Valentine, Skidmore James, Skidmore Joseph, Ward William,
Wise Jacob.

Population of Randolph.

The population of Randolph in 1790 was 951. The first
ten years the population nearly doubled and in 1800 the census figures show Randolph to have had 1826 souls. The rate
of increase in subsequent years was not so large, but in 1810
the population had increased to 2854. When we remember
that the area of the county was so much greater than at present, we know that the population was sparse in 1820 when the
census of that period gives the population of the county as
3357. The assessors for the year 1792 returned 87 white persons and 18 colored as proper subjects for poll tax in John
Jackson's District. In John Hadden's District 57 whites and
4 colored. In the remainder of the county 15 white persons
were eligible for poll tax; making in the entire county 159
whites and 12 colored, or 181 in all. John Hadden's District
embraced very nearly the same territory that constitutes
Randolph County today. In that district according to the
estimate of five persons to each tithe, there was in the present territory of Randolph a population of 305 in 1792. There
were 260 horses in Randolph county that year.

From 1820 to 1910 the population of Randolph County
has varied as follows:

1830	5,000
1840	6,208
1850	5,243
1860	4,990
1870	5,563
1880	8,102
1896	11,633
1900	
1910	

Population of incorporated towns in Randolph County according to the census of 1910:

Beverly	438
Elkins	5,260
Harding	105
Harmon	149
Huttonsville	251
Mill Creek	740
Montrose	112
Whitmer	650
Womelsdorf	665

An Old Field School.

The building was a rude round log structure. A chimney made from split sticks cemented together with mud. A roof of clapboards held on by weight poles. Greased paper covering an aperature caused by the removal of a log was substituted for a window. No floor overhead and none beneath but the bare earth. Puncheon seats, no blackboard and few slates, goose quill pens; pupils reading or spelling aloud. A constant supply of hickory gads to enforce discipline. Such was the first school attended by the writer in Valley Bend District in 1866.

Swiss Colony at Alpena.

In April, 1879, a colony of about one hundred Swiss emigrants settled at Alpena, on the eastern slope of the Shaver Mountain. In a strange environment, unaccustomed to the tillage of the crops suitable to this soil and climate, they became discouraged and all but about half dozen families abandoned the country within the first year. About a half dozen families remained and prospered and constitute a valuable acquisition to our population. Those who became permanent residents of the county are Emiel Knutti, Jacob Ratzer, Christian Herdig, Godfrey Herdig and John Herdig.

HENRY CLAY DEAN.

An Orator in Disguise.

Mark Twain, in his "Life on the Mississippi," published in 1906, in referring to his visit to Keokuk, Iowa, relates an amusing incident in the life of Henry Clay Dean. An account of Dean's relation to Randolph County is narrated in another chapter. Mark Twain says:

"Keokuk, a long time ago was an occasional loafing place of the erratic genius, Henry Clay Dean. I believe I never saw him but once, but he was much talked of when I lived there. This is what was said of him:

"He began life poor and without education, but he educated himself on the curb stones of Keokuk. He would sit down on a curb stone with his book, careless or unconscious of the clatter of commerce and the tramp of the passing crowds, and bury himself in his studies by the hour, never changing his position except to draw in his knees now and then to let a dray pass unobstructed; and when his book was finished, its contents, however, abstruse, had been burned into his memory, and were his permanent possession. In this way he acquired a vast hoard of all kinds of learning, and had it pigeon-holed in his head where he could put his intellectual hand on it whenever it was wanted.

"His clothes differed in no respect from a 'wharf rat's' except that they were raggeder, more ill-assorted and inharmonious (and therefore more extravagantly picturesque) and several layers dirtier. Nobody could infer the master mind in the top of that edifice from the edifice itself.'

"He was an orator by nature in the first place, and later by training of experience and practice. When he was out on a canvass, his name was a lode stone which drew the farmers to his stump from fifty miles around. His theme was always politics. He used no notes, for a volcano does not need notes. In 1862, a son of Keokuk's late distinguished citizen, Mr. Claggett, gave me this incident concerning Dean:

"The war feeling was running high in Keokuk in '61, and a great mass meeting was to be held on a certain day in the new Athenaeum. A distinguished stranger was to address the house. After the building had been packed to its

utmost capacity with sweltering folk of both sexes, the stage
still remained vacant—the distinguished stranger had failed
to connect. The crowd grew impatient, and by and by indig-
nant and rebellious. About this time a distressed manager
discovered Dean on a curb stone, explained the dilemma to
him, took his book away from him, rushed him into the building the back way and told him to make for the stage and save
his country.

"Presently a sudden silence fell upon the audience, and
everybody's eyes sought a single point—the wide, empty, car-
petless stage. A figure appeared there whose aspect was familiar hardly to a dozen persons present. It was the scare
crow Dean in foxy shoes, down at the heels; socks of odd colors, also down; damaged trousers, relics of antiquity and a
world too short, exposing some inches of naked ankle; an un-
buttoned vest also too short and exposing a zone of soiled,
wrinkled linen between it and the waistband; shirt bosom
open; long, black handkerchief wound round and round his
neck like a bandage; bobtailed blue coat, reaching down to the
small of the back, with sleeves which left four inches of the
forearm unprotected; small stiff-brimmed soldier cap hung
on a corner of the bump of whichever bump it was. This figure moved gravely out upon the stage and with sedate and
measured step down to the front, where it paused and dream-
ily inspected the house, saying no word. The silence of surprise held its own for a moment, then was broken by a just
audible ripple of merriment which swept the sea of faces like
the wash of a wave. The figure remained as before, thought-
fully inspecting. Another wave started—laughter this time.
It was followed by another, then a third—this last one
boisterous.

"And now the stranger stepped back one pace, took off
his soldier cap, tossed it into the wing and began to speak
with deliberation, nobody listening, everybody laughing and
whispering. The speaker talked on unembarrassed, and presently delivered a shot which went home, and silence and attention followed. He rivited their attention quick and fast
with other telling things; warmed to his work and began

to pour his words out instead of dripping them; grew hotter and hotter and fell to discharging lightning and thunder, and now the house began to break into applause to which the speaker gave no heed, but went hammering straight on; unwound his black bandage and cast it away, still thundering; presently discarded the bobtailed coat and flung it aside, firing up higher and higher all the time; finally flung the vest after the coat, and then for an untimed period stood there like another Vesuvius, spouting smoke and flames, lava and ashes, raining pumice stone and cinders, shaking the moral earth with intellectual crash upon crash, explosion upon explosion, while the mad multitude stood upon their feet in a solid body, answering back with a ceaseless hurricane of cheers, through a threshing snow storm of waving handkerchiefs.

"When Dean came," said Claggett, "the people thought he was an escaped lunatic; but when he went, they thought he was an escaped archangel."

Stocks and Pillories.

In the pioneer period each court house yard was supplied with stocks and pillories. The pillories were for the punishment of a higher grade of crimes than the stocks. The court house grounds of Randolph County were provided with these primitive methods of penal punishment. At the February term 1794, an allowance of $10 was made for the construction of stocks and pillories. Next year Edward Combs was put in the stocks five minutes for contempt of court. Three years later St. Leger Stout was ordered to the stocks five minutes for the same offense. Stocks consisted of a framework of heavy timbers, having holes in which legs and arms were confined. Pillories were made of a wooden post and frame, fixed on a platform several feet above the ground, behind which the culprit stood, his head and hands being thrust through holes in the frame, so as to be exposed in front of it. The intention of setting a criminal in the pillory was that he should become infamous.

A PRIMITIVE INDUSTRY.

"RANDOLPH Co EXPRESS" DELIVERING HUCKLEBERRIES TO HORTON W.VA

Marks and Brands.

For many years in the earlier history of this country no attempt was made to confine horses, cattle, sheep or hogs in enclosed fields. None except cultivated fields were put under fence. Horses, cattle and sheep were belled and turned loose to roam upon the range. Horses were branded and cattle, sheep and hogs were marked. Each individual owner selected a brand or mark of his own, which he had recorded with the court of the county. Proving this brand or mark was sufficient to recover stock in dispute. Recording ear marks and brands constituted a large part of the business of the court in those days. As an example of these marks, at the June term, 1794, it was ordered that the "ear marks of Jacob Westfall, which consists of a swallow fork in the left ear be admitted to record."

Arrow Heads.

Arrow heads are made from quartz of various colors. Some have been found in the country of such rare quality that it is not known where the Indians obtained the material from which they were made. A quantity of flint would be carried perhaps for many miles and handed down for generations as an inheritance. Maxwell's history says there is a ledge of flint near Brady's Gate in Mingo District. Sprawls are found in some localities, especially about the mounds, showing that the Indians stopped there long enough to replenish their supply. A notable difference between some arrow heads and other arrow heads is that which distinguishes the point made for hunting game from that made for use in war. In the arrow heads, made for hunting, at the base of the triangular part there is an indented portion, enabling the huntsman to fasten the point to the shaft with a thong, so that he could recover the weapon in its entirety. The war points, however, are perfect triangles or triangles with a concave curve at the base. The war points have thus not only one but three sharp points. The war arrow heads were not fastened to the shaft with thongs, but simply inserted in the split end of the shaft. When they struck and wounded a brave he pulled at the shaft, which became loose, but the pronged point remained in the flesh. The war points are long and narrow of design, well calculated to give a death blow to the stoutest warrior who did not know how to encase himself in armor, and was in fact ignorant of the use of iron or any other metal until he met the strangers across the sea. A battle-ax, made of stone, was found near the Indian mound on the Lytle place, about three miles south of Elkins.

Wooden Wagons.

Although the pack saddle was the pioneer's main dependence in matters of transportation, yet for local purposes he constructed a wagon entirely of wood. Therefore, the order of the court that wagon roads were to be constructed did not signify that wagons of modern design were in use. However, the first wagons, in the modern sense, used in this county were built by local workmen. The iron used was brought to the county by pack horses. In the first years of the settlement of the county, wagons constructed entirely of wood were in general use. The axles were made of hickory and wheels were sawed from the swamp gum tree. Harness, especially tugs and traces, were made from raw hide, buffalo skins being a favorite material for this purpose.

Bees and Birds.

The honey bee was inported from Europe to America by the first settlers. Its first home is supposed to have been in Asia. In pioneer days wild bees were found in great numbers far from human habitation. However, in the beginning they escaped from the settlers' apiary. Crows, black birds, and song birds also followed the advent of the white man. The English sparrow, the recent feathered nuisance, is an importation into this country of the last few decades. The common house rat and the common house mouse which have played such an important role in the spread of contagious diseases, belong to the mammalia of India, although some specimens are supposed to be indigenous to China. However, the white man is responsible for their existence in America.

Mill Creek.

Mill Creek has the distinction of being the second town in Randolph county. It has a population of 740 according to the census of 1910. The community had prosperous stores, churches, school house and a blacksmith shop at the junction of the Valley Pike and the Mountain road, many years before the extension of the railroad up the valley. However, the completion of the railroad gave the impetus to the growth of the present town of Mill Creek. For many years the community bore the not euphonious name of "Dog Town." For about a decade before the building of Mill Creek the village was called Crickard, in honor of Patrick Crickard, who was its first postmaster. Mill Creek is now the site of several large saw mills and is quite an important industrial center as well as the emporium of a wide agricultural territory.

Spanish War Volunteers.

Following is a list of the volunteers in the Spanish-American war of 1898. They were mostly in Company E First West Virginia Volunteer Infantry: Zan F. Collett, captain; James Hanley Jr., first sergeant; John J. Nallen, second Sergeant; H. B. O'Brien, third sergeant; C. D. Poling, W. C. Kennedy, T. J. Collett, T. J. Goddin, David F. Foy and J. E. Weese, corporals; F. A. Rowan, C. L. Weymouth and H. Platz, musicians in the Regimental band; G. W. Buckey, Wagoner; privates: Bruce Phares, James R. Collier, C. L. Lewis, Cyrus J. Warner, John S. Garber, Leslie Harding, William Russell, C. Lloyd, J. Lloyd, K. Bennett, W. Welch, S. Knox, Wm. Steffey, F. W. Orris, T. J. Smith, H. Crawford Scott, Braxton O. Meeks, Stewart Anthony, Wamsley. Randolph had three regular soldiers in the battle of Santiago. They were: Robt. L. Hamilton, first lieutenant; Walter Phillips, hospital steward, and a Mr. Wolf, of the Twenty-second

Infantry. Colonel Davis Elkins was on General Coppinger's staff.

The City of Elkins.

The site of the present City of Elkins, was a place of more than local distinction before the railroad was among the prob-

Historical Round Barn, Built About 1832, Elkins, W. Va.

abilities in Tygarts Valley. Leadsville and the Round Barn were the scenes of many stirring events during the Civil War.

The City of Elkins was laid off into lots in 1889. It was named for Hon. S. B. Elkins, who with Honorable H. G. Davis and Honorable Richard Kearns, built magnificent residences on adjacent eminences. On August 18, 1889, trains commenced running into the town. The railroad was extended to Beverly and Belington in 1891, and to Huttonsville a few years later. A branch was also built, known as the C. & I., connecting with the Chesapeake & Ohio railroad at Durbin. The Coal & Coke, though entering the city over the Western Maryland tracks, entered the city over its own road bed in 1911. The county seat, which from the organization of the county, had been located at the ancient town of Beverly, was wrested from that place in an election in 1898, and the records were moved to Elkins eighteen months later. The clerk's offices were kept in the Western Maryland railroad building until the completion of the present court house about two years later.

The Elkins Electric Railway commenced running its cars on December 1, 1909. It is slowly extending its line down the river in the direction of Belington and is at present carrying passengers to Roaring Creek Junction and Harding.

In the fall of 1910, the magnificient Odd Fellows Home was dedicated in the western suburbs of Elkins. In this palatial home, in the midst of parks, driveways, artificial lakes and beautiful landscape, there is cared for the aged Odd Fellow and the orphaned children of deceased brethren. This home is supported by the order in West Virginia.

The same year marked the completion, also, in Elkins, of the Orphans Home, a State institution, supported by general taxation. The population of Elkins according to the census of 1910, was 5,260.

Indian Trail Still Visible.

An Indian trail leading over the mountain from the Valley to Fishing Hawk is still visible according to good authority. The trail followed the divide between the forks of Files Creek for some distance and then took its course along the north side of the mountain to the gap between the heads of Files Creek and Fishing Hawk. Evidences of the existence of this trail can be traced through the pasture fields and in the woods on the mountain side. The information of its existence was orally transmitted by Wm. Daniels to his grand son, Harrison Daniels, who lives near where the trail starts up the mountain side. Several "licks" of salt springs were near the course of the trail, which, perhaps, partially accounted for its location. The county court of Randolph ordered a survey of a road from Beverly up Files Creek to the top of the Alleghany Mountain in 1799, but the grade of the road now traveled is not as good as was the old Indian trail.

Salt.

Salt is an indispensable condiment. It is an essential ingredient of food for most mammals. Obtaining a sufficient supply of salt was one of the most difficult problems that confronted the pioneer. Not a few of the roads leading to older communities were opened for the purpose of importing salt. At an early day some salt was made in this country from saline springs, frequented by deer and buffalo. The water was evaporated by boiling. However, the greater part of the supply was carried on pack saddles from Bull Town, Braxton County. In an inventory of a personal estate, admitted to record in 1803, salt was valued at $6.00 per bushel.

Names of Streams.

Tygarts Valley River was named for David Tygart, who settled on its banks near Beverly, in 1753. In the early records of the county the name is spelled Tygers. After the massacre of the Files family, Tygart abandoned the Valley. However, a family by the name of Taggart was among the first permanent settlers of the county and tradition says they were of the same stock as the David Tygart family. It is therefore probable that the name of the Valley and the river should be Taggart rather than Tygart.

Cheat River is so called from the deceptive appearance of the depth of the river, due to its freedom from foreign substances. Estimating the depth of Cheat River from the standard of other streams the eye is much deceived. The stream was called Wilmoths River for a number of years in the early history of the county for the reason that the Wilmoths were the first settlers on its banks.

Files Creek was named for Robert Files who settled near its mouth in 1753.

Mill Creek was called Currence's Mill Creek in the pioneer period. It was one of the first streams in the county to furnish power for grinding grain. Wm. Currence erected a grist mill on the site of the present mill of Jesse Rosencranse in 1794. In the course of time the word Currence was dropped from the name and it now bears the abbreviated name of Mill Creek.

Gandy Creek was named in honor of Uriah Gandy who was the first settler on the waters of that stream.

Dry Fork is so called for the reason that this stream is wont in many places to seek subterranean passages and leave a dry bed.

The origin of the names of Mud Lick, Gum Lick, Pond Lick, Laurel Fork, Middle Fork, Roaring Creek, Beaver Creek, Elkwater, Leading Creek, Otter Fork, Windy Run, is indicated by the names they bear.

Beccas Creek was named for a man by the name of Becky or Beckay, who settled on that stream in an early day.

Board of Registration.

From 1866 to 1870, the elective franchise in Randolph County was subject to the whims and discretion of a Board of Registration appointed by the Governor. Those charged with disloyalty to the government during the war, then just closed, were tried before the Board. The accused was found loyal or disloyal as the evidence indicated and was either disfranchised or left on the list of eligibles. William Apperson was the first to be tried and being unable to establish his loyalty was disfranchised.

The following are samples of findings of the Board:

State vs. Squire Bosworth.

The defendant, a resident of Beverly District, being called appeared. No witnesses appearing this cause is dismissed.

State vs. Christopher N. Schoonover.

Christopher N. Schoonover having been struck off appeared and asked to be reinstated. Ordered that he stay off.

The Board adjourned to meet no more in 1870 and thus ended an incident that had done much to foster and keep active the passions and prejudices of the war.

Board of Supervisors.

A Board of Supervisors managed the affairs of this county from 1866 to 1872. Their jurisdiction was similar to the county courts. Following is a list of supervisors and the dates of entering office:

1866—Elijah Kittle, John K. Scott, John M. Haney, John M. Crouch, John A. Hutton, Powhatan A. Lolly, Sampson Snyder, Elijah M. Hart, Charles W. Burk, William Rowan, James H. Lambert.

1867—Benjamin F. Wilmoth, William D. Armstrong, Orlando Woolwine, Geo. Buckey, Crawford Scott, Oliver Wilmoth, A. E. Harper.

1869—Samuel Tyre, Eli Kittle, Riley Pritt, A. J. Swecker, Melvin Currence, John W. Phares, Jacob Vanscoy, Elijah Cooper.

1871—John Cain, Adam Yokum.

During the time the county was managed by a Board of Supervisors the county was divided into townships. The districts of Mingo, Dry Fork and Beverly were named and bounded very much as they are today. Clay corresponded to New Interest, Clark to Valley Bend, Reynolds to Huttonsville, Scott to Roaring Creek, Union to Middle Fork, and Greene to Leadsville.

Lorenzo Dow.

Lorenzo Dow, the noted Methodist Missionary, visited Beverly in his annual pilgrimages through the frontier settlements of America. In addition to his enthusiasm as a missionary, Dow had another purpose in visiting Beverly. His brother-in-law, Dr. Benjamin Dolbear, was a resident of that place. Mrs. Dow was a sister of Dr. Dolbear. The house in which Dr. Dolbear lived and which sheltered Dow is still standing on the Archibald Chenoweth lot near the eastern end of the Valley River bridge. Dow made his appointments a year ahead and seldom disappointed his congregation. In Beverly he usually preached in the eastern suburbs near the Creed Butcher homestead. He would lay his hat, coat and watch on a log and would preach about two hours. He was a man of unusual magnetic presence and power. It was not unusual for many of his congregation to become affected with the "jerks" in which the individual would undergo strange and peculiar contortions. These manifestations were variously interpreted. Some believed that these extraordinary expressions of emotion were the wrestling of the spirit of the Evil One with the soul of the convicted sinner. Dow refers to these mental states in his writings and evidently they were as much a mystery to him as to any one else. Today psychologists would readily attribute them to the power of suggestion. These phenomena heralded his reputation and magnified his power and influence. He visited Europe in 1799 and in 1805. His dress and manner was that of the frontierman and he attracted great crowds to see and hear him. His Polemical works were published in 1814, and the history of a Cosmopolite and a short account of a Long Travel in 1823. He was· born in Connecticutt in 1777, and died February 2, 1834.

The Tygarts Valley News.

The Tygarts Valley News made its initial bow to the public September 13, 1889. The first owners and editors were James A. Bent and Floyd J. Triplett. In January, 1891, Zan. F. Collett and John F. Ferguson succeeded Messrs. Bent and Triplett, the latter having been elected clerk of the county court, temporarily left the newspaper field to assume official duties. At the expiration of his term of office Mr. Triplett, with Mr. Collett, conducted the paper until the breaking out of the Spanish American war in May, 1898, when Mr. Collett, having been elected Captain of Volunteers entered the military service. Mr. Triplett a few years later sold the paper to a joint stock company which still owns and manages the paper. The paper has since suspended.

The Randolph Enterprise.

The Randolph Enterprise was the first paper published in Randolph County. The first issue appeared in May, 1874. Its first editor and owner was Geo. P. Sargent. The paper was a five column quarto and was printed on a Washington hand press. The nearest railroad station was Webster, Taylor County, and blank paper and other supplies were hauled from that point by road wagons. Mr. Sargent, after a few years management of the paper sold it to T. Irvin Wells. V. B. Trimble and B. L. Butcher succeeded Mr. Wells. Mr. Butcher, having been elected Prosecuting Attorney, sold his interest to Mr. Trimble. J. L. and A. S. Bosworth purchased the paper of Mr. Trimble. They sold to John Hutton and he sold it to J. L. Bosworth and E. D. Talbott. Mr. Talbott sold his interest to F. J. Triplett, who about two years later sold his interest to A. S. Bosworth. J. L. and A. S. Bosworth conducted the paper about eight years and sold it to a stock company with G. W. Lewis and S. A. Rowan as editors. The paper followed the county seat to Elkins and has been under the editorial management of James W. Weir for several years. and was succeeded by J. Slidell Brown, the present editor.

The Randolph Review.

The Randolph Review was the second paper published in Randolph County. It was founded by J. L. and A. S. Bosworth and after publishing it for about six months purchased the Randolph Enterprise and sold the Review plant to Buckey Canfield, who moved it to Huntersville and started the Times, the first paper published in that county. These events occured in 1882.

Huttonsville.

The town of Huttonsville was named in honor of the Hutton family. Before the war the village was the educational center of the county. Until the coming of the West Virginia Central railroad, it was a county hamlet with post-office, hotel, church, school house and blacksmith shop. It is now an incorporated town with a population of 251 according to the census of 1910.

Coalton.

This town is situated in the center of the Roaring Creek coal fields. The existence of the village is cotemporaneous with the entrance of the railroad into the town in May, 1894. Until recently it was called Womelsdorf for O. C. Womelsdorf, who founded the town and was the pioneer in the development of that section. It is now a flourishing village with a population of 650 according to the census of 1910.

Harman.

The town of Harman is situated near the junction of the Dry Fork and Horse Camp Run. For many years a quiet country hamlet, with the advent of the railroad it has grown into a prosperous village with a bank, hotels, graded school and a system of water piped from an adjacent mountain spring. It is surrounded by a rich agricultural community with neat and attractive farm houses. According to the census of 1910 the town has a population of 159 and is incorporated.

The Frost of '59.

On the morning of June 5, 1859, occurred a notable frost in Randolph County. The spring had been warm and auspicious and the farmers were looking forward to a bountiful harvest. However, on the day previous the weather became unseasonably cold. Furs and overcoats were taken from their winter recesses. Some farmers presaged the coming calamity and entered their corn fields with horse and plow and covered the growing crop with the mellow earth, which was removed when the weather moderated. Their pains were rewarded with the usual harvest. All unprotected crops of corn and wheat and every other green and growing thing were frozen. To compensate for the disaster the farmer went to work with renewed energy. Corn was replanted and partially matured. A large acreage of buckwheat was sown. The local supply of seed was exhausted and the Glades of Preston and Garrett were drawn upon. Winter found the farmer's graneries with their wonted plethora.

First Foreigner Naturalized.

The first foreigner to be naturalized in Randolph was John Lambertson in 1787. He came from Ireland. William Currence witnessed his good character and the fact that he had been a resident of the State one year. The second was Wm. Bock in 1806, and the third was William Nearbeck in 1824.

Emancipation Paper.

So far as the records show the bearer of the following paper was the first negro to receive his liberty in Randolph County:

Randolph County, Va.
Dec. 30, 1791.

I do hereby certify that I have set the bearer hereof, Negro Tom, at full liberty from servitude to act and do for himself as a free man, as witness my hand the day and date above written.

JONAS FRIEND.

Town of Beverly.

The General Assembly of the State of Virginia passed an Act December 16, 1790, creating the town of Beverly, as follows:

That twenty acres of land, the property of James Westfall, as the same are already laid off into lots and streets in the County of Randolph adjoining the land whereon the Court House now stands, shall be established a town by the name of Beverly; and that John Wilson, Jacob Westfall, Sylvester Ward, Thomas Philips, Hezekiah Rosecrouts, William Wormsley, and Valentine Stornaker, Gentlemen, shall be and are hereby constituted Trustees thereof.

The names Rosecrouts, Womsley, and Stonaker, as they

appear in the Act reproduced above, should be Rosencranse, Wamsley and Stalnaker.

The original name of the town was Edmonton, in honor of Edmond Randolph. The Virginia Assembly changed the name to Beverly in honor of Beverly Randolph. The town, as indicated by the charter, consisted of 20 acres. This tract was divided into 40 half-acre lots and were sold at $16.66⅔ each and the purchaser bound himself to build a house 16x16 feet with stone or brick chimney within five years. An annual rent of 36 cents for each lot was to be paid to James Westfall or his heirs forever. There is no evidence that this stipulation in the deeds was ever enforced.

The town has a population, according to the census of 1910, of 438.

Historic Beverly.

In the years subsequent to the Civil War, isolated and unassuming, nestled among the mountains, many miles from the marts of trade, stood the village of Beverly. But this hamlet possessed a wealth of men that entitled it to a higher rank than larger and more pretentious towns—a class of honest yeomanry so aptly described by Dr. Goldsmith in his poem of the "Deserted Village." To each of whom is applicable Mark Anthony's tribute to Caesar: "His life was gentle and the elements so mixed in him that nature might stand up and say to all the world this was a man." Intelligent, honest and upright, with good counsel and good example to the young. they sought neither pelf, place nor power, and living simple and unselfish lives, the higher self unfolded. Such men were B. W. Crawford, Adam Crawford, Adam Rowan, Claude Goff, David Goff, George Printz, Lemuel Chenoweth, Archibald Chenoweth, Dr. Geo. W. Yokum, Nelson Fitzwater, Fountain Butcher, Creed Butcher, Henry Suiter, Geo. W. Leonard, John Leonard, John B. Earle, Elias Earle, Alpheus Buckey, John Buckey, Dr. Squire Bosworth, Chas. W. Russell, C. J. P. Cresap, Parkinson Collett, Isaac Baker, Eli Baker, James H. Logan, Solomon Warner, Samuel Gilmore, Jacob Suiter, L. D. Greynolds, Jacob M. Weese, Calvin Collett, Jacob Collett,

Johnathan Arnold, L. D. Strader, Bernard L. Brown, George Buckey, William Rowan, Judson Blackman, James D. Wilson, Rev. Robert Scott, John B. Morrison, Emmett Buckey, James A. Vaughan.

These men have gone to reap their recompense in that "country from whose bourn no traveler returns," but they merit a permanent place in the annals of their town and county, which they so highly honored. Accepting Walt Whitman's definition of the greatest city, which we append, the ancient village of Beverly should live in history for having produced a superior class of men:

The greatest city is that which has the greatest man or woman.
If it be a few ragged huts, it is still the greatest city in the whole world.
The place where the greatest city stands is not the place of stretched wharves, docks, manufactures, deposits of produce,
Nor the place of ceaseless salutes of newcomers, or the anchor-lifters of the departing,
Nor the place of the tallest and costliest buildings, or shops selling goods from the rest of the earth.
Nor the place of the best libraries and schools—nor the place where money is plentiest,
Nor the place of the most numerous population.
Where the city of the faithfulest friends stands,
Where the city of the cleanliness of the sexes stands,
Where the city of the healthiest fathers stands,
Where the city of best-bodied mothers stands,
There the greatest city stands.

Wild Pigeons.

The wild pigeon or the passenger pigeon appeared in very large flocks in Randolph County until a comparatively recent date, perhaps for a decade following the civil war. They visited this section as a rule in September and October, and were evidently attracted to the wooded districts of Randolph by acorns and beech nuts. They came in such flocks as to obscure the sun light and present the appearance of the sky being overcast by dark and ominous clouds. Trees and their branches were often broken and crushed by the weight of their numbers. Some flocks were estimated to contain many millions of birds. It is supposed their breeding ground was in Western Canada and the backwoods of the Western United States. The passenger pigeon was about the size of the common turtle dove, but with a long wedged shape tail. The male was of a dark slate color above and a purplish bay beneath, the sides of the neck being enlivened by gleaming violet green and gold. The female was drab colored and dull white beneath, with only a slight trace of the brilliant neck markings. This species of pigeon is now supposed to be extinct and fabulous prices are offered for a male and female specimen.

Prisoners at Fort Deleware.

Lenox Camden, William Salisbury and his son, ... Salisbury, Pugh Chenoweth, Levi Ward, Allen Isner, Philip Isner, William Clemm, Smith Crouch, Thomas Crouch, John Caplinger, John Leary and Charles Russell, were sent to Fort Deleware near Philadelphia, to be held as hostages for a number of Union sympathizers taken to Richmond by General W. L. Jackson, in his raid of 1863. All died but the last four from drinking the poluted water of Delaware Bay. Frank Phares went to Philadelphia and secured the release of the survivors.

The Settlement of Adolph.

This settlement was established in 1880-1 by imigrants from Switzerland. However, a few Swiss families that moved to Adolph had lived temporarily in other States of the Union. Fred Iseley, a single man, and the following heads of families were the permanent settlers of the colony: Jacob Ruthenbuler, John Rush, Albert Brenwald, Jacob Pheister, Gotlieb Schorer, Joseph Koefle, and Jacob Schmid. A few families not mentioned above came, but not finding conditions to their liking, settled elsewhere.

The village consists of eleven dwellings, store, postoffice, blacksmith shop, school house and grist mill. Carl Lutz was the John Smith of this colony, having directed and inspired its formation.

Adolph is situated in a picturesque little valley at the junction of Mitchel Lick Run with the Middle Fork of Buckhannon River. The site of the village was a heavy forest of virgin timber.

Helvetia.

In 1869, a real estate company of New York induced a number of Swiss immigrants to establish a settlement on a branch of the Buckhannon River. In honor of their native village, the colony was called Helvetia. In June, 1879, Carl Lutz, agent for the company that owned a large boundary of land arrived. He was a man of practical qualities of mind and his services were invaluable to the colonists.

Among the first to locate in the settlement were: Henry Asper, Ulrich Miller, Mathew Marty, Joseph Zillman, Jacob Halder, John Andregg, J. Benziger, Jacob Zumbach, Max Lehman, Gotlieb Deitwiller, Christian Zumbach, John Engler, John Teuscher, Alfred Teuscher, John Merkle, John Huber, Fritz Zumbach, Ernest Hassig, George Sutton, John Hofer, John Carlen Jr., John Farhner, John Better, George Andregg, Christian Burky, Jacob Andregg, Edwin Vogel, John Wenger, Jacob Loser, and Fritz Hasselbach. Most of these imigrants were craftsmen and without experience in clearing land and agriculture.

For groceries and other supplies the settlers were compelled to go to French Creek, a distance of eighteen miles. Having no horses, this trip was made on foot, requiring two days. These conditions remained until 1872, when Gustave Senhauser arrived from New Philadelphia, Ohio, and established a general store. Soon thereafter another store was established by Randolph See. Still the settlement was handicapped for want of a saw mill, and lumber for building houses and other purposes had to be manufactured by hand.

The larger number of these settlers were members of the German Reformed Church, but a few were Roman Catholics.

In 1872, a Sunday School was organized in Mr. Senhauser's store with store boxes for seats. A little later, Rev. Andreas Kern, from Zurich, Switzerland, organized a German Reformed Church to which about twenty members subscribed. Rev. Kern is still affectionately remembered by his former congregation.

At present the congregation owns a neat and comfortable church and parsonage and one acre of land. Dr. Carl Stuckey, of Bern, Switzerland, the first physician to locate in Helvetia, was much interested in religious matters and was instrumental in organizing churches and Sunday schools in the community. The first public school was opened in 1873-4. The first trustees were Gustav Senhauser, John Dever, and Jesse Sharp. The first teacher was a Mr. Wilson.

By frugality and industry these pioneers succeeded in converting the forests into farms, producing various grains and cereals, but they did not swerve from their original purpose of engaging in the dairy business. Accordingly, John Kellenberger, of Appenzell, Switzerland, imported, at the instance of the settlers, a herd of brown Swiss cattle, and a company was organized to manufacture Sweitzer cheese. The business lasted several years but was abandoned because of the distance from the railroad and the limitations of local markets. John Teuscher, a member of the company remained in the business and is still making Swiss cheese on his own account. In 1873, Geo. Betz, of Wertemberg, Germany, erected a saw and grist mill, but for some reason his enterprise did not flourish and both enterprises have been abandoned.

After nearly half a century, the lumber industry invaded the community, and modern frame houses supplanted the round log structures that had so long sheltered the settlers. Even the painter found opportunity to ply his art. At last the fruits of their earlier hardships began to be realized. In the trying times, son and daughter had supplemented the income of the families at home, by going to older communities and sending home their savings.

These people still retain the customs and usages of the Fatherland, the most civilized country on earth; where laws are made and administered for rich and poor alike; where compulsory education has been in effect for centuries, and from whence comes the progressive laws that recently are being adopted in this and other countries. They think it is no harm to take a drink of wine or cider, but he who would go beyond the bounds of moderation would be disgraced and ostracised by the community. The stranger is always treated to the vintage of the grape. Picnics and sociables are frequent where the people enjoy themselves with music and song.

The best of care is taken of domestic animals and they think it cruel to expose the horse, the cow, or the sheep, to the storms of winter without shelter. The horse was not in common use in the early years of the settlement and it was not an infrequent sight to see oxen single or in pairs hitched to sleds, drawing the plow, or with packsaddles on their backs, at the mill or store.

Before the days of railroads and the lumber industry, produce of the farms commanded very low prices; butter and eggs often as low as six cents per pound and dozen respectively. The first to engage in the lumber business in Helvetia was Floyd Brown, who later gained the sobriquet of Cherry Brown. The extention of the lumber business to their community gave many the opportunity to sell their remaining timber for many times the price they paid for the land in the first place, viz: $3.00 per acre.

A few years subsequent to the coming of the Swiss to Helvetia, a colony was located nine miles southwest of that town on Turkey Bone Mountain. Among the colonists were: Mark Egglison, John Zender, Casper Winkler, John Hartman Sr., and John Hartman Jr., Horles Zimmerly, John Lassy, Peter Swint and a Mr. Stadler, who for a number of years operated a tannery. Although undergoing many privations, this colony did not suffer the inconveniences and hardships experienced by the older colony. However, no preparation was made for their arrival and many lived in tents and houses without windows until better ones could be afforded. Heads of families, in many instances, were compelled to leave home to obtain work in order to maintain their families and pay for their lands. Cloudbursts and thunderstorms were com-

mon and in many instances higher ground had to be reached
in the midst of darkness and downpour by the women and
children, whose husbands and fathers were absent from home.
At least in one instance, a mother of thirty, as the result of
these experiences, had her hair to turn gray in one night.

Let it be said to the credit of the Adolph and Helvetia
colonists that, while under such conditions some bickerings
were inevitable, yet their distance from home amongst a
people of a different tongue, cemented their friendship and
developed a co-operative spirit, and all were ready to give a
helping hand in time of need or distress. Industry and intelligence has triumphed over obstacles and today these people are happy, prosperous, and contented. They are attached
to their homes and their adopted country and have all the at-
tributes and characteristics of good and patriotic citizens.

RELIGIOUS.

Presbyterians.

The first preacher of the Presbyterian faith to hold services in the valley was, perhaps, Rev. Chas. Cummins, who
was licensed to preach by the Tinkling Springs Presbytery
in 1766. His field of labor consisted largely of Albemarle
and Amherst Counties. In 1772 he was directed to preach
eight sermons a year in Greenbrier County and Tygarts
Valley.

Rev. Wm. Foote, in his sketches of Virginia, gives the
following interesting account of the manner in which religious
services were held in that day:

"On Sabbath day morning, Mr. Cummins dressed himself, then put on his shot pouch, shouldered his rifle, mounted
his dun stallion, and rode off to church. There he met his
congregation, each one with rifle in hand. When thus seated
in meeting house it presented a solemn spectacle. The
preacher would walk through the crowd, deposit gun and
pouch in the corner and then commence his discourse." These
precautions were necessary as an attack by Indians was at
all times imminent.

In 1786 Rev. Edward Crawford preached two sermons in the valley. He was from the Valley of Virginia In the following year Rev. William Wilson, of the Old Stone Church of Augusta, preached two sermons. In about 1820, Rev. Asa Brooks, of New England, visited the valley as a missionary. In that year Daniel McLean, Johnathan Hutton and Andrew Crawford met at the latter's residence and organized a church. Mathew Whitman was elected ruling elder. In 1823 Adam See gave three acres on which to build a church. In 1826 Rev. Geo. Baxter, of Lexington, Va., preached in the valley. In 1831 the church had sixty members and five elders: Mathew Whitman, Daniel McLean, Andrew Crawford, Squire Bosworth, and Johnathan Hutton. The Mingo church was organized in 1841 with W. H. Wilson and William Logan as elders.

At that time there were eighty Presbyterians in the valley. Rev. Enoch Thomas was in charge of the churches in the valley in 1844-60. He was also one of the pioneer school teachers of the county. Rev. Robert Scott was in charge of the Presbyterian churches in the county from 1867 to 1875, and was instrumental in organizing churches in the outlying districts. Rev. Plummer Bryan was for many years located at Beverly and later at Huttonsville. He was the leading spirit in the building of the Huttonsville Presbyterian church. In about 1881 he moved to Chicago, in which place he has since held a pastorate. Rev. Samuel J. Baird was pastor of the Beverly church in 1884, Rev. J. N. Vandevander in 1887, Rev. Chas. D. Gilkesson in 1891.

The Methodists.

The Methodists were active in religious matters at a very early day in Randolph. The first society of the Methodist Episcopal church in Randolph was formed in 1786, directed and inspired by Rev. Joseph Chevuront, of Clarksburg.

Rev. Lorenzo Dow also often visited the valley in the thirties. He was a man of magnetic personality and his annual visits were looked forward to with much interest. His name was a household word among the pioneers for many years. His influence over his hearers was marked and his camp meetings were events of great importance in the community. Under the spell of his eloquence the emotions of his audience became uncontrollable and was attributed by many to mysterious agencies.

Hanning Foggy, for nearly half a century, a local preacher of the M. E. church, lived a few miles south of Elkins. He was a man of unusual gifts of mind and character and wielded an influence in his community for many years that falls to the lot of very few men. He died in 1893.

Rev. Samuel Clawson, a pioneer Methodist, often preached in the valley. He was noted for the unreserved manner in which he spoke his mind, his eccentric manner, and his energetic language. In closing a meeting at Mill Creek he thus summarized the results of his efforts: I have been fishing and after thumping and threshing among the thorns and thickets of perdition, and wading and floundering in the nasty pools of abomination, my only reward is that I have caught one shad, two herring, and two old roosters." In another instance he voiced his disappointment as follows:

"Thank God the day is not very far distant when you miserable and unrepentant sinners will be chained down to hell's brazen floor, and the devil with his three-pronged harpoon will pierce your reeking hearts, and pile upon you the red hot cinders of black damnation as high as the Pyramids of Egypt, and fry the pride out of your hearts to grease the gudgeons of the rag wheels of hell."

Again being informed that the residents of the community not of his own way of thinking on theological subjects, had been in the habit of disturbing public worship, he gave notice in opening his discourse in the following vigorous language:

"I understand that there is a gang here who call themselves 'No-Hellers,' and that they are in the habit of attacking preachers who come here to expound the gospel. I serve notice on you that if any of you speak to me here tonight or any other time, I will knock you higher than the Tower of Babel."

The "No-Hellers" discreetly made no effort to interview Rev. Clawson.

Bishop Asbury's Visit to the Valley.

Rev. Francis Asbury, bishop of the Methodist church passed through the valley on his way to Clarksburg in the year 1788. He traveled on horseback from North Carolina by way of Bedford, Greenbrier, and Pocahontas counties to Clover Lick. His destination was Clarksburg where he was to hold a quarterly meeting. His journal describes his impressions of the valley as follows:

Thursday, July 10, 1788.

We had to cross the Allegheny Mountains again at a bad passage. Our course lay over the mountains and through valleys, and the mud was such as might scarcely be expected in December. We came to an old forsaken habitation in Tygarts Valley. Here our horses grazed about while we boiled our meat. Midnight brought us up at Jones after riding forty, or perhaps fifty miles. The old man, our host, was kind enough to wake us up at four in the morning. We journeyed on through devious lonely wilds, where no food might be found except what grew in the woods or was carried with us. We met with two women who were going to see their friends and attend the quarterly meeting at Clarksburg.

Near midnight we stopped at A—s, who hissed his dog at us, but the women were determined to go to the quarterly meeting so we went in. Our supper was tea. Brother Phoebus and Cook took to the woods, old ———— gave up his bed to the women. I lay along the floor on a few deer skins with the fleas.

My mind has been severely tried under the great fatigue endured both by myself and my horse. Oh, how glad I should be of a plain, clean plank to lie on, as preferable to most of the beds, and where the beds are in a bad state the floors are worse. The gnats are almost as troublesome here as the mosquitoes in the lowlands of the seaboard. This country will require much work to make it tolerable. The people, many of them, are of the boldest cast of adventurers, and with some the decencies of civilized society are scarcely regarded. The great landholders, who are industrious, will soon show the aristocracy of wealth by lording it over their poorer neighbors, and by securing to themselves all the offices of profit or honor. On the one hand savage warfare teaches them to be cruel, and on the other the teaching of Antinomians poisons them with error in doctrine. Good moralists they are not, and good Christians they can not be unless they are better taught.

The Primitive Baptists.

This church was one of the leading and influential religious organizations in the early history of the country. Its membership was large and many of the prominent pioneers were adherents of its religious tenets. Elder Thomas Collett, born 1788 and died 1870, was, perhaps, the first preacher of this denomination in Randolph. Other preachers of this church who have occupied a prominent place in the religious affairs of the county may be mentioned: Rev. Ezra P. Hart, Rev. Nathan Everet, Rev. Elam Murphy, Rev. Joseph Poe, Rev. James Murphy, and Rev. Stephen D. Lewis.

Missionary Baptist Church.

This church was organized in Elkins in 1870 by Rev. W. E. Powell. It then had seventeen members. Rev. Amos Robinson was its first pastor. A splendid new edifice has recently been erected. Other prominent preachers who have occupied the pulpit of that denomination in Randolph are, Rev. H. M. P. Potts, Rev. H. P. Loomis, and Rev. W. H. Tiffany.

Left Pulpit for Melon Patch.

Henry Clay Dean preached in the valley in 1846. He is remembered by many now living. More about that eccentric genius can be found in another chapter. A survivor of the days of Rev. Dean's preaching in the valley tells of a protracted meeting held by him at Mill Creek. He was a very

effectual revivalist and it was not an uncommon occurrence
for his congregation to lose control of their emotions and
engage in a general shout. On such an occasion at Mill
Creek, Rev. Dean was noticed by a few to put the meeting
in charge of an assistant and leave the house. His protracted
absence alarmed those who knew of his departure. Some
feared he was ill. Others said he had repaired to the adjoining woods to engage in silent and secluded prayer. Two
members concluded to investigate. Rev. Dean was found
"cutting a melon" in a neighbor's patch nearby the church.

An Old Letter.

Superintendent of Schools Troy Wilmoth has in his
possession a letter that has been handed down in the Wilmoth
family for more than two centuries. It was written in 1697
by Richard Wilmoth, of Derbyshire, England, to Louis Wilmoth, of Rappahannock, Virginia. The name as explained
by its origin in the chapter on surnames, in another part of
this book, was spelled Wilmot. Richard and Louis Wilmot
were ancestors of the Wilmoth family in Randolph.

The Irish Settlement.

"I've heard whispers of a country that lies beyant the say,
Where rich and poor stand equal in the light of freedom's day.
Oh! Erin must we leave you, driven by the tyrant's hand,
Must we ask a mother's welcome from a strange but happy land,
Where the cruel cross of England's thralldom never shall be seen
And where thank God, we'll live and die still wearing of the green?"

No event in the history of the county will leave more
permanent traces than the settlement on Roaring Creek by the
Irish in 1840-50. This is true from a business, educational, political and religious point of view. These settlers, strong of
body and intellectually alert, inured to toil and hardship, soon
converted the wilderness into a prosperous community of
comfortable homes, churches, and schools amid which sprang
up the village of Kingsville, with the conveniences of a store,
postoffice and blacksmith shop. These settlers were not only
eminently successful themselves in their undertakings, but

bequeathed sons and daughters, who took front rank in the business and professional life of the county.

The first to locate in what is known as the Irish settlement was Patrick Flanigan. He was a contractor and was engaged in the building of the Staunton and Parkersburg pike. He lived for a while after the completion of the pike in the valley, and then bought land and moved to Roaring Creek in 1840-50. Perhaps nearer the former than the latter date.

John O'Connell was the next to locate in that vicinity in about 1850. He was a strong southern sympathizer and in attempting to communicate with the Confederate army at Philippi, in the first year of the war, he was shot and killed near Laurel, from ambush, generally supposed by Union sympathizers.

Patrick O'Connor, who had been engaged in the construction on the Staunton and Parkersburg Pike, bought land of Patrick Flanigan and with his family added to the nucleus of a settlement in its earliest days. He lived to the ripe old age of 108 years.

Daniel Tahany, who came in 1852, was among the first settlers. About seventy families in all located in that section, among whom may be mentioned Michal O'Connor, Peter King, Patrick Riley, Patsy King, Miles King, Edward King, Owen Riley, Andrew Durkin, John Madden, Owen Gillooly, Andrew Durkin, Patrick Gillooly, Patrick O'Connor, Richard Ford, John Ford, Patrick Rafferty, Morris Hanifan, John Nallen Sr., Thomas Burke, Alexander Burke, John Conley, Mathew Davis, John Cain, Patrick Moyles, John A. King, Thomas O'Connor, John Staunton.

The following facts have been ascertained concerning some of the members of the Irish settlers:

John Cain, born in County Mayo, Ireland, married in 1848 to Mary Moyle; children, Peter, Ellen, Sarah, Bridget, Theresa, John, James, Patrick, Ignatius and Maggie. He settled on Roaring Creek in 1860 and died in 1871.

John Conley, born in 1834, Ireland, died 1903. Married

Mary McGinnis; children, Patrick, Anna, John, Mary and Joseph. Settled on Roaring Creek in 1866.

Thomas Burke, born 1845, Longfort County, Ireland; son of Michael and Margaret (Rowan) Burke. Married Mary Ellen, daughter of John A. and Margaret Nallen; children, Patrick F., John Thomas, Margaret A., James and Michael, twins; Mary Ellen and Alexander. He settled on Roaring Creek in 1866 and died in 1890.

Chas. Durkin, born in County Mayo, Ireland, 1818; married Catherine Durkin, daughter of Andrew Durkin Sr., in 1847; children, Edward, Catherine, Andrew, Ellen, Mary and Bridget. He settled on Roaring Creek in 1864 and died at Coalton, W. Va. 1908.

Patrick Durkin, born in County Mayo, Ireland, 1830. He married Margaret, daughter of John and Margaret King in 1855; children, Mary A., John T., William V., Catherine, Edward, Margaret, Alice Agnes, Joseph and Teresa. He settled on Roaring Creek in 1857 and died in 1887.

Alexander Burke, born in Ireland 1842, Longfort County. Son of Michael and Margaret (Rowan) Burke. Married Bridgett Burke in 1865; children, Michael W., Mary A., Bridget D., Catherine, Margaret, John D., James, Dennis, Sarah, Elizabeth, Joseph and Agnes. He died in 1900.

Andrew D. Durkin Jr., born in 1841, Mayo County, Ireland. Married Mary Joyce, daughter of Thomas and Mary Joyce. After the death of his wife, Mary Ellen Joyce, he married Ida Nay. He settled on Roaring Creek in 1866 and died in 1902.

Andrew Durkin Sr., born in County Mayo, Ireland. Settled on Roaring Creek in 1854 and died in 1867.

Mathew Davis, born in Roscommon County, Ireland, in 1820. Married Anna Brady; children, James, Peter, Mary, William, Thomas, Patrick, John, Catherine, Ellen, Agnes, Winifred and Mathew. Mr. Davis died in 1906.

Michael H. King was born in Ireland in 1814. He came to this country in 1855 and settled on Roaring Creek. He married in Ireland, to Bridget Morgan. They had children, John A. and Patrick M., both of whom were born in Ireland. He was treasurer of Roaring Creek District 1865-9.

John A. King, son of Michael and Bridget (Morgan) King was born in 1844, County Galway, Ireland. He came to America with his father, Michael H. King, and with him settled on Roaring Creek. In 1867 he married Mary O'Connor, of Philadelphia. Fifteen children were born to this union, Maria, Michael W., Owen J., Anna T., Patrick F., John T., Alice B., Frances G., Stephen, James, Winifred, Oscar B., William V., Alfred G. and Mary A.

Owen J. King, son of John A. and Mary (O'Connor) King, was born in 1872. He was educated in the public schools. Mr. King has been for a number of years prominently connected with the business interests of the city as merchant and in real estate and insurance, and as member of the City Council. In 1913 he was appointed postmaster of Elkins, which position he holds at the present time. He married Gertrude Collins, of Logansport, Indiana, who died February 6, 1913. Children, Madeline, Mildred and Clarence.

Patrick O'Connor was born in Ireland in 1830 and came to America in 1855. He was a contractor in the building of the B. & O. railroad. After practicing law for a while in Grafton, W. Va., he came to Randolph and purchased land on Roaring Creek in 1865. He was an uncle of Hon. John T. McGraw, of Grafton. He died in 1901.

Thomas O'Connor was born in County Galway, Ireland, in 1824. He came to Roaring Creek in 1866. He married at Cincinnati, Ohio, 1854; children, John P., James, Michael V., and Mary. He died in 1891.

Owen Riley, born in County Galway, Ireland, in 1825. In 1845 he married Mary Malia and came to America in 1852. He came to Roaring Creek in 1855. Children, Bridget, Michael, Patrick, Mary, Ann, John, Maggie and James. He died in 1899.

Patrick Naughton was born in County Mayo, Ireland, and came to America in 1845. After working on the construction of the B. & O. railroad from Cumberland to Grafton in 1851, he came to Roaring Creek in 1856. Children, William, Mary, Maggie, Ellen, Anna and Kate. He died in 1899.

Morris Hanifan, born in County Cavny, Ireland, 1820, came to America in 1840. He worked on the C. & O. Canal in its construction to Cumberland, then on the Winchester and Strawsburg Pike to New Market, Va., then on the Staunton and Parkersburg Pike to Huttonsville. He settled on Roaring Creek in 1847. He married Bettie Kittle. Children, John, Patrick and Isaac. He died in 1868.

John Nallen Sr., was born in County Mayo, Ireland, in 1825. He married in 1845 and came to America in 1846 and settled in Roaring Creek in the same year. Children, James, John, Margaret, Mary E. and Elizabeth. He died in 1901.

Patrick O'Connor, son of Michael O'Connor, was born in County Galway, Ireland, in 1844. In 1876 he was married to Mary McCauley. He settled on Pike near Middle Fork River in Roaring Creek District. Children, Mary, Mathew, Thomas, James and Pearl. He died in 1915.

Daniel Tahany was born in the County Sligo, Ireland, in 1815. He came to America in 1835. He married Bridget McCan in New York City in 1837. After working on the construction of the Staunton and Parkersburg Pike, he settled on Roaring Creek in 1846. Children, Mary, Margaret, Patrick, John, Charles and Jane. He died in 1872.

John O'Donnell was born in Ireland in 1817, and came to America in 1834. Married Margaret Foy. Children, John, Margaret and Maria. He died June 5, 1861, from gun shot wound. He worked on S. & P. Pike in its construction through Roaring Creek District.

The first priest to celebrate Mass in the Kingsville Parish was Father Stack, of Staunton, Va., at Patrick Flanigan's house in 1865. In 1863 Father O'Connor with the aid of his people commenced the erection of a log church, the first Catholic church in Randolph. In 1872 Father Dacey came as resident priest, but died soon thereafter. In 1873 Father Fitzpatric came to take charge of the Mission. Soon the growing congregation became too large for the little church and under the leadership of Father Fitzpatrick, they built a commodious church and rectory in the growing village of Kingsville. Father Fitzpatrick also commenced the erection of a church at Coalton, but it was completed by his successor, Father Sauer.

Father Fitzpatrick was twenty-eight years in Kingsville, but has since died at Wheeling, W. Va. Father Fitzpatrick was for many years one of the leading figures of the county and had many friends throughout Randolph and adjoining counties among the Protestants as well as the adherents of his own religious faith.

The Rev. William Sauer succeeded Father Fitzpatrick, who in turn was succeeded by Rev. William Hall, who was succeeded by the present pastor, Rev. John H. Cochran.

The opportunities of a new country with cheap lands, together with the oppression of English landlordism at home were, perhaps, among the principal reasons for Irish immigration to America. The average price paid by Irish settlers for Roaring Creek lands was about $1.25 per acre. These same lands at the present time command fabulous prices, in many instances, as a result of the discovery of very rich veins of coal in that vicinity.

Owen Gilluly, born in 1816, in the Parish of Killgaffin, County Roscommon, Ireland, son of John and Mary (Johnson) Gilluly. He came to America in 1847, landed in New York, and from there came to West Virginia. In 1842 he married Mary White at Weston, W. Va. He was a stone mason and cutter by trade. In 1853 he moved to St. Louis, Mo., from there to Prairie, Wis., and later to St. Paul, Minn. After spending about five years in the west he returned to West Virginia and settled in Roaring Creek District, Randolph County. In 1858 he purchased a farm of 90 acres and made some improvements on it. After the war he returned to his trade and was foreman on the construction work of the Weston Asylum for 13 years, he also did the mason work on the Wesleyan Academy, at Buckhannon, in 1882, and was contractor on the first Catholic church built in Randolph County in the year of 1864. He spent the last few years of his life on his farm. An incident which goes to show that he was not easily outdone happened in 1863 in the time of the Civil War. When General Imboden raided this county one of his soldiers took a horse belonging to him, he being away from home at the time, and on his return he quickly followed after by a near cut, overtaking the soldier on the west bank of the Mid-

dle Fork River and catching his horse by the bridle, commanding the soldier to dismount which he did, and the captain being near by seeing his undaunted courage told the soldier to
let him have his horse.

He died December 25th, 1886, at the age of 69 years, and
was buried in St. Vincents cemetery near Kingsville, W. Va.
His wife died July 2nd, 1903, and is buried at the same place.

Their children's names were as follows: John, Mary, Ella,
James J., Annie, Bridget, Margaret, Katherine, Owen, William, Joseph, Agnes, Elizabeth, Teresa, and Sarah.

Edward Joyce was born in County Galway, Ireland, in
the year of 1833; married Bridget Joyce in 1857. He worked
on the B. & O. railroad for a while, coming to Roaring Creek
District in 1859, and purchased 220 acres of land in the Roaring Creek Coal fields, which he improved and farmed. He
also dealt in cattle and sheep. He spent some time in the employ of the government in repairing roads in 1864, and served
a term as justice of the peace in 1863-1867. He was a remarkable leader and very honorable in all his dealings. Children's names were John T., James, Mary A., William L., Martin, Miles, Edward, Annie, Peter, Stephen and Isaac.

Michael King, born in 1839, in Parish of............................,
County Galway, Ireland, son of Owen and Bridget (Morgan)
King, came to America in 1850, and learned the plastering
trade. He was in the government employ for three or four
years during the Civil War, after which he went to Baltimore,
Md., and in 1865 married Delia Joyce, sister of State Senator
Eugene Joyce, who served one or two terms in that capacity,
and was later elected municipal judge of Baltimore. He then
came to Randolph County, W. Va., settled in Roaring Creek
District, where he erected a house and store, this being the
only store in that district for five or six years. He afterward
bought a farm of 120 acres in the Roaring Creek coal field,
which he improved and farmed for a number of years.
Through his efforts a postoffice was established which was
known as the Kingsville postoffice, and he was appointed postmaster, and served in that capacity during all the time he remained at Kingsville, with the exception of a couple of short
intervals.

In 1895 he purchased eight acres of land at Fisher, (now known as Mabie) and built the Mountain View Hotel, of which he is proprietor. He is engaged in the mercantile business, and is also postmaster at Mabie. His home is located almost on the spot where General McClellan's headquarters were when he camped at Roaring Creek just before the battle of Rich Mountain, July 11, 1861.

Children's names are Eugene, Joseph M., William, Walter, Anna S., Katherine, Ada and Lillian.

Michael H. King, born in County Galway, Ireland, in the year of 1814, son of Owen and Anna King, married in Ireland in 1834 to Bridget (Morgan) King, immigrated to America in 1850, and settled in Roaring Creek District. In 1856 he purchased 400 acres of land which he farmed. He was elected Township Treasurer in 1865 and served a term of four years. Children were John A. and Owen.

Patrick Moyle was born in 1834, Parish of Cross Malina, County Mayo, Ireland, and came to America in 1855, landed at Baltimore, Md. He married Mary Cain, who was also from same Parish. He remained there until 1860, when he came to Roaring Creek and bought 150 acres of land in the Roaring Creek coal fields where he built a home, improved and farmed the land and lived the remainder of his life. He also bought other land and property in Elkins, W. Va.

He died in 1902, and was buried in St. Vincent's cemetery near Kingsville, W. Va. His wife died a year or two later and is also burried at the same place. Children's names are as follows: John, James, Matthew, Daniel, Patrick, William, Mary Anna and Sarah.

Elihu A. Madden, son of John Madden and Cecelia (Dwire) Madden, was born in 1849 in Randolph County, W. Va., and married Anna Gilluly, daughter of Owen and Mary (White) Gilluly, November 5, 1883. He received his education in the public schools. In 1868 he started to work at stone work and learned the stone cutting and masoning trade after which he was employed on the locks on the Little Kanawha River, later by the Edgar Thompson Company in the construction of their steel plant at Braddock, Pa., then on the water works in Pittsburgh, returning to his home in 1880 where he worked on the farm until he was married. He purchased a farm of 100 acres adjoining 72 acres willed to him by his father. Both tracts were in Roaring Creek coal field and he farmed them until the city of Elkins begun to build, when he was employed on the construction of the West Virginia Central Railway shops, the Hotel Randolph, National and Trust Bank buildings, court house, Davis and Elkins College and the central high school building. In 1900 he moved his family to Elkins, which place has been his home since that time. Children, Mary E., B. Gertrude, Patrick F., Thomas J., Elizabeth B., Charles C. A., Leo C., Jerome L. A., Bernard, Agnes and John.

Thomas Madden, son of John and Cecelia (Dwire) Madden was born in 1846. He received his education in the public schools of the state. During the war he was in the employ of the government as teamster and later was made wagon master or manager of a train of wagons. He was present at the battles of Bull Run, Antietem and South Mountain. After the war was over he returned home and again entered school and studied for a couple of terms, and in 1870 took up the profession of teaching, at which he was considered very successful, and taught until the time of his death. He died May 5th, 1887.

Martin Madden, son of John and Cecelia (Dwire) Madden, was born in 1858 in Randolph County, W. Va. He was educated in the public schools. He married Norah Moore in 1882. He taught school for about 20 years. He went west in 1888 and stayed about a year and then returned to West Virginia. In 1894 he went into the mercantile business at Coalton, which he has followed all the time since, either at Mabie or at Coalton. He is located at Mabie at the present time.

William P., son of John and Cecelia (Dwire) Madden was born in Randolph County in 1857. He received his education in the free schools from 1867 to 1870. He worked on public works in Maryland in 1871 and 1872, and in 1873 went to Weston, W. Va., where he was employed on the stone work of the Weston Asylum for a short time, going from there to Pittsburgh where he worked on the Pittsburgh Water Works until 1875. He then returned home and worked on the farm until 1877, when he took up the profession of school teaching at which he was fairly successful. In 1884 he again returned home and went to work on the home farm, later purchasing 50 acres of land in the Roaring Creek coal field, and his father willed him 72 acres adjoining it, making 122 acres in all, which he still owns. At the death of his father, upon him fell the responsibility of keeping up the home, where he lived with his mother and sister until the death of his mother, after which he and his sister Sarah moved to Coalton, W. Va., where they now reside. He served as a member of the Book Board for five years.

Edward D., son of John and Cecelia (Dwire) Madden, was born at Old Town, Md., in 1840. He married Katherine, daughter of Patrick and Bridget O'Connor in 1874. He entered the government service in 1861 and was employed as a teamster until 1865, being present at the battle of Gettysburg. In 1865 he enlisted in the Seventh West Virginia Regiment and served as a soldier until the close of the war, being mustered out of service at Wheeling, W. Va., in July 1865.

In 1871 he purchased a farm of 50 acres in the Roaring Creek coal fields, and on the death of his father was willed 100 acres of land, making a total of 150 acres. He made his home here and farmed until 1908, when he moved to Elkins where he owns property and now resides. Children, Mary, Dennis, Edward D., Annie, Joseph.

Francis P. Madden, son of John and Cecelia (Dwire) Madden, was born in 1856, in Randolph County, W. Va. He received his education in the free schools of the State, and in 1871 he took up the profession of school teaching which he followed for a few years, but wishing to further his education he entered the Flemington College where he studied for a couple of terms, and then returned to teaching. In 1887 he was elected County Superintendent, and in 1889 resigned to accept a position in the Census Department at Washington D. C., where he remained until 1893, at which time he returned to Randolph County and taught school for a short time, and later went into the merchandising business at Beverly and later at Coalton, W. Va., where he remained until the time of his death. He died in 1902 and was buried in St. Vincent's cemetery near Kingsville.

John Madden, son of William and Mary (Brennan) Madden, was born in the Parish of Kiltormer, County Galway, Ireland, in 1815. In 1834 he came to America, landed in New York City, and after a short stay in the State of New York he came to Baltimore, Md., and was employed on the construction of the Chesapeake and Ohio Canal from that point to Cumberland. In 1839 he was married to Cecelia Dwire. He then went to work on the State road from Winchester to Staunton, Va., and later was employed on the Staunton and Parkersburg pike to Huttonsville, W. Va. He then located in Tygarts Valley near Huttonsville, where he worked as a tenant on the farms of Moses and John Hutton, also on the Nagler farm. In 1859 he moved to Roaring Creek District, and in 1863 purchased 350 acres of land in the Roaring Creek coal field from Cyrus Kittle, which he lived on and farmed the remainder of his life. He died February 9th, 1877, and was buried in St. Vincents cemetery near Kingsville, W. Va. His wife died August 15th, 1900, and is buried at the same place. Their children's names were as follows: Edward D., John, Thomas, William P., Elihu A., James, Mary A., Michael, Francis P., Martin, Peter and Sara A.

John Stanton was born in Ireland, County Galway, Parish of Kiltormer, in 1826. He received an education in the National schools of his country, and was married to Bridget Morrisey; immigrated to America in 1850, landed in New York, going from there to Connecticut where he located and being a shoemaker, worked at that trade for three years, then he came to Grafton, W. Va., and worked along the B. & O. railroad from that point to Kingwood, W. Va. In 1857 he came to Randolph County, W. Va., and settled in Roaring Creek district, where he purchased 250 acres of land, improved it and farmed; also worked at the shoemaker's trade. After the war he taught in the free school of the district. He was appointed postmaster at Middle Fork postoffice, Roaring Creek district, in Grant's second administration, 1873, in which capacity he served until 1884, when he was removed by Grover Cleveland but was reinstated under William Mc-

Kinley and served the remainder of his life. He died in 1895 and was buried in St. Vincent's cemetery near Kingsville. Seven of his children lived to be grown. Their names are Patrick, Thomas, George, Peter, Elizabeth, Mary and Catherine.

Luke White, born in the Parish of Kiltevin, County Roscommon, Ireland, came to America in 1854, landing in New York City. He came to West Virginia and married Margaret Burke, a widow. He worked on the B. & O. for a time and later settled in Roaring Creek district, and in 1858 purchased a farm of 100 acres where he made his home for the rest of his life. He donated two acres of land to the Catholic congregation for church property and cemetery, and later when more ground was needed he sold them seven and one-half acres more to be used as garden, pasture, etc. The priests who visited that Parish prior to the time a Parish house was erected, stayed at his house where they were made to feel very much at home. In 1872 a Parish house was built, that being the time at which Rev. Michael Fitzpatrick became pastor. He died in 1881 and was buried at St. Vincent's cemetery near Kingsville, W. Va. His wife died a few years later and was buried at the same place.

CHAPTER XVI.

FAMILY HISTORY.

Origin of Surnames.

OUR surnames, like everything else, had a beginning. In England they were confined to the higher and land holding class prior to the fourteenth century. Many of the names familiar in the history of this county first appeared in Domes Day Book, written in England in 1086. It consisted of a list of land holders at that time. Its authority was not to be questioned in disputes as to title to land and for this reason was called the Domes Day Book or book of judgment.

Surnames were originally written over the other name and is derived from the Latin surnom or the French super nomen.

Many names were derived from their baptismal ones by adding the suffix son to the name of the father as John-son, Wil-son, William-son, Peter-son, Richard-son, Adam-son.

The practice of using diminutives was often adopted by the people to multiply the comparatively limited number of names at their command. The Saxon diminutives commonly used were kin, cock, ock, and the Norman ones at, et, on, or in. Therefore it is ascertainable whether names so ending are Norman or Saxon in their origin.

Before surnames came into vogue it was by no means an uncommon practice to give all the sons of one family one name, as William for example. They would be called Wil-kin, Will-cock, Will-ot, Will-mot, which in the process of time has changed to Wilmoth.

The suffixes ham, nam, an, and er were often used for man. Thus originated the name Rowan, Rose-an, being identical with Rose-man, has passed through changes in orthography, as Rows-an, until we have at present Rowan.

Likewise we have the name Cuningham, derived from Coney, Teutonic for rabbit and ham Norman for man. The old form of spelling Coney was Cunyng. In the regulation of the Scottish Privy Council, August 6, 1602, regulating the Masters and Barons of the University of Glaglow, amongst the viands mentioned were "with ane foull or cunyng or a pair of dovis and ciclyk to their Supper." Another probable origin of the name is from the Anglo-Saxon Cyning for leader and ham, Norman for man. Then we have Cyningham, the leader man.

The suffix lea, leah now ley is Anglo-Saxon, meaning an untilled tract of land or pasturage, used as a shelter for animals. In the origin of the name Woodley we have the Anglo-Saxon word Wudu, meaning wood and lea or leah, meaning land or pasturage. We then have Wudu-lea, now Woodley, meaning a lea on which there is a wood.

Roman names were derived from mental or physical characteristics. Such words are Wise, Sharp, Dear, Able, Long, Crouch, and Armstrong. The Romans were also partial to animals covered with wool. It is probable that such names as Fox, Wolf, and Bear had a Roman origin.

A very large number of other names had their origin in the occupations as Weaver, Carpenter, Miller, etc.

Surnames in some instances had their origin in the sneers of the vulgar, as is evidenced in the name Proudfoot.

ALLEN—Gaelic, exceedingly fair. In Domes Day Book as Alan.

ARMSTRONG—Strength in battle. An ancient King of Scotland had his horse killed under him and Fairburn, his armour bearer, taking him by the thigh, set him in his own saddle. The King gave him the appellation of Armstrong. See Scott's Lay of The Last Minstrel.

AP, MAB, and AB are Welsh words meaning son. In the early history of Randolph we find Morgan ap Morgan.

AT or ATTE was used to describe the place of residence as John-at-Wood, now Atwood.

BENT—English, a plain or Moor.

BELL—The name Bell was taken from the sign of an inn or tavern. The sign of a bell was frequently used to designate that the house was an inn. John-at-the-bell became John Bell. Belle in French means beautiful.

BARNARD—The name Barnard is from Bean or Bairn, a child and ard, Teutonic for nature. The word Barnard, therefore, described one of a child-like nature, or affection.

BING—The surname Bing is from the Danish Binge, an inclosure or a place where supplies are kept.

BOGART—German, Boomelgard, an orchard.

BOSELEY—The name Boseley is derived like Bosworth except that the suffixes "lea" and "worth" have reference to small estates slightly different in their characteristics.

BOSWORTH—The Anglo-Saxon words, wirth, worth, urth, means a small estate. This word combined with the old Norse word Bass, middle English Bose or Boose, "a stall in which cattle are kept in winter," gives us Bose-worth or Booseworth, now Bosworth. Bosworth would then mean a worth on which there is a boose or an estate on which there is a cattle stall. However, there is another probable origin of the word Bosworth. This Bos is from the personal name Bosa or Boso, found more than a score of times in the Onomasticon. In this case Bosworth means the worth or estate of Boso, getting its name from the owner.

BRADLEY—The name Bradley is from the Anglo-Saxon word Bradlea, Brad meaning broad and "lea" or "leah" a pasturage.

BUTCHER—Norse as Buoker, Danish as Boedker, German as Boettcher, Flemish as Buker or Buscher, French as Boucher.

CAR—French as Carre, meaning broad shouldered, Norse as Karr. In Domes Day Book as Carr.

CASSIDY—Gaelic from cassaideach, apt to complain.

CHENY—French, a grove.

COB—German as Kobe, Scotch as Kobbes. The name appears in the Domes Day Book as Copsi. The English Cob originated from Jacob.

COLLETT—The word Collett is from the ecclesiastical word Acolyte, attendant, and is from the Greek. The Acolyte was one of the minor order of clergy in the ancient church. We learn from the canons of the fourth council of Carthage that the Archdeacon at the ordination put into the hands of the Acolyte a candlestick with a taper and an empty pitcher to imply that they were appointed to light the candles of the church and to furnish wine for the eucharist. Their dress was the cossack and the surplice. The name and the office still exist in the church.

COLLIER—French as Coulier.

CRAWFORD—The name Crawford is Gaelic in its origin, and means a pass of blood. From "cru," bloody and "ford" a way. The name was first assumed by the barony of Crawford in England.

CURTIS—The name Curtis is derived from and is an abbreviation of courteous. The name was perhaps first applied to a person noted for his urbanity.

DANIELS—The name Daniels is from Daniel, signifying the judgment of God. The "s" added is a contraction of son.

DAVIS—French as Devis.

DENTON—Denton is derived from "Den" a valley and "ton" a town, meaning a town in a valley.

DICK—Dyck, German bulwark thrown against a sea or river.

DILWORTH—French, Diluerth.

DOVE—Norse, Dufan, German, Dove.

DOWNING—A local name in Worchester, England.

FERGUSON—From the Gaelic and Celtic Feor, meaning man and Guth, meaning voice or word. The two words meaning the man of the word or commander. A fierce and brave chieftain.

GILMORE—From the Irish, McGiolla Muire.

GOFF—Goff is the variation of the German word Gough or Gow, being the German for the English Smith, and is, therefore, occupational in its origin.

HANSFORD—The name Hansford is derived from the Welsh words, "Han" meaning old and "ford" meaning way. The name Hanford, now Hansford, therefore, means the old way.

HARDING—Norse as Haddingr. Harding from "here" or "har," meaning an army and "ing" a meadow. A meadow in which an army is encamped.

HARMAN—The name Harman is from the German "Har" originally meaning soldier and man. The name, therefore, was perhaps first applied to a military man.

HART—Norse as Hyortr. In Domesday Book as Hard.

HARPER—Some names as Harper may be either German or English in their origin. Harper, meaning one who contributes to musical entertainments, would lead to the conclusion that the name is of English etymology, being occupational in its origin. However in the early records of Shenandoah Valley, the word as Herber and Herrber. This makes it probable that the name is German.

HARRIS—Norse as Harri, Domesday Book as Harries.

HAZELTINE, from Hazeldine.

HERON—Welsh, a hero.

HILL—German, Hille.

HUTTON—The Anglo-Saxon words "tun" and "ton" mean small enclosed farmsteads or villages. In the derivation of the word Hough-ton, now Hutton, we have the Anglo-Saxon words "Hough" or "Hoh," meaning a heel and "tun" or "ton" meaning an enclosed village or farmstead. The name Houghton, now Hutton, was probably applied originally to a resident of an enclosed village or farmstead in the shape of a "hoh" or heel.

JACKSON—English, Danish as Jacobson, French as Jackchen.

JOYCE—Irish, Normandy as Joyeus.

KENDALL—An English word derived from the two words Kent and Dale. Kent-dale, now Ken-dall, meant a dale on the River Kent, so the name was probably applied originally to a people living in such a locality.

KELLY—The surname Kelly is derived from the Gaelic and Celtic Kill or Cille, a church. The name was, perhaps, first applied to an individual who was in some manner connected with the church.

KENNEDY—Irish, O'Ceannfhada, originally.

KYLE—The name Kyle is from a district in Scotland, through which the River Coyle flows.

KITTLE—A name introduced into England, perhaps, at the time of the Norman conquest. Thor, the Supreme God of the Norsemen, is the root word of many of our surnames. The sacrificial kettle or cauldron was an important article in the worship of Thor. Thor-Kettle or Thyr-Kittle is a common name in England to this day. The word now appears in this country as Kittle.

LONG—It is said that the name Long originated from a very tall attendant of Lord Treasurer Hungerford. The Longs were very numerous in Oxfordshire, Cambridge, England, in the reign of Edward the First.

LLOYD—From the Gaelic Lhuyd and signifies gray or brown.

MARSHALL—The name Marshall originated in the north of England and was at first spelled Marechal. It means master of the horse.

MAXWELL—The Maxwells took their name from a village in Roxburgshire, England.

McLEAN—The name McLean is derived from MacGilean, a highland chieftain and a celebrated warrior.

McINTOSH—"Mac," son, and "tosh," leader. Then McIntosh means son of a leader.

MOORE—The name Moore is from the Celtic word "morh," meaning big.

MULLENIX—French as Molynix, from "moulin" a mill.

McQUAIN—Irish, and is probably derived from "Mac," son, and "cairn," a heap of stones erected by the early inhabitants of the British Islands as sepulchral monuments. The name was originally McCairn.

PHILLIPS—The surname Phillips is from a Greek word meaning a lover of horses.

PRITT—From the Norse Prudi.

RUSSEL—French from Roussel, a stream or brook. In Domesday Book as Rozell.

RYAN—Normandy as Royan, Danish as Ryan,.

SCHOONOVER—Derived from Schoonoven, a place in South Holland. The word is from "Schoon," an old Dutch word meaning fine and "hoven," a garden or court.

SCOTT—The origin of the name Scott is clouded in doubt. Scotylle, Anglo-Saxon for winnowing fan is given by some writers as the original word. Other scholars say the word meant rulers or possessors. Again it is maintained that the Scotts who invaded Argyle in 360 were so called because the word "Scotti" meant sacred painters or sculptors, an art in which these people were proficient.

SEE—German, lake. Thunersee, the lake of Thun.

SHANNON—The name Shannon is derived from the Shannon River in Ireland. The word was originally Shenabhanon.

SHREEVES—Derived from "Schir," a Shire, division, or township and reeve, the Bailiff. The word then means a Bailiff of a Shire.

S—The Welsh merely appended "s" instead of son as Edwards and Davis.

SMITH—The word Smith was an occupational one; the original word was "smote," the art of striking the anvil. The name is a very common one because, at the time of the adoption of surnames, the smith made almost everything used in the arts of war and peace. A very large number of people were engaged in the trades of gunsmith, blacksmith, tinsmith, silversmith, etc.

STALNAKER—Derived from the German word "Stahal" or "Stahl" meaning steele, and "Nagel," a sharp point or spear. Then the original word was Stahl-nagel, meaning a sharp pointed steele spear. So the name was, perhaps, first applied to a warrior who was armed with such a weapon.

TAGGART—Appears as McTaggart in Scotch.

TALBOTT—English, and appears in the Domesday Book as spelled at present.

TYRE—Derived from "Tyreman," a dresser. From the fact that the Norman suffix "er" is used to abbreviate the word, it is to be presumed that it is of Norman origin.

WARD—From the Anglo-Saxon "weard," a watchman.

WARNER—Appears in the Domesday Book as Warn.

WEESE—From the German "weiss" meaning white, or "waas" meaning bold.

WAMSLEY—Derived from a Lancashire township of that name.

WEYMOTH—The name Weymoth is provincial in its origin, being first, perhaps, applied to residents about the mouth of the small River Wey in England. The City of Wey at the mouth of this river, is very ancient. The Anglo-Saxon word was Wagemuth, from "wage" meaning a wave or passage way, and "muth" meaning a mouth.

WHITE—Derived from the Anglo-Saxon "hweit," meaning fairness of complexion.

WILMOTH—derived from the baptismal name of William as explained elsewhere. Originally the name was spelled Wilmot.

Nicholas was a favorite name in the Wilmot family in England. Sir Nicholas was Knight in the seventeenth century in England. His grandfather was named Nicholas. It is significant that the eldest of the Wilmoth brothers to locate in Randolph was named Nicholas.

YEAGER—Danish, huntsman. Yagere also means a sweetheart.

Variation in Surnames.

Individual peculiarities in pronunciation largely accounts for the variations in spelling of surnames. In the earlier history of the county names were seldom written and the ear was the only guide to the spelling and in some cases the only method of transmitting names from one generation to another. Then the settler often coming direct from European countries, embraced the opportunity to simplify and abbreviate a cumbersome name. This was particularly true of German names. The object was sometimes to change the form into English. Thus we have Armikast changed to Arbogast, Herman tracht to Armentrout, Bauman to Bowman, Kromet to Crummett, Kerper to Carper, Dahle to Dolly, Herber to Harper, Herrman to Harman, Heffner to Hevener, Huber to Hoover, Loch to Lough, Roeder to Rader, Sieman to Simmons, Schaefer to Shaver, Schneider to Snyder, Sponaugen to Sponaugle, Tehudi to Judy, Wetzel to Whetsell, Wildfang to Wilfong, Zwickenfus to Zickafoose.

Classification of Names.

The following classification of names though not free from error is in the main correct:

English.

Ayers.

Blair, Bosworth, Bell, Brown, Bradley, Barlow, Bent, Bennett, Bishop, Bond, Boseley, Blackman, Brandley.

Chenoweth, Cook, Channell.

Daniels, Day, Digman, Davisson, Dawson, Denton.

Earle, Elliott, England, Elza, Elkins.

Findley, Fox.

Goddin, Gibon, Gandy, Gawthrop.

Haymond, Hart, Harding, Hansford, Hunt, Hutton, Harris, Henderson, Hadden, Holder, Howell.

Isner.

Jones, Jackson, Johnson.

Kittle, Kelley, Kimble.

Lamb, Lee, Long.

Marshall, Morris, Mason.

Porter, Powers, Payne, Pennington, Patterson, Potts.

Russell, Roy, Reed, Robinson.

Smith, Summerfield, Skidmore, Shreve.

Taylor, Turner, Taft, Thompson, Triplett.

Woodford, Williamson, Weymouth, Wamsley, Woodley, Ward, Wilmoth, White, Wilson.

Irish.

Adams, Adamson.

Burns, Bodkin, Boggs, Brady, Boyles, Beaty.

Clark, Collier, Connolly, Cain, Coff, Crickard, Cunningham, Currence.

Donohoe, Daugherty, Davis, Durkin.

Ford, Ferguson Flanigan.

Gainer.

Jordan, Joyce.

Keenan, Kinnan, Kee, Kennedy.

Murphy, McLain, McAllister.

Phares.

Rains, Rooney, Ryan, Rowan.

Scott.

Wood.

German.

Alt, Arbogast, Armentrout.

Bowers, Baker, Ball, Buckey, Bowman.

Car, Conrad, Caplinger, Crummett, Carper, Canfield, Collins, Curtis.

Dove, Dolly.

Eberman, Eye.

Fisher, Friend.

Goff.

Haigler, Halterman, Harman, Harper, Hedrick, Hevener, Hinkle, Hoover, Huffman.

Judy.

Ketterman, Kyle.

Lantz, Lough.

Marteny, Moyers, Marstiller.

Rigleman, Rosencranse, Rader, Riffle, Rohrbaugh, Rinehart.

Shaver, Simmons, Sites, Snyder, Sponaugle, Swadley, Smith, Stalnaker, See, Swecker, Schoonover.

Teter, Tingle, Tolly.

Vandevander, Vanpelt.

Westfall, Weere, Wolf, Wimer, Whetsell.

Yokum, Yeager.

Zickafoose.

Scotch.

Anderson, Armstrong.

Collett, Cowgeer, Cunningham, Campbell, Crawford.

Lambert, Logan.

McLeary, McMullen, McClung, McLean, McDonald, McQuain, McCorkel.

Nelson.
Simpson, Skidmore.
Thompson.
Vansoy.
Welch.

Welch.

Davis.
Howell.
Lewis.
Williams.

French.

Capitio, Cassell.
Montony, Mullenix.
Tyre.

Spanish.

Pedro.

Extinct Families of Randolph.

This list includes pioneer families of Randolph that have no descendants of the same name residing within the county. Families of the same name may live in the county, but they are not of the same strain of blood as the names here mentioned. As a rule these families pushed farther west when Randolph assumed the staid aspect of older communities:

Anderson, Armstrong, Adams, Alford.

Barnhouse, Bingham, Blair, Bogard, Baxter, Bell, Blain, Bond, Botkin, Bruff, Bridger, Booth, Breckenridge, Bent, Brian, Buffington, Briggs, Bozart, Bogard.

Connonly, Cutright, Cade, Casto, Carpenter, Casey, Cassity, Claypool, Crane, Combs, Carney.

Donohoe, Dougherty, Dolbeare.

Evick, Eberman England, Friend, Fink, Files.

Gandy, Gibson.

Haigler, Heath, Holder, Hughes, Hiller, Harris.

Kinnan, Kozer.

Lackey, Leeky, Longacker.

Mace, McLeary, McLean, McMullen, Maxwell, Myers, Maddix.

Nelson.

Osborn.

Petty, Powell.

Ralston, Rummell, Reeder, Rollins.

Springtone, Stout, Steers, Slagle.

Taft, Taggart, Taffee, Troutwine, Turner.

Warthen, Warwick, Whitman, Whiteman, Wise, Wolf.

HISTORIES OF FAMILIES IN RANDOLPH COUNTY.

In this chapter will be found a brief history of the pioneer families of Randolph; their origin, place of settlement and such other facts as are now obtainable:

THE ARNOLD FAMILY.

Arnold. In the year 1765 three brothers, Jonathan, Andrew, and Jesse Arnold removed from Chester County, near Philadelphia, the place of their birth, and located in the vicinity of old Fort Redstone (now Brownsville, Pa.). The history of Chester County makes mention of but one family of the name of Arnold residing there prior to the date named, viz: Richard Arnold, who died in the year 1720 leaving a large family. He was presumably the grandfather of the three brothers named. At that time this section was claimed to be a part of Virginia, and the Arnold brothers supposed they were locating in that State. They brought with them their family slaves. Later when the controversy as to the State line was settled, leaving this section in Pennsylvania, their supposed slaves being in free territory were free.*

I. Jonathan, the first of the above named brothers, had married Rachel Scott. There was born to them children as follows: Samuel, Benjamin, Levi, Jonathan, William, of

---

*The county records, of that period, containing enumeration of property includes the slaves and names of owners.

whom further mention is made; James, Rachel, Hannah and Sarah. The said William and James were twin brothers. It may be mentioned as an interesting incident, that in a geneaogical chart of the Arnold family on file in the Congressional Library in Washington, extending back to the eleventh century, inscriptions are copied from four tombstones in England, of about the sixteenth century, and three of the four bear the same family names above given, viz: William Arnold, born 1537, James Arnold died 1631, Sarah Arnold born 1623.

II.   William, son of Jonathan and Rachel (Scott) Arnold, was brought up and resided in what later became Greene County, Pennsylvania. He married Hulda Knotts, daughter of a prominent citizen of the same section. Here he owned a valuable farm and followed that occupation. Children, Jonathan of whom further, William, Rachel, Sarah, Charles Pinkney and Caroline.

III.   Jonathan (III) the eldest son of William and Hulda (Knotts) Arnold was born and raised on his father's farm near West Brownsville, Greene County, Pa., the date of his birth being March 27th, 1802. He settled at Beverly, in Randolph County, then Virginia, in 1822, where he continued to reside until his death which occured July 20th, 1883.

Upon locating in Beverly, Jonathan Arnold established a tannery. He continued in this business a few years only, when he engaged in speculating and cattle grazing, being usually successful in his business ventures. He was an ardent Whig, and was for years one of the leaders of his party in his adopted county. He never sought nor would he accept office, but many a political battle was waged in the county under his leadership, the result leaving no doubt in the minds of the opposition as to his active participation therein. He was a conservative man of the soundest judgment, of unquestioned integrity, of a kind heart, sympathetic and considerate with those in distress, of uncompromising sternness with dishonesty in any place, and a trusted friend who could always be relied upon. His advice and judgment were frequently sought, and given freely to those whom he esteemed, and when observed rarely failing to benefit and profit the recipient.

At the breaking out of the Civil War Jonathan Arnold

was strongly opposed to the State seceding from the Union, and he voted in 1861, with the minority in his county, against the ratification of the Ordinance of Secession. Early in the war, however, when he saw the policy of the Federal administration trending, in his opinion, beyond the limits of the Constitution, he experienced no great change in finding his sympathies more in accord with the seceding states, as they seemed to him more nearly in line with the tenets of the Constitution. He was fearless in adherence to his principles and convictions, and he strongly opposed and voted against the formation of the State of West Virginia, at a time when such a vote stamped one with disloyalty in the eyes of the Federal commanders stationed throughout the State, and subjected him to risk of arrest and imprisonment. In the autumn of 1863, he was arrested by the United States authority; was never informed as to any charge against him except the general charge of disloyalty, and was held as a prisoner until the close of the war. Through the intercession of influential friends he was paroled within narrow limits shortly after his arrest, but was not allowed to return to the vicinity of his home until a short time preceding his release.

Jonathan Arnold possessed one of the largest and most carefully selected libraries in his section of the State. Endowed with an unusually retentive memory, he read his books and between the lines, the result being that he was a man of unusual information.

In the year 1827 he united in marriage with Thursa, daughter of Eli and Elizabeth (Hart) Butcher, a prominent merchant and resident of Beverly. He lost his wife within a little over a year, one child only surviving the mother, but dying in youth. In 1841 he married Phoebe Ann, daughter of Solomon and Edith (Davisson) Collett, and was again unfortunate, his wife dying in a few months. In September, 1844, he was united in marriage with Laura Ann, daughter of Jonathan and Julia (Neale) Jackson, of Clarksburg, West Virginia, and the only sister of Thomas J., afterward General "Stonewall" Jackson.* By this marriage there were four

---

*See sketch of Edward Jackson.

children, the youngest dying in infancy, the three eldest
being Thomas Jackson, Anna Grace, and Stark W., who died
in 1898. Anna Grace became the wife of Major C. H. Evans,
of Springfield, O. She died in 1878, having previously lost
her two little children.

IV. Thomas Jackson Arnold was born at Beverly, No-
vember 3, 1845. He was the eldest son of Jonathan and Laura
Ann (Jackson) Arnold. At the age of thirteen he was placed
in school at Lexington, Va., making his home with his uncle,
Major Jackson, afterward General "Stonewall" Jackson. In
1863-4 he attended school at Parkersburg, West Va., under
Rev. William L. Hyland, rector of Christ Church. In 1866
he began the study of law at Beverly, under Colonel David
Goff, and afterward took the course in law and equity at
Washington and Lee University, Virginia, graduating from
that institution in 1867, with the degree of LL.B. Judge John
W. Brokenbrough at that time filling the chair. The next
year he began the practice of his profession in his native town
and in the autumn of that year was elected Prosecuting Attorney for Randolph. In 1879 he was re-elected by a largely
increased majority, and in 1872 was for the third time elected
with a still larger majority. The last term was for four years,
under the new Constitution, then but recently adopted.

On June 1, 1876, Mr. Arnold married Miss Eugenia Hill,
daughter of Lieutenant-General D. H. Hill, a distinguished
Confederate officer. General Hill was prominent in many
battles of the Civil War. He was in command at Big Bethel,
the first important Confederate victory. As Major-General
his Division did some of the heaviest fighting in the Seven
Days battles near Richmond, particularly at Fair Oaks,
Gaine's Mill, and Malvern Hill; later at Second Bull Run, at
South Mountain and Antietam or Sharpsburg. At Chicka-
mauga, as Lieutenant-General, he commanded an army corps,
the right wing of Bragg's army. He surrendered with Joseph
E. Johnston, April, 1865. After the war he was quite promi-
nent in literary and educational work to the time of his death,
September 24th, 1889. Miss Hill was a native of Lexington,
Va., but from childhood her father's home was in Charlotte,
North Carolina.

In 1880, Mr. Arnold removed to San Diego, California, where he continued the practice of law. In 1886 he was appointed by President Cleveland, Collector of the Port of San Diego, and continued in that position throughout the remainder of Mr. Cleveland's term and for nearly two years under the Harrison administration. The duties of the office during the period of his incumbency were particularly arduous, in consequence of the rapid growth of San Diego from a town of 3,000 to a city of 25,000 inhabitants. The records of the Treasury Department show that during Mr. Arnold's administration the cost of collecting in the San Diego District was reduced to a lower percentage on the dollar collected than had ever been done before or since. The following newspaper extract is from the pen of his successor in office under the Republican administration: "Mr. Arnold yesterday surrendered the office of Collector of the Port of San Diego to his successor. Mr. Arnold has held the office for nearly a full term, and has administered it with his characteristic integrity and fidelity. His rulings on close questions, upon which there were no decisions, have been sustained by the Department with much uniformity, and he has had the pleasure of seeing several of his suggestions adopted as Department rules of administration. The business of the office has increased largely during his term of office, and he turns it over to his successor in good condition."

In 1896 Mr. Arnold, with his family, returned to West Virginia to look after his business interests in that State. He resided on one of his farms at Arnold Hill station, midway between Elkins and Beverly. There were born to Mr. and Mrs. Arnold four children, a daughter, Miss Isabel, and three sons, viz: Daniel Harvey Hill, Thomas Jackson and Eugene H.

V. Daniel Harvey Hill, son of Thomas Jackson and Eugenia (Hill) Arnold, was born at Beverly, W. Va. He was educated at the preparatory schools in San Diego, Calif., later attended Davidson College, North Carolina, then Washington and Lee University, from which he graduated with the degree of bachelor of arts in the year 1900. Later he took a course of law in the office of his uncle, Judge Joseph M. Hill, late Chief Justice of the Supreme Court of Arkansas. From there he went to the University of Michigan, at Ann Arbor, where he completed his law course. He has been engaged since 1902 in the practice of his profession at the city of Elkins, in which he has been successful and is an energetic and leading citizen. He is a director of the Peoples National Bank, is a member of the Ancient Free and Accepted Masons, and of the Benevolent and Protective Orders of Elks.

Mr. Arnold married at Monticello, Fla., October 24, 1906, Mary Ann, born at Monticello, November 29, 1884, died at Elkins, September 1, 1909, without issue; daughter of James and Mary (Hansell) Denham. Her father served in the Confederate Army in the Civil War, and was afterward a merchant and planter, living at Monticello. In Auguest, 1914, Mr. Arnold married the second time, Miss Rebecca Andrews, of Staunton, Va. They have one child, a daughter.

VI. Thomas Jackson, son of Thomas Jackson and Eugenia (Hill) Arnold, was born in San Diego, California. He attended the preparatory schools there and later in Lexington, Virginia. He then entered the A. and M. College at Raleigh, North Carolina, and afterward the Maryland Agricultural College near Washington City. After a few years of business life in Elkins, he decided to become a foreign missionary and was appointed by his church to become their business manager for the American Presbyterian Congo Mission, and is stationed at Luebo, Belgian Congo, Central Africa. In this work for the moral and spiritual uplift of these natives of Africa he is both happy and useful and constantly sees good results and would not exchange places with any one. In other words, life in Central Africa is not a hardship for him, and he has never felt that he was making a sacrifice.

VII. Eugene Hill, son of Thomas Jackson and Eugenia (Hill) Arnold, was born in San Diego, California. He was educated at Davis and Elkins College, West Virginia, graduating with the degree of bachelor of arts. He later studied law at the Georgetown University, and having a strong inclination for newspaper work became a reporter on the Washington Herald. After a few months he changed to the Baltimore Sun and served as one of their Washington City reporters. Later he was assigned by the Sun to report news of the White House and the departments, being called to Baltimore during the National Democratic convention of 1912. After being on the Sun's staff for a year, he resigned this position and again resumed the study of law, this he continued, subject to one interruption. He was prevailed upon to act as press agent for the State of West Virginia for the National Democratic committee in the Wilson campaign. After discharging this onerous duty in the interests of his party, he entered the law department of the State University at Morgantown, and completed the two years course at this institution in a little over one year. Since then he has been in continuous practice, being the junior member of the law firm of Arnold and Arnold, Elkins, West Virginia. He has recently been elected city attorney. Mr. Arnold is a member of the B. P. O. Elks, of the I. O. O. F. and of the Loyal Order of Moose.

Rev. Stark W. Arnold, son of Jonathan Arnold, was born in Beverly, December 20, 1851. Early in life he was appointed to a clerkship in the Interior Department in Washington, where he remained about seven years. During this period he took the course of law, graduating from the Columbia Law School. He then came to Beverly, locating soon afterward at Buckhannon, engaging in the practice of his profession. In the fall of 1876 he was a candidate for the office of Prosecuting Attorney of Upshur County, and was elected by an overwhelming majority, the largest that had been given a candidate in that county at that time. On account of his father failing in health, requiring his personal attention, he returned to Beverly to reside in the year 1879, and continued there until after his father's death in 1883. During this last residence at Beverly he was elected to the senate from that senatorial district, serving out the full term of four years, introducing and successfully carrying through several measures of legislation that attracted considerable attention throughout the State, notably, the election law, the changes then made leading up to the present system. It was while serving in the Senate that he concluded to do that which had long been a subject of deep consideration with him, viz: to go into the ministry. In order to prepare himself for this, he entered

Drew Theological Seminary, where he remained and completed his theological course. Shortly afterward he began his ministerial work in the State of New York, where he continued in active work to the end of his life, August, 1898, preaching his last sermon only three weeks preceding his death. In December, 1880, he married Miss Lizzie Gohen, of Cincinnati, O. She and four children survive him.

THE ARBOGAST FAMILY.

The Arbogast Family. This family, numerously represented in Randolph, is of German descent, and settled in what is now Highland County, Virginia, prior to 1779. The name was originally spelled Armikast. Adam Arbogast was Captain of a company of Pendleton militia in 1793.

THE ARMENTROUT FAMILY.

The Armentrout Family. This family is of German descent. The name was originally spelled Erhmantrout. Christopher Armentrout moved from Rockingham County, Virginia, to what is now Grant County prior to the Revolution. The immediate ancestors of the Armentrouts in Randolph lived in Grant and Pendleton counties.

Hiram, son of Christopher, was born in Pendleton County in 1811. He married Amanda Smith. Their children were, John W., who married Martha Dolly; Christopher, who married Pheoba Mullenix; Aaron, Mary, Martha, Isaac, Anne, Susan, Adina and Nevada.

John W. Armentrout was born in 1843 and was married in 1868 to Martha, daughter of John and Susan Dolly. Their children are Robert E., Laura V., Stella C., Jasper C. and Wilbur E.

Christopher Armentrout was born in 1845. Children, Ola E., Vista G., Carrey L.., Elva T., Viva and Orgie. He came from Pendleton to Randolph in 1872 and was elected a member of the countty court in 1888. His grandfather, Christopher Armentrout, was born in Grant County in 1775. In 1792 he entered 218 acres of land in the vicinity in which his grandson, Christopher, is now a resident, but he did not occupy it. His greatgrandmother, Catherine Peterson, was captured at Fort Seybert by the Indians in 1758. About forty settlers were in the fort and all were massacred but two who were held in captivity and taken to their village near Chilicothe, Ohio. Catherine Peterson was among the number spared. The Shawnee Trail by which they returned to Ohio passed through or near the city of Elkins. A brave had pity on Mrs. Peterson and gave her a pair of moccasins that she might travel with greater comfort. She remained in captivity for six years. Two hundred captives were rescued by General Boquet, who attacked the Indian towns in Ohio in 1764. They were returned to Fort Pitt. Mrs. Peterson was among the number and from there returned to her home in Pendleton.

In 1788 Uriah Gandy sold to Christopher Armentrout 131 acres on Gandy Creek, Randolph County. The name was spelled in the conveyance Hermantrout.

THE BOSWORTH FAMILY.

The Bosworth Family. The first of the Bosworth family to locate in what is now West Virginia were Joshua and a brother whose name is now not known. The brother after a brief sojourn in Virginia, moved farther west and located at Marietta, Ohio. Joshua Bosworth married in Massachusetts a Miss Squire and to this union were born, in the native State, the following children: Joshua, Amaziah, Squire, Parley, Harriet, who married John Phillips, of French Creek, Upshur County; Delaney, who married Alpheus Rude and moved to Illinois; Rhoda, who married a Mr. Allen and moved to Ohio.

Squire Bosworth was born in Montgomery, Massachusetts in 1785 and died at Beverly, West Virginia, in 1870. He married Hannah, daughter of Peter Buckey, in 1816. Unto this union were born John W., Squire Newton, George W., Elam B., Rebecca, who married Rev. C. S. M. See; Lucy, who married Capt. T. A. Bradford; Harriet, who married Charles See; Martha, who married .... McGuffin, Christina, who married William Brown; Mary, who married Adam Crawford.

Dr. John W. Bosworth married Mattie Dold. Child, Annie, who became the wife of Dr. Chas. Williams.

Geo. W. Bosworth married Mary, daughter of John and Ann (Conrad) Currence. Children, Drs. John L., Albert S. and Perry.

Joshua Bosworth came to Virginia with the New England colony that settled on French Creek. He located on Turkey Run, near the Upshur-Harrison line. Among the families that comprised that settlement were the Goulds, Burrhs, Morgans, Phillips, Brooks, Sextons and the Phillips. They were well educated and devout Christians and were of the best material for a new country.

DR. SQUIRE BOSWORTH.

Dr. Squire Bosworth after teaching school for a time in Parkersburg and Beverly studied medicine under Dr. Dolbear and attended lectures in Richmond, Virginia. He was for nearly half a century the only physician in Randolph. He was clerk of the county court of Randolph as well as deputy for a number of years under Archibald Earle. He also represented Randolph and Tucker in the Virginia Assembly prior to the Civil War.

Dr. J. L. Bosworth married Rachael, daughter of Randolph and Katherine (Hutton) Crouch. Children, Mary, who married Tracy Fling, of Gilmer County, and Hallie and John Woodbridge.

Dr. Perry Bosworth married in Pocahontas County, Lucy, daughter of Joseph Samuel and Abigail (Curry) Smith.

Dr. A. S. Bosworth married in 1882, Julia M., daughter of Geo. W. and H. Keziah (Boyers) Davis. Children, Stella M., who married Blake Taylor. Mrs. Bosworth died in 1885. He married his second wife, Miss Eleanor, daughter of Henry and Elizabeth (Snyder) Weisgerber, of Baltimore, in 1894. One child, Stanley, has been born of this union.

The original home of the Bosworths in England was in Leicester County, an inland town. Bosworth Field and Bosworth Market are historic places in Leicester. Benjamin was perhaps the first of the name to come to America in about 1630, settling at Highham, Massachusetts. The Bosworths in New England intermarried with the Mortons, Childs, Sturdevants and Mathers.

Squire N. Bosworth, son of Dr. Squire and Hannah (Bucky) Bosworth, was born in 1841, married (1867) Florence A., daughter of Bernard L. and Mary (Daily) Brown. Children, Lutie Lee, Florence A., Mary Eva, Ada, Charles B., Carroll L., Hellen, Nina and Willie.

Mr. Bosworth served through the war as a Confederate soldier, belonging to the Thirty-first Virginia Infantry, of which company he was Sergeant. He still has in his possession the flag of his regiment, presented by Stonewall Jackson, May 5, 1862. The flag was pierced by a shell.

Mr. Bosworth was for many years postmaster of Beverly.

THE BAKER FAMILY.

Isaac Baker was the first representative of this family to locate in Randolph, coming here from Pendleton about 1825. He married Naomi (Morgan) Stalnaker. The children of this union were, Isaac, Harriett, Eli, Catherine, Ellen, John and Daniel R.

Isaac, son of Isaac and Naomi (Stalnaker) Baker, was born in 1833, and died in 1910. In 1859 he married Harriet, daughter of Zirus Weese. One child, Stark L. Baker, was the result of this union.

Stark L. Baker was born in 1860; married Mable S., daughter of J. J. and Margaret (Stuard) Burns. One child, James. Mr. Baker was educated in the public schools and the Fairmont Normal, from which institution he graduated. He was deputy collector of Internal Revenue from 1889 to 1893; chairman of the Republican County Committee sixteen years; was U. S. District Court Commissioner and represented the Tenth District in the State Senate, being elected in 1898.

Eli Baker, son of Isaac, born 1835, died 1898; mother's name, Maria Stalnaker; married in 1862, Upshur County, Rebecca J., daughter of William Sexton. She died in 1867. One child, Jessie B., who married Clay Daniels, was born of this union. His second marriage was to Maggie E. Sexton. She died in 1916. The issue of this marrige were Wm. E., Chas. C., George C. and Anna G.

Mr. Baker was postmaster at Beverly 24 years.

Anna Greta married L. R. Fowler. Children, William, Richard and Baker.

Dr. Geo. C. Baker married Katherine, daughter of J. Bier Wells, of Baltimore. Children, Frances Margaret, Katherine, Elizabeth and Virginia.

Wm. E. married Martha Davidson, of Evansville, Indiana. Children, Janet Davidson.

Charles C. married Hattie, daughter of A. D. and Bell (Russell) Barlow. Children, Charles Baker, Margaret Bell.

William E., son of Eli and Margaret (Sexton) Baker, was born February 25, 1873. He was educated at Wesleyan University and State University, where he received the degrees of A.B. and L.L.B. He was admitted to the bar in 1896. He is a director and a member of the finance committee of Davis Trust Company of Elkins. On March 28, 1906, he married Martha, daughter of William Davidson, of Evansville, Indiana. Mr. and Mrs. Baker have one child, Janet Davidson.

Daniel Randolph Baker, son of Isaac and Maria (Stalnaker) Baker, was born in 1846. He married, in 1868, Margaret Christina, daughter of Lemuel and Nancy (Hart) Chenoweth. Children, Nora Lee, who married F. A. Parsons. Children, Margery, Hallie, Christina, Sally, Randolph and James who is dead; Hattie Maria, who married Dr. H. Yokum. Children, Baker, Virginia, George, Christine, Gertrude and Katharine are dead; Edgar D., Bernard L. and John Ulysses, who married Lena Mae (Schuyler) of New York. Children, Rosalind Randolph, Margaret Christine and Daniel Randolph.

The Westfall Fort stood on Baker's farm near the mouth of Files Creek.

THE BOOTH FAMILY.

The Booth Family. The names of Isaac, William, James and David Booth appear in the records of Randolph prior to 1796. Isaac Booth was sheriff in 1813. James Booth was married to Pheobe Osborn in 1797. William Booth married Debora, daughter of Edward Hart, in 1803.

GEORGE E. BOND.

George Elmer Bond, son of Wm. H. and Rebecca (Judy) Bond, was born May 11, 1866; married Ida J., daughter of C. S. and Amanda (Jeffries) Bowers.

Mr. Bond has been chief of police at Huttonsville two years, assistant chief at Elkins for one year, and chief at Whitmer seven years. He is now a farmer and poultry raiser at Whitmer.

THE BOGARD FAMILY.

The Bogard Family. This family moved to Randolph at a very early day. The Bogards and Pettys came together from Pennsylvania. The exact date is not known. Samuel Currence son of the first William, married Elizabeth Bogard, daughter of Cornelius Bogard in 1795. Cornelius Bogard entered land on Glady Fork in 1789. He was assessor of Randolph in 1783 and sheriff in 1796.

THE BUFFINGTON FAMILY.

The Buffington Family. Jonathan and William Buffington were early settlers of Randolph. They located on Leading Creek. The Buffingtons, Rooneys, Hornbecks and Doughertys were neighbors on Leading Creek, in the vicinity of the present village of Gilman. The Buffingtons came to Randolph from Hampshire. Johnathan Buffington's wife and children were murdered by the Indians in the Leading Creek massacre of 1781. He escaped to Friends Fort. Mr. Buffington married for his second wife Madaline, daughter of Jacob Helmick, in 1801.

THE BLAIR FAMILY.

The Blair Family. Wm. Blair came from Eastern Virginia prior to 1789, as in that year the County Court ordered the sheriff to pay Mr. Blair his pension for the years from 1786 to 1789. He received a pension of $33.33⅓ for wounds received in the battle of Point Pleasant, October 10, 1774.

THE BUCKEY FAMILY.

The Buckey Family. The Buckey family was one of the pioneer family of Randolph. Peter Buckey immigrated from Germany to Maryland. After a few years residence at Hagerstown, that State, he moved to Beverly, a short time after the formation of the county. He was a tailor by trade, but there being no demand in a pioneer community for an individual of his occupation or trade he engaged in the hotel business and for more than a century his descendants were engaged in that business in Beverly, or as long as it was the county seat of Randolph.

Peter Buckey married a daughter of Wm. Marteny. Children, George, William, John, Marteny, Eunice, Hannah, Christina and Mary. Eunice married a man by the name of Carter; Hannah married Dr. Squire Bosworth; Christina married David Goff; Mary married Archibald Earle; Wm. Buckey moved to Sydney, Ohio; John moved to Knoxville, Tennessee; Daniel, son of Peter, married Virginia Ball; Marteny Buckey never married; Geo. Buckey, son of Peter and................(Marteny) Buckey, married Elizabeth, daughter of Daniel Hart. Children, John, Alpheus, Emmett, Eugene, Daniel, Edith.

Wirt Buckey, son of Alpheus and Rebecca (Chenoweth) Buckey, was born in 1860; married Eliza Alice, daughter of John B. and Elizabeth (Currence) Earle. Children, Wilbur, Clara, Stella and Lena R.

Mr. Buckey is a great grandson of Peter Buckey, one of the pioneers of Randolph. Mr. Buckey was was many years foreman of the painters crew on the Western Maryland Railroad.

THE BUTCHER FAMILY.

The Butcher Family. This family became indentified with Randolph County in 1790, when Samuel Butcher moved from Loudon County, Virginia, to Randolph, locating on a farm where the Odd Fellows Home now stands. Samuel Butcher had moved to Virginia from Lancaster County, Pennsylvania, in about 1750. The Samuel that located in Randolph was the youngest son of the first Samuel. Samuel Butcher lived in Randolph until 1815, when he moved to Wood County, where he resided until his death in 1846, in the 92nd year of his age.

Samuel Butcher had three sons: Ely, Thomas and Balis G. Balis G. married Patsy McNeil, of Pocahontas County. Their first born, Oscar G., became a prominent physician of Randolph. (See chapter of Physicians and Surgeons.) Ely Butcher married Elizabeth, daughter of Edward Hart, in 1804. Children, Creed W., Fountain and Baxter.

THE BROWN FAMILY.

Brown Family. Bernard L. Brown was born in Albemarle County, Virginia, near White Hall. His ancestors came to

Virginia as early as 1621. They were men and women who were prominent in the early affairs of the colony; most of them settling in Hanover County, and in and near Richmond; but when the County of Albermarle was formed, and settlers began to flock to that locality, Benjamin Brown and Sarah (Thompson) Brown his wife, with their large family, removed from

MR. BERNARD L. BROWN.

Hanover County as early as 1747, and entered the land on both sides of Moorman's River in Albemarle County—more than six thousand acres—twenty miles from Charlottesville. This land was divided among his sons, and all builded homes except one, William or Benjamin, Jr., who had his home in Hanover or Louisa County. Some of these homes are still owned and occupied by their descendants, and the neighborhood was and is still known as Brown's Cove.

Benjamin Brown, the father, had his home called "Trini-dad," at the head of this valley, and his sons had theirs along the sides of the stream known as Moormans River.

Bernard, Sr., married Elizabeth Dabney, daughter of Gen. John Dabney, a Revolutionary soldier, and granddaughter of Cornelius Dabney or D'Aubigne. (The name has been angli-cized to Dabney). His second wife, grandmother of Eliza-beth, was Sarah Jennings. The mother of Elizabeth was Anne Harris Dabney, daughter of Major Robert Harris, mem-ber of the House of Burgesses from Hanover County, 1736, 1738, 1740, 1742. His wife was Mourning Glenn. He was born 168...., died 1765. He was a son of William Harris and Temperance Overton, his wife, who was a daughter of Wil-liam Overton. William Harris was the son of one Robert Har-ris of Wales, and his wife who was·Mrs. Mary Rice, a widow, daughter of William Claibome and his wife Elizabeth (But-ler) Claibome. This Robert Harris was born in 1630, died 1700. William Claibome was born in 1587, died 1676. He came to Virginia with George Wyant in 1621, was secretary of the Colony of Virginia, 1625, 1635, 1652, 1660; treasurer, 1642, 1660; surveyor general, 1621, 1625; J. P. York & North-umberland, 1653; member of the Council, 1623; commanded an expedition against the Indians, 1629, again in 1644. In the Northumberland records April, 1653, is an order referring to the Worshipful Col. William Claibome Deputy Governor.

Bernard Brown, Sr., husband of Elizabeth Dabney and grandfather of Bernard L. Brown, was a soldier in the struggle for American Independence whose duty was to carry dis-patches from New York to Charleston, South Carolina. He was born January 28th, 1750, died February 26th, 1800. His wife, Elizabeth Dabney, was born June 18th, 1751, died June, 1826, 75 years of age. Bernard Sr. and Elizabeth, his wife, had twelve children, one of whom, Bernard M., married Mi-riam Maupin, also of French descent.

Bernard L. Brown, the subject of this sketch, was their son. Their home was near White Hall, at or near the home of the first Bernard. (The name had been given to father and son through three generations and is still given to one child in almost every family of the descendants.) Bernard L. Brown was left an orphan at the age of nine years. He was the seventh of nine children. The others were, Thompson, Sarah Pyrena, Sidna, Allen Smith W., Elizabeth Dabney, named for her grandmother, the wife of Bernard Sr. The youngest was James Dabney, who distinguished himself at the battle of Manasses, carrying dispatches from Beuregard to Jackson through such a heavy fire that four horses were shot down under him while he escaped unhurt and received an honorable parole from his General Beureguard.

Bernard L. Brown was born August 9th, 1816. After the death of his parents, both dying almost within a year, he lived with his uncle, Thomas H. Brown, in Albemarle, until he obtained a position as clerk in a store with a Mr. Moore in Scottsville, Virginia, and afterward moved to Beverly, Randolph County, in company with John S. Carlisle, the politican, with whom he was in partnership in a store for sometime. He was licensed to practice law in 1840. On account of loss of hearing he was compelled to relinquish the profession of law.

Bernard L. Brown was county surveyor of Randolph and clerk of the Circuit Court for about twenty years prior to the Civil War. At the beginning of the Civil War he returned to Albemarle County, Virginia, where he remained until the close when he returned to Beverly to find his home demolished. He was of a very ingenious turn and was therefore enable to furnish his family with various conveniences during the war.

When Wm. J. Jackson made his raid into Beverly he captured the records of the office of the Circuit Court and took them to Brownsburg, Virginia, where Col. David Goff and Judge Gideon D. Camden resided. They notified Mr. Brown that they were there and requested him to come and get them. He took his daughter, now Mrs. Earl, with him. They met a colony of their old friends, viz: Col. Goff and family, Judge Camden and wife, B. W. Crawford and family, Absolem Crawford and family, Elam Bosworth and family and Eli Chenoweth and wife. They took the records to Albemarle County. At the close of the Civil War he returned to Beverly with a large amount of wild mountain land his only possession. Unable to hold office on account of the "Test Oath" which he was unable to take conscientiously, he found it hard to provide for his large and helpless family, and although one of his Union friends, John B. Earle, who was Circuit Clerk at the time, had him appointed deputy under himself, it was still a struggle. Broken down in health and spirits, he died February 10th, 1868 at the age of 52 years. He married March 4th, 1842, Mary Elizabeth Dailey, daughter of Hugh Dailey of Louden County, Virginia, and Edith Butcher who was the daughter of Eli Butcher, of Beverly, West Virginia, and Elizabeth Hart, his first wife, who was a daughter of Edward Hart and Nancy Stout, his wife, and a granddaughter of John Hart, signer of the Declaration of Independence from New Jersey.

Mary Dailey Brown, wife of Bernard L. Brown, was born January 20th, 1825. Long after Mr. Brown's death she married her cousin, Summers McCrum, of Aurora, Preston County, West Virginia, and died at the home of her daughter, Mrs. Page R. McCrum, May 18th, 1907.

The children of B. L. Brown and Mary Dailey his wife were, first, Edith who died in infancy. Second, Adeliza who married Archibald Earl, Jr., of Fort Worth, Texas. (Both living at Fort Worth.) Three children, Bernard, Charles and Clay, deceased. Third, Florence, married S. N. Bosworth, Beverly, West Virginia; nine children, Mrs. E. D. Talbott, Elkins; Mrs. Dr. L. W. Talbott, Elkins; C. Bernard Bosworth, Beverly; Mrs. Clare Harding, Elkins and Beverly; Mrs. Helen Harding, Elkins; Carroll L. and Miss Nina Bosworth, Beverly; Florence and Miller, dead. Fourth, Laura Sidna, died when 13 years of age. Fifth, Oscar L., died 1888. Married Edith Dailey of Illinois. Two children, Bernard L. and Jesse Harold, of Pomona, California. Sixth, Lucy B., married Page R. McCrum, Aurora, West Virginia. Two children living, Summer D., Aurora, and Harold Bernard, Fairmont, West Virginia. Clare and Paul deceased. Seventh, Edwin A., who died in infancy. Eighth, Charles Bernard, of Clinton, Iowa, married Mary Smith, of Albany, Illinois. Four sons, Earl F., Clarence, Leonard and Alva. Ninth, Clarence Hugh Dailey, died unmarried. Tenth, Alice G., married Porter, of Chariton, Missouri. Two living children, Clarence R. and Mrs. Edith Vedder, of Seattle. One child, John, died in infancy. Eleventh, Roberta L., married Erastus Williamson, Cordora, Illinois. Two living children, Mr. Augusta Simpson, Cordova; and Ray Brown, Williamson. Two children, Frederick and Alma died in infancy.

THE CROUCH FAMILY.

The Crouch Family. Three brothers by the name of Crouch immigrated to the American colonies from Wales in 1750. Their names were John, James, and, perhaps, Andrew. James Crouch, in 1780, in company with a number of men who were escorting John and William Warwick to their homes in Greenbrier County, was ambushed by the Indians as related in another chapter of this book. Prior to this time Andrew Crouch was living in the vicinity of Haddan's Fort and it is known that his son, Joseph, was a man of maturity at that time. It is therefore probable, coupled with the fact that their lands were among the choicest in the county, that they came with the general rush to the Valley in 1772-4. The Crouch brothers were neighbors of the Warwicks, Haddans, Currences and Whites.

John Crouch had three sons, John, Jacob and Andrew. Andrew is known to have had one son, Joseph. James Crouch escaped immediate death at the hands of the Indians in the tragedy near Haddan's Fort, but whether he finally recovered or died of his wounds is not known. John Crouch, the pioneer, died from the effects of a snake bite. He lived at the time on his farm a mile or so below Huttonsville on the east side of the river, near the mouth of Shavers Run.

John, son of the first John, married Judy Westfall. Their children were, Isaac, Abraham, Andrew, Marshal and one daughter whose name is not known.

Andrew Crouch, son of John the pioneer, married Elizabeth Hutton. Their children were Johnathan Jacob, Kitty, Moses, John and Abraham.

Johnathan, son of Andrew and Elizabeth (Hutton) Crouch, married, in 1830, Delilah, daughter of Adam and Christian (Harper) Haigler. Children, Dorothy, Almira, Cyrus, Martha, Christina, Elizabeth, Mary, Robert, Eli H. and Henry Clay.

Abraham Crouch.   The Crouch family, one of the wealth-
iest and most prominent in the county, was first represented
by three brothers, John, James and Andrew.   Abraham
Crouch, son of Andrew and Elizabeth (Hutton) Crouch, was
born in 1832 and died in 1901.   He married Elizabeth, daughter of John and Harriet (Lockridge) McNeal.   Children, Lee,
Ada, Lina, Bettie, May, Grace and Jackson.   Abraham was

ABRAM CROUCH.

the grandson of John and the great grandson of John, the pioneer.   He was a member of a family that has been identified
with the county from its earliest settlement to the present
time.   A family that has been prominent in every movement
of interest and stands today in the front rank of prominent
and substantial families.

Abraham Crouch typified a class of an earlier day citizen,
the greatest asset and product of any community, who sought
neither place nor prominence, whose exemplary lives were em-
bittered neither by poverty nor encumbered by wealth, whose

counsels were invaluable and whose only ambition was to live honestly, serve their fellow man and leave the heritage of a good name.

Lee Crouch, son of Abraham and Elizabeth (McNeal) Crouch, was born in 1859, married Amanda, daughter of John and Mary (Blake) Wallace. Children, Mary E., Wallace M., Maude and Eva.

Mr. Crouch was deputy sheriff under A. J. Long and Warwick Hutton. He was elected county clerk in 1896 and re-elected in 1900, but resigned to accept a position as cashier of the First National Bank of Elkins, which place he held until 1916 when he succeeded Hon. Henry G. Davis as president of that institution.

THE COLLETT FAMILY.

The Collett Family. This was a pioneer family in Randolph and Pendleton. Thomas Collett was the first of the name to locate in Pendleton. He had two children, Thomas and Gabriel. Thomas Collett lived in Buffalo Hills in Pendleton in 1780. Gabriel Collett was constable in Pendleton in 1788. Thomas Collett is mentioned among the tithables of Pendleton in 1790. Thomas Collett in 1782 rendered a claim for material, food, etc., furnished the American troops in the war of the Revolution. Thomas Collett was on the muster rolls of Pendleton in 1794.

Rev. Thomas Collett, the pioneer Baptist minister of Randolph, was the son of Thomas Collett and perhaps the grandson of Thomas Collett. He married Nancy, daughter of Henry Pedro. Rev. Collett died December 31, 1870. His wife Nancy Pedro Collett died during the Civil War.

Parkison Collett, son of Rev. Thomas and Nancy (Pedro) Collett, was born in 1828, married 1866, Anzina, daughter of Alba and Emily (Wilmoth) Chenoweth. Children, Zan, Mittie, Thomas J., Emma, Louise Alba and Florence, who died in infancy.

Mr. Collett was in the Confederate service and participated in the battle of Gettysburg and other important engagements. He was First Lieutenant in McClanihan's battery. He was four times assessor of Randolph, twice prior and twice subsequent to the Civil War.

A. J. Collett, son of Rev. Thomas and Nancy (Pedro) Collett, was born in 1837, married (1868) Xantippe, daughter of B. W. and Anzina (Earle) Crawford. Children, Beulah, who married Geo. W. Leonard; Susan, who married Dr. Thompson; Ora, who married Geo. Curtis; Katherine Ward, who married John Emmart; Albert, Bushrod C., and Howard L,, and Laura, who is a graduate of Jefferson College Hospital Training School for Nurses, Philadelphia.

Calvin C. Collett, born in 1818, son of Rev. Thomas and Nancy (Pedro) Collett, and died in 1880. Married (1859) Louise, daughter of William and Emaline (Vandevander) Hyre. Children, Columbus, Christina, Florence, May, Lena, Birdie and William Thomas.

Alba, son of Parkison and Anzina (Chenoweth) Collett, was born in 1882. On November 20, 1916, he was united in marriage to Nina, daughter of S. N. and Florence A. (Brown) Bosworth. Mr. Collett is descended from three prominent pioneer families of Randolph, the Colletts, Chenoweths and Pedroes. He is at present with the H. L. Manning Drug store, Elkins, West Virginia.

Howard L., son of A. J. and Xantippe (Crawford) Collett, was born in 1883. Mr. Collett was educated in public schools and Mountain State Business College where he graduated in 1904. For twelve years he has been teller in the Davis Trust Company, Elkins, West Virginia.

Bernard C. Collett, son of Solomon and Mary (Hill) Collett, was born in 1885, married Bessie, daughter of Martion Weese. Children, Russell.

Mr. Collett is in the employ of the Crawford and Corrothers Lumber Company near Elkins.

Chas. H. Collett, son of Solomon and Mary (Hill) Collett, was born in ...., married Stella, daughter of Geo. and Christina (Weese) Hill. Children, Richard.

Mr. Collett is a foreman for Crawford and Corrothers Lumber Company near Elkins.

THE CHANNELL FAMILY.

The Channell Family. The Channell family was among the first settlers of Randolph. Jeremiah was the first of the name to locate in this county. He came from Hardy in the first decade of the pioneer period in Randolph. He married Sallie Steele and they were residents of the county at the time of the massacre of the Connolly family by the Indians. Jeremiah located on land opposite the town of Huttonsville. The farm is now owned by Patrick Crickard. The children of Jeremiah and Sallie (Steele) Channell were, John, Samuel, Andrew, Susan, Elizabeth and Jemima.

Enoch W., son of Noah S. and Mary (Crickard) Channell, married Eliza, daughter of Martin and .... (Bell) Wamsley. Children, Elenor and Carl.

Mr. Channell is of English and Irish descent and is a member of the pioneer family of Channells of Randolph. Mr. Channell is postmaster at Huttonsville.

G. N. Channell, son of Samuel and Susan (Taylor) Channell, was born in 1849, married Jemima Jane, daughter of James M. Wilmoth. Children, Tippie, Belva, Clay, Fletcher, Cletus and Grover. Bernice and Clyde died in infancy. Mr. Channell was born and raised in the vicinity of Kernes, and is a grandson of Samuel Channell, the pioneer.

G. Clinton Channell, son of Noah S. and Mary (Crickard) Channell, was born in Huttonsville, Febuary, 1884, married April 25, 1905, to Dora, daughter of Zacharia and Margaret Talbott. Children, Marguerite, Earl, Woodrow and Garland.

Mr. Channel came to Elkins in April, 1912. He is proprietor of the Grove Feed and Storage Co., and is vice-president of the W. Va. Feed and Flour Co. at Clarksburg.

THE CRICKARD FAMILY.

The Crickard Family. The Crickards are of Scotch-Irish descent. My great grandfather was a resident of that part of Ireland known as Ulster. He was an officer in King James army and fought at the battle of the Boyne, July 1, 1690. The Irish forces were defeated by William III of England. After this battle many of the estates of the Irish were confiscated and divided among William's followers who were largely

Protestants. My great grandfather, being loyal to Ireland and a Catholic, his estate was confiscated. My grandfather resided in the County of Doun. My father, John Crickard, and his brothers came to America in 1834-40. They settled in Augusta County, Virginia. My father, John Crickard, and my uncle, Peter Crickard, built the Staunton and Parkersburg Pike from Greenbrier to Cheat Bridge. After the completion of this work, my father located on Shavers Run in Valley Bend District. My only brother, Peter Crickard, lived and died there. He was the father of the present sheriff of Randolph, A. T. Crickard. Thos. Michael Plunkett, member of the British Parliament is a cousin of the Crickards of Randolph. My mother's name was Mary (Plunkett) Crickard. My grandfather, Michael Crickard, took part in the Emmett Rebellion of 1803.—Patrick Crickard.

John R. Crickard, son of Patrick and Amanda (Currence) Crickard, was born in 1860, married Alverda, daughter of John and Hannah (Currence) Bell. Children, Patrick E., Nixon J., Robert B., Eva B., Peter W., Mary A., Jonas F., Anne C. and Rose P.

Mr. Crickard was educated in public schools and at Rock Hill College, Maryland. He was for several years one of the prominent school teachers of the county and served several terms as president of the Board of Education of Mingo District. He was also justice of the peace of Mingo District for twelve years. In 1910 he was elected justice of the peace of that district on the Socialist ticket, giving him the distinction of being the only man having been elected by the adherents of that political faith in Randolph. Mr. Crickard is prominent in fraternal circles and is a member of the A. F. and A. M., I. O. O. F., K. P..and M. W. W.

THE CAPLINGER FAMILY.

The Caplinger Family. This name is of German origin and was originally spelled Keplinger. In the early records of Pendleton the name was spelled Caplinger, Kaplinger, Keplinger and Coplinger. The Caplingers were among the pioneers of Pendleton. Samuel Caplinger was the first of the name in Pendleton. He died in that county in 1769. He had a son named George, who died in 1773. He was a soldier in the French and Indian war of 1754-60, from Augusta, now Pendleton County. George, son of the first George, resided in Pendleton and was relieved from military duty on account of physical disability in 1792. Whether he was a soldier in the Revolution is not known, however, he submitted a claim for supplies furnished the American army in that war.

George, grandson of the first George, was born February 3, 1784. He moved to Randolph from Pendleton in about 1800. He was the first of the name to locate in Randolph and founded the Caplinger settlement. Many of his descendants still live in the community and the original homestead remains in the possession of members of the family.

George Caplinger married Sarah Collett in 1804. Their children were, Thomas J., George W., Solomon C., Adam D., Margaret and Elizabeth.

Thomas J. Caplinger married Margaret Chenoweth, daughter of Jehu Chenoweth. Children, George, John, Jehu, Lloyd, Adam, Rachel, Eliza and Ann.

Geo. W. Caplinger married Jane Heavener of Upshur County. Children, Alice, who married Marion Grose, and Caroline, who married Jacob Chenoweth. Two children, Elias and Jacob died in youth.

Adam D. Caplinger married Elizabeth, daughter of William B. Wilson. Children, Theodore, Edwin Duncan, William B., Ida E., Pattie C. and Lee Duncan. His second wife was Sabina Saulsbury. Children, Mary, Perry L., Hattie B. and Addie W. Mary married Iddo Ward; Hattie B. married Fritz Hanger and Addie W. married Michael Weese.

Edwin Duncan Caplinger died when 18 years of age. Ida, daughter of Adam D. Caplinger married Randolph M. Harper. Pattie C. Caplinger, daughter of Adam D. Caplinger, married Henry A. Harper.

Wm. B. Caplinger married in 1839 Phoeba, daughter of Henry A. Harper. She died the same year and some years thereafter Mr. Caplinger married Elva Riggleman.

Lee Duncan, son of Adam D. and Elizabeth (Wilson) Caplinger, married Lucy, daughter of Henry A. Harper. Children, Frank and Hoke. Frank died when 12 years of age.

Thomas J., son of George and Sarah (Collett) Caplinger, married Margaret Chenoweth. Children, Lloyd, George C., John C., Jehu C., Adam C., Rachel, Ann and Eliza.

Lloyd Caplinger, born in 1849, married in 1892, Bernice, daughter of John B. and Bettie (Currence) Earle. Children, Earle. Some years later after the death of his first wife Mr. Caplinger married Ida Durett. Rachel, daughter of Thomas Caplinger, married Elisha Talbott; Ann, daughter of Thomas J., married Augustus Moore; Eliza. daughter of Thomas J., married Edward Skidmore.

John C. Caplinger, born in 1844, son of Thomas J. Caplinger, married in 1873, Sydney, daughter of John W. and Mary Wood Moore. Children, Lena, Rizpaw, Lawrence and Ada.

Jehu, son of Thomas J. Caplinger, born in 1848, married in 1873, Ida W., daughter of Joseph Harding. Children, Viva, Marion F., Roberta B., Belva, Bernice F. and Geo. H.

Adam C., son of Thomas J., married Mary Grose. Children, Martha, who married a McDaniel and Nettie, who married Charley Skidmore.

Solomon Chenoweth Caplinger was born in 1811, died in 1893. His first wife was Mary, daughter of Gabriel Chenoweth. Children, Laban D., Phoeba C., Sarah E., Calvin L., Margaret and Maryette. The wife of his second marriage was Mary A., daughter of John Ryan. Children, Solomon C., Julius C., Delia W. and Robert Bruce. Laban D. and Sarah E. died in youth. Martha B. married Hanning Foggy; Phoeba C. married A. C. Rowan; Calvin L. married Belle Wilson. Children, Lillie, who married Lee Chenoweth; Grace, who married a Mr. Lough; Daisy married a Mr. Eslack, Rosa married S. M. Kendall; Margaret married John Hart. Maryette, daughter of Solomon C. and Mary Chenoweth Caplinger, married Rev. S. D. Lewis. Solomon C. Caplinger, Jr., went West when a young man and is now in Dawson City, Alaska. Robert Bruce, son of Solomon and Mary A. (Ryan) Caplinger, married Jesse May, daughter of John W. Detter. Children, Hilda, St. Clair, Clyde, John, Guy, Mary Edith, Julius and Richard died in early childhood. Julius, son of Solomon and Mary (Ryan) Caplinger, married Alema, daughter of Eli H. Rowan. Delia, daughter of Solomon and Mary (Ryan) Caplinger, married Vernon Lough.

Solomon C. Caplinger was sheriff of the county in 1857 and commissioner of the County Court in 1880. He was one of the prominent, intelligent and substantial citizens in the early history of the county.

THE COFF FAMILY.

The Coff Family. Patrick Coff came to America from Ireland in about 1800, settling on Mill Creek, Bath County, Virginia. He married Martha Lyle. To this union were born eight children, all living except second daughter. James Lyle Coff was born October, 1844. He learned the carpenter trade and later studied vocal music at Singers Glen, Virginia, under Joseph Funk and Aldine S. Keifer. Mr. Coff is prominent in the councils of the Democratic party and was justice of the peace of Mingo District four years. He married Diana F. Jordan, daughter of George and Frances Jordan, of Green Valley, Virginia, and moved to Randolph in 1877.

Eight children have been born to Mr. and Mrs. Coff. James W., farmer, who lives with parents at Mingo; Martha, who married P. O. Louk and lives in Elkins; Lena died in 1893; Mary, who married K. D. Marshal and lives in Mingo. They have one child, Nina, who is a student of the Wesleyan University, Buckhannon. Theodore L. never married and is orderly to Col. Treat of the U. S. Army, now stationed at Fort Sam Houston, Texas. John K., also single and lives with his parents at Mingo. Jacob F. married Laura Beale and lives at Dunmore, West Virginia. She was the daughter of James Beale of Linwood, West Virginia. Commodore Coff, the third, son of James Lyle and Diana Coff is a photographer in Elkins.

THE CURTIS FAMILY.

Thomas P. Curtis was born in Pittsylvania County, Virginia, in 1804. He died in Randolph in 1856. He came to Randolph in 1828. He married Mary, daughter of Peter Conrad. She was born in 1815 and died in 1880. Children, J. Milton, Laban B., Sarah, Thomas C., America, David Blackman, Emma, John C. and Almeda.

Thomas P. Curtis had a store in what is now Elkins in 1834. His storehouse was located in what is now known as Park View Addition.

John Milton Curtis was assessor in 1864 and was twice re-elected. He was township clerk in 1865. He was collector of Internal revenue in 1862, 1863, 1864 and 1865. His territory embraced Randolph, Tucker and Webster counties.

David Blackman Curtis, born in 1841, died in 1893. Mr. Curtis was for many years one of the prominent educators of the county. In 187....he married Virginia, daughter of George McLean.

George McLean Curtis was born in 1872. He studied law and was admitted to the bar in 1895.

Mr. Curtis married Ora, daughter of Andrew and Xantippie (Crawford) Collett. He is connected with the Inter-State Commerce Commission, Washington, D. C., as chief clerk.

THE CASSITY FAMILY.

The Cassity Family. John and Peter Cassity located in Valley Bend District prior to 1780. In the early records of the county the name is spelled Cashedy. They settled on land now owned by Lee Rosecranse. Peter Cassity was commissioner of the Revenue in 1789, and was a member of the first County Court of Randolph County. He was captain of the militia at the time of leaving the State in 1792 and was succeeded by John Haddan.

THE CONNOLLY FAMILY.

The Connoly Family. Wither's Border Warfare mentions the Connolly family as being among the first settlers of Randolph. They settled in what is now Mingo District on a creek that has since borne their name. They were of Irish ancestry. Withers and other historians were in error in stating that the Darby Connolly family were killed by the Indians. Connolly himself was killed but his family had not come to Randolph at that time. He was placing the roof on his cabin when he was shot and killed by the Indians. The murder occurred December, 1772. Jacob Conrad became the owner of the Connolly land and it has remained in possession of his heirs for more than a century.

THE CHENOWETH FAMILY.

The Chenoweth Family. The Chenoweth family in America has descended from John Chenoweth, who came to this country from Isle of Wright in 1652. He settled in Maryland and married Mary Calvert, daughter of Lord Baltimore. William, a son of this marriage was a member of a colony that settled in Frederick County, Maryland, prior to 1750. John, a son of Willaim was born in 1755. He was a soldier in the Revolutionary War and drew a pension. He was in Pendleton in 1790 and entered 50 acres of land in that county in that year. The Pughs who were related to the Chenoweths and came to Randolph with them, also entered land in Hampshire in the year of 1790. John Chenoweth entered land in Randolph in 1792, but perhaps he had been a resident of the county a few years previous.

A monument was unveiled to the memory of John Chenoweth about three miles south of Elkins on the Job Daniels place October 16, 1915. On one side is the inscription: John Chenoweth, Born November 15, 1755, Died June 16, 1831. A Soldier of the Revolution. On another side is the inscription to his wife as follows: Mary Pugh, Wife of John Chenoweth, Born January 29, 1762, Died February 1, 1849. They were married on January 7, 1779.

On another side are the names of all the children as follows: Robert, William, Mary, John, Jehu, Gabriel, Nellie.

John Chenoweth was captain of the militia in 1794; coroner in 1803; sheriff in 1810; justice of the peace in 1799. His son Robert was commissioner of the Revenue in 1816; sheriff in 1827. Z. T. Chenoweth was sheriff in 1884.

THE CRAWFORD FAMILY.

The Crawford Family. Andrew and Robert Crawford, two brothers, came to Randolph a few years prior to 1800. The Crawfords immigrated to Augusta County, Virginia, a few years previous to the revolution. They were of Scottish ancestry. Andrew Crawford was twice married. His first wife was a Miss Stephenson, who died in 1829. His second wife was a Miss Hyre, of Upshur County. Their children were, James C. Crawford, W. H. Crawford, Absalom Crawford, Adam Crawford, J. W. Crawford, Eliza Crawford, Robert Crawford, Jennie Crawford, Andrew Crawford. Robert and Andrew Crawford located on Shavers Run on the farm at this time owned by D. R. Baker. Robert, a short time afterward, moved to Lewis County this State and settled near Walkersville. J. S. Crawford moved to Clermont County, Ohio, and W. H. Crawford moved to Tuscaroras County, the same State.

Absalom, son of Andrew, married Emily, daughter of Joseph Hart. Children, Emmett, Rush, Amanda, Cora, Delia, Jennie and Maggie.

John W. Crawford married Edith, daughter of Peter Buckey. Children, Clay and Columbia.

Adam, son of Andrew Crawford, married Mary, daughter of Dr. Squire Bosworth. Children, Kent Bosworth Crawford, Lucy, Florida, Harriet, Augusta and Emily.

Eliza, daughter of Andrew Crawford, married Elias Wilmoth.

Jennie, daughter of Andrew Crawford, died in youth.

Bushrod W. Crawford, born in 1818, died in 1893; son of Andrew Crawford, married first, a Miss Wilson. Children, Xantippe, who married Andrew J. Collett. Some years after the death of his first wife Mr. Crawford married in 1850, Anzina, daughter of Archibald Earle. Children, Laura, Earle, Jefferson and Andrew.

Kent B. Crawford, born in 1848, son of Adam, married in 1876, Mary A., daughter of Franklin and Lucinda (Earle) Leonard. Children, Herbert and Stella.

Emmett Crawford, son of Absalom and Emily (Hart) Crawford, married in 1869, Margaret, daughter of Mathew and Eunice (Harper) Wamsley. Children, Burns, Rossie, Maggie, Ocia, Leah, Maud, Matie and Emmett. In 1882, after the death of his first wife, he married Minerva, daughter of Sampson Shifflett. Mr. Crawford was a soldier in the Confederate army and was a participant in many of the hard battles of that war. He was highly esteemed by his comrades in arms as well as by his neighbors in civil life.

Jefferson A. Crawford, son of Bushrod and Anzina (Earle) Crawford, married in 1887, Nora, daughter of George W. and Keziah (Boyers) Davis. Children, Earle, Davis, George Watts and Annie Laura.

Rush Crawford, born in 1855, son of Absalom, married in 1880, Melissa Shreeve, and after her death he married in 1895, Emma Yokum. Children, Plummer B., Dale W., Asa Fl and Clinton.

Andrew Crawford, the pioneer, was an adherent of the Presbyterian faith and was an active organizer of that denomination in Randolph. The early Presbyterians of Randolph were of scrupulous Purintanical piety and did much to enforce and make respected the civil laws against immorality and the violation of Sabbath observance.

Andrew Crawford was sheriff in 1820; commissioner of Revenue in 1818. John W. Crawford was county clerk in 1845. B. W. Crawford was assessor in 1843. Absalom Crawford was assessor in 1849. K. B. Crawford was commissioner of the County Court.

THE COBERLY FAMILY.

Coberly. James Coberly was the progenitor of the Coberly family in Randolph. He married Julia Vanscoy. The name is of German origin. The children of James and Julia Vanscoy) Coberly, were Aaron Levi, born 1824, married Mary Canfield in 1846; John, born 1829, married in 1854 to Janet Gainer; Randolph, born 1830, died 1884, married in 1853 to Jane M., daughter of Archibald Wilson. Children, Helen, Martha E., John, Alfred T., Archibald, James, Wm. H., Ida J. and Julia E.

James A., son of Randolph and Jane M. (Wilson) Coberly, born in Barbour County, 1864; came to Randolph in 1883, locating in Elkins in 1894. He was deputy surveyor four years; elected justice of the peace of Leadsville District in 1892. After studying law at State University he was admitted to the bar in 1898.

Mr. Coberly married (first) Delphia, daughter of Nicholas and Amanda (Taylor) Marstiller. She died in 1895. Children, Otto Glen, who is deputy assessor of Randolph County, Cleon Edwards, Ohley Francis, and Virgil J. Mr. Coberly married (second) Mary Hannagan, of Monroe County, West Virginia.

THE CUNNINGHAM FAMILY.

The Cunningham Family. In 1753, John, James and William Cunningham, three brothers from Dublin, Ireland, settled on the North Fork in what is now Pendleton County. James Cunningham had several sons and daughters among whom was William. Solomon, son of the second William was born in 1830. He married in 1857, Mary J., daughter of Lenox and Elizabeth Lantz. Children David S., James I., Abraham, Absalom M., Charles B. Y., Mary E., Arthena, Martha P., Anna B. and Solomon T.

James Cunningham, the pioneer, was captured by the Indians in 1758. He was kept a prisoner for seven years and became nearly blind as a result of starvation while in captivity. After his release and return to his people he moved to Randolph. John, James and William Cunningham were in the French and Indian war of 1754-60. John, James and William Cunningham had their claims certified by the County Court of Augusta for supplies furnished the American Army in the Revolutionary War.

Joseph Arnold Cunningham, a member of another branch of the Cunningham family, but a descendant of the pioneer family of Pendleton, was born April 27, 1861; son of Andrew J. and Eleanor (Wimer) Cunningham, was married September 2, 1888, to Rosa Anna, daughter of Jacob and Catherine Knutti. Mr. Cunningham was constable of Dry Fork District for several years and later represented Randolph and Tucker in the State Legislature. He is at present a prominent farmer and stock raiser of Alfena.

Absalom Marion Cunningham, son of Solomon and Mary Jane (Lantz) Cunningham, born in 1864 in Upshur County, West Virginia. Mr. Cunningham was educated in the public schools of the State and at the age of sixteen entered the profession of teaching which he followed for twelve years. During the last four years of his school work he applied himself to the study of law. In 1892 he opened a law office in Davis and subsequently moved to Parsons. In 1909 he moved to Elkins.

Mr. Cunningham was prosecuting attorney of Tucker from 1893-7, and represented that county in the Legislature in 1903-4.

Mr. Cunningham married first, Maude, daughter of Daniel and Eliza (Lantz) Auvil. Children, Eugene Blaine, Stanley Charles, Neil, McKinley Hobart and Absalom Marion Jr. Mr. Cunningham married second, Grace Isabel, daughter of John W. and Mary (Coston) Keith. Children, Marion Keith and Ruth Lantz.

George W. Cunningham, son of Jackson and Eleanor (Wimer) Cunningham, born in 1858, married Mollie Hamick. Children, Babel, Delmar, Lois S., S. Lutie, Reta, Hurst J., Ella and Wimer W. Mr. Cunningham has taught school thirty-seven years and has always held a first grade certificate. He has taught three terms in Barbour and fifty-five terms in Randolph County. The first school attended by Mr. Cunningham was in a building without floor or chimney. Mr. Cunningham has gained a place among the prominent educators of the county.

Abraham L. Cunningham, son of Solomon and Mary (Lantz) Cunningham, born in Gilmer County, 1861, married Catherine B., daughter of Wm. and Martha (Waybright) Hinkle. Children, Lelsa and Vista, Zenia, died aged 26; William H., died at age of four, and Edith in the fifth year of her age. Mr. Cunningham is an undertaker and cabinet-maker at Job.

THE COWGER FAMILY.

The Cowger family live in the southwestern part of Randolph and are of German descent. Michael Cowger was, perhaps, the first of the name to locate in Virginia. He entered 900 acres in the Shenandoah Valley in 1753. His descendants moved to Pendleton where many families of that name now reside. Michael Cowger lived in Pendleton prior to 1782. George Cowger lived in Pendleton in 1775, when Pendleton was a part of Augusta.

THE CONRAD FAMILY.

Conrad. The Conrad family moved to Randolph from Pendleton prior to 1792, the exact date is not known. Peter Conrad, the progenitor of the Conrad family in Randolph, settled on the farm which had been owned by Darby Connolly before he was murdered by the Indians. Peter Conrad, the pioneer, was the son of Jacob Conrad and the grandson of Jacob Conrad, who came to America and settled in Pendleton in 1750. He was born in 1705 and died December 1, 1775. He had a brother, Ulrich, who came to Pendleton with him. They were from Canton Berne, Switzerland. The Conrad brothers located on the South Branch, Jacob selecting a tract of land on which there was a "squaw patch," or a small clearing made by the Indians.

Ulrich Conrad was a soldier in the French and Indian War from Pendleton, and represented that county in the Virginia Assembly in 1792-3.

Jacob Conrad was foreman of the first grand jury in Pendleton in 1787.

Children of the first Jacob: Barbara, who married Chas. Hedrick; Elizabeth, who married Geo. Fisher, and Jacob, who married first, Hannah Bogard, and second, Barbara Probst.

The second Jacob Conrad had the following children: Sabina, Frances, Barbara, Jacob, Benjamin, Peter, Daniel, John, Ulrich, Mary and Phoeba. Peter moved to Randolph; Daniel, John and Benjamin moved to Braxton; Ulrich lived in Pendleton and married Sarah Currence. He was born in 1786, and died in 1867. Sabina married John Colaw; Barbara married Adam Harper; Jacob married Magdalena Hedrick; Benjamin married Barbara Hedrick; Mary married Geo. Kyle, Phoeba married Samuel Kyle; Daniel married Margaret Shieldh; John married Elizabeth Currence.

Peter Conrad, who located in Mingo District at an early date, was born in 1777. He had three sons, John, Jacob and Peter. His daughters were Elizabeth, who married David Saulsbury; Sarah, who married Joseph Wamsley; Phoeba, who married Jeremiah Cowger; Alcey, who married Daniel Wamsley; Diana, who married Lewis Cowger; Maria, who married Isaac Dodrill; Polly, who married Thomas Curtis and Syrena, who married Marshall Clarke. Two girls, Nancy and Barbara never married. Peter married Elsey Arbogast; Jacob married Ann Bailey; John B. Conrad married Mary Wilson. Children, Harmon J., Peter B., Samuel and William H.

The second Jacob was born in 1744.

Mrs. W. H. Conrad, of Mill Creek, has in her possession the family Bible, which was the property of the second Jacob, and is one hundred and eight years old. The first Jacob was a weaver by trade.

John Conrad, son of the second Jacob Conrad, married Elizabeth, daughter of John and granddaughter of the first William Currence. Children, Currence, Rush, Jacob, Ann D., who married John Currence; Eliza, who married William Currence; Nancy, who married John Crawford; Sarah, who married a Mr. Haymond; Jemima married Crawford; Mandy, who married Marshall Clark and moved to Missouri; Currence Conrad married a Miss Haymond; Rush married a Miss Shingleton; Jacob married a Miss Haymond. *Rush Conrad was county clerk of Braxton many years. Currence moved to Gilmore and was clerk of the County Court for about thirty years. Benjamin, son of Jacob, was clerk of the Circuit Court of Webster for many years.

Bailey M., son of Johnathan and Mary (Beasley) Barco, was born in 1870, married in 1903 Estelle, daughter of Harman and Mary Conrad. Children Mary C. and Ruth M.

Lewis C., son of Jacob and Ann (Baily Conrad, was born in 1850, married Mary, daughter of Johnathan and Delila (Haigler) Crouch. Children, Grace, Harry and Bruce.

Mr. Conrad is a merchant at Mill Creek. He has been four times mayor of Mill Creek; constable of Huttonsville District, and member of Board of Education. Mr. Conrad's mother at the advanced age of 89, is still active physically, with no diminution of her mental faculties.

Hiram J., son of John B. and Mary Ann (Wilson) Conrad, born 1847, married Mary, daughter of Jacob and Ann (Baily) Conrad. Children, Louella Ann, Estella Cecil and Jacob Wilton.

Mr. Conrad is a grandson of Peter Conrad, the pioneer,

*Omar Conrad, son of Rush, married Alice, daughter of Conrad Currence. He is a prominent resident of Randolph. He is an ex-member of County Court and has held other positions of trust and honor.

and first of the name in the county. Peter Conrad married Ann, daughter of the first William Currence.

William Hall, son of John B. and Mary (Wilson) Conrad, was born in 1849, married 1892, Alice, daughter of Bryson and Mary (Stalnaker) Hamilton. Mr. Conrad selected his second wife in the person of Effie, daughter of Randolph and Katherine (Hutton) Crouch. Mr. Conrad has traveled extensively in Colorado, California, Florida and other Southern and Western States. He is constable of Huttonsville District.

Wirt P. Conrad, son of Jacob P. and Elizabeth (Alkire) Conrad, was born in 1853. In 1873 he married Lydia Sargent and some years after her death he was united in marriage to Mary E. Brady. Children, Fenton, Fletcher, Ross W., Hettie A., George P., John B., Grover L., C. O., Mary, Charles, Boyd, Myrtle and Laura. Mr. Conrad was justice of the peace of Huttonsville District, and his father was for many years a lawyer and clerk of the Circuit Court of Webster County.

THE CURRENCE FAMILY.

The Currence Family. William was the paternal ancestor of the Currence family in Randolph. He immigrated from Ireland to the colonies, locating in Maryland. He left his native land when 16 years of age. After remaining in Maryland for a few years he pushed farther into the wilderness and settled in the Valley, occupying the land where the town of Beverly is now located. Believing that the county seat would be located farther up the Valley, he traded lands with the Westfalls, obtaining 600 acres where the town of Mill Creek is now located. He built a tub mill on the river, near the mouth of Mill Creek. This is supposed to have been the first water mill within the present limits of Randolph County. Some years later his son, William, built a grist mill on Mill Creek, on the site of the present steam flouring mill of Jesse Rosencranse. That stream for many years in the pioneer period bore the name of Currence's Mill Creek. Later the word Currence was dropped and it has since borne the abbreviated name of Mill Creek. He built the Currence Fort, which was located a few hundred yards southeast of the railway station in the present town of Mill Creek. It was built in 1774. Withers incorrectly refers to it as Cassino's fort. In the early days of Randolph, the pioneers carried their iron, salt and other necessities that could not be manufactured at home, from Clarksburg on pack horses. It was while on one of these trips that William Currence met a Miss Steele of Harrison County, whom he married.

William Currence was killed from ambush by the Indians May 12, 1791. Frank Riffle was killed by the savages on the same day, on the same road, and in the same immediate vicinity. Whether they were together when they were attacked is not known. They were killed on the flat between Beccas and Riffles Creek, near where the Old Brick Church stood. Mr. Currence was on his way to Haddan's fort, several miles up the river. He then lived in the vicinity of Currence's Fort. The settlers were apprehensive that Indians were in the community and Mr. Currence's family in vain entreated him not to venture on such a perilous trip. His son was sent to the field for the horse and returned with the excuse that the animal could not be caught. But the father was obdurate and under threats of punishment the lad brought the horse to his father. Mr. Currence was shot and killed by a shot from an Indian's rifle and the tradition that he came to his death by falling against a tree when his horse was shot from under him, is incorrect.

Disagreement with his step mother was the cause of William Currence leaving home and coming to America. In the absence of his father a misunderstanding arose between the two. Believing that harmony was no longer possible, he at once entered upon his journey to America. When a short distance from home he met his father, who enquired where he was going. The son replied, "To America." The father after finding admonition unavailing, dismounted and a spirited foot race was the result. The young man finally leaped a ditch which the parent could not cross and eluded the pursuit of his father.

Ten children were born to Mr. and Mrs. William (Steele) Currence. They were as follows: John, Willliam, Samuel, Sydney, Jane, Sally, Ann, Lydia, and two girls whose names are not known. One of these girls married Samuel Bonner, of Elk, and the other married a man by the name of Shaw. John married a daughter of Jonas Friend; Samuel married Elizabeth, daughter of Cornelius Bogard; William married Mary, daughter of Sylvester Ward, Sydney married Nicholas Wilmoth; Jane married Johnathan Smith; Sally married Mathew Wamsley; Ann married Henry Mace; Lydia married Benjamin Hornbeck.

Samuel, son of William and Lydia (Steele) Currence, married Elizabeth Bogard. Children, Cornelius, Henry, John and William. All went West except Henry, who married a Miss Zicafoose. Their children were Amanda, who married Patrick Crickard; Mary, who married Adam Hornbeck; Andrew, Haymond and Eliza, who married John Fox.

John, son of William and Lydia (Steele) Currence, had six children; John, who married a Miss Crouch; William, who married Miss Nellie Daniels; Ann, who married Peter Conrad; Elizabeth, who married John Conrad; Delilah, who married a McLean and Sarah, who married Ulrich Conrad.

The children of John Curence, who married Miss Crouch, were Abraham, Bettie, who married a Parsons; Sarah, who married a Bell; Mary, who married a man by the name of Weese, and Elizabeth, who married Aaron Bell.

William, son of the first William, who married Miss Mary Ward, and after her death married the widow Dyer, had by his first wife, John,* Johnathan and William, and Elizabeth, who married Gabriel Chenoweth; Jemima, who married Adam Carper; Virginia, who married Benjamin Scott. By his second marriage, Nancy, who married James McCall; Mary, who married Absalom Kyle; and Catherine, who married Jesse Haigler.

William, son of William and Mary (Ward) Currence, married Eliza Conrad. Children, Jacob C., Melvin, Johnathan, Eliza and Elizabeth. Adam married a Miss Dodrill, Anthony married Mary, daughter of Aaron Bell, in 1870. Children, Eliza, William, Louisa, Melvin, Retha, Reuben D., and Addie.

Col. Melvin Currence, son of William H. and Eliza Conrad Currence, was born in 1829. In 1863 he married Matilda V., daughter of John B. Earle. Children, Flora, Frederick,

*John, son of William and Mary (Ward) Currence married Ann Conrad, daughter of John and Elizabeth (Currence) Conrad Children: Laban, who married Alice Ward, Conrad, who married Edith Buckey, and who was killed in the civil war, Perry, who married ...., Nancy who married Stephen Shaver, Mary, who married Geo. W. Bosworth, Millie, who married Eli Crouch, and Rush, who died in youth.

Elizabeth, William H., Hiram A., Albert B., Eliza A. and Felix E.

Jacob C. Currence married Virginia, daughter of William and Nellie (Daniels) Currence. Children, William D., Page B., R. E. Lee, Marion Harding, Arthur, Melvin, Maud, Effie, Eliza, Elizabeth and Nellie. Page B. Currence married Diana Swecker. Children, Christopher, Leland, Jacob, Hugh, Marion, Ruth, Missouri, Virginia and Rusia. He died in 1906.

William, son of Jacob, married Ann Conrad. Children, Humboldt, Alice, Garland and Warren.

Lee Currence, son of Jacob, was born in 1864, married in 1891, Annie, daughter of Whitman Bradley. Children, Mary.

Nellie, Melvin, Arthur and Eliza are dead. Eliza and Arthur died when adults, the others in childhood.

Johnathan, son of William H. and Eliza (Conrad) Currence, was born in 1832. He married in 1857, Nancy Geer. Children, William, Rhoda, Charles, Adam, Austin, Eliza.

William Currence, son of John and grandson of the first William, married Nellie Daniels. Children, Lorenzo Dow, Squire Bosworth, William Dolbeare, Ulrich, Virginia, Thony, Ellen and Allen.

Lorenzo D. Currence moved to Nebraska subsequent to the Civil War. He married Mary Leeper. Children, Florence and Brownson.

William, son of William and Nellie (Daniels) Currence, married Adaline, daughter of William and Mary Bradley. He was born in 1822 and died in 1809. Children, Maria, and Ann Laban. By a second marriage to Ellen Stalnaker, children, Delphie and Lewis.

Squire B. Currence married Margaret Wamsley. Children, L. D. John.

Laban Currence, son of William D. and Adaline Bradley Currence, married Edmonia Woolwine. Children, William, Ida, who married Wm. Phares; Sallie, who married R. E. Newlon, and Daisy.

John Currence, son of William, who was killed by the Indians, was a member of the first grand jury drawn in Randolph County in 1787. He was sheriff in 1806, captain of the county militia in 1805, overseer of the poor of John Haddan's District in 1803.

William Currence, son of the first William, was lieutenant of militia in 1807.

Jacob C. Currence was captain of the militia in 1853 and constable in 1854.

William Dolbear Currence was constable for about twenty-five years, performing the duties of that office up to within a short time of his death, at the advanced age of 88 years.

Col. Melvin Currence was justice of the peace in 1884. He was Colonel of the 107th Virginia Regiment at the beginning of the Civil War.

C. S. Currence, son of Page B. and Dianah (Swecker) Currence, was born June 18, 1885. Mr. Currence lives on part of the Currence homestead, near Daily, that has been in possession of the family for more than a century.

William D., son of Jacob and Virginia Currence, was born April 30, 1857, married Ann, daughter of Peter Conrad. Children, Alice, Humboldt, Grace and Warren. The family name has passed down to him from the pioneer William Currence, who was killed by the Indians. Mr. Currence is proprietor of the Cassidy Coal Mines that supplies the Upper Valley with duty diamonds. He is a voluminous reader and is well informed on past and passing events of the world.

John W., son of Squire Bosworth and Margaret (Wamsley) Currence, was born January 20, 1877, married, first, Mary Catherine Cooper, second, Floretta May Painter. Mr. Currence having misfortune in the loss of his first and second wives, choose a Frances Vandevander for his third wife. One child, John Franklin, survives his second wife and by Miss Vandevander he has a son, Lotry Clyde, and Jenneatta and Winnona. Mr. Currence has been policeman at Mill Creek for twelve years. He is a descendant of two prominent pioneer families of Randolph.

R. E. Lee Currence, son of Jacob and Virginia Currence, was born May 10, 1864, married, first, Anna, daughter of Whitman Bradly. Children, Mary. Married, second, Arsella, daughter of George and Mary (Doyle) Pingley. Mr. Currence is a prosperous farmer living near Huttonsville. Mr.

Currence is a member of the pioneer Currence family of Randolph.

Johnathan J. Currence was born in 1843. Mr. Currence was a Confederate soldier in the Civil War and belonged to the 19th Virginia Cavalry, and was Sergeant of Couriers in Lonox Division of Early's Corps. Mr. Currence was constable of Huttonsville District seven years and served one term as Mayor of Mill Creek.

THE DANIELS FAMILY.

The Daniels Family. William Daniels was the first of the name to locate in Randolph County. The exact date is uncertain, but it was prior to 1795, perhaps in 1792. John Chenoweth and William Daniels came to Randolph together. William Daniels located on Files Creek, a few hundred yards east of the present residence of Richard Wamsley, two miles east of Beverly. He married Catherine, daughter of Jacob Stalnaker, in 1795.

William Daniels was a typical man of his day. Casting his lot in the wilderness, at the age of 16, remote from relatives, he learned to read by his own unaided efforts, and became an intelligent and prominent citizen. He represented Randolph in the Virginia Assembly, when the capital at Richmond was reached by a perilous trip through the wilderness on horseback. He was sheriff of Randolph in 1818, justice of peace in 1808, constable in 1803. The family originally came from England where several of them were distinguished as poets, historians and scientists.

The children of William and Katherine (Stalnaker) Daniels were, Earle, Jacob, Johnathan, Madison, Nellie, who married William Currence; William, Elmere, Eli and Mary.

Children of Madison: Rev. William P. Daniels, Harrison, Harper, Allen, Bushrod, Samuel, Mary, who married Achem Harper; Elizabeth, who married Alpheus Buckey, and Christina, who married Geo. Elbon.

Children of Johnathan: Jacob, Squire William, Elam, Hamilton, Catherine, Mona and Mattie.

Children of Jacob: Welton, Parsons and Job.

Children of Allison: Washington, John, Elijah Lafayette, Elmore, Isom David, Nancy, who married Absalom Pritt; Harnett and Mary.

Earle Daniels moved to the West. Children, James, Ambrose, Isom, Bernard, Rebecca, Mary and Elizabeth.

Children of Eli: Orlando, Gabriel and Melvina.

The children of the first William married as follows: Jacob married a Miss Parsons, Johnathan a Miss Weese, William a Miss Chenoweth, Madison a Miss Skidmore, Allison a Miss Chenoweth, Earle a Miss Parsons, Elmore a Miss Cooper, Eli a Miss Harper.

Rev. Wm. P. Daniels, son of Madison and Ellen (Skidmore) Daniels, was born in 1849, married in 1869, Minerva, daughter of Hoy and Elizabeth McLean. Children, Dr. H. W., ·Floyd A., Dorsey M., Byron H. and Willie.

Rev. Daniels was for years a minister of the Methodist Episcopal church. He rendered particularly valuable services to the church in his day, it seeming to appeal to his sense of duty to visit and serve the weak, isolated and neglected fields.

Byron H., son of Rev. Wm. P. and Minerva (McLean) Daniels, was born May 19, 1883, married June 12, 1914, Sara Virginia Ellifitts. Mr. Daniels was educated in the public schools. For twelve years Mr. Daniels has been in charge of the money order and registry department of the Elkins postoffice.

Dorsey M. Daniels, son of Rev. Wm. P. and Minnie (McLean) Daniels, was born in 1877, married Earnie N. (Johnson) Ray. Children, Edgar, Eugene and Charles Cletus. Mr. Daniels' efficiency and faithfulness is attested by the fact that he has been in the employ as clerk of the Elkins Hardware and Furniture Company for thirteen years.

Page Cameran Daniels, son of Solomon W. and Mary (Gum) Daniels, was born in 1856, married Annie Grace, daughter of Fountain and .... (Hamilton) Butcher. Children, Howard L., Ulah, Mabel, Ethel and Hallie B. are deceased. Mr. Daniels is the great grandson of the first William. Mr. Daniels has been mayor of Beverly and member of town council.

Martin L. Daniels, son of G. H. and Susannah (Semple) Daniels, was born in 1868, married Carrie Shobe. Children, Ralston and Mary. Mr. Daniels was educated in public schools and Fairmont Normal. He taught school several terms and was principal of Pickens public school. At present he holds a responsible position with the Western Maryland Railroad.

Oliver C. Daniels, son of George Harrison and Susannah (Semple) Daniels, was born in 1872, married 1898, Lovet, daughter of J. H. and Sydney (Weese) Schoonover. Mr. Daniels is the present postmaster of Beverly.

William G. Daniels, French descent, was born in Augusta County, Virginia, in 1846; came to Randolph in 1878. His grandfather, Joseph Daniels, was seven years a soldier under Napoleon and though wounded many times, survived the war. Mr. Daniels was justice of the peace in Huttonsville in 1908. Mr. Daniels belongs to a family that is not related to the other Daniels family in Randolph.

George Harrison Daniels, son of Madison Daniels and grandson of William Daniels, was born in 1840, married in 1862, Martha I, daughter of Martin and Susan Stemple. Children, Flora A., Jessup, Loretta E., Martin L., Calvin H., Oliver C., Louie B., George H., Plummer B., Lizzie M., Alta G. He represented Randolph and Tucker in the State Legislature in 1893.

THE EARLE FAMILY.

The Earle Family. Archibald Earle, son of Isaiah Earle, was the first of the name to locate in Randolph. He was born in Clark County, Virginia, in 1788, and died in 1842. He came to Randolph when quite a young man and was elected county clerk in 1810, when 22 years of age. He was clerk of the County Court twenty-nine consecutive years. The Earle family is of English descent and the name is derived from the Anglo-Saxon, Eorle, a title of nobility. In 1812 Archibald Earle married Mary, daughter of Peter Buckey. Their children were John B., Sally Ann, Lucinda, Maria, Christina, Edith, Elias, Anzina, Archibald, Jefferson, Mary E. and Creed L.

Creed Luther Earle, born in 1837, son of Archibald and Mary (Bucky) Earle. In 1878 he married Columbia J., daughter of William Harrison and Ruth Ann (Hart) Coberly. Children, Charles, Harrison, Delbert, Archibald, Pearl and Mary Ruth. Mr. Earle was constable of Leadsville District in 1886 and was postmaster of Leadsville under Cleveland. He owned the land which was the original site of the City of Elkins.

John B. Earle was for many years clerk of the Circuit Court of Randolph. Arch and Jefferson Earle moved to Fort Worth, Texas, at the close of the Civil War.

THE EBERMAN FAMILY.

The Eberman Family. This family was among the early settlers of Randolph. The name is not represented in the male line in Randolph today. John and Jacob Eberman, brothers, located on Eberman's Creek, now Chenoweth Creek, at an early day. They came from Pendleton. The Ebermans were of German ancestry. They were soldiers from Pendleton in the French and Indian War of 1754-60.

THE ELZA FAMILY.

The Elza Family. This name is of English origin and in the early records of the County was spelled Elsey and Elzay. The Elza family was among the first settlers in the eastern part of the county. Thompson Elza moved to Randolph from Mineral the first decade of the county's history. Thompson Elza was captain of the militia in 1844. Sampson Elza was captain of the militia in 1860.

Thompson Elza married Sarah White, and to this union were born Solomon, Taylor, William, Sampson, Alfred, Lafayette, Joseph, Adam and Caroline.

Floyd Elza, son of Taylor Elza, was born in 1895. Mr. Elza is single and is a woodsman by occupation.

Eli Elza, son of Taylor Elza, was born in 1888, married Ockie, daughter of Malcom and Sally A. Henry. Children, Emma, B. Y. and Hansel. Mr. Elza resides at Wymer, West Virginia, and his occupation is that of a woodsman.

Adam Elza was born in 1854, married Almeda, daughter of Albertus White. Children, Sarah C., Victoria, Oliver Y., Lafayette, Albert N., Lustie, Selma, Wilbert, Lusta, Sana,

Leon, Folsie, William and Rockford. Mr. Elza is engaged in farming and has lived twenty-six years in his present location.

JAMES H. ELDER.

James H., son of John W. and Clara (Huber) Elder, was born September 11, 1872, at Chambersburg, Pennsylvania. Mr. Elder married Miss Mae, daughter of Martin and Elizabeth (Sensney) Brown. Children, Ruth and Huber. Mr. Elder's ancestors were pioneers in Franklin County, Pennsylvania. His paternal grandfather, J. G. Elder, was colonel of the 126 Pennsylvania volunteers in the war between the states. Mr. Elder came to Elkins in 1901. He is a stationer and book seller, having his place of business at Third Street, Elkins.

THE FRIEND FAMILY.

The Friend Family. The Friends were of German descent and came to Randolph from Pendleton. The date of their arrival is not certain, except as to Joseph, who settled in Randolph in 1789. Jonas Friend vas Sergeant from Pendleton in the French and Indian W.r of 1754-60. He was constable of that County in 1767, when a part of Augusta. Jacob Friend was the father of Jonas, Joseph, Thomas and Johnathan. Jonas Friend settled on Leading Creek, near its mouth, on the south side of that stream, where Friends Fort was located. He was a neighbor of Robert Maxwell, who lived on the opposite side of the Creek. In 1789 Robert Maxwell gave notice to the County Court that he had applied to the General Assembly for the privilege of constructing a ferry across Leading Creek, between the lands of Jonas Friend and his own. A ferry across Leading Creek would not seem to be necessary today, however, all streams were, perhaps, larger a century ago than today because of their more heavily timbered water basins. The Friend family is extinct in the male line in Randolph. They moved to the West. Their names appear in the records of Randolph for the last time in 1807.

THE FERGUSON FAMILY.

The Ferguson Family. Robert Ferguson was the first of this name to locate in Randolph. He came from Greene

County, Pennsylvania, in 1780. His father, James Ferguson, immigrated from Ireland to the colonies at an early day. Robert Ferguson was a blacksmith, and when a youth, shod a horse for General Washington near Pittsburgh. Robert Ferguson married Deborah, daughter of Thomas Wilmoth, in 1807. He was a soldier in the war of 1812, and died in 1868. His children were, Archibald, who married Anna Triplett; Nancy, who married Elizabeth De Garmo; Wyatt, who married Edith Schoonover; Solomon, who married Mary J. Tripplett; Robert, who married Nancy Gainer; Susan, who married Abel H. Kelly; and Elizabeth, who never married.

THE GIBSON FAMILY.

The Gibson Family. James, Dudley, John and Virginia Gibson, three brothers and a sister, came to Randolph prior to the Civil War from Virginia. Later Betsy, with her husband, James Trainum, also moved to the Valley. The children of James were, Alexander, Francis and Catherine Dudley twice married and had twenty-four children, none of whom reached manhood. James and Dudley were soldiers of the was of 1812. Alexander married Margaret, daughter of John and Joan (Harris) Currence. Children, J. N., Mary, J. A., Thomas, Alice, William, Samuel, Lafayette and Lottie. Alice married John Fansler, Willliam married Jane Fansler. Lafayette married a Miss Everett. Samuel and Thomas moved to the western part of the State. Mary married William Gibson; Lottie married Sampson Day.

J. N. married Gilsae McLeod. Children, Rose, Dold, Daisy, Emerson, W. W., Kent, Alonzo and Sallie. J. Newton Gibson was a teamster in the Civil War at the age of......years. J. A. Gibson married Virginia, daughter of John W. Mullenix. Children, Effie V., John, Ethel, Eddie, Flossie, Catherine and Dollie. Eddie died in early childhood, Effie and Dollie died at the age of 24.

J. A. Gibson was the nominee of the Republican party for the Legislature in 1908 and more than carried the strength of his party. He also taught in the public schools of this County and the State of Nebraska for a number of years.

Francis Dold Gibson, son of Jasper N. and Rosae (Mc-

Lead) Gibson, was born at Beverly in 1872, married Maggie Collett. Children, Ruth, Martha, Blanche, Frances D. and Eugent. Mr. Gibson was on the police force, regular and extra, in the City of Elkins for five years. He was policeman for the Coal & Coke Company for three years. He is now engaged in the real estate business in Elkins.

THE GODDIN FAMILY.

The Goddin Family. The Goddin family is of English descent and were pioneers in the mother state, being among the first settlers of New Kent County, Virginia. Jefferson Goddin came to Randolph in 1827 and settled near Elkins. He married Rachel Chenoweth. Their children were, Andrew J., Isaac P., Judson C., Thomas J., Clitis, George, Emmett, Melissa E., Virginia, Mary and Eliza.

Judson Chenoweth Goddin, born in 1841, married Susan (Ray) Corley. Children, Rachel J., Jacob L., Thomas J., Benjamin F., Hattie Lee and George Judson.

Jesse W. Goddin, son of Jefferson and Rachel (Chenoweth) Goddin, married in 1856, Mary E., daughter of Daniel and Sallie Ann (Earle) Harper. Children, Floyd, Lucy, Ida, Betty, Jefferson, May and John. He was a member of the Board of Supervisors in 1870-1, and was president of the County Court in 1872-6. He was justice of the peace of Leadsville District 1884-92, and was again a member of the County Court in 1892-93.

THE GANDY FAMILY.

The Gandy Family. Uriah Gandy was the leader of a band of Tories during the Revolution. He was active in behalf of the mother country in Pendleton, the eastern part of Randolph and adjoining counties. With a number of British sympathizers he established a camp on Tory Camp Run, a few miles south of the present town of Harmon. Notwithstanding the fact that he was not in harmony with the early settlers in the matter of politics, he attained a place of prominence in the early history of Randolph. Subsequent to the Revolution he settled on a branch of Dry Fork, which has borne the name of Gandy Creek. At that time he was miles from any other human habitation. His wife was a daughter of Jesse Hughes, the noted Indian fighter. He was one of the justices of the peace appointed by the Governor in the organization of the County in 1787. Being the oldest justice of peace in point of service, he was promoted to sheriff in 1793. He moved to Kentucky in 1797. Mr. Gandy located his cabin about fifty yards from the junction of Gandy Creek with Dry Fork between the two streams.

THE GOFF FAMILY.

The Goff Family. The Goff family, one of the most prominent and influential in the State, was first represented in Virginia by Job Goff, who settled in Harrison County in 1805. The Goff family is of German descent and settled in Rhode Island is an early colonial period.

David Goff, son of Job Goff, located in Randolph prior to 1829, when he was united in marriage to Christina, daughter of Peter Buckey. Their children were Claude, Cecilla and Vernon. David Goff became prosecuting attorney in 1835, superintendent of schools in 1853. He represented the County in the Virginia Assembly and also in the Senate after the formation of the new state. He was Colonel of the Virginia militia in 1844. General Nathan Goff, ex-Secretary of the Navy, and now United States Senator, is a nephew of David Goff and studied law in his uncle's office at Beverly.

Claude Goff, son of David and Christina (Buckey) Goff, was for many years a practitioner at the Beverly bar and was a highly esteemed citizen. He married Anna, daughter of Franklin and Lucinda Leonard. Their children were Chas. P., David and Ralph Waldo.

Ralph Waldo Goff, a very promising young man who was preparing himself for the legal profession, died in the twenty-first year of his age at Beverly.

THE HUTTON FAMILY.

The Hutton Family. Abraham Hutton was, perhaps, the first of the name to come to America. He was of Welch descent, and located in what is now Hardy County. He married a Miss Evans, of Philadelphia. The children of this marriage were Isaac, Moses, Peter and Johnathan. Moses Hutton entered 200 acres of land on Stony River in Hampshire County in 1789. Abraham Hutton was living in Hardy County in 1794.

Johnathan Hutton was born June 3, 1769, and married Mary, daughter of Frederick and Barbara Troutwine, in Hardy County in May, 1790. He moved to Randolph and settled on the west side of the river, near the present village of Huttonsville in 1795. The children of Johnathan and Barbara (Troutwine) Hutton were Moses, Abraham, John A., Elizabeth, Sarah, Nancy, Catherine, Fannie and Mary. Elizabeth married Andrew Crouch, Catherine married Chas. C. See, Mary married W. J. Long.

Moses Hutton, son of Johnathan and Barbara (Troutwine) Hutton, married Mary Haigler. Their children were Mary, Alfred, Elihu, Eugene, Virginia and Mozella. He died in the sixty-sixth year of his age.

John A. Hutton, son of Johnathan and Barbara (Troutwine) Hutton, married Dorothy See in 1834. Their children were Margaret, Catherine, Rachel, Lucy, Caroline and Warwick.

Abraham Hutton, son of Johnathan and Barbara (Troutwine) Hutton, married Phoeba Ann Wilson in 1836. Children, Mary Catherine, Phoeba, Amelia, Albert E., James S. Decatur B. and John.

Lieutenant Eugene Hutton, son of Moses Hutton, gave his life to the lost cause at the battle of Bunkerhill, September 3, 1864. He was a brave and intrepid soldier and was highly esteemed for many excellencies in civil life.

Elihu, son of Moses and Mary (Haigler) Hutton, was born December 31, 1837, died April 19, 1916. He was reared on his father's farm in the vicinity of Huttonsville and was educated under private tutors and at the Huttonsville Acadtmy, then the principal seat of learning in this section of the State. At the age of 24, in 1861, he organized Company C of the 20th Regiment Virginia Cavalry. He was elected Captain of his Regiment and by meritorious service arose to Colonel of the Regiment at the close of the war. He participated in the principal engagements of the war. He was wounded several times; severely at Smithfield, Virginia. His brother, Eugene, a young man of much promise was killed at Bunker Hill in 1864. At the close of the war he resumed the pursuits of husbandry on the home farm.

COLONEL ELIHU HUTTON.

In 1872 he married Miss Sophrina, daughter of Harvey Woodford, of Barbour County. To this union were born two daughters, Mrs. Laone, wife of Capt. W. H. Cobb, of Elkins, and Mrs. Beryl, wife of Floyd Strader, of Elkins; and three sons, Woodford, Forest and Ernest.

Col. Hutton represented his county two terms in the State Legislature and his genial and generous nature, coupled with qualities of mind that incited admiration, made him very popular, alike in private and public life.

Col. Hutton was prominently identified with the Confederate service during the Civil War. He was with Lee at Elkwater. He accompanied Gen. W. L. Jackson in his raid in the Valley in 1863, and was with Gen. Imboden in his raid in West Virginia the same year. Col. Hutton was one of Gen. Early's subordinates upon whom he much depended in his campaign in the Valley against Sheridan.

John A. Hutton was justice of the peace in 1841. He represented Randolph and Tucker in the Legislature subsequent to the Civil War. He was assessor of lands in 1880. Warwick, son of Johnathan, also represented Randolph and Tucker in the State Legislature and was sheriff of Randolph in 1888.

John A. Hutton in association with Mathew Whitman, Dr. Squire Bosworth, Andrew Crawford and others, were among the leaders in the organization of the Presbyterian church in Randolph and made it a power in moulding a moral and religious sentiment in the earlier years of the County. The Hutton family also deserve credit for fostering education in Randolph prior to the Civil War. It was largely through their efforts that the academy was established in antebellum days. In this school, taught by Capt. Jacob I. Hill, many men of Randolph received an education which enabled them to take a leading part in the professions of teaching, law, medicine, the pulpit, as well as in the civic affairs of the County and State.

H. Woodford, son of Col Elihu and Sophina (Woodford) Hutton, was born February 26, 1876, married Lena, daughter of Seymour McCarty. Mr. Hutton was educated at Fairmont Normal and at State University. He is engaged in farming and stockraising near Huttonsville.

Bedford Forrest, son of Elihu and Sophina (Woodford) Hutton, was born in 1885, married Ethelyn Virginia, daughter of A. J. and E. V. (Robinson) Bonnafield. Children, Elihu Bonnafield, Frances Haigler and Ethelyn Virginia. Mr. Hutton was educated at Potomac Academy, Stetson University, Florida, Pantops Academy, Washington, and Washington and Lee University, where he matriculated in the department of law.   Mr. Hutton is engaged in farming and stock-raising.

THE HARDING FAMILY.

Joseph French Harding, born November 9, 1838, in Anne Arundle County, Maryland, son of Joseph and Alice (Elliott) Harding.   He married in 1869, Luceba, daughter of Archibald and Caroline (Taylor) Wilmoth.   Children, Clare W., French Leslie, Luceba M., Roella, Jo L. and Vie Owen. Mrs. Harding died April 8, 1910. Jo Lile died January 26, 1906. The name had a military origin and the Hardings have always had a bent toward the profession of arms, many of the name distinguishing themselves in military life. Maj. Harding entered the Confederate service at the beginning of the war, when 23 years of age. He remained until the close of the war firing the last shot of that conflict, perhaps, at Knapps Creek, in an engagement with Capt. Badger. He was in many hard fought battles and had many seeming miraculous escapes. Although several times wounded, Maj. Harding is today physically superior to the average man twenty years his junior. He rose to the rank of Major and was named for promotion to Colonel when the war closed. Maj. Harding has no characteristics of the man who yields and after Lee's surrender made an effort to reach the country beyond the Mississippi, where he believed the Confederates were still holding out, but on learning that all had surrendered, he wrote his own parole May 23, 1865.

Subsequent to the Civil War, Maj. Harding twice represented Randolph and Tucker counties in the State Legislature and was a member of the Constitutional Convention of 1872. He was Sheriff of Randolph from 1877 to 1881. Since 1885, with his son Clare W. Harding, as junior member of the firm, he has been an attorney at law.

Clare W. Harding, son of Major and Luceba (Wilmoth) Harding, was born in 1872, married Ada, daughter of S. N. and Katherine (Brown) Bosworth. Children, Mildred, Evelyn, Neil, Lyle and Josephine. Mr. Harding has served two terms as prosecuting attorney of Randolph County and was appointed commissioner in chancery by Judge Kittle.

THE HARPER FAMILY.

The Harper Family. The Harper family is of German ancestry. The name was originally spelled Herber or Herrber. Three brothers, Adam, Jacob and Phillip immigrated from the Rhine to the Shenandoah Valley in about 1750. They were in the French and Indian War from Pendleton. Henry, a son of the first Jacob, was born in 1788 and died in 1850. He was the ancestor of the Harper family in Randolph. He married Elizabeth Mouse. Their children were Jacob, Jehu, Moses, Henry, Eva, Elizabeth, Abraham and Daniel. In 1799, Jacob C. Harper purchased two tracts of land of Abraham Claypool on the east side of the river in the Caplinger settlement. The Harpers and Caplingers were neighbors in Pendleton and it is probable that the report that the Caplingers gave of the country induced the Harpers to follow them to Randolph. There were two Jacob Conrad Harpers. The Jacob Conrad Harper who lived on Horse Camp Run was the son of Moses and Phoeba Conrad Harper and grandson of the first Jacob Harper. Jacob Harper also purchased 402 acres of land in what is now the Caplinger settlement in 1799. The grantor was Geo. See of Hardy County, who had received a patent for the land in 1783.

Geo. W. Harper, son of Daniel and Sally Ann (Earle) Harper, was born in 1849. Mr. Harper was married in 1870 to Louisa Ann Taylor. Children, W. G., Burtie M. and John T., who was a machinist and was killed by a boiler explosion in the Western Maryland yards at Elkins. Mr. Harper was deputy sheriff in 1866-7, and was constable from 1881-7.

W. W. Harper, son of Miles N. and Christina Lawrence Harper, was born in Pendleton County in 1881. He was educated in the public schools of his native county and came to Randolph in 1914. Mr. Harper married Margie Christina Teter. Two children have blessed this union, Freda and Lena. Mr. Harper was clerk of the Circoit Court of Pendleton in 1913, and deputy sheriff in 1908-12. At present he holds the responsible position of cashier of Stockman's Bank at Harmon.

Seymour Harper, son of Jacob C. and Susan (McDonald) Harper, was born in 1865, married Sallie (Shober) Ours.

Children, Carl, Earle C., Pearl S., William Jennings Bryan, Mabel, Brooks, Madaline, Neil Wood, Gail, Ruth. Dale died in infancy. Mr. Harper came to Elkins in 1907 and has been prominently identified with the business interests of the city.

Isom Harper, son of Jacob C. and Susan (McDonald) Harper, was born near Harmon in 1868; married Phoeb (Bright) Carr. Children, Minor, Delia, Lexie, Theodore R., and Guy. Calvin died in the twenty-ninth year of his eage; Claudie died, aged 21; Holmes R. died, in the eleventh year of his age, and Otos died in infancy. Mr. Harper was constable of Dry Fork District in 1895.

Daniel A. Harper, son of A. E. and Amanda Virginia (Hinkle) Harper, was born in 1867; married Minerva, daughter of Nicholas and Eliza (McLean) Wilmoth. Children, Caudy,, Mittie Virginia and Benton E. Mr. Harper was born and raised on what is known as the Harper Triangle in the City of Elkins. He was also the founder of Harper Town, a thriving suburb of the City of Elkins.

Philip D. Harper, son of John D. and Ellen (Simmons) Harper, was born in Harmon, W. Va. in 1868; married Mintie E. (Goff) Lantz. Children, Harmon, Iva, Nela, Nellie, Wilbur, John, Bessie, Maggie, Lester, Ernest, Snowden, Ross, Scott. Five children of Mr. and Mrs. Harper died in infancy, making 18 children. It is a peculiar coincidence that Mr. and Mrs. Harper were born on the same day in the same year.

THE HART FAMILY.

Hart Family. The Hart family is of English descent and has been identified with the county since 1785, when two brothers, Daniel and Edward Hart, located at the present town of Beverly. Daniel settled about a mile above Beverly on Files Creek near the old Buckey mill site. They came to Randolph from New Jersey. John and Daniel Hart were soldiers in the Revolution, and were sons of John Hart, who signed the Declaration of Independence.

Joseph Hart, son of Edward Hart, was born and reared near Beverly. He became a prominent lawyer, having been admitted to the bar of Randolph in 1837, and was also prominent in public and political affairs. He twice represented his county in the State Legislature and was president of the county court. He moved to the summit of Rich Mountain in 1855 for the benefit of his health, but continued to practice law until the beginning of the Civil War. His farm on the mountain top became the site of the battle of Rich Mountain and his residence was between the lines of the contending forces. He died April 4, 1881.

Squire Bosworth Hart, son of Joseph and Susan (Pickens) Hart, was born near Beverly in 1841. He enlisted in Battery E First West Virginia Artillery and served in the Valley of Virginia. After the close of the war he taught school until 1867, when he was elected county superintendent of schools, and was re-elected in 1869. In 1849 a coal mine was opened a short distance west of the summit of the mountain on the Hart farm and supplied the demand in Beverly and vicinity until the building of the railroad up the Valley. In 1868 Mr. Hart married Maria L. Morgan, of Upshur County. They had one child, who became the wife of Hon. Clyde Johnson, a prominent attorney of St. Marys, this state.

William Camden Hart, son of Calvin C. Hart and Julia Hart, was born December 19, 1868; married Marietta E. Logan, daughter of William Thomas Logan and Elizabeth F. Logan. Children, Shirley D. Hart, Logan D. Hart, Dorothy Julia Hart, Marion L. Hart, Sheffey B. Hart, and Calvin E. Hart. William Camden Hart has been constable twice and justice of the peace of Beverly District once.

THE HAIGLER FAMILY.

The Haigler Family. Though the family name in the male line is no longer represented in Randolph County, the Haigler strain of blood is transmitted in several prominent families in Randolph. The forebears of this family, Benjamin and Jacob Haigler, were soldiers in the French and Indian War from Pendleton County. The Haigler family is of German ancestry.

Jacob and Perry Haigler moved to Iowa in 1856. Jacob Haigler, Sr., died April 9, 1842, aged 53 years. He died from the effects of a burn received while burning brush in a clearing. Henry Clay Dean married a daughter of Jacob Haigler.

THE HAYMOND FAMILY.

The Haymond Family. Creed Haymond was born in Beverly, Randolph County, April 22, 1836. His father was Calder Haymond and his mother was Martha, daughter of Ben Wilson. Calder Haymond located in Beverly in 1830 for the practice of law. When Creed Haymond was sixteen the family moved to California. In 1859 he entered upon the practice of law in his adopted state and rapidly rose to the leadership of his profession. He was counsel for Leland Stanford and prepared the papers for that gentleman's donation for the foundation of that noted institution, the Leland Stanford University. He also became a national figure in politics.

THE HADDAN FAMILY.

The Haddan Family. Withers in his Border Warfare, mentions the Haddans as among the first settlers to occupy the Valley in 1772-4. There were three brothers, John, William and David Haddan. They came to Randolph from New Jersey. The Haddans located above Huttonsville in the vicinity of the mouth of Elkwater, and built a fort on the farm now owned by Forrest See. Mary, daughter of David Haddan, married Edward Jackson. She was the grandmother of General Stonewall Jackson. She was the child of the first wife of David Hadden. For his second wife David Haddan married Rebecca Barr. They had three children, David, Margaret and Elizabeth. David died in youth. Margaret became the wife of Isaac White in 1797. Elizabeth married John Stalnaker in 1804. John Haddan was one of the justices of the peace appointed by the Governor in the formation of the county. He was also assessor in the same year. He was one of the first representatives of Randolph in the Virginia Assembly. He was captain of the militia in 1795 and major in 1800. In 1806 he moved to Indiana. The Haddan families moved to the west and although extinct in Randolph in the male line, the strain of blood is represented in several prominent families of the county.

THE HARRIS FAMILY.

The Harris Family. Jerome B. Harris, son of Barnabus Tunis and Rachael Marquis Harris, was born in 1836. He married Mary Crocket. Six children were born unto them, Lenora, Gaylord, Jerrold, Tunis, Mary and Raphael. This branch of the Harris family is decendant of James Harris, who was born in Bristol, England, in 1700. Imigrated to New Jersey in 1725. He married a Miss Boylen. A son, George Harris, was born in 1745. He married a Miss Tunis. A son, Barnabus Harris, was born at Pulaski, Lawrence County, Pennsylvania, in 1768. He married Ester Miller. Of this marriage Barna C. Harris was born in 1811. Barna C. Harris married Rachael Marquis, and unto them was born Barna Tunis Harris, who married Rachael Marquis. Their son, Jerome B. Harris, was the ancestor of this branch of the Harris family in Randolph.

Jerrold Harris, son of Jerome B. and Mary J. Harris, was born in Pennsylvania in 1876; married Birdie McGee, daughter of Adam and Mary A. McGee. Children, Frank, Clarence and Edith. Mr. Harris is an employe of the Laurel River Lumber Company, Jennington, West Virginia.

THE HORNBECK FAMILY.

The Hornbeck Family. Benjamin Hornbeck was the first of that line to locate in Randolph. He was of Irish ancestry and came to Randolph from Pendleton. Benjamin Hornbeck settled on Stalnakers Run, near where White Station is now located on the Western Maryland Railroad. The remains of the chimney of his cabin is still visible on the farm of Obidiah Taylor on the north bank of Stalnaker Run. His wife and children were massacred by the Indians in 1781. His first wife was a Miss Vanscoy. His second wife was the daughter of William Currence, the pioneer.

Benjamin Hornbeck was born in 1754, and died September 6, 1827. He was buried at the old Currence graveyard on the farm now owned by John Weese. The children of Benjamin and Lydia (Currence) Hornbeck were Sarah, who married Samuel Channell in 1804; Ann, who married James Carr in 1810; Mary, Joseph, Moses, John and Elizabeth.

Moses moved to Upshur County, Joseph moved to Illinois. John remained on the patrimonial estate.

John, son of Joseph, who moved to Illinois, married Bettie, daughter of William H. Currence. They had one son, John, who now lives in Beverly.

John, son of Benjamin and Lydia (Currence) Hornbeck, married Margaret Stalnaker. Their children were Adam, who married Mary, daughter of Henry Currence; Margaret, Dorcas and Elizabeth, who married William Miles of Greenbrier County.

Adam, son of John and Margaret (Stalnaker) Hornbeck, lives on the Benjamin Hornbeck homestead near Daily Station. He had one son, William, who was justice of the peace of Valley Bend District. He was killed by lightning in 1898.

THE ISNER FAMILY.

The Isner Family. William Isner was the first of the name to locate in Randolph, perhaps. He lived in the Valley in 1775 on lands adjoining the lands of Benjamin Wilson (See Early Land Patents in another chapter.) Thomas Isner applied for a pension in the year 1833 on the grounds that he was an Indian spy in the Revolution. Michael Isner entered 190 acres of land in 1789 in Tygarts Valley. Michael Isner was a member of the first grand jury in Randolph County in 1787.

THE JACKSON FAMILY.

The Jackson Family. The first of this Jackson family to come to America was John Jackson, who was from the north of Ireland. Upon his arrival in America in 1748, he secured employment on the plantation of Lord Baltimore, in Calvert County, Maryland, where he met and married Elizabeth Cummins, a native of London, England, and a woman of intelligence and great force of character. After a time, John Jackson moved to Hardy County, thence to Randolph, now Upshur County, where the town of Buckhannon now stands. Eight children were born to them. Five sons, George, Edward, Henry, Samuel and John, and three daughters. Edward Jackson married Mary, raughter of David Haddan, who resided in the vicinity of Elkwater; Edward Jackson moved to Harrison, now Lewis County, in about 1800. Three sons were born to Edward and Mary Haddan Jackson, George, David and Johnathan.

George Jackson moved to Clarksburg and his parents made their home with him until their death. The father died in 1801, in the eighty-fifth year of his age. The mother died in 1825 at the very unusual age of 105 years.

Johnathan, son of Edward and Mary (Hadden) Jackson, was an attorney of Clarksburg and married Julia Neal, of Parkersburg. Two sons and two daughters blessed this union, Warren and Thomas Johnathan and Elizabeth and Laura Ann.

Warren and Elizabeth died in early life. Laura Ann became the wife of Johnathan Arnold, of Beverly.

Edward and John Jackson were members of the first County Court of Randolph County, and with their associate justices of the peace organized the county in 1787. Edward Jackson was the first surveyor of Randolph County; was assessor in 1791, and sheriff in 1792. He was captain of the militia in 1787. Henry Jackson was surveyor in 1793. John Jackson was lieutenant of the militia in 1787. Edward Jackson moved to the West Fork about five miles below the present town of Weston in about 1800. He died in 1827.

THE KYLE FAMILY.

The Kyle Family. This family is numerously represented in Randolph and is of German ancestry. The name was originally spelled Keil. The Keils came to Randolph from Pendleton. George and Valentine Kyle were soldiers in the French and Indian War from Pendleton. They lived at Upper Tract in Pendleton and moved there from Rockingham in the early days of Pendleton when it was a part of Augusta. The Kyles, Friends, Bogards, Harpers and Caplingers were all decended from Pendleton County ancestors.

THE LOGAN FAMILY.

The Logan Family. This family became identified with this county in 1823, when William and Elizabeth Logan, husband and wife, located in Mingo District. They came from

Rockbridge County, Virginia. William Logan erected and operated the first grist and saw mill in that section of the county. Mr. Logan was an elder in the Presbyterian church and co-operated with Mathew Whitman, Dr. Squire Bosworth, Johnathan Hutton, Adam See, Daniel McLean and others in organizing that denomination in Randolph. He died in 1858 and his wife in 1831.

James H. Logan, son of William and Elizabeth (Crawford) Logan, was third in order of birth of seven children, and was born in Rockbridge County, Virginia, in 1818, and was five years old when he came to Randolph with his parents. He was educated at Washington and Lee University and for many years was a school teacher in Randolph. Many of his pupils in after life became prominent at the bar, in the pulpit and other professions. In later years, he followed surveying and civil engineering. While never an aspirant for office, he was president of the board of education, member of city council and mayor of Beverly. He was a classical scholar and was apt at quoting the best productions of poets and orators. His foresight was evident by obtaining large holdings in timber lands, which with the development of the county made him a man of wealth. Four children were born to Mr. and Mrs. Logan, two of whom died in infancy. The eldest, Frances Irvine, married Cyrus H. Scott. She died August 5, 1893. Emma, the only surviving child, also became the wife of Cyrus H. Scott.

THE LEVITT FAMILY.

The Levitt Family. Little is known of this family. Withers does not mention the well authenticated fact that this family was massacred by the Indians. William Levitt entered 200 acres of land on the east side of Tygarts Valley River, May 30, 1780. It is probable that he had occupied the land several years prior to that time. His land was joined on the south by the lands of John Cassedy and on the north by the lands of Cartine White. The Indians secreted themselves behind a cluster of bushes that surrounded the spring, which was about one hundred yards south of the cabin. They waited for some member of the family to appear in the yard, when the Indians fired. Mrs. Levitt and her children were killed and scalped. Mr. Levitt escaped and when he returned to the scene with some neighbors, Mrs. Levitt had revived, tied a handkerchief about her head and made her way to a clump of underbrush nearby where she was in hiding. However, she survived her injuries but a few hours. The date of the tragedy is uncertain. The land is now owned by Drs. J. L. and Perry Bosworth.

THE LOUGH FAMILY.

The Lough Family. This family is of German ancestry and came to Randolph from Pendleton in about 1840. The original German name was spelled Loch. Adam Lough was perhaps the first member of the family to come to America. He settled on Deer Run in Pendleton in 1772 and died in 1789. His wife's name was Barbara Conrad—perhaps. They had seven children, Elizabeth, Catherine, Barbara, Adam, George, John and Conrad. John married Sarah Harpole. They had eleven children. The fifth son, Elias R. Lough, was born in Pendleton in 1815 and died in Randolph in 1886. In 1843 he married Dorcas, daughter of George and Ruth (Morgan) Weese. Children, Angeline, Rebecca, John Vernon, Leslie J. and George Morgan.

John Vernon Lough was born in 1850 and in 1894 married Delila Wilson, daughter of Solomon and Abigail (Ryan) Caplinger. They had one child, Wilson.

Geo. M. Lough, son of Elias and Dorcas (Weese) Lough, was born in 1845. He married Louisa, daughter of Alba and Emily (Wilmoth) Chenoweth. Children, Guy and Leslie. Leslie, son of Geo. M. Lough, married Eva L. Grose.

THE MARTENY FAMILY.

The Marteny Family. This was one of the prominent pioneer families of Randolph and was related by marriage to many of the early settlers of the county. William Marteny was born about 1770 and lived to be about 80 years of age. His first wife was Eunice Estburn. There children were William, Daniel, Washington, Joseph, Charles, Jane, Lucretia, Deborah, Sarah, Ellen. Joseph died in Indiana, Charles was drowned in Leading Creek in childhood. Jane married Dr. Dolebar, Lucretia married Robert Ball, Deborah married William Corrick, Sarah married Thomas Wilmoth, Ellen married John Phares. William Marteny lived near the Leading Creek bridge, on what is now known as the Reed place. His second wife was a Miss Earle, sister of Archibald Earle, who was for many years clerk of the Circuit Court of Randolph County. Peter Buckey married a sister of William Marteny. William Marteny, the pioneer, represented Randolph County in the Virginia Assembly for four years and was sheriff in 1830.

THE MARSTILLER FAMILY.

Nicholas Marstiller, the first representative of the Marstiller family in Randolph, came from Pennsylvania. The exact date is not known. The name is of German origin. The first Nicholas was appointed master of brands and measures in 1798. The position was an important one at that time. He was elected overseer of the poor in 1803 for the Second District of Randolph. The Second District extended down from Files Creek, including Wilmoth's settlement and the Dry Fork. At that time overseer of the poor was practically the only office in the county that was elective, all other offices were appointive until the adoption of the constitution of 1852. Nicholas Marstiller, the pioneer, owned and lived on the farm now owned by Charles Crouch a few miles below Beverly.

John Marstiller, son of the first Nicholas, had six children, Nicholas, William, Godfrey, John, David Blackman and Squire Bosworth.

Nicholas, son of John and grandson of the first Nicholas Marstiller, married Amanda, daughter of John Taylor. Children, Charles M., Lee, John D. and Delphia B.

Charles M. Marstiller, son of Nicholas and Amanda (Taylor) Marstiller, married Agnes, daughter of David and Pernie (Skidmore) Gilmore. Children, O. G., Clare H., Pearline W. and Jeanne. The second Nicholas Marstiller was county surveyor about forty years from 1840-80. His son, C. M. Marstiller, was county surveyor for twelve years, deputy sheriff twelve years and mayor of Elkins in 1912-14.

Stewart L. Marstiller, son of Page and Sarah C. (Collett) Marstiller, married Mary Grace Ramsey. Children, Richard J., Calmor P., Ina Lee and Katherine D. Marl S. died in infancy. Mr. Marstiller was constable of Leadsville District two terms, from 1904-12. He was deputy sheriff from 1912 two terms, from 1904-12. He has been deputy sheriff from 1912 to the present time. He was elected sheriff in 1916.

THE McCOLLUM FAMILY.

The McCollum Family. The McCollums were among the first settlers of Pocahontas County. From the best information obtainable the first of the name in America was Daniel McCollum, who settled in New Hampshire. He was Scotch-Irish and a son of a physician who was a graduate of the University of Edinburg. The McCollum family settled near Driscol on Brown's Mountain, in Pocahontas county in 1770. They came to Virginia from New Jersey. The children of Daniel McCollum, the pioneer, were Daniel, Jacob, William, Rebecca, Mary and Sarah. Isaac, son of William and grandson of Daniel, married Margaret Thomas and moved to Randolph.

Newton B. McCollum, son of Isaac and Margaret (Thomas) McCollum, was born in Greenbrier County, West Virginia, 1854; married Martha J. Marteny in 1875. Children, Clinton, Fenster, May, Ada. Children deceased, Ruth, Allie May and Della. Mr. McCollum is in the employ of Pugh & Beavers Wholesale Grocery Co., at Elkins.

J. Floyd, son of W. H. and M. E. (Simmons) McCollum, was born October 19, 1886, at Mill Creek; married July 2, 1911, Lena, daughter of C. C. and Sarah (Elza) Carr. Mr. McCollum is a member of the McCollum family of Randolph and is of Scotch-Irish descent. Mr. McCollum is at present an employe of the Laurel River Lumber Company at Jenningston.

THE MORGAN FAMILY.

The Morgan Family. Zedekiah Morgan was born in Connecticut in 1744. He was an officer in the Revolutionary War and came to Randolph subsequent to that period. He was twice married. His first wife was Ruth Dart of Con-

necticut. His second wife was Rebecca Watson of Boston.
Two of his daughters married into Randolph families, Ruth,
who married George Weese and Naomi, who married Adam
Stalnaker. They were both children of his first marriage.
Zedekiah Morgan was a participant in repelling the Indian
raid in which Adam Stalnaker was killed between Elkins and
Beverly. His descendants have been influential in West Vir-
ginia.

Clark, son of J. R. and India (Rice) Morgan, was born
in Taylor County, September 14, 1879; married Mary, daughter of John J. and Nannie (Galvin) Gallohr. Children, Mildred, Velona and Geraldine. Mr. Morgan graduated from
the Grafton high school in 1889. He came to Randolph in
1909 and is general manager for West Virginia and Eastern
Telephone Company. He is a descendant of David Morgan,
the Indian fighter.

Camden J. Morgan, son of J. P. and Virginia (Morgan)
Morgan, was born in 1886, married Barbara, daughter of
Dexter and Maude (Crites) Cutright. Children, Ralph and an
infant not named. Mr. Morgan is clerk in the B. & O. Railroad office at Pickens. He was educated in public schools.
Mr. Morgan is of English descent and a member of the Morgan family that was prominent in the Monongalia Valley in
the pioneer period. His grandfather, David Morgan, moved
to Randolph from Marion County in 1856. He is also a descendant of David Morgan, the noted Indian fighter.

Hugh O., son of Chester W. and Mary (Talbott) Morgan, was born at French Creek, West Virginia, in 1863; married Isabelle M., daughter of John (Gallman) Light. Children, Chas. E., Troy C. John L. died aged 10 years. Mr.
Morgan moved to Randolph in 1868 and resides at Pickens.
The paternal grandfather, Joshua Morgan, moved to Randolph with the Massachusetts Colony that located in Upshur
County in about 1800. Among those who came with this
colony were the Burrhs, Philips, Goulds, Sextons and Bosworths. Mr. Morgan's father, C. W. Morgan, was one of the
first to settle in the section of Pickens. The nearest store and
postoffice was twenty-two miles distant for years.

THE MAXWELL FAMILY.

The Maxwell Family. The Maxwell family as presently represented in Randolph were of Scotch descent and came from Pennsylvania to the Monongahela Valley in 1800.

Thomas Maxwell, son of Robert Maxwell, of Chester County, Pennsylvania, married Jane Lewis, near Germantown. Their children were Abner, Levi, Lewis, Robert, Mary and Amy. Thomas Maxwell made a journey into Western Pennsylvania and was never heard of afterward. It is supposed he was drowned. His widow and six children moved from their home in Pennsylvania to Harrison County. Her son Lewis was three times elected to Congress. He lived at West Union. Rufus Maxwell, son of Levi Maxwell, was born in 1828, died in 1907, was the first prosecuting attorney of Tucker County. He was also a member of the Legislature from Tucker. He married Sarah L. Bonnifield and reared a family of six children.

Wilson B. Maxwell, son of Rufus and Sarah (Bonifield) Maxwell, was born in 1853. He was educated in the State University and began the practice of law at St. George in 1876. He married in 1876 Miss Carrie Lindsay. He is an attorney of Elkins.

Mr. Maxwell's grandfather, Levi Maxwell, married Sarah Haymond, whose mother, Mary Wilson, was the daughter of Col. Ben. Wilson, the Randolph pioneer. This explains the origin of the Wilson name in the Maxwell family.

Claude Wilson Maxwell was born July 28, 1877. He graduated from the State University in 1897. He located in Elkins in 1900. Mr. Maxwell married Miss Nell M. White, daughter of Prof. I. C. White, of Morgantown. Children, May M., Chas. W. and Dorothy B. Mr. Maxwell is not only a successful lawyer and business man but finds time to indulge a natural fondness for delving into the subjects of science and phylosophy.

Earle Maxwell, son of W. B. and Carrie (Lindsay) Maxwell, was born September 7, 1888. He was educated at the State University. He has been associated with his father in the practice of law for six years. He received the Democratic nomination for prosecuting attorney in the 1916 primaries.

THE McLEAN FAMILY.

The McLean Family. Two distinct and non-related McLean families have lived in Randolph. John McLean was killed by the Indians near Haddan's Fort when Warwick's Company was ambushed. Abner McLean, who in 1807, married Rhoeba Daniels was, perhaps, a member of this family. This branch of the family spelled their mane McLain.

Daniel McLean was the first representative of the other branch of the family to locate in Randolph. He was of Scotch-Irish ancestry. Daniel McLean came to Randolph from Annarundell County, Maryland, at a very early day. He married a Miss Wilmoth of this county. Their children were George, William, Joseph, John, Dawson, Hoy, Noah, Elizabeth, Ann and another daughter, whose name is not remembered, married Adam Westfall. Elizabeth married Daniel Weese. Ann married William Foggy.

George McLean married a Miss Ryan. Children, Julia Sarah, Jane, Virginia and James E.

James E. McLean studied law and although he died when a comparatively young man, he attained prominence at the bar. He was practicing his profession at Buckhannon when a fatal illness brought to a close a promising career.

William McLean married a Miss Weese. Their children were Retus, Sarah, Martha, Mary, Jacob, Elizabeth, Minerva and Fleming

Joseph, son of Daniel, moved to Illinois. Dawson died in infancy.

John McLean married Delila Currence, daughter of John Currence, in 1815.

Hoy McLean was twice married. His first wife was Rachael, daughter of Daniel Weese. Children, Emaline. His second wife was Miss Elizabeth Lytle. Children, Minerva, who married Rev. W. P. Daniels; Martha, who married Dr. Thos. L. Daniels, and Anna, who married F. M. A. Lawson.

Noah McLean, son of Daniel, married Julia Meek of Augusta County, Virginia. Children, Eliza Ann, who married Nicholas Wilmoth, and Perry H. McLean, who moved to Miami County, Indiana, in 1865.

Perry H. McLean, son of Noah and Julia (Meek) McLean married Ustena Myers of his adopted state of Indiana. Their children are Alonzo and J. F. McLean.

THE POTTS FAMILY.

The Potts Family. In the year 1847 Mathias C. Potts bought a tract of land on the foothills of Cheat Mountain, about three miles from Valley Head, and moved from Bath County, Virginia, upon it with his family, consisting of himself and wife and six children, five boys and one girl; the oldest boy, Franklin, being about 14 years old. Mr. Potts was at that time a very vigorous man, about 40 years old. It required much courage, rigid economy and much hard work to clear up a farm in the wild woods and support so large a family, but he and his wife and the older boys addressed themselves to the task and succeeded. In a few years he had a comfortable home and his farm stocked with horses, cattle, sheep and hogs. No one in the upper end of Randolph had more friends than he or was deserving of more. His house being the most commodious in the community, became a preaching place. On one occasion when the question of character was being discussed in the "living room" in front of a great blazing log fire, he made this remark, "I do not expect to have very much property to leave to my children, but I want to live so that when I am gone it will be said of me 'he was an honest man.'" He was for a long time justice of the peace in his Magisterial District and his counsel was often sought in settling difficulties between neighbors.

When the war broke out in 1861 his sympathies were with the South and in consequence he was compelled to leave his home and much of his property to the mercy of the enemy. He went as far into the interior as Bath County, but on the way his only daughter died from sickness caused by exposure. He remained in Bath County till the fall of 1865 when he returned to his devastated farm where he continued to make his home until his death which occurred in 1881 while he was on a visit to his son, Newton, in Huntington, West Virginia.

His second son, Warwick, was a very highly respected young man, a carpenter by trade, and died in Upshur County in the winter of 1861-2. Franklin and Newton entered the Confederate Army in May 1861 and served with distinction till the close of the war; Franklin as Orderly Sergeant in McClannihan's Battery and Newton as Lieutenant in Company G Eighteenth Virginia Cavalry, and in the fall of 1864 he was promoted to the position of Adjutant. He had five horses shot under him during his service in the army. Gatewood Potts enlisted in Company G Eighteenth Virginia Regiment. He was wounded and captured in Pennsylvania a few days before the battle of Gettysburg. He was kept in prison until the close of the war.

Hamilton Potts enlisted in the Twentieth Virginia Cavalry and served until the close of the war.

Franklin Potts married Miss Mary Ann Mathews. Three children, one daughter and two sons, were born of this union. The younger son, James O. Potts, is a minister in the U. B. church.

Newton Potts married Miss Maggie Stewart of Virginia and moved to Huntington, West Virginia. He has been a member of the city council, city clerk and police judge of the City of Huntington.

Rev. L. Gatewood Potts married, first, Miss Jane Woods, of Mingo, Randolph County. Of this union one child, Vernon Brown Potts, was born. He is at present a resident of Florida. After the death of his first wife, Mr. Potts married Miss Anna Waugh, of Pocahontas County, West Virginia. Three children were born to this union, George, who resides in Cincinnati, Ohio, J. Forrest Potts, who holds a position with the Western Maryland Railroad at Elkins, and Mrs. Maggie Isner, who is a popular school teacher. Rev. Gatewood Potts, while living on his farm near Elkins, is a prominent local preacher in the Methodist Episcopal church.

Rev. Hamilton Potts was twice married. His first wife was Miss Lizzie Logan and after her death he married Miss

Maggie Baxter. Rev. Potts was unfortunate in the death of both of his wives and he is now living alone in Alabama. Six children, four of whom are living, were born to them. His eldest daughter became the wife of Mr. Joe Bartlett, of Elkins. His youngest daughter, Miss Lizzie, is a school teacher. His son, Broadus, lives in Upshur County and Bucy lives in Clarksburg. While Rev. Potts is an ordained minister of the Baptist church he at present fills no regular pastorate, but preaches as a supply. He was one of the pioneer hotel men of Elkins and the Temperance Hotel was one of the land marks of the town.

THE PHARES FAMILY.

The Phares Family. This family is of Irish descent and came to Randolph from Pendleton in about 1796. This family was among the prominent pioneers of Pendleton, settling on Hedricks Run in that county in 1781. John, Robert and Johnson Phares were among the tithables in Pendleton in 1790. Johnson Phares was a captain of the Pendleton militia in 1793. In the organization of Pendleton in 1787, Johnson Phares was selected as one of the constables of the county.

Robert, who married Susannah Minnis in Pendleton in 1795, was the first of the name to locate in Randolph. They settled on Leading Creek. Their children were Benjamin, Johnson, John, Jesse and Susan.

John Phares, son of Robert and Susan (Minnis) Phares, married Martha Marteny. Their children were William, Benjamin I. and Johnson.

Benjamin I., son of Robert and Susannah (Minnis) Phares, was born in 1805, and married in 1834, Catherine, daughter of Jacob Slagle. Children, Jesse F., John R., William S., Melissa E. George W. and Jasper W.

Johnson, son of Robert and Susannah (Minnis) Phares, never married.

Susan, daughter of Robert and Susannah (Minnis) Phares, married Edward Pritt.

Wm. Phares, born in 1826, died 1892, son of John and Martha (Marteny) Phares, married Mary E., daughter of

John B. Earle. Children, May, John T., Catherine, W. B. and Chas. H. Catherine married Hon. W. L. Kee, for several years a prominent attorney of Randolph.

Benjamin I., son of John and Martha (Marteny) Phares, was born in 1826 and married Hellen, daughter of Geo. W. Ward. Children, Inez, Robert L., L. W., Maria, Page, Grace, Columbia, Tucker J. and Maud E.

Johnson W. Phares, son of John and Martha (Marteny) Phares, was born in 1836; married in 1872 to Mary A., daughter of Levy D. Ward. Children, Bruce, Nettie B., Flora H., Charles, James Pindall, John L., Burl R., Flossie H. and Nellie R.

George W. Phares, born in 1824, son of William, married Eliza, daughter of William Wilmoth in 1848. Children, Squire B., William P., Hannah, Anzina, Mary Jane, Alice M., Amanda, Ella M., Columbia A. and Philadelphia.

Abel W. Phares, born in 1826, son of William and Anna (Stalnaker) Phares; married Elizabeth, daughter of Archibald and Jane (Corley) See. Children, Harriet, Angelina, Emmeline, Patsy Jane, Archibald Wilson, Xantippe, Lucy Ellen, William R., Laura Virginia, Caroline, Augusta, Elizabeth, Bird and Charles Bruce.

Jacob Phares, son of William, born in 1831. In 1853 he married Jemima, daughter of William and Mary (Taylor) Wilmoth. Children, Delia, Lydia, Anna, Leonard, Jasper N., Marian, Robert, Warner, Luceba, Dora and Walter.

Jasper N. Phares, son of Jacob and Jemima (Wilmoth) Phares, born in 1861, near Elkins; married Addie I., daughter of Eli and Margaret (Triplett) Taylor. Children, Stroller, May, Dora, Reta, Jemima, Arthur Clay and Ruth. Mr. Phares has been assessor and deputy assessor of Randolph County.

THE PEDRO FAMILY.

The Pedro Family. The Petro or Pedro family was perhaps the only representative of the Spanish nationality among the pioneers of Randolph. The names of Henry, Leonard and Nicholas Petro appear in the early records of Randolph. Nicholas Pedro was a member of the first grand jury of Randolph. Thomas Butcher married Susan, daughter of Henry Petro in 1807. Solomon Collett married Sarah, daughter of Henry Petro in 1815. Leonard Petro was captured by the Indians, while guarding a trail that lead into the Valley, in 1777. He was taken to Ohio and never heard from afterward. Although the name is extinct in Randolph the strain of blood is represented in several prominent families of the county.

THE PRITT FAMILY.

The Pritt Family. John Pritt was the first representative of the Pritt family in Randolph County. He settled in Valley Bend District. He married a Miss Miller. Mr. Pritt came from Bath County, Virginia, in about 1812. Their children were John, Edward, James, William and Jane. James Pritt married Sydney McLaughlin. Their children were Riley, Edward, Joseph, Cornelius, Amelia and Sallie.

Edward Pritt married Susan Phares. Their children were Holman, John, George, Benjamin, Robert, Johnson, Martha, Naomi, Virginia and Margaret. Virginia married Seymour Phares; Margaret married Jefferson Marteny.

William Pritt, son of the first John, married Bettie Woolwine. Children, Absalom, Washington, Sallie, Mary, Susan, Elizabeth and Agnes. Mary married Edmond Kittle; Susan married Seymour Stalnaker and Elizabeth married Hiram Hill.

John Pritt, son of John the first, married Nancy Phillips. Their children were Wirt, Pierce, John Haddan, Margaret and Jane. Margaret married David Kelly; Jane married Draper Stalnaker.

Riley, son of James and Sydney (McLaughlin) Pritt, married Katherine, daughter of Isom Channell. Children, Branch, Howard, Ernest, Warwick, Hellen and Hattie.

Edward Pritt, son of James and Sydney (McLaughlin) Pritt, married Mary Jane Lloyd. Children, Charles, Bert, Humboldt, Ford, Lora and Clem.

Joseph Pritt, son of James and Sydney (McLaughlin) Pritt, married Margaret, daughter of Isom and Margaret Channell. Children, Katie, Ida, Vernie and Odie.

Cornelius never married and died in middle age. Sallie married Jasper, son of Benjamin Phares. Amelia married William Herron.

Holman Pritt married Columbia Woolwine. Children, Bruce, Clay, Minnie and Nina.

John "Dixie" Pritt married a Miss Crickard. Children, Thadeus, Albert, Wade, Lenora, Ella and Anna.

Benjamin Pritt married Abbie Stalnaker, daughter of Seymour and Susan Stalnaker. Children, Ruth.

Robert Pritt married Georgia, daughter of George and Melissa (Phares) Long.

Johnson Pritt married Hannah Harper, daughter of Henry Harper. Children, Hugh, Maggie, Susan, Hope and Edward.

Absalom Pritt, son of William and Betty (Woolwine) Pritt, married Nancy, daughter of Allison Daniels. Children, French, Eli and George W.

Washington Pritt, son of William and Bettie (Woolwine) Pritt, married Amelia Stalnaker, daughter of John Stalnaker. Children, Jefferson and Laura.

Edmond Pritt, son of the first John, married Susan Ryan. Children, George.

George, son of Edmond, married a Miss Stalnaker. Children, Frank, Bessie, Edmond and Wayne R. Wayne Pritt was clerk of the Circuit Court of Tucker for many years and is now a prominent attorney of that county.

Riley Pritt was lieutenant of the county militia in 1866, and justice of the peace and member of the County Court in 1873. He represented Valley Bend District as a member of the board of supervisors in 1869. Holman Pritt was justice of the peace and as such member of the County Court in 1876. Thadeus Pritt was sheriff in 1910 and is the present clerk of the County Court.

Guy Pritt, son of Hadden and Mary Elizabeth Pritt, was born November 1, 1876; married Josie, daughter of John Smith. Children, Beulah, who died aged 7 years, Mary Edith, Roy Hadden, Bessie Marie, all living. Mr. Pritt is track foreman on the Valley Bend section of the Western Maryland Railroad.

THE RYAN FAMILY.

The Ryan Family. The Ryans were among the early settlers of Randolph County. The first of the name to locate in this county was Solomon. He located on a farm west of the Valley River near Beverly.

THE RIFFLE FAMILY.

The Riffle Family. Jacob Riffle settled in Randolph in about 1772. Withers mentions the Riffles as being among the earliest settlers of the county. They located on the stream that still bears their name in Huttonsville District. They were neighbors of the Crouches, Currences, the Warwicks and the Haddans. Jacob Riffle was one of the first constables of the county in 1787. Frank Riffle was killed by the Indians on the same raid in which William Currence and several members of the Kinnan family were murdered.

THE ROONEY FAMILY.

The Rooney Family. The Rooneys, Hornbecks, Dougherties and Buffingtons were a necleus of an early settlement on Leading Creek. They were all of Irish descent and were perhaps acquainted in Pendleton and Hampshire before coming to Randolph. A man by the name of Rooney was among the victims of the Fort Seybert massacre. Alexander Rooney was killed in the Indian raid of 1781. He lived on Rooneys Run near where it empties into Leading Creek on the east side a quarter of a mile south of Gilman station.

THE ROWAN FAMILY.

The Rowan Family. The Rowan family is of Irish ancestry. Rev. John Rowan was the first of the name to locate in Randolph. He was born in Maryland, April 12, 1749. He was a soldier in the Revolutionary War and was wounded by being trampled upon by the British Cavalry at the battle of Brandy wine, and bore the impress of a horse shoe upon his body to the time of his death. Subsequent to the Revolution he married Elizabeth Howard of Anne Rundell County, Maryland. On April 12, 1809, he located one and one-half miles north of Beverly and lived there about three years. He then moved to Roaring Creek and located on 300 acres of land which he had purchased where the town of Coalton is now located. He lived there about ten years and lost his land in a law suit with Daniel Stringer. He then returned to the Valley and taught school and preached until the infirmities of age compelled him to abandon his labors. His death occurred at Beverly, December 29, 1833. His wife survived him about ten years, dying February 19, 1844. Their children were John, Thomas, Joseph Francis, William, Nancy, Elizabeth, Bathany and Labannah. He was a minister of the Methodist Episcopal church and officiated at many weddings in the pioneer period.

William Rowan, son of John and Elizabeth (Howard) Rowan, was born August 17, 1804, and married Anna, daughter of John S. and Anna Goff, in what is now Barbour County, April 10, 1827. Their children were John Addison, George W., David B., Eli H. and Adam C. Mr. Rowan was constable and deputy sheriff for more than thirty years. His wife, Anna Goff, was born September 2, 1804, and lived to be 94 years of age. She had living at the time of her death three great great grandchildren. George W. Rowan moved to Bath County, Virginia.

John Addison Rowan, born in 1828, is still living on Roaring Creek. In 1832 he married Ellen, daughter of John and Ellen (Skidmore) Chenoweth. Children, Burns, William, Eli C., Kent, Lee, Delphia, Martha, Mary, Thomas, Peggy and Ida.

THE STRADER FAMILY.

The Strader Family. Lorenzo Dow Strader, for many years one of the leaders of the Randolph County bar, was born in Upshur County, November 13, 1839. He came to Randolph in 1869 and opened a law office in the town of Beverly. In 1871 he married Maria S., daughter of Judson and Philadelphia (Reese) Blackman. Before studying law Mr. Strader was a soldier in the Federal Army, belonging to Company E First West Virginia Cavalry and was a participant in the battle of Rich Mountain as well as many other important engagements of the war.

The Strader family came from Holland at an early period in the history of America. They first settled in New Jersey, later moving to the South Branch. John Strader, the paternal grandfather of L. D. Strader, moved to Upshur County from the South Branch, settling near the mouth of Little Sand Run.

Valentine Strader, son of John and father of L. D. Strader, was born in 1818 and married Mary Jackson, daughter of Edward H. Jackson. Edward Jackson, who was the grandfather of Stonewall Jackson, was the uncle of Edward H. Jackson. L. D. Strader died at Beverly, January 10, 1905. Unto Mr. and Mrs. L. D. Strader were born Judson Floyd, Wilbur J., Philadelphia R., Mary Dow and Helen B.

Judson Floyd Strader is a member of the law firm of Strader & Tallman. He was educated at State University and at Wesleyan College at Buckhannon. He represented Randolph in the Legislature in 1907-8 and is at present chairman of the Democratic Executive Committee of Randolph County. He was born September 13, 1872.

Wilbur Jackson Strader was born at Beverly, December 2, 1879. He was educated at the Wesleyan College at Buckhannon and at the State University.

THE STALNAKER FAMILY.

The Stalnaker Family. Jacob was the first of the name to locate in Randolph. Withers mentions him in connection with the Haddans, the Connellys, the Whitmans, the Warwicks, the Nelsons, the Riffles and Westfalls as being the first occupants of the Valley after the murder of the Files family. The Stalnaker came to America from Holland. They were pioneers of Greenbrier, Augusta and Rockingham before coming to Randolph. Jacob Stalnaker's children were John, Adam, Andrew, Jacob, Eunice and three daughters whose names are not remembered.

Adam Cooper Stalnaker, born in 1832, son of George W. and Elizabeth (Piercy) Stalnaker; married Drusilla, daughter of William and Elizabeth (Yokum) Isner. They had one child, Wilbur Lee. Mr. Stalnaker died in 1914. He was the grandson of John W. and Mary (Chenoweth) Stalnaker and the great grandson of John and the great great grandson of John, who was killed by the Indians. John W. Stalnaker, grandfather of Adam C., was born May 19, 1783. Mr. Stalnaker was a Conferedate soldier, participating in many of the hard fought battles. He lived on a farm near Elkins and owned property that became valuable because of its proximity to Elkins. He was an intelligent and upright citizen.

Leonidas Stalnaker, son of Nimrod G. and Mildred (Thorne) Stalnaker, was born in 1866; married Icy, daughter of R. C. and Delilah (Canfield) Moore. One child, Opal, has been born to this union. Mr. Stalnaker is a member of the pioneer family of Stalnakers in Randolph. His grandfather, Edward Stalnaker, at one time owned the old Hart mill, east of Beverly, built by one of the first settlers, a Westfall.

Thomas W., son of Alba and Rebecca (Mouse) Stalnaker, was born in 1869; married Marietta, daughter of Johnson and Mary (Hinkle) Phares. Children, Grace, Thomas W. Jr., Mary Rebecca. Squire Stalnaker was educated in the public schools. He has served three terms as justice of the peace of Leadville District, being elected in 1900, 1904 and 1908. He is a descendant of the pioneer family of Stalnakers. His parental grandfather was Asbury and great grandfather was Isaac.

Wilbur L. Stalnaker, son of Adam C. and Drusella (Isner) Stalnaker, born June 18, 1870, was educated in the public schools and for a number of years engaged in teaching. He graduated in pharmacy from the Ohio Normal University in 1898, since which time he has conducted a drug store in the city of Elkins. He was a member of the Elkins city council in 1910. Mr. Stalnaker married in 1898, Ota, daughter of Randolph and Ida (Caplinger) Harper. Children, Alva, Winnie, Camille and Harold.

THE SIMMONS FAMILY.

The Simmons Family. This family is of German origin and came to Randolph from Pendleton. The name was originally spelled Sieman. The Simmons family came to Randolph subsequent to the war of 1812. Leonard Simmons located on the South Fork in Pendleton in 1763. The Simmons family is very numerous in Pendleton.

Josiah Simmons represented Randolph in the first West Virginia constitutional convention, which assembled at Wheeling, November 26, 1861, and adjourned February 18, 1862. He was a farmer and resided at Leadsville.

THE SNYDER FAMILY.

The Snyder Family. Two distinct families of this name have lived in Randolph since 1845. Harmon Snyder moved from Highland County, Virginia, to Randoph in 1845. He located in Mingo District. Mr. Snyder was born in Highland County in 1821 and in 1865 married Elizabeth (Teter) Lawson. Children, John B., Elizabeth, Mary C., Harmon E., Martha W., Blaine R., George W., William I., and James. Harmon Snyder was justice of the peace of Mingo District for many years. He also served as president of the Board of Education of that district. In 1884 he represented Randolph and Tucker in the state Legislature. The greatest elevation in Randolph, Snyders Knob, was named for him. It is located in Mingo District on the Snyder homestead.

William L., son of Harmon and Melvina (Lawson) Snyder, was born in 1881 in Mingo District; married Mamie, daughter of Arthur and Alice (Daft) Male. Children, Verl and Vernon. Mr. Snyder was educated in public schools and at Wesleyan University, Valpariso University and at Mountain State Business College. Mr. Snyder taught in the public schools of the county six years and at present is clerk in the Gouthap store at Huttonsville. Mr. Snyder is the nominee of the Republican party for the House of Delegates from Randolph in the approaching election.

Another branch of the Snyder family settled on the Dry Fork in Randolph County in about 1800. Snyder is a German name and was originally spelled Schneider. John Snyder, whose father was also named John, moved from the South Branch to Randolph. He married Lucinda Hensley of Albemarle County, Virginia. Children, Elizabeth, Sampson, Mary Jane, George W., Henry, Pheoba, Lorenzo Dow and Hannah. During the Civil War he was prominently identified with the Union cause and was a member of the Independent Scouts and had many thrilling experiences and hair breadth escapes. At one time he was thought to be mortally wounded but recovered.

Capt. Sampson Snyder, son of John and Lucinda (Hensel) Snyder, was captain of a company of Independent Scouts during the Civil War. When the company disbanded at the close of the war it was composed of the following persons: Captain, Sampson Snyder; First Sergeant, John W. Summerfield; Second Sergeant, Geo. W. Snyder; corporals, Jesse Keller, John Middleton, Jesse Harmon and Joseph Roy; privates, Geo. Arbogast, Daniel Bennet, Geo. Bishop, John S. Darnall, Absalom Echard, Henry Echard, Geo. Jennings, Chas. Gray, Samuel Harmon, Joseph Harmon, William Helmick, John W. Harper, Mathias Helmick, H. D. Jordan, Noah Jordan, Philip Keller, John Keller, John W. Long, Samuel Long, Absalom Mick, Elijah Nezelrod, Jesse Penington, John P. Roy, Isaac Roy, Solomon Roy, Henry Snyder, John Snyder, Benjamin Snyder, Laban Smith, Isaac Smith, Alfred Stalnaker, Adam Wolf, Geo. Wolf, Geo. L. Rimer, Mathew Collins and Solomon Hoffman.

THE SMITH FAMILY.

The Smith Family. Johnathan Smith came to Randolph soon after the first permanent settlement, the exact date is uncertain. He married Jane, daughter of William Currence. Their children were William, Jane, Lydia, Samuel Currence and John. Johnathan Smith lived to be 99 years old.

William, son of Jonathan and Jane (Currence) Smith, married Ester, daughter of Joseph Pitman. He was born in 1777 and died in 1852. Their children were Jane, who married Bennoni Lazure; Samuel, who married Katie Mace; Nancy, who married Jacob Wilmoth; Judy, who married Ferdinand Mace; Christina, who married John Smith; Elizabeth and Mary who died young.

William, son of John and Mary Smith, had four children. John, who settled in Randolph, was born in 1755, and died in 1831. He married Mary Pugh.

John D. Smith, son of Ambrose and Mary (Bland) Smith, was born in Pendleton in 1887; married Mary, daughter of

Marian Sponaugle. Children, Virginia and Levince. Mr. Smith is a merchant at Whitner.

THE SKIDMORE FAMILY.

The Skidmore Family. The Skidmores were pioneers in Pendleton as well as Randolph. James and Joseph Skidmore were in the French and Indian War from Pendleton. John Skidmore was president of the first County Court of Pendleton in 1787. Joseph Skidmore was a member of the first grand jury of Pendleton. James, John, Joseph and Andrew Skidmore were, perhaps, brothers and sons of Andrew Skidmore, who emigrated from England to Norfolk, Virginia, at an early period. John Skidmore was a captain under General Andrew Lewis at Point Pleasant, and Andrew, his brother was a private in his company and both were wounded. Andrew settled in Randolph a few miles north of the present city of Elkins. He undertook to construct a mill race by digging a ditch across the narrow neck between the two channels of the river about two miles below Elkins, but finding the fall insufficient he abandoned the enterprise. He died at Sutton, Braxton County in 1826.

John Skidmore mentioned above was born in 1725. Andrew Skidmore was born in 1750. John Skidmore married Polly Hinkle, in Pendleton. The children of John Skidmore were John, who died on Holly River in Braxton County; Eddie, who married Canfield; Polly, who married George Bickle; Mahala, who married Edward Robinson; Edith, who married John Chenoweth, and Phoeba, who married Alexander Taylor.

After the Revolution, old soldiers would meet at Circuit Courts, general musters and other public gatherings. On these occasions incidents of their soldier lives were rehearsed. Tradition says that at these reunions of former soldier comrades, Andrew Friend was wont to tell an incident of the Battle of Point Pleasant. During this battle some of the soldiers resorted to a hollow log for shelter. Andrew Skidmore and Andrew Friend and others had taken refuge in the log and it was becoming crowded. As Andrew Skidmore pointed to another log near by as a possible place of retreat, an Indian shot off his finger.

Andrew Skidmore married Margaret Johnson of Randolph, and settled on Tygarts Valley River, where he entered 400 acres of land on November 24, 1777. His brother, Joseph, entered 350 acres adjoining. Margaret Johnson was a daughter of Andrew Johnson and was the grandmother of President Johnson. She had six brothers, John, Charles, Robert, Oliver, Jacob and Levi. Jacob moved to Raleigh, North Carolina, and married a Miss McDonald. Jacob died in 1812, leaving one son, Andrew, four years old. He was born and reared in poverty and his wife learned him to read while he was an apprentice to a tailor. He moved to Greenville, Tennessee, and worked at his trade as a tailor. He entered politics in 1828, and ascended the political ladder as member of the Legislature, Congressman, Governor of Tennessee, United States Senator and Vice President, succeeding to the presidency upon the assassination of President Lincoln.

The Skidmores intermarried with the Chenoweths, Johnsons, Coberlies, Kittles, Hinkles and Scotts. Rachael, daughter of Andrew and Margaret Johnson Skidmore, was the mother of the Scott family of Randolph. The father, John K. Scott, weighed 225 and the mother 208 pounds. The weight of the sons were Jefferson, 240; Charles, 275; Hugh, 250; James S., 258; Olover J., 276; Winfield, 225; John J., 276 and Edwin 340.

Garfield I., son of D. E. and Martha V. (Corley) Skidmore, was born in Roaring Creek District in 1880; married Mary, daughter of James and Mary Brady. Children, Joseph, Leona and Margre. Mr. Skidmore was educated in public school. He is prominent in politics and is the nomineee of the Democratic party for justice of peace in Leadsville District. He is a member of the pioneer family of Skidmores of Randolph.

THE SEE FAMILY.

The See Family. Adam and Michael Frederick See were the first of the name to come to America. In 1734 they came to this country to escape religious persecution. They belonged to the Baptist sect and fled from Prussian Silessia with the colony of Schwenkfelders and first settled in Bucks County, Pennsylvania. The persecution under which they fled is described in the ninth edition of the encyclopedia Britanica under the title of Schwenkfeld. Adam See's wife's was Barbara and Michael Frederick See's wife's name was Catherine. In 1745 they moved to Hardy County. In 1760 Michael Frederick See moved to Greenbrier County and was killed by the Indians, July 17, 1764. His wife and four children were carried by the Indians to Old Town, now Chilicothe, Ohio. They were all restored to their people after the treaty of peace at the close of the French and Indian War of 1765, except John See, a child seven years old, who eluded his relatives and returned to an Indian family, which had adopted him, but was ransomed by his uncle, Adam See, some years later. He became a soldier in the Revolution and was wounded at the battle of Brandywine. He died at Peoria, Ill., in 1845, aged 90 years. The first Adam See had one son, George, and several daughters. In about 1767 George See married Jemima Harness of Hardy County. He had a family of nine children, Adam, Michael, George, Charles and John; daughters, Barbara, Hannah, Elizabeth and Dorothy. Michael See married Catherine Baker and raised a family of nine children, Adam, Anthony, Jacob, John, Solomon and Noah, and daughters, Mary, Elizabeth and Barbara. George See and son Charles were killed by lightning while stacking hay in 1794. Adam and Michael moved to Randolph in 1795. The second Noah See was born September 19, 1815, and was educated at Beverly. He moved to Missouri in 1837, and was soon followed by his father, mother and three brother and two sisters.

This family is of German descent and immigrated to Pennsylvania in the colonial period. Frederick Michael See was, perhaps, the first of the See family to come to America. His son, Michael See, was the first of the name to locate in Randolph. The Sees were pioneers in that part of Hampshire County that is now embraced in the territory of Hardy County. Sees Run is an historic stream in Hardy County.

The children of Michael See were Anthony, Adam, George, John, Noah and Barbara. Anthony married Julia Leonard, Adam married Margaret Warwick, Barbary married Wm. McLeary, the first prosecuting attorney of Randolph County; John married a Miss Stewart.

Adam See, son of Michael, married Margaret Warwick. Their children were George, Jacob, Warwick, Charles C., Eliza, Dolly, Christina, Mary, Rachael, Hannah and Margaret.

Chas. C. See, son of Adam and Margaret (Warwick) See, married Harriet, daughter of Dr. Squire Bosworth.

Jacob, son of Adam and Margaret (Warwick) See, married a daughter of Rev. Geo. A. Baxter.

Dolly, daughter of Adam C. and Margaret (Warwick) See, married Hon. John A. Hutton.

Christina, daughter of Adam C. and Margaret (Warwick) See, married Washington Ward.

Hannah, daughter of Adam and Margaret (Warwick) See, married Henry Harper.

Margaret, daughter of Adam C. and Margaret (Warwick) See, married Hon. Washington Long.

Rev. C. S. M. See, son of Jacob See, married Rebecca, daughter of Dr. Squire Bosworth.

Rachel, daughter of Adam C. and Margaret (Warwick) See, married Hon. Paul McNeil.

George See, son of Adam C. and Margaret (Warwick) See, married .... Children, Adam, who married Dolly Crouch, Georgiana, who married Captain W. Marshall.

George See, son of Michael, the pioneer, disposed of his farm of 383 acres in Hampshire County in 1785 and purchased 218 acres on the west side of the Tygarts Valley River, in the Caplinger settlement, in 1787.

Adam C. See, son of George, was admitted to the bar of Randolph County in 1793, and was prosecuting attorney of the county in 1798. He was captain of the county militia in 1800.

Lee Roy See, son of Randolph and Sarah E. (Hall) See, was born in French Creek, Upshur County, in 1873. Mr. See was educated in the public schools, Wesleyan College and State University. He was the Democratic nominee for sheriff of Upshur County in 1896; represented the same party as their candidate for prosecuting attorney in 1904. He was also the Democratic nominee for state Senate in the Thirteenth District in 1906. Although more than carrying his party strength in each of these contests, he was defeated by the greatly superior vote of the opposing party. He occupied the bench as special judge in Randolph Circuit Court in 1916.

THE SCHOONOVER FAMILY.

The Schoonover Family. This pioneer family is of German ancestry, Benjamin Schoonover was born in Connecticut in 1755 and settled at the mouth of Horse Shoe Run in Randolph, now Tucker County. A few years later he moved to Shavers Fork. His children were Joseph, David, Henry, Daniel and Amy. David married Susan, daughter of Thomas Wilmoth; Henry married Mary, daughter of David Canfield.

Joseph Schoonover married Anna, daughter of Nicholas Marstiller. Children, Marshall, Eli, Assyrian, Charles, Leonard, Anna, Etna and Fredricka.

Thomas Schooner, son of David and grandson of Benjamin, married Bashaba, daughter of Dr. Thomas C. Nutter of Barbour County.

Coleman J. Schoonover, born in 1839, son of Thomas and Bashaba (Nutter) Schoonover, married in 1865 Susan, daughter of James R. and Mahala Parsons. After her death he married in 1870 Rachel E., daughter of Henry V. and Margaret (Wilmoth) Bowman. Children, Carl W., Harriet E., James T., Lillian Adaline, A. Ward, Sampson E. and Leslie Clare.

Eli, son of Joseph and Anna (Marstiller) Schoonover, Currence. Children, Holman, William, Mary, John, Thomas married Julia Stemple. Children, John H., Sarah, Anzina and Leda B.

John Schoonover, son of Eli and Anna (Marstiller) Schoonover, married Sydney, daughter of John Weese. Children, Lucetta, Violet, Lovett, Summaville, Lorena and Willis R.

THE SCOTT FAMILY.

The Scott Family. John and Mary Scott, of Irish descent, lived in that part of Hampshire County now embraced in Hardy County, prior to the Revolutionary War. Their son, Benjamin T. Scott, was born in 1788. He came to Randolph and married Jane, daughter of William and Mary (Ward)

B. and Catherine. William married Susan Channell, Holman married a Miss Parsons.

Thomas B. Scott was born near Huttonsville in 1823. He married Mary Ann, daughter of Moses and Mary (Haigler) Hutton. His second marriage in 1866 was to Martha, daughter of Elias Wilmoth, and his third marriage was in 1875 to Rebecca, widow of Solomon Hull Parsons. Children of Thomas B. and Mary (Hutton) Scott, Felix S., Lucy E., Cyrus Hall, Virginia, Annie, George Clinton, Clyde and Evaline C. Thos. B. Scott was justice of the peace in 1856 and was also president of the County Court.

Cyrus Hall Scott was born in 1856. He was educated in the public schools and graduated from the Fairmont Normal in 1877 and from Roanoke College, Salem, Virginia, in 1877. He was admitted to practice law in 1879 and was elected prosecuting attorney in 1880. He was elected to the state Senate from the Tenth District in 1892. Senator Scott has been twice married. His wives were sisters and the daughters of James H. Logan. His daughter Edna (Logan) Scott became the wife of Hon. H. G. Kump. Two children, Mildred and Logan, the issue of his marriage to Emma (Logan) Scott, remain at home.

THE TRIPLETT FAMILY.

The Triplett Family. The Triplett family came from England and was among the settlers of Jamestown. John Triplett, the first in Randolph County, was born in Baltimore, Maryland, August 28, 1778. He came to Virginia when a boy eighteen or nineteen years old, having run away from his master, a tanner to whom he was bound. He was married young to a Miss Kittle, who seems to have been of a different family from Abraham Kittle. To them were born fourteen children, two of whom died in infancy. Of those who lived to manhood and womanhood, Ephrain, Jacob, Moses and Job spent their lives and reared families in Randolph County. William and Loami settled in Kanawha County, where they spent their lives. Eli and James went to Missouri after marrying in Randolph, Eli to Margaret Hart, a daughter of James Hart, and James to Deborah Harris, a daughter of Henry Harris, of

Leading Creek. Ann was the wife of Archibald Ferguson, and Mary, the wife of Solomon Ferguson. Eunice was the wife of Isaac Taylor.

In April, 1829, after the death of the first wife, John Triplett and Nancy Kittle were married. She was a Bennett, and came from Fauquier County, and was born in 1798. Her first husband was the brother of his first wife. Her son by the first marriage was Maj. Ben Kittle, and a daughter was the mother of Lloyd and Hamilton Ismer. To this union were born Martha, who married Amasa Kittle, Rachael, who married Arnold Wilmoth, Harriet, who married William Ferguson, (John J. Ferguson is the only living child) ; John J., who went to Montana when the trouble between the North and South came up and died there in the eighties; Randolph Triplett, born August 28, 1837; Hickman, who went to Nebraska about twenty-five years ago and now lives in British Columbia; and Anthony, who lives near Grafton in Taylor County.

Jasper and Owen Triplett were sons of Job. Elijah Triplett was the son of Jacob, and the sons of Ephriam were Milton and David.

Floyd J. Triplett, son of Randolph and Sarah (Kittle) Triplett, was born in 1863. He married Ella May, daughter of Archibald and Caroline (Taylor) Wilmoth. Children, Eva Belle, Samuel, Lucebia Maria, Sallie and Clare. Mr. Triplett has been editor of the Randolph Enterprise and Tygarts Valley News, and was county clerk in 1891-7. He is now editor of the Plymouth, N. C., Independent.

Jasper W. Triplett, son of Job and Sydney (Wilmoth) Triplett, was born in 1842 and died in 1914. He married Eliza Chenoweth. Children, Wade H., George and Delphia, who married Rev. Wm. Flint. Wade married Louie Lambert. Children, Delphia, Mary, Hellen, Preston and Revely. Graydon died in infancy. Jasper Triplett was assessor of Randolph twelve years.

THE TALLMAN FAMILY.

The Tallman Family. In the veins of this family flows the blood of the old pioneer and hero, Daniel Boone, of Kentucky, Boone Tallman having married Mary Logan, a sister of the late James H. Logan of Randolph County, and become the father of Robert L. Tallman, who was a farmer and surveyor of Barbour County, West Virginia. The latter married Harriet L. Blake, daughter of Herod and Elizabeth Blake, of which union there were born Floyd Ellis Tallman and four other children.

Floyd Ellis Tallman, son of Robert L. and Harriet (Blake) Tallman, residents of Barbour County, West Virginia, was born March 9, 1882, in Barbour County, West Virginia. He spent his early years on the farm, during which time he attended the rural schools until the year 1900, when he became a teacher in the public schools of his native county, and during the years 1900-1905 he was a teacher in the rural schools of Barbour County and a student of Wesleyan College at Buckhannon, West Virginia, from which institution he graduated in the year 1905. In the fall of 1905 he entered the college of law of the West Virginia University, where he continued for the school year of 1905-1906. In September 1906, he was married to Bess Lillian Talbott, daughter of George E. and Ellen E. Talbott of Barbour County. During the winter of 1906-7 he taught in the public schools of Barbour County. In the fall of 1907 Mr. and Mrs. Tallman moved to Elkins, Randolph County, where they have since resided. Mr. Tallman held the position of principal of the grammar school of the city of Elkins for the years 1907-8 and 1908-9, returning to the West Virginia University in the fall of 1909, where he again resumed his law studies, completing his course in the spring of 1910. He was admitted to practice law in Randolph County in November, 1910, and soon thereafter entered into partnership with the Hon. J. F. Strader under the firm name of Strader & Tallman, and has remained in the active practice of his profession since. In August, 1911, he was appointed commissioner in chancery of the circuit court of Randolph County, a position which he still holds, and in 1912 he was elected as a member of the Elkins city council from the Second ward, having been the candidate of the two leading parties. He is also a member of the Republican party.

Mr. Tallman is a member of Delta Chapter of the Phi

Sigma Kappa college fraternity at Morgantown, West Virginia; a member of Elkins Chapter Royal Arcanum, and a member of the Masonic Blue Lodge and Chapter at Elkins, West Virginia. His wife, Bess Lillian (Talbott) Tallman graduated from Wesleyan College at Buckhannon in the year 1904 in the literary and elocution courses, and is very active in the Methodist Episcopal church and its societies. Mr. and Mrs. Tallman have two daughters, Lucille and Mary Louise. Their home is at 220 Boundary Avenue.

THE TAYLOR FAMILY.

The Taylor Family. The progenitor of the Taylor family in Randolph was Isaac, who moved to the South Branch from Kentucky in about 1800, and thence to this county. He married Elizabeth Hays of Hardy. Children, John, Washington, Polly, Jemima, Elizabeth, Sarah, Caroline, Susannah, Nimrod, James and Isaac.

John married Susannah, daughter of Levi Coberly. Their children were, Alfred, Amanda, Allen, Felix, Andrew, Wm. H., who died while in the Confederate service during the Civil War, Elam B., and Percy. Washington married Melvina Chenoweth, Polly married William Wilmoth, Jemima married Samuel Wilmoth, Elizabeth married Edwin Stalnaker, Sarah married Hamilton Skidmore, Caroline married Archibald Wilmoth, Susannah married Samuel Channel, Nimrod married Margaret Coberly, James married Deborah Skidmore, Isaac married a Miss Triplett, Rebecca never married.

Andrew, son of John and Susannah Taylor, was born in 1835. In 1858 he married Louise Dyer daughter of Jacob and Elizabeth (Dyer) Ward. Mrs. Taylor's grandfather, James Dyer, was at the Fort Seybert massacre in Pendleton and was captured by the Indians. He remained in captivity three years when he made his escape and returned to his people. He was fourteen years old at the time of the massacre and capture. James and Nancy (Hall) Dyer had but one child, who married Jacob Ward. The children of Andrew and Louise (Dyer) Ward were Blain W., Annie Laurie, Ida B. and Gretta V.

Ida B. married J. G. Nestor, Gretta V. married W. L. Wilhide.

The children of John and Susannah Coberly Taylor were Alfred, Amanda, Allen, Felix, Andrew, Wm. H., Elam B. and Perry.

Nimrod Taylor, born 1815, son of the first Isaac, married 1834 Margaret, daughter of Levi Coberly. Children, Martha, Washington Kiner, Lucinda, Phoeba M., Hamilton S., John Columbus, James Monroe, Columbia Jane, Isaac Louis and Margaret E.

Allen Taylor, born 1831, son of John and Susannah (Coberly) Taylor, married first, Elizabeth Ward, and after her death Eltha, daughter of John K. and Sarah Chenoweth. Children, Louisa, Elizabeth, Rebecca, Florida and William C.

Hamilton S. Taylor, son of Nimrod and the grandson of the first Isaac, was born in 1844. He married in 1866, Elizabeth M. Vanscoy. Children, William C., Dorsey F., Lacey M. and Lucy B.

Felix Taylor, son of John and Susannah (Coberly) Taylor, was born in 1833, married in 1859 to Lucinda, daughter of Nimrod Taylor. Children, Sheffey, William Haymond and Emma Harriet.

Washington Coyner Taylor, born in 1838, died in 1896, son of Nimrod and Margaret (Coberly) Taylor; married in 1861 Jane, daughter of Elijah Nelson. Children, Elam, Samuel Lee, Nimrod, Lizzie, French, Alice, Delphia, Maud and Ella.

Elam E. Taylor, born in 1862, married in 1885 to Lydia Ann, daughter of Levi and Mary (Canfield) Coberly. One child, Marvin Lucius, who is a civil engineer in the government service.

Isaac, son of the first Isaac Taylor, married a Miss Triplett. Children, Judson, Levi, Eli and Elizabeth, who married Jesse Coberly.

John, son of Isaac and Elizabeth (Hays) Taylor, was a prominent man in Randolph. He represented Randolph in the Virginia Assembly two terms and was a member of the West Virginia Legislature also two terms.

Blain Ward Taylor, son of Andrew and Louise Dyer (Ward) Taylor, was educated in the public schools and the Fairmont Normal school, where he graduated in 1886. He taught in the public schools of the county a number of terms, teaching his first school when 14 years old. He served two terms as superintendent of schools of Randolph. He served two terms as committee clerk in the West Virginia Legislature. In 1882 he was appointed to revalue the lands in the second assessment district of Randolph County. During Governor Fleming's administration he was chief clerk in the Department of State. In 1885 he was mail clerk on the B. & O. between Grafton and Baltimore, which position he held until 1888. In 1894 he was appointed chief clerk in the Dead Letter Office in Washington. In 1895 he was promoted to the position of superintendent of the division of postoffice supplies. In 1897 he was again promoted to chief clerk in the postoffice department, which position he held for eight years, resigning to assume the management of part of the state of West Virginia for the campaign of Parker and Davis for President and Vice President. Mr. Taylor was secretary of the Second District Democratic congressional committee during the campaign of Col. Thomas B. Davis. Mr. Taylor has been engaged in the practice of law in Elkins for the past ten years.

Mr. Blain W. Taylor was united in marriage February 13, 1889, to May (Paxton) Jackson, daughter of Col. Alfred H. Jackson of Weston, West Virginia. Col. Jackson was Lieutenant Colonel of the Thirty-first Virginia Regiment under Stonewall Jackson, and was killed at the battle of Slaughter Mountain. Mr. and Mrs. Taylor have the following children: Mary Louise, Elizabeth Jackson, Beatrice Washington, May Jackson, Jean Stuart died aged 3 years, and Beatrice Washington died aged 16 years.

Children of Washington and Melvina (Chenoweth) Taylor were David B., who married Mary Ward, daughter of the second Jacob Ward; Hayes, who married Mary Yoke. Of this union was born Francis M. Taylor, who was the father of Howard, a merchant of Elkins.

Louise, daughter of Washington and Melvina (Chenoweth) Taylor, married Oliver Wilmoth.

Emaline, daughter of Washington and Melvina (Chenoweth) Taylor, married Hyre Stalnaker, who were the parents of Rufus Stalnaker of Elkins.

Mary, daughter of Washington and Melvina (Chenoweth) Taylor, married Isaac Stalnaker.

Blake, son of O. W. and Virginia (Wamsley) Taylor, was born June 2, 1879. He was educated in the public schools and Fairmont Normal where he graduated in 1893. After teaching a few years he entered the West Virginia University where he graduated in the department of civil engineering. He was for three years city engineer of Elkins and spent one year in Central Kentucky in the engineering department of railroad construction. For a number of years he has been engaged in highway work as a profession and is now engaged in permanent road improvement in Wyoming County. He married Stella, daughter of Dr. A. S. and Julia (Davis) Bosworth. Mr. Taylor is the grandson of Washington and the great grandson of the first Isaac Taylor. Mrs. Stella (Bosworth) Taylor is a graduate and post graduate of Emerson College of Oratory, Boston, and has taught in Glenville Normal school, Randolph Macon, Danville, Virginia, and two years in Great Falls, Montana, high school.

Captain W. H. Taylor of the Eighteenth Virginia Cavalry was killed in the battle of Winchester. His brother, Elam B. Taylor, first lieutenant, was severely wounded in the same engagement. The command of the company then fell upon the Second Lieutenant, Job Parsons. Captain Taylor is spoken of by his comrades as having been a brave soldier and much above the average in military ability.

Sheffey, son of Felix and Lucinda Taylor, was born in 1860. In 1883 he married Mary Ellen, daughter of Job and Martha (Chenoweth) Daniels. Children, Earle, O'Ferrell, Della, Wesley, Odbert, Haymond, Mary Jackson, Opal Mamie and Marion Francis. He was a merchant for a number of years at Kerens, taught in the public schools of the county for a number of years, and was assessor of Randolph County in 1892.

THE WEESE FAMILY.

The Weese Family. This family is of German descent. For the origin of the surname see another chapter. Jacob Weese was the progenitor of the Weese family in Randolph. He was born in 1733 and died in 1826. He came to Randolph in the early days of the county and the family had recourse to the Wilson Fort in times of Indian raids into the Valley. The sons of Jacob Weese were Jacob, George, Daniel and John. The sons of the second Jacob were Absalom, Jacob, John and Eli. The sons of George were Zirus, Zaiba and Jacob, and the daughters were Rebecca, Catherine, Dorcas and Martha. Daniel's sons were Judson, Haymond and Duncan. John's sons were Elijah, John and Job.

Zirus Weese, son of George and Ruth (Morgan) Weese, married in 1828 Abigail, daughter of John L. and Deborah Hart. Children, Harriet, Deborah, Ruth, Ziba and Perry Hart.

Perry Hart Weese was born in 1840. In 1865 he married Alice Jewel, daughter of Joseph and Alice (Elliot) Harding. Children, Boyd, Kirk, Clyde, Glenn and Hope.

Boyd Weese was born in 1866. He was educated in the public schools and at the State University. Mr. Weese is a merchant and his store has grown from a cross-roads country store to one of the largest department stores in Elkins. Mr. Weese was the nominee of the Democratic party for the State Senate in 1908. He has twice been mayor of the city of Elkins and has served on the city council. Mr. Weese married Knight, daughter of James J. and Margaret Stewart Burns of Fairmont, West Virginia. Children, Dorothy Burns and Donald Stuart.

THE WHITE FAMILY.

The White Family. This family of Whites was among the first settlers in the Valley in 1772-4. The Border Warfare mentions John and William White as prominent participants in Indian warfare in Randolph in pioneer days. Lieutenant John White was shot and killed from ambush by the Indians in 1778. In October of that year, in the upper part of the Valley, the savages, in hiding near the road, fired several shots at Lieutenant White but only wounded his horse which caused him to dismount. On foot in open ground he was shot, tomahawked and scalped. William White was captured by the Indians in 1777. He was taken to their villages in Ohio where he procured a gun by artifice, shot an Indian, took his horse and made his way safely to the settlements in Randolph. At a later period he was killed by the Indians near the present town of Buckhannon.

John and William White settled in the Valley above Huttonsville and were the neighbors of the Crouches, the Haddans, the Currences and the Warwicks. Price's history of Pocahontas says: William White would frequently visit the home of Andrew Crouch, senior, and the Major had a vivid recollection of the impression White's appearance made upon his youthful mind as he walked the floor, he was so very tall and portly.

Isaac, son of John White, was born near Huttonsville in 1776. He moved, when a young man, to Beverly District, about a mile southwest of Beverly where he lived the remainder of a long life. This land had been entered prior to 1780 by Cartine and Jacob White.

Isaac White, was born September, 1776; married Margaret Haddan, February 1, 1798. Children, Polly H., born November 9, 1798; John B., born April 27, 1800; Rachel, born February 28, 1802, and Eliza, born December 4, 1804.

Children of John B. and Mary (Reger) White, Amanda, born November 9, 1831; Lorenzo Dow White, born January 5, 1834; Margaret White, born September 2, 1836; F. M. White, born May 3, 1838, and Columbia White, born February 12, 1849.

Amanda White married Mathew Ward; L. D. White married Emeline McLean; Margaret White died in youth; F. M. White married Lewis Woolwine.

F. M. White married Mary E. Buckey; Columbia White married Lewis Woolwine.

Children of F. M. and Mary (Buckey) White, Kent, Lizzie and Effie. Lizzie married S. P. Scott; Effie died young. Rev. Kent White is a prominent minister in Denver, Colorado.

Children of L. D. and Emeline (McLean) White were

John B. and Laura. John B. White married Lucy, daughter of Job Daniels. Children, Beulah, Nellie and Howard. Beulah and Howard died in infancy.

Eliza, daughter of Isaac and Margaret (Haddan) White, married Nathan Devine.

Polly, daughter of Isaac and Margaret (Haddan) White, died July 22, 1885, aged seven years.

Isaac White was justice of the peace in 1809. L. D. White was clerk of the Circuit Court in 1860; sheriff in 1873-6. F. M. White was sheriff in 1871-2.

Nellie White, daughter of John B. and Lucy (Daniels) White, married Marion Ross Payne, April 16, 1913. One child, Cecil Arlington, has been born of this union, the date of its birth being September 9, 1914. Mr. Payne was born in Webster County, West Virginia, January 1, 1886. A second child, Marion Ruth, was born to Mr. and Mrs. Payne April 3, 1916.

The best information now obtainable indicates that Thomas White was the first of the White family that is now numerous in the eastern part of the county to locate in Randolph. He located on the head of Whites Run on the summit of the Allegheny Mountains, the exact date of which is not known. He made his will in 1802. He devised his property to his children, William Thomas and David. His wife's name was Abigail Summerfield. He immigrated to America from England says tradition.

L. D. White, son of Laban and Katherine (Roby) White, was born May 28, 1870; married Frances, daughter of Aaron Day, in 1890. Children, Omer C., Davy G., Page L., Lester, Londa May, Alpha, Dawson, Lula and Hansford. Mr. White is a farmer residing in Job.

James W. White, son of S. L. White and Etta White, was born 1878; married Cleo, daughter of A. L. and Katie Cunningham, in 1914. Mr. White was a farmer's son. He taught school three years, made an extensive trip to the west, returning to Randolph County and engaging in the mercantile business. Mr. White is notary public and postmaster at Wymer, West Virginia. He is acquiring considerable real estate.

George White, son of James and Catherine E. (Nelson) White, was born March 16, 1873; married Julia Speck. Children, Dessie, Beulah, Don, Clare, Paul, Dale, Emerson, Stella M. and Letitia L., who died in infancy. Mr. White is a member of the numerous White families of this section and is a grandson of Levi White and great grandson of Soldier White. He is a farmer living on Middle Mountain.

Isaac C., son of Emanuel and Margaret White, was born in 1876; married a daughter of Sylvester and Elizabeth (Vandevander) Powers. Children, Nola, Carl, Chester, Thelma, Zellie and Wilson. Edgar Edison died in infancy.

B. Y., son of James B. and Sarah (Carr) White, was born in 1878; married Hettie C., daughter of Cyrus and Rachael E. (Harper) Teter. Children, Odbert, Sarah, Pauline and Raymond. Mr. White has been a merchant and school teacher. He was deputy assessor under A. W. Zinn.

Daniel, son of James and Ellen (Nelson) White, was born in 1875; married Ada, daughter of Noah and Malinda (Smith) Montony. Children, Eva, Carl, Vistie, Edith, Hersell, Opie, who died in the seventh year of her age; Foster, who died in the fourth year of his age. Edith died in infancy. Mr. White is a blacksmith at Job.

Grover C. White, son of James and Ella (Nelson) White, was born in 1893; married Mabel, daughter of Andreas and Sallie (Calhoun) Hartman. Children, one child, Othie, has been born unto them. Mr. White is a farmer near Job.

Grover S. White, son of G. W. and Mary S. White, was born in 1886; married Ada, daughter of John and Frances (Harman) Kimmell. Children, Robert, Gladis, Frank, Guy, Mary and Ronald. Mr. White is a farmer near Whitmer.

Geo. W. White, son of Henry and Sarah C. (Roy) White, was born in 1860; married Mary S. White, daughter of Laban and Katherine White. Children, Lenora C., Olive L. Grover Scott, Dennis, Dixon Carl, Roy and Jared. Mr. White was constable for twelve years. He was mayor of Whitmer for three years and town sergeant two years and for three years he was deputy assessor.

Benjamin F. White, son of Laban and Catherine White, was born in 1865; married Permelia, daughter of Joseph and

Hannah (Eye) Elgard. Children, Phoeba, Lena, Charles and Virgil. Two children, Preston and Izetta died in infancy. Mr. White is a farmer and lives near Job.

John W. White, son of Levi and Mary Ann (Davis) White, was born in 1850; married Columbia Jane Nelson. Children, Alonzo, Elizabeth, Sarah, Catherine. Mary Margaret died aged 35 years; Susan A. died at the age of 22 and Francis died in the thirtieth year of her age. Mr. White has lived on the farm on which he now resides for forty-five years, having cleared his entire farm from an unbroken forest.

Bernard, son of Edward and Mary A., (Houchin) White, was born in 1878 in Randolph County; married May E., daughter of Rillis and Elizabeth (Gawthrop) Hermon. Mr. White is of English descent. His father moved to Randolph from Highland County, Virginia, in 1877. Mr. White is proprietor of a garage at Mill Creek.

S. L. White, son of Harvey and Martha White, was born in 1864. Children, James W., Gertie, Amos, Corbett, Jason, Mason, David, Sallie, Arthur and Stanley. Mr. White is engaged in farming.

THE WILSON FAMILY.

Benjamin Wilson was born in Shenandoah County, Virginia, in 1747. His father, William Wilson, emigrated from Ireland in 1737, and located on Trout Run in what is now Hardy County. In about 1774 he moved to the Valley and located on what has since borne the name of Wilson Creek. He built the Wilson Fort in 1777. To retain his position of clerk of the County Court of Harrison County he moved to Clarksburg when Randolph County was formed. He was a Federalist in politics and was the leader of his party in Western Virginia until lines were obliterated by the War of 1812.

For his first wife Col. Wilson married Ann Ruddell of Hampshire County. Twelve children were born to this union. For his second wife Col. Wilson married Phoeba Davisson. Seventeen children blessed this union. Colonel Wilson died in Harrison County, Virginia, in 1827, in the eightieth year of his age.

Three brothers of Benjamin Wilson seem to have lived in Randolph, William, John and Moses.

William Wilson, born in 1754, died in 1851. He held many offices in Randolph.

John Wilson, born 1756, died 1827. He was the first county clerk in 1787 and first circuit clerk in 1809.

Moses Wilson, born in 1761, died in 1784.

William B. Wilson, son of Benjamin and Ann (Ruddell) Wilson was born in 1773. He married Elizabeth Davisson of Harrison County. Children, Prudence, who married Judge Edwin S. Duncan, Patsy, who married Lenox Camden; Ann, who married Abraham Hutton; Elizabeth, who married Adam D. Caplinger; Alexander, Frederick, Daniel and Edwin Duncan.

Edwin Duncan Wilson married Martha Weese. Children, James Duncan, Florida, Rose Ann and Elizabeth.

Below is an extract from an address made before the trustees and patrons of the Randolph Academy at Clarksburg, delivered on the 29th day of December, 1799, by Col. Wilson, who was one of the trustees of the institution:

"Sir: We give you assurance that nothing shall be wanting to render you assistance to make this institution respectable. Therefore permit us to enumerate some of the dangerous ills which is to command your attention as well without the Seminary as within, viz: the wilful breach of the Sabbath Day, lying, cursing, swearing, quarreling, frequenting taverns or still houses by night or by day and in particular the infamous ills of gaming, together with all other ills not enumerated. You will also please inspire such of your youths as have arrived at the age of discretion to avoid all low company, and at all times and places to sequester themselves from such."

James D. Wilson, son of Edwin D. and Martha (Weese) Wilson, was born in 1844, and died in 1895. In 1866 he married Delia, daughter of Absalom and Emily (Hart) Crawford. Unto this union was born Lottie Lee, who died in 1912, and Jessie May, who married Homer Houston and after his death Lee J. Sandridge, a prominent business man of Barbour County. James D. Wilson was a member of a distinguished family, being the grandson of William B. Wilson, who was the son of the first Benjamin Wilson. Living in the formative period of Western Virginia, no other family, perhaps, has left, in so marked degree, the impress of their lives and influence upon the region now embraced in the state of West Virginia. During the active period of his life no other individual in Randolph wielded a greater influence than James D. Wilson. With more than ordinary ability and with a peculiar fitness for clerical

MR. J. D. WILSON.

work, Mr. Wilson for eighteen years discharged the duties of county clerk with entire satisfaction to his constituents. In the true sense of the word, he was not a politician as he was open and fearless, following his convictions and opposing or espousing a cause in utter disregard of the consequences to himself. The county has not produced a more unique or noted personage.

Colonel Ben. Wilson, who for many years represented the Clarksburg District in Congress was a son of Josiah Wilson and a grandson of the first Benjamin Wilson.

William Woodrow, an ancestor of the Woodrow family, a member of which was the mother of President Wilson, in an early day entered land on Wilson Creek, this county, but it is not known whether he ever resided on his possessions.

William H. Wilson, son of John Q. and Harriet (Wood) Wilson, was born in 1840; married Rachael, daughter of Abram and Catherine (McNeal) Crouch. Mr. Wilson was justice of the peace, deputy sheriff and clerk of the Circuit Court in 1884-96.

THE WOOLWINE FAMILY.

The Woolwine Family. This family is of German ancestry and the name was originally spelled Eolvine. Orlando Woolwine was born about 1805. He lived in Valley Bend District. He had two sisters, Peggy, who married Isom Channell, and Elizabeth, who married William Pritt. Orlando Woolwine married Sallie Clark. Children were Judson E., William, Columbia, Lucinda and Edmonia.

William Woolwine died in a Federal prison during the Civil War. Edmonia Woolwine married Laban, son of William Dolebear Currence. Lucinda married Carper Ward, Edmonia married Holman Pritt.

Judson B. Woolwine married Amanda Smith. Children, Herman, Maynard, Stanley, Stella.

Louis Woolwine was born in 1848. He married Columbia, daughter of John B. and Mary Reger White. Children, Lee, Nora, Icy, Tucker, Dorpha, John, Howard, Burr, Guy, Kent and Merlie. He owns the land on which was situated the Round Barn, a land mark of ante-bellum days.

Orlando Woolwine was a member of the Board of Supervisors of Randolph County in 1867.

THE WARTHEN FAMILY.

The Warthen Family. Raphael Warthen was among the first settlers of Randolph. His home was on the banks of Kings Run near the Staunton and Parkersburg pike, in Beverly District. He died in 1798, leaving a widow and two children. Elizabeth and Chlotilda. Chlotilda was born in 1798. The widow with her children moved to Kentucky in 1800. Chlotilda married a Montgomery, a member of a Maryland family. One son of this union, Hon. Zacharia Montgomery, moved to California in 1849. He became a prominent citizen of his adopted state, and gained distinction as a writer on political and other subjects and was assistant attorney general under Cleveland's first administration. A grandson of Chlotilda Warthen Montgomery is the Right Reverend George Montgomery, a Catholic Bishop of Southern California.

Prof. John J. Montgomery, son of Hon. Zacharia Montgomery, gained world wide fame as a pioneer in the field of aerial flight. Prof. Montgomery was recognized by aviationists of every nation as one of the greatest inventors of heavier than air flying machines. He was in fact the father of the flying machine, but the Wright brothers following in his footsteps and infringing on his patents received popular credit that belongs to Prof. Montgomery. He met his death in an effort to solve the problem of gliding without the use of power, after the manner of the eagle and other soaring birds.

THE WESTFALL FAMILY.

The Westfall Family. George, Jacob, Job, William, James and Cornelius Westfall settled in the Valley as early as 1772. They were, perhaps, brothers and came to Randolph from Pendleton. Withers says that one of the Westfalls found and buried the remains of the Files family who were murdered by the Indians nearly twenty years previous. This is improbable from the fact that the Westfalls settled near the mouth of Mill Creek and William Currence first owned and occupied the land where Beverly now stands and which had been abandoned by the Files family. Some years later William Currence and the Westfalls exchanged lands. Jacob Westfall was a justice of the peace and a member of the court appointed by the Governor in the organization of the county. In the same year he was elected sheriff by his associate justices of the peace, and thus became the first sheriff of Randolph. The residence of James Westfall in Beverly was designated as the court house of Randolph County, May 29, 1787, the first session having been held the day previous at the residence of Benjamin Wilson. Cornelius Westfall was the second sheriff of Randolph in 1789. George and James Westfall were captains of the militia in 1787. Jacob Westfall was one of the trustees of the town of Beverly in 1790. James Westfall was major of the militia in 1794. The Westfalls were of German origin and the name was spelled Westphal in the mother tongue. The Westfalls settled in Pendleton in 1752. Cornelius Westfall moved to Hamilton County, Ohio.

THE WHITMAN FAMILY.

The Whitman Family. The Whitman family was among the first settlers of Randolph. Mathew Whitman was the first deputy sheriff of Randolph. He was captain of the militia in 1800 and was elected sheriff by the court the same year. He assisted in the organization of the first Presbyterian church in Randolph in 1820. He was commissioner of revenue in 1831. The Whitman family was of English descent and came from Bucks County, Pennsylvania, stopping temporarily in Hampshire County. Mathew Whitman was a soldier in the Revolutionary War and received a pension.

THE WARWICK FAMILY.

The Warwick Family. The Warwick family came to Randolph in the first years of its settlement. Jacob Warwick came from England to Williamsburg, Virginia, in 1740-50. He was employed by the Crown to survey land grants in Pocahontas County. It is to be presumed that he was the father of Jacob Warwick, who settled in Randolph. The Warwicks became connected by marriage with the Sees, the Marshalls, the Crouches and other prominent families of Randolph. A descendant of this family of Warwicks became a prominent politician of the Buckeye State and had the distinction of defeating Wm. McKinley for Congress some years before he was elected to the Presidency.

THE WILMOTH FAMILY.

The Wilmoth Family. The Wilmoth settlement was among the first permanent colonies in Randolph. The date is fixed by the records of Monongalia County, which show that the Wilmoths obtained certificates for land on Cheat River on which they settled in 1776. These certificates were given by the commissioners of unpatented lands in 1781. They were of English descent and consisted of four brothers and two sisters. Their names were Nicholas, Thomas, James and John, and the sisters, Deborah and Susan. They immigrated from England to Virginia and thence to Randolph, sojourning, perhaps, in Pendleton. Thomas Wilmoth received a patent for 71 acres of land in Pendleton on Hedricks Run in 1771. The Wilmoths probably lived in Pendleton from 1771 to 1776. For many years subsequent to their settlement on the river, the stream was called Wilmoths river.

Nicholas, the eldest of the Wilmoth brothers, married Sydney, daughter of William Currence, the pioneer. The children of Nicholas and Sydney (Currence) Wilmoth were, John W., Sarah, Thomas, William, Eli, Samuel, James and Currence.

Thomas, brother of the first Nicholas, married in 1798 Amy, daughter of Benjamin Schoonover. He owned the land where the stone house now stands. The stone house was built by Levi, son of Thomas. The children of Thomas and Amy (Schoonover) Wilmoth were, Absalom, John, Edmund, Levi, and three daughters whose names are not remembered.

John Wilmoth, one of the pioneer brothers, married in 1799 Mary Cunningham, daughter of James Cunningham. The names of their children were Elias, Peggy, James, Prudence, Wilson, Solomon, John Adam, Mary Ann and Dewy. James married Nancy Smith.

James Wilmoth, the pioneer, was murdered by the Indians. The date of the tragedy is uncertain, but it was probably at the time of the Leading Creek massacre. The Wilmoth settlement was apprehensive of a raid by the Indians and had sought safety at Friends and Wilson's Fort. However, James Wilmoth ventured to make a visit to the settlement, when his whereabouts was betrayed to the savages lurking in the community by the barking of a dog with him. The Indians killed him from ambush near where the stone house now stands. Susan Wilmoth married David Schoonover.

Eli, son of Nicholas and Sydney (Currence) Wilmoth, married Rebecca, daughter of Aaron Vanscoy. Their children were Archibald, Emily, Currence, James, Arnold, Louisa, Isbern, Oliver and Elizabeth.

Nicholas Wilmoth, born in 1824, son of William and Mary (Taylor) Wilmoth; married in 1853 to Eliza, daughter of Noah McLean. Children, Simpson, Haymond, Theodore, Virginia, Emiline, Minerva, Lou A. and Julia.

Benjamin F. Wilmoth, son of Wm. and Mary (Taylor) Wilmoth, was born in 1829. He was a member of the Board of Supervisors during the Civil War.

Oliver Wilmoth, son of Eli and Rebecca (Vanscoy) Wilmoth and grandson of Nicholas and Sydney (Currence) Wilmoth, was born in 1835. He was a member of the Board of Supervisors in 1861-8 and was town sergeant, chief of police and city treasurer of the city of Elkins, holding one of these positions almost continuously during the first two decades of the city's growth.

Archibald Wilmoth was born in 1824 and was the son of Eli and Rebecca (Vanscoy) Wilmoth. He died in 19..... He married Caroline, daughter of Isaac Taylor, in 1847. Children, Luceba, Alonzo, F. Ella and Rebecca.

Luceba E. Wilmoth married Major J. F. Harding; Ella May Wilmoth married Floyd J. Triplett; Rebecca C. Wilmoth married Ziba Weese.

Alonzo F. Wilmoth, son of Archibald and Caroline (Taylor) Wilmoth, was born in 1854; married Nancy, daughter of Thomas G. and Emily L. Black. Children, Emily, Josephine, Russell Woods, Edith Loraine. Mr. Wilmoth graduated from Fairmont Normal school in 1881. He was principal of the New

Martinsville public schools in 1882; from 1884-8 he was secretary to State Superintendent of Public Schools, B. L. Butcher. For years Mr. Wilmoth was a representative of the publishing house of Ginn & Co. He was elected county superintendent of schools in 1878 and served two terms.

THE WARD FAMILY.

The Ward Family. Sylvester was the ancestor of the Ward family in Randolph. He came to Randolph from Pendleton in 1788 and married Mary Cunningham of that county. He was one of the trustees of the town of Beverly in 1790. The children of Sylvester Ward were Jacob, Jemima, Phoeba, Levi and Adonijah. Adonijah, Levi and two sisters, Phoeba and Jemima, moved to Ohio at an early date. They launched a boat on the Monongalia and floated down that stream and Ohio was their destination. The boat was constructed with sides too thick to be penetrated by the bullets of enemies. Tradition says that the Wards had more than one encounter with the Indians on their journey and that friends and companions of the trip, who were not so well prepared to repel attacks, perished on the way.

Mary, daughter of Sylvester Ward, married William Currence. Unto this union were born John J., who married Ann Conrad and moved to Braxton; William, who married Elizabeth Conrad; Virginia, who married Benjamin Scott; Jemima, who married Adam Carper; Elizabeth, who married Gabriel Chenoweth.

Jacob Ward, son of Sylvester, married first, Elizabeth Scott of the South Branch. Children, Scott, killed by falling on pitchfork; Adonijah, who married Miss Hull; Jacob, who married Miss Dyer; Levi, who married Miss Stalnaker; Katie, who married William Parsons; Mary, who married Solomon Parsons, and Jemima, who married Job Parsons. The children of Jacob and Elizabeth Whitman Ward were, Whitman, William L., Washington G., Jesse and Phoeba.

The children of Jacob and Elizabeth (Dyer) Ward were Levi D., Catherine, Mary, Jemima, Louisa D., Morgan Blaine and William Thomas.

Levi, son of the first Jacob Ward, married Katie Whitman. Children, Adonijah, George and Whitman.

The children of Adonijah and Hannah (Hull) Ward were Hull, Levi and Scott Ward.

Whitman Ward, born April 9, 1803, married Mary Weese, daughter of John Weese. Children, Washington G., born October 28, 1831; Squire Bosworth, born October 10, 1833; John W., born February 28, 1836; Mary E., born August 7, 1838; Phoeba C., born July 8, 1840; Job, born January 28, 1843; Mathew W., born December 28, 1850; William K., born November 13, 1853.

Whitman Ward was killed at Kerens, June 14, 1862, while attending a muster. He was shot from ambush by Confederate scouts, who mistook him for a Union sympathizer, who had been active in reporting Confederate partisans.

Squire B. Ward, born in 1833, married in 1856 Mary Jane, daughter of Daniel and Catherine Dinkle. They had one child, Iddo. Mr. Ward married after the death of his first wife Ida Huffman.

John Baylis Ward, an attorney of Beverly, was born in 1852. He is the son of George W. and Maria (Earle) Ward. In 1882 he married Angelia, daughter of Andrew and Susan (Foggy) Scott. Children, George A., William M., Wilson P., John Baylis, Edgar Foggy and Mary Genevieve.

James A., son of Levi D. Ward and Rebecca (Wamsley) Ward, was born in 1860. Mr. Ward lives in Idaho.

Elihu B. Ward, born in 1838, son of Jesse C. and Elizabeth Ward, married first, Eliza A. Crouch and after her death Eugenia Crouch. Children, Mittie L., Kent C., Jubal E., Mary, Emma Nora, Lenna, Bessie, Randall and Bruce. Mr. Ward served through the Civil War as a Confederate soldier.

Lee M. Ward, born in 1846, son of Wm. L. and Eliza (Myers) Ward. In 1867 he married Virginia, daughter of Moses and Mary (Haigler) Hutton. He served in the Confederate army from 1862 to the close of the war. To Mr. and Mrs. Ward have been born Tucker H., Russie L. and Lucy. Tucker Ward is a graduate of the law department of the State University. He married Aneath, daughter of Edwin

Butcher of Parkersburg, West Virginia. Children, Wm. L. and Brownie B.

Levi Scott Ward, son of Adonijah and Hannah (Hull) Ward, was born in 1819. In 1841 he married Martha, daughter of John and Mary (Hornbeck) Wood. Children, Hannah, John, Luther, Asa, Paul and Sabina. Mr. Ward was the great grandson of Sylvester Ward. For many years he resided near the head of Files Creek in Valley Bend District.

Hull Adam Ward was born in 1825. He was the son of Adonijah and Hannah (Hull) Ward. He married Melvina Weese.

Sterling Price Ward, son of George and Margaret E. (Wamsley) Ward, was born May 12, 1867; married May Martha, daughter of Charles and Virginia (Wilmoth) Crouch. Children, Maggie, who married John Petit. Mr. Ward was educated in the public schools and at Bingham Military Academy, North Carolina. Mr. Ward is a prominent farmer of Huttonsville District, residing near Mill Creek.

Ray Ward, son of Job and Catherine (Chenoweth) Ward, was born in 1873; married Hattie, daughter of Randolph and Sarah (Kittle) Triplett. Children, Lanier Ferrel, Freda Helen, Austin Job, Ada C., Dorotha May and Waldo Triplett. Mr. Ward is a farmer and lives near Elkins.

THE YOKUM FAMILY.

The Yokum Family. This family is of German descent and was among the first settlers of the Valley. The name as it appeared in the early records was spelled Yoakum. The first ancestor of this family of which we have any record was Phillip Paul Yokum, who lived on the South Branch of the Potomac in what is now Hardy County, and married a Miss Harness.

John and Michael Yokum settled in what is now Barbour County at a very early date. They were brothers, perhaps. The commissioners appointed to adjust land titles, certified that John Yokum was entitled to 400 acres on Barker's Creek to include his settlement made in 1773, and that Michael Yokum was entitled to 400 acres to include his settlement made in 1772 on Sugar Creek. Their names appear in the early records of the county and it is to be presumed that they moved to the Valley shortly after their settlement in what is now Barbour.

William Yokum, grandson of Phillip Yokum, married Sally, daughter of Solomon Ryan, who lived near the Beverly bridge on the west side.

John Yokum, grandson of the first John, married a Miss Kuykendall. George W. Yokum, for many years a prominent physician of Beverly, was a son of this union.

Bruce, son of Dr. G. W. and Mary C. (Ward) Yokum, was born in 1860; married in 1893 Mary Ervin, daughter of Morgan and Sallie (Long) Kittle. Mr. Yokum was educated at Washington and Jefferson College. He lives in the ances tral home in Beverly and is extensively engaged in farming and stockraising, owning some of the best agricultural and grazing lands in the county.

Palmer R., son of Elam and Martha (Stalnaker) Yokum, was born November 15, 1888; married Nellie, daughter of Lafayette and Lucy (Clem) Daniels. Mr. Yokum is proprietor of the railroad restaurant and hotel at Mill Creek. He is of German descent and a descendant of the pioneer family of Yokums.

PERSONAL SKETCHES

ALEXANDER ADDISON.

Alexander Addison was the second Prosecuting Attorney of Randolph. He succeeded William McCleary and held that office from 1787 to 1790. At the August term of the court, 1787, he was licensed for one year to practice law. At that time the recommendation of some court was necessary to obtain a license. Mr. Addison was given one year to meet this requirement. Nothing is now known of his previous or subsequent history.

MAXWELL ARMSTRONG.

Maxwell Armstrong was Prosecuting Attorney of Randolph from 1795 to 1798. He was practicing at the Randolph County bar as late as 1795, when he was engaged by the County Court to bring suit against Edward Hart for failure to complete the court house in the time specified in the contract Another family of the same name settled in Randolph about this time. They were from Prince William County, Virginia Whether relatives of Maxwell Armstrong is not known.

JOHN M. BALL.

John Marshall Ball, son of George W. and Malinda (Parsons) Ball was born in 1836, married (1860) Christina, daughter of Adonijah and Patsy (Carper) Ward. Children, Hattie and Maggie, both deceased.

Mr. Ball has traveled extensively in the West and lived for several years in Kansas in the pioneer days of the Sunflower State, when the homesteader came in conflict with hot winds, cyclones, grasshoppers and Indians. He is the only living representative of a pioneer family in Randolph.

ANDREW D. BARLOW.

Andrew D., son of Alexander Barlow, was born in Pocahontas County in 1847, married (1874) Jennie Bell, daughter of C. W. and Mary (Collett) Russell. Children, Hattie, who married Chas. Baker; Willis D., Agnes, Mattie, Russell, Ralph and Dr. C. A. Barlow who is superintendent of the Spencer Insane Asylum. Mattie is a graduate of Emerson College of Oratory, Boston, and for a number of years has been a teacher in a college in Oklahoma.

HARRY N. BARNARD.

Harry N. Barnard, son of Nathaniel and Nancy E. (Speers) Barnard, born in Rockwood, Pa., 1872, married Stella, daughter of D. P. and Caroline (Chenoweth) Harper. Children, Paul H., Chas. E., Harry N., Jr.

Mr. Barnard came to Randolph in 1889 and is a dealer in hardware and plumbers' supplies. He is an active member of the Presbyterian church and is president of the Randolph Sunday school Association.

REV. FREDERICK H. BARRON.

Rev. Frederick H. Barron, A.M., D.D., son of J. L. and Agnes (Jackson) Barron, was born in St. Marys, Province of Ontario, Canada, January, 1870. Rev. Barron took the degree of bachelor of arts from the University of Toronto, in 1897. In 1900 he graduated from Knox Theological Seminary. From 1900 to 1902 he was pastor of Reid Memorial Church, Baltimore. Since 1902 he has been pastor of the Davis Memorial Presbyterian Church. Rev. Barron was president of Davis and Elkins College, 1905-6, and has been professor of Biblical Literature in that institution since 1904.

Doctor Barron married Mary C., daughter of Capt. O. N. and Mrs. Mary S. Butler. Children, Mary Spence, Frederick Minto and William Wallace.

AMOS J. BENNETT.

Amos J. Bennett, son of Aaron and Elizabeth (Bennett) Bennett, was born in Pendleton County in 1849; married Elizabeth, daughter of Reuben and Margaret (McLaughlin) Teter. Children, Harrison, Gordon, Lottie, Annie Izerna, Macie, Odie, Mamie. Mary died at the age of 29; Strigh died in the 13th year of his age; Mamie and Lester A. died in infancy.

Mr. Bennett came to Randolph in 1870. He served several terms as president of the Board of Education of Dry Fork

District; was constable eigh years and was the nominee of the Republican party for deputy sheriff in 1908. He is at present engaged in farming and stockraising.

JAMES APPLETON BENT.

James Appleton Bent, son of George B. and Elizabeth Bent, was born July 15, 1853, Roane County, West Virginia, married Maggie C. Butcher, daughter of C. W. and Manda Butcher, November 27, 1888, Beverly, W. Va. Children, Myrtle M. Bent, Laura Gertrude Bent and Edgar M. Bent. Mr. Bent became a resident of Randolph County September, 1883.

Mr. Bent has attained a place of prominence at the Randolph county bar. He has been honored by his fellow practitioners by being chosen as special judge in important cases. He is also a law writer of note, being the author of Bent's Digest.

JEFFERSON SLIDELL BROWN.

Jefferson Slidell Brown. The subject of this sketch was born at the old "Fairfax Manor" house near Kingwood, West Virginia, during the throes of the Civil War. His father, Charles Mercer Brown, a lawyer, who died at the age of 32 years, leaving a widow and two sons, the other, Ben L. Brown, now postmaster at Kingwood. The mother of the subject of this sketch was Virginia Caroline Fairfax, a granddaughter of Col. John Fairfax of Virginia, who was superintendent for seven years for Gen. Geo. Washington at his plantation at Mount Vernon, Virginia, and Lawrence Washington, a half brother of General Washington, married a sister of Col. Fairfax. The latter was a son of William Fairfax, a cousin to Lord Tom Fairfax of Greenaway Court, near Winchester, Virginia. The great grandfather of the subject of this sketch was Capt. Thomas Brown of Prince William County, Virginia, who served in the Revolutionary War and was wounded at the battle of the Cowpens in South Carolina while fighting under General Morgan. He came to Preston County, this state, in 1805, and took up a large tract of land adjoining his friend and neighbor in Old Virginia, Col. John Fairfax, who moved to Preston County in 1790. J. Slidell Brown, purchased the West Virginia Argus at Kingwood in 1889 and edited it for almost a quarter of a century, when the late Congressman W. G. Brown purchased the paper, and Slidell Brown came to Elkins in May, 1914, and took charge of the Randolph Enterprise, as editor and manager. Mr. Brown served as postmaster of Kingwood for over four years, having been appointed by President Grover Cleveland. He was the Democratic nominee for State Senator twice, once in the old Preston-Taylor-Monongalia District and once in the Fourteenth District composed of Preston, Tucker, Grant, Mineral and Hardy. He served as chairman of the Democratic committee of Preston County for sixteen years and served on all the various committees, congressional, senatorial, judicial and was an alternate-at-large from West Virginia to the National Democratic Convention at Chicago that nominated Bryan the first time. Mr. Brown served five terms as president of the West Virginia Editorial Association and is a prominent member of the Knights of Pythias, Masons, Odd Fellows, Red Men, Maccabees, Junior Order, Daughters of Rebekah, Pythian Sisters, etc. In 1902 he was married to Stella Maud Parsons, daughter of Capt. J. W. Parsons, formerly of Rich Mountain, Randolph County, and now residing at Kingwood. Five children, four boys and a girl, are the fruits of this union.

MILFORD CARR.

Milford Carr, son of John and Isabel (White) Carr, was born in 1892, married Martha, daughter of Chas. and Carrie (Day) White. They have no children. Mr. Carr has taught in the public schools three years.

RICHARD CHAFFEY.

Richard Chaffey, born at Pittsburgh in 1850, son of H. F. and Hopewell Chaffey, was married in 1882 to Laura L., daughter of A. W. and Caroline Couse. Children, Ruth, Laura and Florence. He came to Randolph in 1889. In 1897 Mr. Chaffey was elected to the Elkins City Council. He is president of the Peoples National Bank of Elkins. Although an active and successful business man, Mr. Chaffey is prominent in civil and church affairs, and much credit should be accorded him for the adoption of the prohibition amendment in West Virginia.

ABRAHAM CLINGERMAN.

Abraham Clingerman, son of Peter and Julia Ann (Smith) Clingerman, was born in Bedford County, Pennsylvania, married, first, Maggie E. Smith. Children, Oda E. For his second wife Mr. Clingerman married Bertha Ellen Eliff. Children, Herschell, Virgie V., Pearl and Denver. Mr. Clingerman has been a carpenter and builder since locating in Elkins.

CAPT. WILLIAM H. COBB.

Capt. Wm. H. Cobb. William Henry Cobb was born June 30, 1859, in Hall County, Georgia. He was united in marriage in 1896 to Laone, daughter of Col. Elihu and Sophrina (Woodford) Hutton. This union has been blessed with four children, Elihu Hutton Cobb, Marion Cobb, William Henry Cobb, Jr. and Langly Woodford Cobb.

Capt. Cobb was reared on the typical southern plantation on the Oconee River, and received such early education as was afforded by the Old Field Schools of that time. Later he attended the North Georgia Military Academy and took his degree from the Georgia State University at Athens. Subsequently he took a course in law and located in Southern Florida for the practice of his profession.

With military mien, talent and training, Capt. Cobb has always had a native bent toward the profession of arms. Accordingly, when war with Spain was declared, he raised a company in his home town of Arcadia. Capt. Cobb's company saw service in Santiago and Guantanimo, Cuba. He has held commissions from the President of the United States and from the Governors of three States, and was preparing to enter the service in the recent anticipated unpleasantness with Mexico. At the close of the Spanish American War Capt. Cobb's company was mustered out and he located in Elkins to practice the profession of law. Capt. Cobb has been active in the affairs of the city and has been a member of city council, mayor and six years president of the Board of Trade. He has been also, vice-president of the State Board of Trade.

In a practical way he has been active in the upbuilding of the city by erecting several modern business blocks.

The Cobb family is an old English one and the Cobham estates remain as landmarks in the mother country. The family came to America in 1655 and settled near Norfolk, Virginia, moving to the Carolinas prior to the Revolution. Representatives of this family have been prominent in the councils of both branches of the National law-making bodies and furnished governors for several States in Dixie. Capt. Cobb is also related to the Tanner and Langley families of Virginia that trace their lineage back many centuries.

H. T. CONNER.

H. T. Conner, son of William and Minerva (Layman) Conner, was born in Frostburg, Maryland, 1883, married Mary Bowers. Children, Cathaline, Mildred and William G.

Mr. Conner is proprietor of Elkins Bakery and Confectionery, and has been a resident of Elkins since 1905.

C. L. CORDER.

C. L. Corder son of Elam G. and Martha (Hodges) Corder, was born in Upshur County in 1872, married Lula, daughter of Rev. C. B. and Marian (Maxwell) Meredith. Children, Paul, Frances and Effie.

Mr. Corder was educated in public schools, Buckhannon Academy and graduated from West Virginia Business College in 1893. After teaching school a number of years, he came to Elkins and engaged in the insurance business. He is now a member of the clerical force of the Western Maryland Railroad Company at Elkins and also maintains an insurance office.

A. WATT CURRY.

A. Watt Curry, son of William H. and Mary (Wilson) Curry, was born December 14, 1849, married Jennie, daughter of James and Rachel (Davis) Moyers. Child, Maud.

Mr. Curry was born at Rock Cave, Upshur County. Mr. Curry is one of the substantial citizens of Beverly, and has a jewelry store on Main street. The Curry family was a pion-

eer family in Augusta. James and Rebecca Curry, children
of William Curry, were baptised by Rev. John Craig, D.D., in
Augusta, in 1746. These names are in Rev. Craig's records
of baptism.

GIDEON C. CORLEY.

Gideon C. Corley, son of N. E. and Louisa (Wilson) Corley, was born in 1840 in Barbour County, married Lydia
Thorn. Children, Edward, Henry, Stella, Dora, Garfield, Mer-
ta, and Lonna.

Mr. Corley was a member of the County Court of Bar-
bour County four years and justice of the peace eight years.
Mr. Corley attended the convention that nominated Abraham
Lincoln for first term.

DR. JAMES L. CUNNINGHAM.

James Lancashire Cunningham, born September 1, 1863,
Pittsburgh, Pa.; graduated from high school of Belmont
County, Ohio, in 1881, and in medicine from the University
of Baltimore in 1892. Dr. Cunningham located in Pickens in
June of the same year where he has since engaged in the
practice of his profession. Dr. Cunningham is a son of John
and Selena (Cowell) Cunningham, who imigrated to America
in 1836, locating in Pittsburgh. At the age of 21, Dr. Cunningham engaged in the profession of teaching and taught
many terms, leaving the profession to take up the study of
medicine as a student under Dr. John T. Huff. He was appointed enumerator of the census for Hackers Valley District, Webster County, in 1890. At present he is a member
of the Board of Education of Middle Fork District and is
surgeon for the B. & O. Railroad.

Dr. Cunningham married Mary, daughter of William and
Margaret (Reese) Roberts, in 1894, in the Pickens Presbyterian church by Rev. Brooks, and have children, Mabel Marie and Ethel Selena. Dr. Cunningham has been successful
in his profession and owns a beautiful home overlooking the
town of Pickens. No physician in the State perhaps, serves
so large a clientele in a non-competitive field. Socially and
fraternally Dr. Cunningham has been a member of the Masonic and K. of P. orders for many years.

HON. HENRY G. DAVIS.

Henry G. Davis. Henry G. Davis, second son of Caleb and Louisa (Brown) Davis, was born November 16, 1823. He was of Welch decent. He worked on a farm from early boyhood until he was 19 years of age. He then became a freight brakesman on the Baltimore and Ohio Railroad between Baltimore and Cumberland. He was successively passenger conductor and supervisor of trains.

At the age of 28 Mr. Davis married a daughter of Judge Bantz, of Frederick, Maryland. In 1854 he was made agent for the B. & O. at Piedmont. Soon thereafter, in partnership with his brothers, Thomas B. Davis and Wm. R. Davis, he engaged in business in shipping coal and lumber. Mr. Davis also founded the towns of Deer Park and Keyser.

In 1866 Mr. Davis entered politics and was elected to the Legislature. Two years later he was elected to the State Senate. He succeeded Waitman T. Wiley in the United States Senate in 1870, which position he held until 1883. He was the leading spirit in the building of the C. I., C. & C. and Western Maryland railroads.

Five children were born to Mr. and Mrs. Davis. Hallie, who married S. B. Elkins; Kate, who married Lieutenant Brown, and Grace, who married Arthur Lee; and two sons, Harry and John T. John T. Davis represented Randolph in the Legislature in 1910-2.

In 1904 Mr. Davis was the vice-presidential candidate with Judge Parker on the Democratic ticket.

Mr. Davis died in 1916.

A. E. DANN.

A. E., son of William Henry and Christina A. (Hannah) Dann, was born in Kansas in 1877, married Eva (Hatfield) Wainer. Children, Martha and Dortha. Mr. Dann was educated in the public schools of Kansas. He is at present and has several times previous represented his ward in the Elkin's city council and is manager of the Elkins Furniture and Hardware Company. His father, William H. Dann, came to America from England in 1871. He was clerk of Grego County, Kansas, in 1885, and for a number of years has resided at Beltsville, a suburb of Washington.

RALPH DARDEN.

Ralph Darden, son of Geo. G. Darden, was born in North Carolina in 1867, married Ada May, daughter of E. C. Harwood. Mr. Darden was educated in the colleges of his native State and entered upon the study of law, but defective eyesight precluded close application to study and Mr. Darden engaged in business pursuits. Mr. Darden has been prominent in the affairs of his adopted county. He was a member of the city council in 1896.

CHARLES E. DULANEY.

Chas. E., son of J. L. and Mary (Cain) Dulaney, was born February 9, 1875, married, first, Hedig, daughter of Mathas and Ada Sulsi. Children, Roy, Franklin and Thamer.

The first wife of Mr. Dulaney died in 1901. Mr. Dulaney for his second wife married Bessie M., daughter of David and Mary Jane (Armstrong) Riffle. Children, Cecil, Charles, Norval, Claude and Mary Louise. Mr. Dulaney was born in Ritchie County and came to Randolph in 1894. He is of French descent. For fifteen years he has held his present position of engineer of Pickens and Webster Springs Railroad.

WILLIAM F. DOERR.

William F. Doerr, German descent, son of Henry and Ida (Lessenger) Doerr, was born in Butler County, Pennsylvania, in 1873, married Ida S. McCauly. Children, Roy I. and Ralph M. Mr. Doerr came to Randolph in 1895 and for nine years has been in the employ of the Gulland Clarke Wholesale Grocery Company at Elkins.

WALTER C. DILWORTH.

Walter C. Dilworth, son of James G. and Alcinda (Ratliff) Dilworth, was born in Barbour County in 1879, married Daisy, daughter of Newton Gibson. Children, Mamie L., Hersell L., Kent G., Wanda and Marie. Mr. Dilworth came to Randolph in 1900. He is in the employ of the Elkins Electric Railway Company as conductor and motorman.

Henry Clay Dean.

Henry Clay Dean. Henry Clay Dean was a native of Pennsylvania and came to Randolph when a young man. He married a Miss Haigler of Valley Bend District. He taught school, then became a minister of the Methodist church. He moved to Missouri in about 1850. He soon gained prominence and was elected Chaplain of the United States Senate, which place he held for twelve years. He studied law and gained a national reputation as a criminal lawyer. At one time he was a candidate for the United States Senate from the State of Missouri and only lacked three votes of election against the combined opposition. The press commenting on his defeat said he would have been elected, without opposition if he had donned a clean shirt at any time within six weeks prior to the election.

During the Civil War Dean's oratorical battery was ever on duty in behalf of the Southern cause and the Federal Government was very anxious to get hands on the man who was giving them more trouble than a regiment of soldiers. His presence in Keokuk, Iowa, became known to the Federal authorities and while he was upon the streets of that city, some dark forms came out of the gloom and took Dean in custody. Rapidly he was hurried up to the tall bluffs overlooking the Mississippi River. A 100-foot drop and eternal silence. It was a magnificient place for an execution—picturesque, sublimely beautiful, fatal. The vitriol throwing Southerner looked piteously around at the determined avengers, but read no compassion in their countenances. He raised his hand.

"No speech," said the Captain peremptorily. He knew the danger of that marvelous tongue. "Just a short prayer, Dean, and then to the fishes."

"Thank you Captain," said the condemned, as if impressed with the soldier's magnanimity, "I have no speech to make, nor will I take up your time to pray. I have only this to ask." He began fumbling in his pocket, seemed perplexed for a moment as if something had been mislaid, and then brought out an old fashioned Barlow knife and a leather pocket book.

"This knife, Captain," he said, "I would have sent to my

son, back on the old farm in Putman County. I promised to make him a kite when I got back home with it, but——well, I don't want to disappoint the lad, you know. He'll be expecting me tomorrow and will be down to the—the gate. Excuse me comrades, but I love the boy——I can't help it."

The voice grew husky and the man under sentence of death turned and looked out over the great river. Some of the men shifted around to the rear.

"It's childish weakness, I know," resumed Dean, turning his face toward the soldiers. "Don't mind it friends." The Captain took the old knife sheepishly. "Now this book contains an old picture of mine and some verses; maybe a dollar or two also. I don't think you'll regard it of much consequence, but the dear angel back in old Missouri—my wife gentlemen—the sweetest, truest, gentlest woman that ever blessed the life of man: I can see her now as she kneels beside her couch, praying to the God of the unfortunate to protect her husband and bring him safely back to the old roof tree, where we've stood beside a cot over which the death angel hovered, and where we walked arm in arm through the clover fields to garland the grave of our dead. This is all I can send her comrades——I'm poor. But she'll prize it beyond the gift of kings. She'll——why where are your men, Captain? Come! I'm ready."

During Dean's pathetic reference to his wife the militiamen had one by one slunk into the night shadows, leaving the orator alone with the leader.

"Oh, they got tired and went home," said the Captain wearily. "Dean if you and the devil ever meet my sympathy will be with the gentleman of the forked tail."

Mr. Dean died in Missouri in 1886, aged 63 years.

NEWTON L. DOWNS.

Newton L. Downs, son of Wm. H. and Elizabeth (Chisholm) Downs, was born October 26, 1874, in Flintstone, Md. married, June 14, 1899, Minnie, daughter of W. F. and Racheal McClaskey. Children, Genevieve, Walter and Julia.

Mr. Downs was educated in common schools. Has been an employe of Western Maryland for twenty years as operator and clerk at Coketon, Thomas and Mill Creek. Has been a member of town council of Mill Creek and is at present president of the Board of Education of Huttonsville District.

Hon. S. B. Elkins.

Hon. Stephen B. Elkins. Stephen B. Elkins was born in Perry County, Ohio, on the 26th of September, 1841, and died at Washington, D. C., January 5, 1911. During the childhood of Mr. Elkins his father removed with his family to the State of Missouri, where young Elkins attended the public school and was fitted for college. Entering the Missouri University, he graduated in 1860, at the age of eighteen. He was admitted to the bar in 1863. When the war broke out he joined the Union forces and attained the rank of Captain. In 1864, young Elkins removed to New Mexico, where at that time dangers, hardships, and discomforts had to be met and overcome, but along with these came opportunities for success. Barely had the first year of his residence elapsed when he was elected to the Territorial Legislature. In 1867 he was made Attorney General of the Territory. In 1869, President Andrew Johnson made him United States Attorney. After holding this place nearly four years, he resigned under the Grant administration.

Mr. Elkins was elected a Delegate in 1873 to represent the Territory in the Forty-third Congress of the United States. During Mr. Elkin's first term in Congress he visited Europe and while abroad was re-elected for a second term to the Forty-fourth Congress. In 1869 he became president of the First National Bank of Santa Fe. While in Congress he wedded Hallie, daughter of Senator H. G. Davis.

His greatest national prominence came to him during the campaign of 1884, when he was chosen Chairman of the Executive Committee of the National Republican Committee.

In December, 1891, Mr. Elkins was nominated by President Harrison for Secretary of War to succeed Mr. Proctor.

Mr. Elkins' father, Col. P. D. Elkins, was a native of Virginia. His mother, Sarah (Withers) Elkins, was a member of a prominent Virginia family. By his first wife Mr. Elkins had two children, Mrs. A. E. Oliphant, of New Jersey, and

Mrs. E. E. Brunner, of New York City. By his second wife Mr. Elkins had five children, four boys, Davis, Stephen B., Jr., Richard and Blaine, and one girl, Katherine.

In 1878 Mr. Elkins became a citizen of West Virginia and associated himself with his father-in-law, Senator Davis, in building the West Virginia Central Railroad.

In 1895, January 23, Mr. Elkins was elected as a Republican to represent West Virginia in the United States Senate. He served continually until the time of his death in 1911. His son, Davis Elkins, was appointed by Governor Glasscock to fill the unexpired term.

ENOCH J. EVANS.

Enoch J. Evans, born in Green County, Pennsylvania, in 1865, son of Alfred S. and Elizabeth (Brewer) Evans. He came to Randolph in 1883, married Mary M., daughter of Lovell and Phoeba (Taylor) Kelley. Children, H. B., Kent T., Clyde R., Barron L. and Ray, who died in the seventeenth year of his age. Mr. Evans has been a successful farmer and fruit grower. He has been road commissioner twenty-two of the thirty years he has resided in the county.

A. ROSS ELLIS.

A. Ross Ellis, son of Powell and Winnie Ellis, was born in Braxton County, 1876, married Linnie May Dingess. Children, Theron, Andrew, Wendel, Burl and Zudora. Mr. Ellis came to Randolph in 1906 and since has been in the employ of the Western Maryland Railroad as brakesman and conductor.

JOHN L. EBERLY.

John L. Eberly, son of Wm. and Martha (Barnard) Eberly, was born in Moorefield in 1873, married Lillian May Weese. Children, Myron, Arthur Lee, John L., Jr. He is proprietor of Eberly News Stand on Third Street.

CLAY FITZWATER.

Clay Fitzwater, son of Nelson and Sarah (White) Fitzwater, was born in 1854, married Anzina, daughter of Jacob and Catherine (Phillips) Daniels. Children, Walter Nelson,

Minnie, Clarence, Holland, Hattie, James, Herbert. Mr. Fitzwater is descended from a prominent pioneer family of Garrett County, Maryland. His brother, Rev. Holland Fitzwater,
is an able minister of the Methodist Episcopal church in Ohio,
filling some of the highest offices in the church.

H. F. FISHER.

H. F. Fisher, son of J. H. and H. E. (Simmons) Fisher,
was born in 1874, married Della J. (Elliott) Johnson. Children, Loula Grace and Mary Louisa. Mr. Fisher has been a
plumber in Elkins for eight years.

W. C. FOWLER.

W. C. Fowler, son of Joseph C. and Margaret (Jones)
Fowler, was born in 1885, at Town Marlborough, Md., mar-
ried Tosa E. Brittan. Children, William Allan, George, Ben-
jamin, Margaret, W. C. Jr., died at age of four years. Mr.
Fowler has been proprietor of a tailoring establishment in
Elkins since 1913.

DELLAS GAINER.

Dellas Gainer, son of Matthew Gainer, is one of Randolph
County's best products. As a young man he was employed
in the paymaster's office of the West Virginia Central Railroad in Elkins. In 1909 he entered professional baseball,
joining the Grafton (W. Va.) team, where his excellent playing attracted the attention of the Detroit managers of the
American League. He was purchased from the Grafton
management in the fall of 1909 for $1500.00, and finished the
season with Detroit, assisting that team to win the league
championship, and participated in the World's series against
the Pittsburgh Pirates.

In 1910 Dell played with the Ft. Wayne Club, of the
Central League, but was taken back to Detroit in 1911. That
year he was the baseball sensation until he had his right arm
broken, which practically kept him out of the game the remainder of that season. At the time of his injury he was batting for an average of .376.

In 1913 he was sold to the Boston Red Socks, of the
same league, for $75000, and is still a member of that team,

his. batting average being .317. In 1915 he participated in the World's series against the Philadelphia National League team, assisting his club materially in winning the championship.

By his consistent performance in his chosen profession, by his modest, unassuming, clean living, Mr. Gainer has a host of friends in every city he visits as a professional ball player, and, above all, is honored by the people of his home city and county.

GEO. E. GREYNOLDS.

George E., son of Joseph and Rowana (Blair) Greynolds, was born in Harrison County in 1851, married in 1876, Verna M., daughter of John D. and Rachel (Dawson) Romine, of Harrison County. Children, Delbert L., Joseph, Mary C., John D. and Robert Lee. Mrs. Greynolds, Mary C. and Joseph are deceased.

Mr. Greynolds has been justice of the peace of Beverly District for a number of years. Rev. Robert Greynolds is a minister of the Methodist Episcopal church.

S. H. GODWIN.

S. H. Godwin, son of William S. and Mary (Cox) Godwin, was born in Barbour County in 1858. The first wife of Mr. Godwin was Sarah M. Gainer, and the children of this union were Raymond, Morris, Dennis, Austin and Belva Alice. Some years after the death of his first wife Mr. Godwin united in marriage Miss Nancy E. Phillip. To them were born Ora Maude, Martha Effie, Stark Daily, Cleet Durkin and Prentiss Page. Mr. Godwin taught school for several years, was justice of the peace in Tucker eight years. He was elected justice of the peace in Barbour in 1904 but resigned to come to Elkins to become manager of Elkins Marble and Granite Works.

ALBERT GEAR.

Albert Gear, son of Adam and Frances (Shifflett) Gear, was born in 1871 at Huttonsville, married Laura, daughter of John and Jane (Smith) Herron. Children, Lela, Ethel, Arthur Sewel, Phelix, Nora, George and Adaline. Mr. Gear is of Irish descent and his parents moved from Virginia to West Virginia before the Civil War. Austin Gear was the first of the name to come to Randolph. The maternal grandfather, Absalom Shifflett, was the first of the Shifflett family to locate in Randolph. Mr. Gear is a merchant at Mill Creek. Mr. Gear takes an active part in religious affairs and is an elder in the Presbyterian church.

ALBERT R. HICKS.

Albert R., son of Franklin and Mary Hicks, was born April 13, 1879; married first Margaret, daughter of John and Socia (Gladwell) Rothenbughler. Children, James Earle and Mary May. Mrs. Hicks died November 5, 1907. Mr. Hicks married for his second wife Nancy, daughter of Casper and Ida (Morgan) Winkler. Children, Casper Albert, Nancy Ida, Jesse Woodrow and Thadeus Cunningham. Mr. Hick's parents moved to Randolph from Braxton in 1888. The Hicks are of English descent and the family moved to West Virginia from the mother state before the Civil War.

WICKHAM HANSFORD.

Acra and Katie (Wimer) Hansford came to Randolph from Rockingham County, Virginia, in 1820, and settled in what was then Randolph but is now Tucker County. Their children were William, Mary, Wesley, John, David, Charles, Levi, Sarah and Julia. Chas. S. Hansford first married Sarah Allender. Children, Katherine, who married David Canfield. Married, second Amanda Hyre; no children to this union. For his third wife Mr. Hanford married Amanda (Conrad) Curtis. Children, Laban, Wickham, Walter and Corder, who died young.

WALTER A. HEDRICK.

Walter A. Hedrick, son of J. C. and Martha (Berkely) Hedrick, was born in 1881, in Pendleton County, West Virginia. Mr. Hedrick never married. He has traveled extensively in south and west and was engaged in the real estate business in Florida for several years. In partnership with his brother, Frederick R. Hedrick, he is engaged in the restaurant business in Elkins.

REUBEN H. HOWELL.

Reuben H. Howell, son of Andrew and Frances (Rains) Howell, was born in 1860; married Verna, daughter of Eugenis Isner. Children, Harley and Mary. Some years after the death of his first wife, Mr. Howell choose his second wife in the person of Mrs. Jones, of Barbour County. Mr. Howell is is an employee of the Western Maryland Railroad.

HOWARD HARMON.

Howard Harmon, son of Samuel and Eva (Bible) Harmon, was born in 1871; married a daughter of Jacob and Susan (McDonald) Harper. Children, Neal, Handy and Cornell. Mr. Harmon has been a merchant at Harmon eight years and was at one time elected mayor of the village, but refused to serve. When 18 years of age Mr. Harmon drove a wagon from Summer County, Kansas, to Randolph, a distance of 1800 miles, and was ten weeks on the journey.

GEO. W. HINCHMAN.

George W. Hinchman, son of Joseph and Caroline (Riffle) Hinchman, was born in 1872; married Lottie L., daughter of John Haddan and Mary E. (Shufflet) Pritt. Children, Sterling W., Wilford and Clay. Mr. Hinchman has been a resident of Elkins about ten years. He is mail porter for Coal & Coke and Western Maryland railroads.

JOSEPH C. HEDRICK.

Joseph C. Hedrick, son of Leonard Hedrick, was born in Pendleton in 1848; married Martha Beckly. Mr. Hedrick came to Randolph in 1883. He is the grandson of Frederick Hedrick, who immigrated from Germany to Pendleton County, Virginia, in the pioneer period.

ANDREW HEDRICK.

Andrew, son of Adam C. and Rachael (Davis) Hedrick, was born in 1874, married Virginia, daughter of Michael and Catherine (Turner) Hedrick. Children, Bertha F., Ethel M., Thomas B., Merril G., Iva and Elaura. Mr. Hedrick was justice of the peace in 1908-12, and mayor of Whitmer, 1912-15.

JOHN W. HELTZEL.

John W. Heltzel and Cora (Johnson) Heltzel moved to Randolph from Rockingham County, Virginia, in 1885. Children, Jas. P., John W., Jr., Mona C., Glen D., Dona M., Connie M., Thomas P., Perry R., Nina, Bruce Woodrow and Mary E. who died at the age of three years.

JAMES P. HELTZEL.

Jas. P. Heltzel was born in 1886, married Eliza (Seitz) Robinson. Children, Lillian Wanda and Cane Keith. He has been deputy sheriff since 1908.

HERMAN G. JOHNSON.

Herman G. Johnson, born in Barbour County in 1875, son of Levi and Helen A. (Poling) Johnson, was educated in public schools, Fairmont Normal, Peabody Normal College, Nashville, Tennessee, and the University of Tennessee. After teaching school several years, he entered the field of journalism and accepted a place on the editorial staff of the Nashville American. Mr. Johnson has been editor of the Intermountain since 1898.

CHARLES T. JEFFERS.

Charles T. Jeffers, son of James C. and Sarah N. (Mathews) Jeffers, was born in 1884 in Monongalia County; married Carrie, daughter of Hamilton and Sarah C. (Schoonover) Isner. Children, Ruth H. and Sarah Margaret. Mr. Jeffers has been clerk in Elkin's postoffice for ten years.

WAYNE JACKSON.

Wayne Jackson, son of Geo. S. and Jessie (Faun) Jackson, was born in 1893, in Salem, West Virginia. Mr. Jackson was educated in public schools and Davis & Elkins College. He is employed as bookkeeper for Peoples Hardware Co. at Elkins. He came to Randolph in 1905.

JUDGE WARREN B. KITTLE.

Judge Warren B. Kittle. In the legal profession the man who rises to a position of prominence by his own efforts must necessarily possess more than ordinary ability. This is especially true in a community where his competitors are learned and abled men. A man of this class is Judge Warren B. Kittle of Philippi. Although a resident of another county, he is identified with Randolph by his lineage, his association at our bar, and by his official position. By descent and intermarriage Judge Kittle possesses the same strain of blood with most of the old families of Randolph County.

The first of the Kittle family of Randolph and Barbour counties was Abraham Kittle, Sr., who was born in New Jersey in January, 1731, and died in Randolph County, September 16, 1816. The exact date is not now known when Abraham Kittle, Sr., settled in Randolph, but it was prior to 1781, for a deed of record bearing that date, shows he acquired lands here in that year; and other records testify that members of his family took part in defending the community against the Indians about the same time. The children of Abraham Kittle, Sr., were Abraham, Jr., Richard, Jacob, George, John and a daughter who married Henry Pedro.

Judge Kittle is a direct descendent of Abraham Kittle, Jr., who was born in Randolph County, February 18, 1773, and married Margaret Marteney, and died April 17, 1814. His children were James, born January 6, 1803, died April 9, 1839; Mary, who married a Mr. Skidmore, was born July 30, 1795, died September 5, 1849; Elizabeth, married a Mr. Yates, was born March 29, 1804, died December 10, 1850; George, born July 20, 1809, date of death unknown; Ellenor married Mr. Holder, born January 7, 1798, date of death unknown; Prudence, married Mr. Holden, born April 24, 1801, date of death unknown; Elijah, born December 24, 1796, and died in 1856; and Eli, born January 6, 1800, died November 12, 1863. Elijah Kittle was the father of six children, Cyrus, Amasa, David, Hulda, Harriet, Sallie, Louise and Emaline. Cyrus Kittle was the father of George M. Kittle, who was the father of Judge Warren B. Kittle.

Judge Kittle was born December 23, 1872, was educated in the common schools and the West Virginia University where he graduated with the degree of LL.B. in June, 1894, since which time he has been constantly in the practice of the law. He was married June 30, 1897, to Zona Wilson, and is the father of three children, Virginia, born in 1898, Nellie, born in 1900, George born in 1904.

Judge Kittle was elected prosecuting attorney of Barbour County in 1904, served four years; was appointed Judge of the Nineteenth Judicial Circuit by Governor Glasscock on May 24, 1911, to fill the newly created Barbour-Randolph Circuit; was elected in 1912, for a term of eight years as Judge of said circuit by 1167 majority, and has served as judge ever since. Judge Kittle is known as an incessant student, and owns one of the largest law libraries in the state. He takes great interest in and devotes his entire time to his profession; is the author of two well known law books, and is a member of the American Bar Association.

Hon. H. G. Kump.

Herman G. Kump, son of Benjamin Franklin and Frances Margaret (Rudolph) Kump, was born at Capon Springs, Hampshire County, West Virginia, October 31, 1879. He was educated in the public schools and the University of Virginia from which institution he graduated in 1903. In 1905 he received the degree of B.L. from the law department of the University of Virginia, and was admitted to the Randolph County bar the same year. He has served as prosecuting attorney since 1908. Mr. Kump married in 1907, Edna, daughter of C. H. and Fanny (Logan) Scott. Children, Cyrus Scott and Frances. Mr. Kump's father, B. F. Kump, was a soldier in the Confederate Army, his grandfather, Jacob Kump, was a solider in the War of 1812, and his great grandfather, Henry Kump, was a soldier in the Revolutionary War from Virginia.

Hon. N. G. Keim.

Noah G. Keim was born in 1862, Elk Lick, Pennsylvania; son of Silas C. and Annie (Arnold) Keim. Mr. Keim was educated in the public schools and at Ashland College, Ohio and Juniatti College, Pennsylvania. He entered the profession of teaching and for a number of years was principal of the Sommerset, Pennsylvania schools. He came to Elkins as tutor for the sons of Senator Elkins. He has been a Republican in politics and was presidential elector on the McKinley ticket. He represents the Thirteenth Senatorial District in the State Legislature. Senator Keim was- the Progressive party's nominee for Congress in 1914.

Senator Keim married Clara, daughter of Kennedy H. and Sarah E. (Rizer) Butler. Children, Howard H. and Elizabeth. Senator Keim's grandfather, James J. Keim, was an early settler in Western Pennsylvania. He was a member of the State Legislature and was for many years one of the judges of the court.

LELAND KITTLE.

Leland, son of Eli and Rebecca (Weese) Kittle, was born January 28, 1846; married Mary Margaret, daughter of James and Rachael (Davis) Moyers, in 1873. Children, Ruth Morgan, a graduate of Mary Baldwin Seminary, Staunton, Virginia. She is a member of the D. A. R. and W. D. C. From 1873 to 1878 Mr. Kittle was clerk of the Circuit Court of Randolph, and was admitted to the bar in 1879. His father, Eli Kittle, was justice of the peace and member of the County Court.

ORVILLE E. KERR.

Orville E., son of William B. and Mary E. (Burnside) Kerr, was born in 1880; married Jessie L. (Spanaugle) Lank. Children, Martha E., Oscar W., Uniah and Cretus. Mr. Kerr resides at Bemis and is an employe of the Bemis Lumber Company.

J. E. KILDOW.

J. E. Kildow, son of Michael V. and Mary (Root) Kildow, was born in 1862, German ancestry, married, Minnie, daughter of Benoni Jordan. Children, Edna, William LaVelle, Eunice and Beulah. Mr. Kildow is a newspaper man of extensive experience. He has edited the Kingwood Argus, Randolph Enterprise and other newspapers. He is an ordained minister in the Methodist Protestant church. Mr. Kildow was the first active propagandist in the Socialist movement in Randolph County.

ISAAC S. KIMMELL.

Isaac S. Kimmell, son of Adam and Lucinda (Shirk) Kimmell, was born in Pendleton in 1870; married Melcena

T., daughter of Christian and Amanda (Jefferson) Bowers. Children, Estella, Howard and Myrtle. Hammond died in childhood. He has been in the lumber business for fourteen years.

L. H. KEENAN.

L. H. Keenan, Irish descent, son of John Payne and Mary (Lazelle) Keenan, was born in 1854; married Irene Donnelly of Albany, N. Y. Mr. and Mrs. Keenan have one child, J. Ed. Keenan. Mr. Keenan was educated in public schools and Mt. Morris Academy. He graduated from the law department of the State University in 1887. Prior to coming to Elkins in 1892, Mr. Keenan practiced law four years at Wichita, Kansas. He has a predilection for political economics but has refused to become a candidate for public office, and is a Progressive in his political affiliations. He wields a trenchant pen.

B. F. KNAGGS.

Benjamin F. Knaggs, son of John R. and Mary (Mathews) Knaggs, was born in Taylor County in 1880; married Bessie Talbott Newlon. Children, Hazel E. and Owlan. Mr. Knaggs is a freight conductor on the Western Maryland Railroad.

CAM LLOYD.

Cam Lloyd, son of James Madison and Louisa (Aimes) Lloyd, was born April 9, 1860; married Maggie, daughter of James McGuire. Children, Annie F. and Tolbard. Louisa died in infancy. Mr. Lloyd lived in Pittsburgh thirteen years. The Lloyds are of English ancestry; the first of the name in America settled at Jamestown. The present generation is the sixth in America. Mr. Lloyd came to Randolph with his parents in 1866. Louisa was the home county in the mother state of Mr. Lloyd's parents. Mr. Lloyd was a member of the town council of Mill Creek from its incorporation until he was promoted to the mayorality in 1914.

H. GRANT LUCAS.

H. Grant Lucas, son of Joseph P. and Eliza J. Lucas, was born at Brooksville, Pennsylvania, 1869. Children, Joseph P., Jr., Frank Philip, Mary Edith and Gertrude. Mr. Lucas has been a resident of the county since 1896, during which time he has been superintendent of the Parsons Pulp and Lumber Company, and has actively identified himself with the interests of his adopted county. Mr. Lucas received his education in the public schools of Brookeville.

MARTIN LANTZ.

Marian Lantz, son of Henry and Elizabeth (Radabaugh) Lantz, was born June 6, 1859; married first, Sarah Radabaugh. Children, Lee Roy, Martha Jane and Julia Ann. Married, second, Martha Jane, (Heavener) Ward. Children, Lloyd, B. F., Albina, Ellen Bettie, Nora Odella, Everett; Kinsy died aged one year and Zona died in the eighteenth year of her age.

GEORGE CASSELMAN LONG.

George Casselman Long, son of Washington J. and Polly (Hutton) Long, was born January 20, 1843; married Malissa Ellen, daughter of Benjamin and Catherine (Slagel) Phares. Children, Catherine, Anna Grace, O'Brien Branch and Carl are dead. The children living are W. J. Long, A. B. Long and George Ann, wife of Robert L. Pritt. Mr. Long's grandfather was George Long and his grandmother was Sarah Casselman. The Long family is of German descent and came to this country from Lancaster County, Pennsylvania. A. B. Long married Russel, daughter of Z. T. Wamsley. W. J. Long married Evangeline, daughter of Webster Wamsley. Grandchildren, Ruby, daughter of R. L. Pritt, and Wilson J. and Gertrude, children of Mr. and Mrs. A. B. Long. Mrs. G. C. Long died in 1915. W. J. Long was county superintendent of schools of Randolph several terms.

LINDLEY B. McLAUGHLIN.

Lindley B. McLaughlin, son of R. M. and Susan, (Gilleland) McLaughlin, was born in 1861, in Pennsylvania; married in 1878 to Sarah, daughter of Robert Boyer. Children, Levy E., Robert M., Annie E., who married Roy Davis, Orlando D., Wilbur R. and Roy R. Mr. McLaughlin came to West Virginia in 1892. He has been justice of the peace of

Beverly District and is one of the Democratic nominees for that office at the present time.

LEVI WILMOTH MCQUAIN.

Levi Wilmoth McQuain, son of Joshua and Mary Ann (Leary) McQuain, was born in 1864; married in 1891 Mary Elizabeth, daughter of Hiram and Elizabeth (Pritt) Hill. Children, Lutie, Hiram W., Elam Dowden. Mr. McQuain was constable in 1892 and has served several terms as assessor and deputy assessor.

PATRICK F. MARTIN.

Patrick F. Martin, son of James and Anna (Cain) Martin, was born in Baltimore in 1862; married Mary, daughter of Edward and Catherine Cogan. Children, Harry, James, Francis, Eleanor, Eileen, Ann and Edward. Edward died in infancy. Mr. Martin came to Randolph when a year old. He is janitor of the Randolph county court house and owns valuable land in the Roaring Creek coal belt.

ALEXANDER MILLER.

Alexander Miller, son of Christian and Margaret (Smith) Miller, was born in Bedford County, Pennsylvania, in 1855; married Mary Ellen, daughter of Charles and Homer (Martin) Fletcher. Children, Guy, Emmett, Pearl, Charles, Carl and Espy. Mr. Miller came to Randolph in 1896. He has been a resident of Mill Creek fourteen years and is at present an employe of the Wilson Lumber Company.

B. FRANK MILLER.

B. Frank Miller, son of B. B. and Amanda (O'Rouke) Miller, was born in Harrisburg, Virginia, in 1870; married Virginia (Hoover) Smith. Children, Charles, Olive, Lessie, Lillie, Mary, Georgia, Minnie, Lucile, Elsie, who died at the age of five. Mr. Miller is now foreman in the mill of the Parsons Pulp and Lumber Co.

JOHN D. MOORE.

John D., son of G. M. and Sarah A. (Simmons) Moore, was born in 1886; married Annie L., daughter of George and

Elizabeth (Simpson) Beatty. Children, Maud, George, Fannie, Ralph, Edgar, Gladdis, Harry, Irene and Walter who died in infancy. Mr. Moore is superintendent of Alton Mill at Mill Creek. He is of English descent. Wood Moore, the paternal grandfather, moved to Mingo District from Botetot County, Virginia, in about 1800. Joseph Moore, a brother of Wood Moore, came with him.

EARLE MORRISON.

Earle Morrison, son of Jerome and Susan (Heck) Morrison, was born at Buckhannon, West Virginia, May 9, 1879; married Lizzie, daughter of John and Kate Winger. Children, Harry, Hazel, Mabel, Helen and Willard. Mr. Morrison holds a responsible position with the Laurel River Lumber Co., Jenningston, West Virginia. Mrs. Morrison is a daughter of Mr. and Mrs. Winger, who were members of the Swiss Colony at Helvetia. Mrs. Morrison died March, 1916.

H. L. MANNING.

H. L. Manning, son of J. A. Zerniah (Jefferson) Manning, was born in 1877 at Moundsville, West Virginia; married Chloe Failor. Children, Joseph, Robert and Helen. Mr. Manning was the nominee of the Republican party for county clerk in 1914-15, and more than carried the strength of his party. He was a member of the city council 1914-15. Mr. Manning's mother was a Jefferson and a distant relative of the author of the Declaration of Independence.

CAPTAIN JACOB WILLIAMSON MARSHALL.

Captain Jacob Williamson Marshall. Captain Jacob W. Marshall was born April 6, 1830, at Cairo, Ritchie County, West Virginia. He was the son of Joseph and Hannah (McKinney) Marshall. William Marshall, the paternal grandfather, lived in New York and was a brother of the renowned Chief Justice John Marshall. The names Williamson and Piatt in the Marshall family came down from John Piatt, who married Jane Williamson March 27, 1863. He lived at Trenton, New Jersey, and was high sheriff of Middlesex. They had five children, Jane, Frances, William and Catherine.

Frances moved to Virginia and married William McKinney, and their daughter, Hannah, was the mother of Captain Marshall.

In 1855, Capt. Marshall married Georgiana, daughter of George and Mary See. They were the parents of nine children. Joseph, Dixie, Mary E., Piatt, Cecil E., Ligon, Adam, Lucy and Arthur. Mrs. Marshall was the granddaughter of

CAPTAIN JACOB W. MARSHALL.

Michael See, who with his brother George, came at an early day to Randolph from Hardy County. Mrs. Marshall died May 6, 1888, aged 56 years.

At the age of 20 years, Captain Marshall sought higher altitudes for the benefit of his health and came to Randolph. For a time he clerked in the store of William Hamilton and then engaged in the mercantile business on his own account. He later retired to give his exclusive attention to his extensive landed estate. At the opening of hostilities between the

states, Captain Marshall entered the service of his native
state. For a time he was scout and guide for General R. E.
Lee in his campaign in the Upper Valley. In 1862 he organized a company and was elected its captain. This company was attached to the Nineteenth Regiment, W. L. Jackson's Brigade. His command took part in the engagements
at Strasburg, Winchester, Monocacy and Fishers Hill, where
he was severely wounded in the righ lung from the effects of
which he never fully recovered. Although a captain, he frequently commanded his regiment. In battle he was cool,
daring and resourceful with many of the other qualities of
the great soldier. He was particularly kind and thoughtful
of the poor soldiers in his company, who had families at home
and granted them furloughs at every available opportunity.
He was never a candidate for office but held the position of
deputy collector of internal revenue under Cleveland's administration.

SAMUEL MULLENIX.

Samuel Mullenix, son of William and Susan (Teter) Mullenix, was born in 1879; married Stellar M., daughter of Job
and Sarah (White) Smith. Children, Grover C., William G.,
Preston, Galden H. (dead), Hoy A. (died, aged 11) and Mar-
ven G. (died, aged 4). Mr. Mullenix is an employe of the Parsons Pulp and Lumber Company at Horton.

MARTIN MULLENIX.

Martin, son of John W. and Katherine (Judy) Mullenix,
was born in 1865. Children, Dixon, Lena, Stella, Charles, Lillie, Vallie, Kenna, Martin and Rachael. Mr. Mullenix is one
of the most extensive farmers and stockraisers of his section.

WILLIAM MORRISON.

William Morrison, son of John B. and Sidney (Wamsley)
Morrison, was born in 1867; married in 1896 to Hattie, daughter of Riley and Catherine (Channell) Pritt. Children, Byron
and Hattie. Mr. Morrison's father, John B. Morrison, was a
man of influence and prominence for many years in Randolph,

and served several terms as clerk of the Circuit Court. Mr. Morrison is at present proprietor of a hotel in Beverly and has been a successful business man.

J. G. NESTOR.

J. G. Nestor, son of Jacob J. and Rachel (Poling) Nestor, was born in Barbour County in 1870; married Ida B., daughter of Andrew and Ida B. (Ward) Taylor. Children, Ersell G., Margaret and Edna Lee. Mr. Nestor came to Randolph in 1890. He is a photographer on Randolph Avenue.

GEORGE H. NEAL.

George H., son of John and Lucina I (McConaughy) Neal, was born September 20, 1878, in Birmingham, Ohio; married Susie P., daughter of Graham and Nettie (McCleary) Buchanan. Children, Winifred Louise, born May 8, 1914. Mr. Neal was educated in the public schools and graduated from Ohio Northern University in 1901 in the department of pharmacy. He came to West Virginia in 1904 and located in Elkins in 1906. Mr. Neal has drug stores at Elkins and Mill Creek. Dr. Neal's ancestors were among the early settlers of the Buckeye State, moving there from Virginia.

CHARLES W. PARRISH.

Chas. W. Parrish, son of Richard G. and Julia (Zernian) Parrish, was born in Parkersburg, West Virginia, in 1875; married Mary Bell, daughter of George and Mary (Hill) Chenoweth. Children, Sylvan G., Eva M. and Carl W. Mr. Parrish came to Randolph in 1897 since which time he has been in the employ of the Western Maryland Railroad as engineer. He was in the 1915 wreck, on the Blackwater grade, in which some of his companions lost their lives and with serious injury narrowly escaped with his own.

JAMES PICKENS.

James, youngest son of James and Rachael (Talbott) Pickens, was born at Duffie, Lewis County, December 29, 1840, and died in Randolph, December 2, 1912. Mr. Pickens's ancestors were among the early residents of Barbour County, this state.   He married Miss Mary (Hamilton) Heavener of Bath County, Virginia.   Some years subsequent to her death, he was united in marriage to Miss Mary (Horner) Vander-

MR. JAMES PICKENS.

vort, of Weston, Lewis County, who survives him and occupies the beautiful Pickens Homestead near the town which bears his name. Both marriages were without issue.

Mr. Pickens made some improvements on his holdings in Randolph in the fifties, but did not move to the county until 1868. He was a leading spirit in the location of the Swiss Colony at Helvetia and Florence and was largely instrumental in the building of the railroad from Buckhannon to Pickens, and was a director of the road before it was absorbed by the B. & O. He brought the first steam saw mill to the county in 1873.

Mr. Pickens served through the war of the rebellion as a member of Company A Tenth West Virginia Volunteer Infantry. Mr. Pickens was a leader in the development of the southwestern part of the county and the prosperous town which was named for him stands as a monument to his enterprise and ability.

JOHN W. POLING.

John W. Poling, son of Sanford and Seyerna (Jones) Poling, was born in Barbour County in 1873; married Selma A. Hill in 1903. They have no children. Mr. Poling is engaged in the mercantile business in Elkins.

SAMPSON PENNINGTON.

Sampson Pennington, son of V. R. and Phoeba (Flanigan) Pennington, was born in Harmon, West Virginia, in 1867; married Christina, daughter of John W. and Emil (Lantz) Thompson. Mr. Pennington has been constable of Dry Fork Districk for six years.

DAVID T. PROBST.

David T. Probst, German descent, son of Levi and Catherine (Weiner) Probst, was born in Pendleton County in 1859; married Mary J. Lambert. Children, Birdie C., Alice, Mattie S. and Lucie J. Mr. Probst married Louise H. Lambert for second wife. Mr. Probst has been a resident of Randolph since 1883.

HERBERT E. QUICK.

Herbert E., son of William Henry and Polina Ann (Strickland) Quick, was born in Valley Bend District in 1880; married Lula Savannah, daughter of C. P. and Esta (Lrye) Gatrell. Children, Ernest Doyle, Algie Elane, William Hugh, Mildred Geneva, Lonnie Herbert and Charles Eugenia. Mr Quick is of English ancestry and the family moved to Randolph from Virginia in 1860. Mr. and Mrs. Henry Quick with their children were enroute from Nelson County, Va., to Iowa. While passing through Randolph Mr. Quick was taken sick and the trip was abandoned and they made Randolph their permanent home.

SCOTT G. RINGER.

Scott G. Ringler, son of Cyrus E. and Columbia C. (Barttell) Ringler, was born in Grafton, West Virginia, in 1883; married Mary J. Conley. One child, John J., has been the result of this union. Mr. Ringler is the manufacturer of the famous Ringler stogies and is also engaged in a general mercantile business. He came to Randolph in 1908.

WILLIAM G. RAINS.

Wm. G. Rains, son of J. F. and Ellen (Sites) Rains, was born in Pendleton County in 1879; married Rosie, daughter of John and Virginia (Rains) Thompson. They had one child, Caroline. Mr. Rains has taught several terms in the public schools of Randolph.

MARTIN J. ROY.

Martin J. Roy, son of Adam R. and Margaret (Carr) Roy, was born in 1875; married Zadie (McDonald) Cooper. Children, Herbert, Byron, Ernest and Ralph. Howard died in infancy. Mr. Roy has been a merchant at Harmon seven years. He was the Republican party's candidate for deputy sheriff in 1910.

THOMAS C. RUSSELL.

Thomas C., son of Chas. W. and Mary E. (Collett) Russell, was born August 17, 1868; married Nannie, daughter of W. H. and Polina (Strickland) Quick. Mr. Russell married

Nannie, daughter of Geo. W. and Sarah (Crickard) McCall for his second wife. Children of first marriage, Willa L. and Clarence. Children of second marriage, Stanley Hugh, Ida Marie, Grace, Georgia, Helen, Missouri and Thomas C. Jr. Chas. W. Russell, father of Thomas C., moved from Winchester, Virginia, to Randolph at an early day. He was a man of influence and prominence in the community. Mr. Russell's mother was a sister of Dr. William Collett, the noted surgeon of Beverly before the Civil War.

CLAY C. ROSENCRANSE.

Clay C., son of Jesse and Mary (Riggleman) Rosencranse, was born in 1887; married Lena, daughter of Albert Gear. Mr. Rosencranse is one of the owners of the Tygarts Valley Flouring Mill near Mill Creek. This mill is located on the site of one of the first mills in the county owned by Wm. Currence, who was killed by the Indians. Mill Creek was then called Currences Mill Creek. Mr. Rosencranse is a descendant of Hezekiah Rosencranse, who was one of the first trustees of the town of Beverly. He first located in what is now known as the Caplinger settlement and is buried in the Baptist burying ground on the east side of the river near Arnold Station.

J. G. S. SHAFFER.

J. G. S. Shaffer, son of Christopher and Elizabeth (Hardesty) Shaffer, was born in Preston County, Virginia, in 1843; married Christina S. Nine in 1863. Children, Sarah J., Pearl, Bessie M., Clinton C., Verba (deceased), Lawrence (deceased), Harold (deceased). Mr. Shaffer came to Randolph in 1891. With the exception of three or four years he has been in the service of the city of Elkins since coming to this county. He has served as assessor, street commissioner and as policeman.

SQUIRE M. M. SMITH.

Milton M. Smith, son of Abram W. and Caroline (Michael) Smith, was born in 1859 in Grant County; married Fannie G., daughter of Henry and Sophronia (Iman) Thalaker. Children, Boyd, Milford and Helen Irene. Mr. Smith came to Elkins in 1889 and was the first recorder of the city. He was postmaster of Elkins under Grover Cleveland and is now justice of the peace of Leadsville District.

HON. HOWARD SUTHERLAND.

Howard, son of John Webster and Julia P. (Reavis) Sutherland, was born in Kirkland, Missouri, September 8, 1865. He was educated in the schools of St. Louis and received the degree of A.B. from West Minister College, Fulton, Missouri, in 1889. He was editor of Daily Republican, Fulton, Missouri, one year. He was chief of the Population Division of Census Department from 1890-3. From 1903 to 1912 he was employed by the Davis and Elkins interests and made his home in Elkins. He was State Senator from 1908 to 1912, when he was elected Congressman at large; was Congressman at large from 1912-16, when he received the Republican nomnation for United States Senate. Mr. Sutherland married at Fulton, Missouri, May 28, 1889, Effie, daughter of James B. and Lucy (Crockrell) Harris. Children, Natalie, Richard K., Virginia, Katharine, Margaret Lindsay, Maria Elizabeth. Four children died in infancy. Mr. Sutherland was elected to the U. S. Senate.

RUFUS SWECKER.

Rufus, son of Charles and Adelphia (Currence) Swecker, was born in 1902; married Jessie, daughter of George Newhouse. Mr. Swecker is a member of the family that moved to Randolph from Pocahontas and settled on the west side in Mingo District.

FRANK SEITZ.

Frank Seitz, son of Frederick and Josephine Seitz, German ancestry, was born in Williamsburg, New York, in 1869; married Clementine Edwards. Children, Frances, Eunice and Franklin. One daughter, Rose, died aged 6 years. Mr. Seitz came to Elkins in 1900 and is a bricklayer by trade.

WILLIAM A. STURMS.

William A., son of L. D. and Annie M. (Stephens) Sturms, was born in Calhoun County, West Virginia, in 1866; married

Louisa (Price) Sturms. Children, D. H., Ada, Jessie, Otto, Dewey, Lula, Russell, Merrill, Jeraldine and Ruth. Mr. Sturms came to Randolph in 1889. He is a track foreman on the West Virginia Southern Railroad at Job.

LEMUEL STURM.

Lemuel Sturm, son of David and Rebecca (Moore) Sturm, was born January 25, 1827; married first, Matisonia Martin. Mr. Sturms married second, Miss Ida Yokum. By his first marriage the following children were born: W. T., Carrie Keighron, Lourena, Minnie, Maud, Charles R., died aged 27. Mr. Sturm came to Randolph in 1894. The name is German in its origin. The paternal grandfather, Jacob Sturm, immigrated to America prior to the Revolution and settled in what is now Marion County, but then a part of Monongalia County. Mr. Sturm was mayor of Mill Creek in 1908. Notwithstanding his advanced age Mr. Sturm retains his mental faculties to a marked degree.

HON. E. D. TALBOTT.

Elam Dowden Talbott, son of William Woodford and Sarah (Simons) Talbott, was born in Barbour County, November 8, 1857; married June 15, 1886, Lutie Lee, daughter of S. N. and Florence A. (Brown) Bosworth. Children, Eva Bosworth, who married E. O. Fling; Marguerite, who married B. F. Downing; Eugenia Arnold, who married James Baker; Winifred Dewing, who married Clifford Gross, and Donald.

William Talbott, the great great grandfather of E. D. Talbott immigrated to Virginia from England, settling in Fairfax County. Richard Talbott, the great grandfather of E. D. Talbott, settled in Barbour County in 1780.

Mr. Talbott was educated in the public schools and in the universities of Virginia and West Virginia. He practiced law at Beverly a number of years and came to Elkins with the removal of the county seat to this place. Mr. Talbott has been mayor of Elkins and represented Randolph in the state Legislature and has been for a number of years president of the Elkins Commercial Club.

Dr. L. W. Talbott.

Dr. L. W. Talbott, son of William W. and Sarah (Simon) Talbott, was born November 25, 1855; married in 1893 Mary Evelyn, daughter of S. N. and Florence A. (Brown) Bosworth. Children, Richard Bosworth, William Brown, Virginia, Lewis, James and Sara. Dr. Talbott has been engaged in the practice of medicine in Randolph thirty-three years; longer than any other practitioner. He has attended more than 1,000 births.

Simon Teter.

Simon Teter, son of Joshua and Mary E. (Harper) Teter, was born in Randolph County in 1870; married Rebecca, daughter of Samuel and Phoebe (Spielman) Mullenix. Mr. Teter is employed by the Parsons Pulp and Paper Company at Horton.

Aaron Teter.

Aaron, son of Cyrus and Annie (Harper) Teter, was born in 1868 in Pendleton County; married Florence, daughter of Columbus and Jemima (Carr) Kernes. Children, Rosa Hoster, Columbus, Thamar, Lillie, Daisy, Sylvia, Lennie, Cyrus and Elsie. Howard Paul died in infancy. Mr. Teter was a merchant at Wymer nine years. He is now postmaster and merchant at Job.

W. W. Tyree.

W. W. Tyree, son of W. W. and Virginia (Stinespring) Tyree, was born in 1871, in Bath County, Virginia; married Mary Ellen, daughter of Uriah and Susan (Hudson) Bird. Children, Ward B., Mary Gale and William Bird. Mr. Tyree came to Randolph from Pocahontas in 1906 and is at present engaged in general insurance business.

W. D. Tyre.

W. D. Tyre, son of J. M. and Mrs. Elizabeth J. Tyre, was born in Randolph County, West Va., near Elkins, July 4th, 1879. Taught school in Randolph County for 11 years, was married to Miss Maud B. Curtis, youngest daughter of Mr. and Mrs. J. Milton Curtis, April 17th 1902. To this union six children have been born: Lela May, born May 5th,

1903; Alma Louretta, May 23, 1905; Glenn Lawrence, January 19th, 1908; Gladys Pearl, September 3, 1909; Earl Washington, born February 22, 1912 and died June 24, 1913, at the age of 16 months of a complication of diseases; Raymond Robert Bruce, born January 26, 1914.

Was a member of the Randolph County School Book Board from Roaring Creek District from 1906 to 1910.

Was Census Enumerator in Leadsville District in 1910. Was appointed as City Letter Carrier in Elkins, July 4th, 1910 and has remained in the Government Service ever since.

His father was a Union Soldier, belonging to Co. E, First West Virginia Light Artillery.

ULYSSES G. TREMBLY.

Ulysses G. Trembly, born in Preston County, 1867, son of Michael and Margaret (Smith) Trembly. Came to Randolph in 1905. Mr. Trembly married Mary, daughter of T. B. and Isaac (Stalnaker) Webster. Children, Mary and Harry. Mr. Trembly is a jeweler and is proprietor of a store on Third Street.

GLENN TETER.

Glenn, son of D. K. and Alice (Harmon) Teter, was born at Harmon, Randolph County in 1896. Mr. Teter is at present a clerk in the Whitmer Drug Company Store.

ELMER G. TETER.

Elmer G., son of D. K. and Christian (Bennett) Teter, was born in 1869; married Almeda, daughter of Isaac and Mary Raines. Children, Russell and Musa, who died in infancy. Mr. Teter is at present a clerk in the Parsons Pulp and Paper Company Store at Horton.

JOHN L. THOMAS.

John L. Thomas, son of William R. and Catherine (George) Thomas, was born February, 1878; married Iva, daughter of John W. and Anna (Martin) Morrison. Children, John, aged 10 years, and Owen Beryl, who died in infancy. The father, William R. Thomas, was born in Connorthenshire, Wales, in 1846, and came to America in 1868, locating in Pittsburgh, Pennsylvania. Father and son came to Randolph in 1902. They are at present prominent citizens of Pickens.

PHELIX R. TUNING.

Felix R., son of Thomas and Sarah (Tidd) Tuning, was born in Highland County, Virginia, in 1893. Mr. Tuning is a farmer and stockman. He is the Democratic committeeman for Middle Fork District.

DR. E. H. UPDIKE.

Dr. E. H. Updike was born in Bentonville, Virginia, in 1877, and came to West Virginia in 1906. Dr. Updike received his professional education at West Virginia University, Baltimore Medical College, University of Maryland and Loyola University of Chicago. Dr. Updike has practiced his profession at Elkins and Elk Garden and is now located at Mill Creek, West Virginia.

HON. WILLIAM G. WILSON.

William Grant Wilson, son of Isaac and Harriet Wilson, was born in Marion County in 1864. He married Mabel, daughter of Major J. H. and Katherine (Harwood) Fout. Mr. Wilson was educated in the public schools and at the Fairmont Normal school. He was among the first residents of Elkins and was for several years the only representative of the legal profession in the city. He was three times Mayor of Elkins and represented Randolph in the state Legislature. His prominence in that law making body is evidenced by the fact that he was made speaker of the house, which position he filled with marked ability. For a number of years he has been president of the Davis Trust Company.

DR. JOHN H. WEYMOUTH.

John H. Weymouth, D.D.S., son of John S. and Henrietta D. (Jenkins) Weymouth, was born at Richmond, Va., in 1843; married in 1873 Mary, daughter of Lemuel and Nancy (Hart) Chenoweth. Children, Myra May, who married G. N. Wilson; Henrietta Blanche, who married Barton Jones; Charles Lee, and Nannie Chenoweth. After the death of his first wife, Dr. Weymouth chose his second wife in the person of Miss Marian Smith, daughter of Abraham and Margaret Harding Smith. Dr. Weymouth's family were pioneers in Richmond and the first house built in that city belonged to the family. Dr. Weymouth was a captain of artillery in the Confederate service. He is a gifted writer and is the correspondent for several Metropolitan dailies. He was educated at Philadelphia Dental College.

JOHN B. WILT.

John B. Wilt, son of Wm. F. and Mary (Lantz) Wilt, was born in Preston County, West Virginia, in 1873. Mr. Wilt married Carrie, daughter of Mr. and Mrs. Geo. Heed. Children, Carrie and Mary Jane. Mr. Wilt taught school a number of years before coming to Elkins. He is now general manager of the large mercantile establishment of Posten & Co.

JARED L. WAMSLEY.

Jared L., son of Captain Jacob S. and Minerva (Hamilton) Wamsley, was born in 1854, died 1916; married Florence M., daughter of Eli B. and Elizabeth (Hutton) Butcher Mr. Wamsley graduated from the Fairmont Normal School and attended Roanoke College at Salem, Virginia. He was admitted to the bar in 1882 and was three times elected prosecuting attorney of Randolph. For years Mr. Wamsley stood in the front rank of Randolph County attorneys.

HON. JAMES W. WEIR.

Hon. James W. Weir, son of S. E. and May (Frothingham) Weir, was born in New Brunswick, New Jersey, in 1882, was educated in public schools at Covington, Virginia and Washington D. C. Prior to coming to Elkins Mr. Weir was on the staff of the Wheeling Intelligencer and Columbus, Ohio, Dispatch. He was editor of Randolph Enterprise from 1905 to 1911. From 1913 to the present time he has been editor and publisher of the Randolph Review. He was private secretary to Senator Watson from 1911-13. Mr. Weir has represented Randolph in the Legislature two terms, in 1909 and 1913. In 1909 Mr. Weir married Vie, the youngest daughter of J. F. and Lucebie (Wilmoth) Harding.

J. A. WEIMER.

J. A. Weimer, son of Peter and Catherine Ellen (Kyle) Weimer, was born in 1878 in Pendleton; married Lena A., daughter of Jacob L. and Jeanetta (Thompson) Nelson. Children, Theodore Willard. When Mr. Weimer was two years old his parents moved to Lincoln, Nebraska. He returned to Randolph in 1900 and is now an engineer on the Western Maryland Railroad. His grandfather, Philip Weimer, emigrated from Germany to Pendleton County, Virginia, in the early history of the county.

C. H. WYMER.

C. H. Wymer, son of Perry and Catherine (Zebaugh) Wymer, was born in 1865, in Grantsville, Maryland; married Martha, daughter of Archibald and Virginia (Hinkle) Harper. Children, Carrie Leta, Mary Marvin, Frank C., Elma and Alma, Charles and Thomas. Mr. Wymer came to Randolph in 1889. For several years Mr. Wymer has been a member of the livery firm of Wymer & Reynolds.

B. F. WHETZEL.

B. F. Whetzel, son of Ruckner P. Whetzel and Charlotte (Trembly) Whetzel, was born in 1863, in Preston County, West Virginia; married Bettie L., daughter of Jesse W. and Mary E. (Harper) Goddin. Children, Chas. V., Robert L., Dana C., Mary G., Cress E., Helen I. and Floyd G. His great grandfather, John Whetzel, moved from Frederick, Maryland, to four miles east of Kingwood, Preston County, in 1800 and founded what has since been known as the Whetzel settlement. He came to Randolph in 1889, before the advent of railroads. He started the first livery stable in Elkins. He is at present engaged in farming and fruit growing, and is the pioneer fruit grower in this section in a commercial way. He owns extensive apple and peach orchards near Elkins and has demonstrated that such an enterprise can be made to pay in this county if directed by energy and intelligence.

WILLIAM LEE WYMER.

William Lee Wymer, son of Joseph and Catherine (Spanaugle) Wymer, was born in Hunting Grounds in 1866; married first a Miss Cooper. Children, Clarence, Frank, Lexie, Alpha, Margie, and Blanche, who died in infancy. Clarence died at the age of 21. From his second marriage, Mr. Wymer had no children. Mr. Wymer chose for his third wife, Malinda, daughter of M. G. and Elizabeth White. The children of this union are Mona, Vernon, Blake, Raymond and Althea.

INDEX

In this index no reference is made to Personal and Family sketches. These sketches are arranged alphabetically.